SUSTAINING REFORM WITH A US-PAKISTAN FREE TRADE AGREEMENT

Gary Clyde Hufbauer and Shahid Javed Burki

PETERSON INSTITUTE
FOR INTERNATIONAL ECONOMICS
Washington, DC
November 2006

Gary Clyde Hufbauer, Reginald Jones Senior Fellow, was the Marcus Wallenberg Professor of International Finance Diplomacy at Georgetown University (1985–92), deputy director of the International Law Institute at Georgetown University (1977–81), deputy assistant secretary for international trade and investment policy of the US Treasury (1977–79), and director of the International Tax Staff at the US Treasury (1974–76). He is coauthor or coeditor of *US-China Trade Disputes: Rising Tide, Rising Stakes* (2006), *The Shape of a Swiss-US Free Trade Agreement* (2006), *NAFTA Revisited: Achievements and Challenges* (2005), *NAFTA and the Environment: Seven Years Later (2000)*, *Western Hemisphere Economic Integration* (1994), *NAFTA: An Assessment* (rev. ed. 1993), *Economic Sanctions Reconsidered: History and Current Policy* (2d ed. 1990), and others.

Shahid Javed Burki, former finance minister of Pakistan, is the chief executive officer of EMP Financial Advisors, LLC. He served at the World Bank for 25 years (1974–99), as division chief and senior economist, Policy Planning and Program Review Department; senior economist and policy adviser, the Office of the Vice President of External Relations; director, International Relations Department of that vice-presidency; director of China and Mongolia; and vice president of the Latin American and Caribbean region. His publications include *Pakistan: Development Choices for the Future* (1986, Oxford University Press); *Pakistan: Continuing Search for Nationhood* (1991, Westview Press, Boulder, CO); *Pakistan: Fifty Years of Nationhood* (1999, Westview Press); and *Pakistan: A Historical Dictionary* (1999, Scarecrow Press, London).

**PETER G. PETERSON INSTITUTE
FOR INTERNATIONAL ECONOMICS**
1750 Massachusetts Avenue, NW
Washington, DC 20036-1903
(202) 328-9000   FAX: (202) 659-3225
www.petersoninstitute.org

Typesetting by ATLIS Graphics
Printing by Automated Graphic Systems, Inc.

Printed in the United States of America
08 07 06   5 4 3 2 1

Library of Congress Cataloging-in-Publication Data

Hufbauer, Gary Clyde.
    Sustaining reform with a US-Pakistan Free Trade Agreement / Gary Clyde Hufbauer and Shahid Javed Burki.
        p. cm.
    Includes bibliographical references and index.
    ISBN 0-88132-395-0 (978-0-88132-395-5 : alk. paper)
    1. Free trade—Pakistan.   2. Tariff—Pakistan.   3. Agriculture—Economic aspects—Pakistan.   4. Pakistan—Commerce—United States.   5. United States—Commerce—Pakistan.   I. Burki, Shahid Javed.   II. Title.

HF2330.5.H84 2006
382'.97305491—dc22   2006027591

Contents

Preface

Since the mid-1980s, trading nations have increasingly used bilateral and regional agreements both to liberalize commerce with their immediate partners and to spur systemic reform. The process has come to be called "competitive liberalization." Even as the Doha Development Round attempts to struggle to a conclusion, numerous World Trade Organization members are negotiating new trade and investment agreements on a bilateral or regional basis. Unlike the first wave of bilateral free trade agreements (FTAs), many recent pacts have sealed commercial relations between distant partners, such as the United States and Singapore or Korea and Chile or Japan.

The first US bilateral FTA was concluded with Israel (1986), and the second with Canada (1989), but the North American Free Trade Agreement (NAFTA) was the watershed pact. Others followed as the United States contemporaneously pursued multilateral liberalization in the Uruguay Round (1986–94) and now the Doha Round (2001–07). In addition to NAFTA, the United States has 13 FTAs in force or awaiting ratification and is conducting FTA talks with more than 20 potential partners.[1]

---

1. Current US FTA partners (in chronological order) include Israel, Canada, Mexico, Jordan, Chile, Singapore, Australia, Morocco, Central America and the Dominican Republic, Bahrain, and Oman. Awaiting ratification are pacts with Colombia and Peru. Under negotiation are agreements with Ecuador, Malaysia, Panama, South Africa and its customs union partners (the Southern African Customs Union), South Korea, Thailand, and the United Arab Emirates. Possible US FTA partners in the intermediate term include the Caribbean Community (Caricom), Egypt, Indonesia, New Zealand, Pakistan, Philippines, Qatar, Switzerland, Taiwan, and Uruguay.

Recent and prospective FTA partners for the United States are mainly developing countries. The US Trade Representative has actively engaged Latin American, Middle Eastern, and Southeast Asian countries with a view toward constructing larger regional trading alliances, namely the Free Trade Area of the Americas, the Middle East Free Trade Agreement, and the Enterprise for ASEAN Initiative. Despite recent progress toward economic reform, however, the countries of South Asia (including Pakistan) have not yet been included among US negotiating priorities.

This Policy Analysis previews the case for more decisive US economic engagement of Pakistan and suggests that a US-Pakistan FTA could reinforce existing reforms and push the envelope in economic areas where Pakistan (and South Asia more generally) have lagged. In keeping with the Institute's extensive research agenda on prospective US FTAs, we present a detailed analysis of the costs and benefits of a US-Pakistan FTA for the signatory countries, for regional integration, and for the world trading system.[2]

Political relations usually dominate economic ties, and nowhere is this more true than in dealings among South Asian nations and between these nations and the United States. Relations between Pakistan and the United States have alternated between episodes of close partnership and sharp friction, reflecting the ups and downs of global and regional geopolitics. The tides of foreign policy have correspondingly affected trade and investment. Post–September 11 diplomacy has reinvigorated the economic ties between Islamabad and Washington, beyond bilateral aid packages and support in international financial institutions. In 2003 the United States and Pakistan signed a trade and investment framework agreement, establishing a joint council designed to facilitate the discussion of bilateral issues. In 2004, following the recommendations of the council, the United States and Pakistan began to negotiate a bilateral investment treaty (BIT); however, negotiations have stalled over certain provisions in the new US model BIT.

Looking to the future, and assuming the geopolitical alliance remains solid, both the United States and Pakistan might decide to explore a comprehensive FTA. An FTA would add a sturdy economic leg to the political alliance. Serious FTA discussions could commence after the conclusion of the BIT and the Doha Development Round (one would hope in 2007). The preliminary findings of this study—authored by a team led by Gary Clyde Hufbauer and Shahid Javed Burki—were posted on the Institute's Web site and previewed at an Institute luncheon in August 2006. We an-

---

2. Our initial work focused on North America, with indepth studies of the Canada-US FTA and NAFTA. Subsequent studies included US-Korea (2001), US-Taiwan (2004), US-Egypt (2004), US-Switzerland (2006), and US-Colombia (2006). Current studies in progress include US–Middle East and US-Indonesia.

ticipate this publication will prove useful to US and Pakistani officials if they choose to conduct exploratory talks.

The Peter G. Peterson Institute for International Economics is a private, nonprofit institution for the study and discussion of international economic policy. Its purpose is to analyze important issues in that area and to develop and communicate practical new approaches for dealing with them. The Institute is completely nonpartisan.

The Institute is funded by a highly diversified group of philanthropic foundations, private corporations, and interested individuals. Major institutional grants are now being received from the William M. Keck, Jr. Foundation and the Starr Foundation. About 33 percent of the Institute's resources in our latest fiscal year were provided by contributors outside the United States, including about 16 percent from Japan.

This project is part of the Institute's overall program of research on possible free trade agreements between the United States and developing countries, supported by the Ford Foundation and the GE Foundation. Partial funding for this study was provided by the Government of Pakistan.

The Institute's Board of Directors bears overall responsibilities for the Institute and gives general guidance and approval to its research program, including the identification of topics that are likely to become important over the medium run (one to three years) and that should be addressed by the Institute. The director, working closely with the staff and outside Advisory Committee, is responsible for the development of particular projects and makes the final decision to publish an individual study.

The Institute hopes that its studies and other activities will contribute to building a stronger foundation for international economic policy around the world. We invite readers of these publications to let us know how they think we can best accomplish this objective.

C. Fred Bergsten
Director
October 2006

Acknowledgments

This book reflects not only the work of the authors but also the very able research assistance of Agustin Cornejo, Claire Owen, and Maya Shivakumar. Particular thanks are due to Madona Devasahayam and Marla Banov for their thorough review in preparing the manuscript for publication.

Introduction

The United States and Pakistan established diplomatic relations in 1947, shortly after Pakistan gained its independence. Since then, relations have alternated between episodes of close partnership and sharp friction, reflecting the ups and downs of global and regional geopolitics.[1] The tides of foreign policy have correspondingly affected trade and investment.

Post–September 11 diplomacy has now created a strong relationship between Pakistan and the United States. In this new setting, a free trade agreement (FTA) could promote economic reform in Pakistan and thereby strengthen bilateral political ties, which have otherwise been largely based on confronting enemies—first communism, then the Soviet invasion of Afghanistan, and now al Qaeda.

We begin with a short review of the diplomatic history between the two countries. Any proposal for an FTA will stir up, in Pakistan, memories of a checkered bilateral relationship dating back 50 years, and it is useful for American audiences to understand why Pakistani sentiments are strong. US leaders, for their part, will entertain a proposal only if it fits within the larger policy framework of US diplomacy toward the Middle East and South Asia.

In this chapter we offer an overview of the context for a US-Pakistan FTA, including factors such as geographical distance, political impacts, timing, and compliance with Article 24 of the General Agreement on Tariffs and Trade (GATT). We also consider the priority of a US-Pakistan FTA among concurrent multilateral and bilateral negotiations.

---

1. This introduction draws heavily on Kux (2001).

Diplomatic Ups and Downs

Against the backdrop of the Cold War, Pakistan's strategic geographic position made the country a valuable partner in the Western alliance to contain the spread of communism. Accordingly, during the first decade of the Cold War, Pakistan was considered one of Washington's closest allies in Asia, was a keystone of two security alliances, the Southeast Asia Treaty Organization (SEATO) and the Central Treaty Organization (CENTO),[2] and received nearly $2 billion in US assistance from 1953 to 1961, one-quarter of this in military aid.

However, when the 1965 Indo-Pakistan war erupted, the United States suspended military assistance to both countries. This decision affected Pakistan much more severely than it did India, and generated a widespread feeling in Pakistan that the United States was at best a fair-weather ally.

The next landmark event was the 1971 Indo-Pakistan war. Despite the widely publicized US "tilt" toward Pakistan, the United States did not lift its embargo on arms shipments to the country until 1975. US foreign policy of that era held that the intervention of outside powers should be avoided in the South Asian conflicts—both the civil war that led to the creation of Bangladesh and the ensuing Indo-Pakistan war.

In April 1979, based on concerns about Pakistan's nascent nuclear program, the United States suspended economic assistance (but not food assistance), as required under the Symington amendment to the Foreign Assistance Act of 1961. This amendment called for a halt to economic assistance to countries that were nonnuclear weapon states but nevertheless imported uranium enrichment technology.

The Soviet invasion of Afghanistan in December 1979 turned things around and revived the close relationship between Pakistan and the United States. The two countries shared a common interest in forcing the withdrawal of Soviet forces and fostering peace and stability in South Asia. Under President Ronald Reagan, the United States agreed in 1981 to provide $3.2 billion to Pakistan over a period of six years, divided equally between economic and military assistance. The president invoked a national security clause to waive the Symington amendment, but assistance was still subject to the annual congressional appropriation process.

A second economic and military assistance program was announced in 1986, this time for over $4 billion, with 57 percent for economic assistance (Library of Congress 1994). The ongoing war in Afghanistan ensured presidential waivers of legislative restrictions on aid to countries with possible nuclear weapons programs.

Following the Soviet withdrawal from Afghanistan in 1989 and the end of the Cold War, the United States took a harder line on the nuclear

---

2. Pakistan joined SEATO and CENTO, the successor of the Baghdad Pact, in 1955.

weapons issue. The Pressler amendment of 1985 required that US assistance to a country be suspended if the president could not certify to Congress, on an annual basis, that the country did not possess a nuclear weapon. For several years, the president, resting on Pakistan's assurances that its nuclear program was solely for peaceful uses, made this certification. But in 1990 President George H. W. Bush, after reviewing intelligence from several sources, was unable to make the required certification and all military assistance and new economic aid to Pakistan were terminated. However, in 1992, when Pakistan suffered devastating floods in the north, the United States relaxed its restrictions to allow food and economic assistance to nongovernmental organizations in Pakistan.

The decision by India to conduct nuclear tests in May 1998, followed by Pakistan's matching response, triggered the next big turning point. Under the mandatory terms of the Glenn amendment, the Clinton administration restricted the provision of credits, military sales, economic assistance, and loans to both governments, as well as credit guarantees to US agricultural exporters.

The overthrow in October 1999 of the democratically elected government of Prime Minister Nawaz Sharif led to an additional layer of US sanctions (under Section 508 of the Foreign Appropriations Act), including restrictions on military financing and economic assistance. Accordingly, US assistance to Pakistan was largely limited to refugee and counternarcotics programs. Although the United States urged General Pervez Musharraf to restore civilian rule, the administration opted to engage the new regime so that strategic concerns—nuclear and missile proliferation, regional instability, and Islamic terrorism—could be addressed.[3]

The terrorist attacks on September 11, 2001, again transformed relations between the two countries. Pakistan's important strategic position bordering Afghanistan, its vital role as a Muslim ally in the US-led "war on terror," and General Musharraf's willingness to support the US military effort in Afghanistan overrode all other US concerns, including the objective of spreading democracy throughout the Muslim world.[4] Remaining US sanctions were lifted in October and November 2001, allowing the United States to support multilateral lending to Pakistan. With US leadership, the Paris Club rescheduled $2.3 billion of Pakistan's debt on

---

3. While President Bush has called on President Musharraf to deliver free and fair elections in 2007, his efforts have not satisfied US prodemocracy advocates who are deeply suspicious of President Musharraf's intentions, and continue to lobby Congress for a more "muscular" promotion of democracy in Pakistan.

4. According to press reports, General Musharraf's forthcoming memoirs claim that his government was subject to crude pressure by the US State Department to join the post–September 11 alliance. Former Deputy Secretary Richard Armitage has denied the claim ("Musharraf memoirs launched in US," BBC News Online, September 25, 2006).

generous terms and provided up to $1 billion in soft loans and grants.[5] Meanwhile, the United States persuaded the International Monetary Fund (IMF) and the World Bank to extend more than $2 billion of assistance for poverty alleviation and growth over the following three years (Economist Intelligence Unit 2004).

During President Musharraf's visit to the United States in 2003, President George W. Bush announced that the United States would provide Pakistan with $3 billion in economic and military aid over five years, and the assistance package was implemented in 2005. In June 2004, in response to Pakistan's efforts to cement relations over the long term, the United States accorded Pakistan the status of a major non-NATO ally.[6]

In January 2004, the exposure of a nuclear technology proliferation network headed by the renowned Pakistani scientist A. Q. Khan renewed tensions between the United States and Pakistan. Khan admitted to overseeing the illegal transfer of nuclear technology and materials, beginning in 1998, to countries hostile to the United States, including North Korea, Libya, and Iran. Khan was placed under house arrest, but President Musharraf granted him immunity from prosecution because of his prior service in making Pakistan a nuclear power. The Pakistan government denied any involvement in the Khan network and launched its own investigation. In 2005 the government confirmed that Khan had supplied nuclear centrifuges—which can be used to enrich uranium for nuclear weapons—to Iran.[7] In April 2006 the government released the last Pakistani scientist detained for his role in the network, Mohammed Farooq, an action that likely signals the end of Pakistan's investigation. But given current alarms over Iran's nuclear program, Western diplomats and the International Atomic Energy Agency (IAEA) have stated that they do not consider the case closed. The Pakistan government has not allowed the IAEA or investigators from any foreign government access to Khan, nor has any action been taken against members of the network, about a dozen of whom were detained and released by the authorities.[8]

Further frictions erupted in early 2006 when, on January 13, a Central Intelligence Agency (CIA) Predator missile strike targeting al Qaeda sus-

---

5. The Paris Club is an informal group of official creditors that find coordinated and sustainable solutions to the payment difficulties experienced by debtor nations. Permanent members are governments with large claims on various other governments throughout the world, including the United States.

6. NATO stands for the North Atlantic Treaty Organization. Non-NATO ally is a special designation by the US government for countries that enjoy close military relations without being NATO members.

7. See "A.Q. Khan Relative Held over Attack," *BBC News*, August 12, 2005, http://news.bbc.co.uk.

8. See Farhan Bokhari and Stephen Fidler, "Pakistan Release Seen as Closing Khan Inquiry," *The Financial Times*, May 3, 2006.

pects in the Bajaur region of Pakistan killed at least 18 civilians. The action took place amid continuing allegations in the American press that terrorists lurking in northwest Pakistan. Pakistani officials said that the intended target of the attack, al Qaeda second-in-command Ayman al-Zawahri, was not at the site, contrary to US intelligence. Although Pakistani intelligence sources claimed that four other al Qaeda leaders may have been killed, their deaths remain unconfirmed. US and Pakistani intelligence circles believe that the Pakistani leadership were forewarned of the attack and that the military's Inter-Services Intelligence (ISI) agency provided information that prompted the CIA to launch the airstrike.[9]

To repair relations following this incident in March 2006 the two countries, following a visit by President Bush to Islamabad, issued a joint statement affirming their long-term, strategic partnership. In addition, President Bush indicated that the United States had dropped its opposition to the proposed gas pipeline from Iran to India via Pakistan. The $6 billion project for the 1,625-mile pipeline will bring gas revenues to Iran, transit fees to Pakistan, and energy to India. The three nations plan to start construction in 2007.

Context for a US-Pakistan FTA

Great distances and sharp differences might seem to argue against a US-Pakistan FTA. Pakistan and the United States do not share a common border or even the same continent. While the United States is one of the foremost advocates of market capitalism, Pakistan began only in 1985 to liberalize its trade and investment regimes (see tables 1.1, 1.2, and 1.3 to compare economic, cultural, trade, and development data). Political institutions have very different origins in the two countries.[10] (See box 1.1 for a brief timeline of political events in Pakistan.) Moreover, in the closing months of the World Trade Organization's (WTO) Doha Development Round,[11] it might not seem sensible to drain diplomatic and legislative energy from the overarching goal of global trade liberalization.

Some observers, in both Pakistan and the United States, will conclude from such observations that a bilateral FTA makes no sense. Others will

---

9. For details, see David Morgan, "U.S. Targeted-Killings of al Qaeda Suspects Rising," Reuters, January 18, 2006. See also David Morgan and Simon Cameron-Moore, "CIA Unlikely to Back Off al Qaeda Attacks in Pakistan," Reuters, January 29, 2006, available at www.alertnet.org.

10. Since Pakistan's creation in 1947, the army has been the country's most influential institution and the ultimate guarantor of national stability and presidential power. Many Pakistani leaders, like General Musharraf, have come to office with military backgrounds.

11. US trade promotion authority (TPA), as written, expires on June 30, 2007. Therefore, the Doha Development Round should conclude by spring 2007, to be ratified by the US Congress under the existing TPA legislation.

Table 1.1 Comparative indicators, Pakistan and the United States, 2004

Indicator	Pakistan	United States
GDP (billions of dollars)	95.0	11,734.0
GDP per capita (dollars)[a]	455.0	39,959.0
Exports (billions of dollars)	13.4	807.5
Imports (billions of dollars)	16.7	1,472.9
Inward FDI stocks (billions of dollars)	7.6	39,473.9
Outward FDI stocks (billions of dollars)	0.7	2,018.2
Population (millions)[b]	162.4	295.7
Labor force (percent by sector)		
Agriculture	42	1
Manufacturing	20	22
Services	38	77
Literacy (percent)[c]	49	97
Male	62	97
Female	35	97
Life expectancy at birth (years)	63	78
Religious groups (percent of population)		
Muslim	97	1
Sunni	77	n.a.
Shi'a	20	n.a.
Other	3	20
Protestant	n.a.	52
Roman Catholic	n.a.	24
Mormon	n.a.	2
Jewish	n.a.	1

n.a. = not applicable

a. Pakistan data are for 2003, at the market exchange rate.
b. July 2005 estimates.
c. Literacy is defined as age 15 or older and able to read and write.

Sources: OECD Economic Survey: United States, October 2005; Economist Intelligence Unit Country Report: Pakistan, October 2005; UNCTAD, *World Investment Report 2005,* www.unctad.org/wir; CIA World Factbook, Pakistan and the United States, www.cia.gov.

be less critical but question the timing: Why not wait until after the Doha Round is sealed and South Asia gets a better sense of its economic and political direction? Still others will argue that each skeptical question can be turned into an argument for a bilateral FTA. This study will be of most interest to those in the second and third camps—that is to say, observers who do not foreclose the possibility or desirability of a US-Pakistan FTA.

Table 1.2 Pakistan: Trade in goods, 2003
(billions of US dollars and percent)

Country/region	Value	Share
Major export market		
European Union	3.7	30
United States	2.9	24
United Arab Emirates	0.9	8
Hong Kong	0.6	5
Afghanistan	0.5	4
Saudi Arabia	0.3	3
China	0.3	2
Turkey	0.2	2
Bangladesh	0.2	2
Others	2.6	21
Total	12.3	100
Major import source		
European Union	2.4	15
Saudi Arabia	1.8	11
United Arab Emirates	1.7	11
United States	1.3	9
China	1.2	7
Kuwait	1.0	6
Japan	0.9	6
Malaysia	0.6	4
Singapore	0.5	3
Others	4.2	27
Total	15.6	100

Source: Government of Pakistan, Federal Bureau of Statistics, www.statpak.gov.pk (accessed November 9, 2005).

Before launching into the chapters, issue by issue, it's worth seeing how the broader skeptical questions can be addressed.

Is the Geographic and Political Distance Too Great?

To start, can support for an FTA gain traction—given the certainty of economic hurdles between the two countries in agriculture and textiles—if the partners are not steadfast political or military allies and are separated by thousands of miles? Prior to the mid-1990s, FTAs and customs unions were dominated by pacts between countries that were already, or in the process of becoming, political allies—the European Common Market and

Table 1.3 US trade in goods, 2004
(billions of US dollars and percent)

Country/region	Value	Share
Major export market		
Canada	189.9	24
European Union	172.6	21
Mexico	110.8	14
Japan	54.2	7
China	34.7	4
South Korea	26.4	3
Taiwan	21.7	3
Singapore	19.6	2
Hong Kong	15.8	2
Others	161.8	20
Total	807.5	100
Major import source		
European Union	282.0	19
Canada	256.4	17
China	196.7	13
Mexico	155.9	11
Japan	129.8	9
South Korea	46.2	3
Taiwan	34.6	2
Malaysia	28.2	2
Venezuela	24.9	2
Others	318.2	20
Total	1,472.9	100

Source: US Census Bureau, Foreign Trade Statistics, www.census.gov.

then the European Union, the Association of Southeast Asian Nations, the Australia–New Zealand Closer Economic Relations Trade Agreement, the North American Free Trade Agreement, and Mercosur.[12]

In short, experience up to the mid-1990s led many commentators to forecast a three-bloc world: contiguous customs unions and FTAs organized around the European Union, the United States, and Asian powers

---

12. Unlike its counterparts listed here, the European Free Trade Area (EFTA) was, from its inception, a purely economic venture without the overlay of a political alliance. In a way, it seems to be the exception that proves the rule: In the 1970s, 1980s, and 1990s, several EFTA members peeled off to join the European Union. In 1960, the original members of EFTA were Austria, Denmark, Norway, Portugal, Sweden, Switzerland, and the United Kingdom. Finland joined in 1961, Iceland in 1970, and Liechtenstein in 1991. In 1973, the United Kingdom and Denmark left EFTA to join the European Communities. They were followed by Portugal in 1986, and by Austria, Finland, and Sweden in 1995, leaving only Iceland, Liechtenstein, Norway, and Switzerland as members in 2005.

Box 1.1 Timeline of political events in Pakistan

Year	Event
1947	Formation of East and West Pakistan.
1948	War with India over disputed territory of Kashmir. Muhammed Ali Jinnah, the first governor general of Pakistan, dies.
1951	Jinnah's successor, Liaquat Ali Khan, is assassinated and military rule is established.
1954	Amid concerns about Soviet expansion, the United States and Pakistan sign a mutual defense agreement.
1955	Pakistan joins the Southeast Asia Treaty Organization (SEATO) and the Central Treaty Organization (CENTO).
1958	Martial law declared; General Ayub Khan becomes de facto president. The United States and Pakistan sign a cooperation agreement.
1960	General Ayub Khan is elected president.
1965	Second war with India over Kashmir. President Ayub Khan wins reelection.
1969	President Ayub Khan resigns and General Yahya Khan (no relation) becomes president.
1971	East Pakistan attempts to secede, leading to civil war and the creation of Bangladesh. The third Indo-Pakistani conflict ensues.
1973	Zulfiqar Ali Bhutto becomes prime minister.
1977	Allegations of vote rigging by Bhutto's Pakistan People's Party (PPP) lead to widespread rioting. General Zia ul-Haq stages military coup.
1978	General Zia becomes president.
1985	Martial law and ban on political parties is lifted.
1988	General Zia, the US ambassador and top Pakistani army officials die in an airplane crash of mysterious origin.
1988	Benazir Bhutto, Zulfiqar Ali Bhutto's daughter, and the PPP win general election. Benazir Bhutto becomes prime minister.
1990	Benazir Bhutto is dismissed as prime minister on charges of incompetence and corruption. Nawaz Sharif becomes prime minister.
1993	President Ghulam Ishaq Khan and Prime Minister Sharif both resign under pressure from the military. A general election brings Benazir Bhutto back to power.
1996	The Benazir Bhutto government falls again in the wake of corruption allegations. Nawaz Sharif assumes power.
1997	A general election brings Nawaz Sharif back to power.
1999	Prime Minister Sharif is overthrown in a bloodless military takeover led by General Pervez Musharraf.

(box continues next page)

Box 1.1 Timeline of political events in Pakistan *(continued)*

Year	Event
2001	General Musharraf names himself president while remaining head of the army. Parliament is dissolved.
2002	General elections are held. President Musharraf wins another five years in office in a referendum.
2003	The centrist Pakistan Muslim League (Q) assumes power under Prime Minister Mir Zafarullah Khan Jamali.
2004	General Musharraf announces that he will retain his military role. In August, former Citibank executive Shaukat Aziz is sworn in as prime minister.
2005	General Musharraf declares that he will seek reelection as president when his term expires in 2007.

(China and/or Japan). FTAs came to be seen as building blocks for the sort of economic and political integration that characterizes modern geographically contiguous nations. These economic blocs might, in turn, fortify political alliances while erecting walls that divide the global economy.

Simply put, this vision proved wrong, even though FTAs have flourished. By one count, some 176 new trade agreements have been notified since the birth of the WTO in January 1995, and the total number may soon exceed 300 (WTO 2005a). Yet many of the post-1995 FTAs are "out of area" and not motivated by existing or anticipated political alliances; indeed, partners are often separated by thousands of miles, distinct cultures, and the lack of a common language. Examples of recent agreements include US FTAs with Chile, Australia, and Singapore; EU FTAs with Mexico and Chile; and Japanese FTAs with Mexico and Singapore. Even China's menu of prospective FTA partners—the Association of Southeast Asian Nations (ASEAN), India, Pakistan, Australia, New Zealand, the Gulf Cooperation Council (GCC), and the Southern African Customs Union (SACU)—seems devoid of political alliances (Hufbauer and Wong 2005).

In fact, the United States has adopted a strategy of "competitive liberalization" based in part on concluding bilateral and regional FTAs with a large number of partners, many of them outside the Western Hemisphere. Rather than forming tightly knit geographic units, centered on a major power, FTAs are creating criss-cross networks spanning the globe, where there is no clear separation between "hubs" and "spokes." Thus, a US-Pakistan FTA is perfectly compatible with current FTA trends.

As mentioned, post–September 11 diplomacy also plays a major role. The Bush administration and many members of Congress place a very high priority on measures that buttress US national interests in Muslim countries generally and the Middle and Near East specifically. The administration believes that prosperous market-oriented economies, run on democratic principles, are far less likely to breed terrorists or threaten world peace. That view is at the apex of policy and explains why the administration favors new FTAs with countries in the Middle and Near East. Morocco was first on the list, followed by Bahrain, Oman, and the United Arab Emirates. Egypt, Pakistan, Malaysia, and Indonesia are all prospects. FTAs with these countries are valued by the United States for the role they can play both in promoting broad economic reform and in averting the "clash of civilizations" that Samuel Huntington has predicted will dominate global politics in the 21st century.[13]

Are There Real Benefits to an FTA?

An FTA between Pakistan and the United States is fundamentally about large political gains for the United States and potentially large economic gains for Pakistan.

While the political payoff is crucial, it would be wrong to focus the FTA analysis on politics alone. Even if FTA signatories are mainly interested in political benefits, they must appraise the pact's economic merits. The costs of trade diversion and trade adjustment need to be weighed against the gains from trade creation, investment promotion, and productivity growth, as well as—most importantly—the role an FTA might play in fostering reform.

For Pakistan, an agreement could spur measures to liberalize the domestic economy and integrate the country into world markets.[14] For the United States, which has historically based its relationship with Pakistan on political and military considerations, an FTA would nourish the economic dimension.

As described in the chapters that follow, both countries retain significant trade barriers. Many of their important barriers operate behind the border as nontariff barriers. Commerce in agriculture, manufactures, some services, and government procurement is often conducted on terms far from the ideals of free trade and investment. Econometric research—using both a gravity model and a computable general equilibrium (CGE)

---

13. In his 1993 *Foreign Affairs* article, Samuel P. Huntington argued that the primary axis of conflict in the 21st century will be along cultural and religious lines. The fault lines between civilizations, he wrote, will be the battle lines for the future. He further developed the case in Huntington (1996).

14. See Ferrantino (2006) for the argument that FTAs between large countries and developing countries can serve as "policy anchors" by acting as a mechanism for the smaller country to make credible commitments to policy reform that it might not otherwise make.

model—suggests that reducing these barriers will substantially augment commerce between the United States and Pakistan.[15]

To preview the econometric research presented in chapter 8, elimination of *all* bilateral barriers between Pakistan and the United States might double two-way merchandise trade.[16] Companion estimates, using CGE analysis, suggest that a US-Pakistan FTA could significantly improve economic performance in Pakistan, resulting in annual gains of around 1.5 percent of GDP. Deeper trade and investment links would erode the power of oligopolies in both economies, especially in Pakistan, and thereby reduce markup margins and spur productivity. Deeper links would also spur the exchange of technology and skilled personnel, and thus enhance economic efficiency.

Is the Timing Wrong?

Perhaps the strongest argument against a US-Pakistan FTA is the matter of timing. Why distract attention from the final push to complete the Doha Development Round? For both countries, the political and economic payoff from a successful WTO negotiation far exceeds whatever achievements can be realized on a bilateral basis.[17] As a related point, it must be mentioned that the US congressional battle over the Central American Free Trade Agreement–Dominican Republic (CAFTA-DR) was prolonged and bruising, and the agreement only narrowly won approval from the US House of Representatives on June 28, 2005, by a tight 217 to 215 vote. In the aftermath of the prolonged CAFTA-DR polemic, there is a certain amount of "trade fatigue" among US business and legislative proponents of greater liberalization. These stalwarts doubtless need time to "rest up" before they take on the "big battle"—congressional ratification of the WTO Doha Development Round package.[18]

---

15. The first section of chapter 8, authored by Dean DeRosa, applies the gravity model technique to a prospective US-Pakistan FTA. While the technique has been well known since the 1960s, it has been applied to assess the effect of FTAs only since the late 1990s. The second section of chapter 8, authored by John Gilbert, applies a static CGE framework using the GTAP6 database.

16. One reason for such large gains may be an "announcement" effect—the wake-up call that an FTA conveys to potential investors, exporters, and importers. Another reason could be the "lock-in" effect that results when firms place greater certainty on a country's trade and investment policies once commitments are made in an FTA.

17. This seems obvious for the United States. Even for Pakistan, better terms of access to world markets for its large textile industry, and its growing agricultural production, are the foremost commercial priorities.

18. The scarcest resource in US trade negotiations is not bureaucratic talent but congressional time and energy. The next scarcest resource is top-level support from leading CEOs in the private sector.

Like CAFTA-DR, a US-Pakistan FTA may in the end be voted up or down in a hot and highly partisan congressional battle. For these reasons, this debate should be put off until the WTO Doha Round has been ratified.

The timing arguments would be persuasive if the US-Pakistan FTA and the WTO Doha Round were alternatives. But the two agreements can be complements, not substitutes. If a political decision is made to go forward during 2006, the central focus of the US-Pakistan FTA should be negotiation, not ratification, either by the US Congress or the Pakistani legislature. Ratification might well occur after approval of the Doha package.

A US-Pakistan FTA can liberalize trade in goods and services to a far greater extent than the Doha Round can. In the WTO, modest progress at best seems possible on agricultural market access barriers.[19] WTO services negotiations have made so little headway that private firms have declared a crisis.[20] WTO members are dickering over tariff-cutting formulas to improve nonagricultural market access (the NAMA group), but the foreseeable outcome will not lead to zero tariffs on a wide range of manufactured goods.[21] By contrast, in all these areas and others (e.g., government procurement, investment, sanitary and phytosanitary barriers), the US-Pakistan FTA should go far beyond what can be achieved in the WTO. In fact, US-Pakistan FTA liberalization should start where the Doha Round foreseeably ends.

Will the Agreement Comport with GATT Article 24?

As indicated above, the United States has entered into numerous FTAs. Apart from NAFTA, these include FTAs with (in chronological order) Israel, Jordan, Chile, Singapore, Australia, Morocco, CAFTA-DR, and

---

19. Former US Trade Representative Robert Portman has described proposed tariff-reduction formulas as too modest in their ambitions, although cuts may be agreed in farm subsidies (progress that cannot be made in FTA talks). See "Key Ministers Make No Progress in WTO Talks as U.S. Criticizes EU," *Inside U.S. Trade* 23, no. 42, October 21, 2005. Most recently, US Agriculture Secretary Mike Johanns and Ambassador Portman acknowledged that countries will miss their goal, articulated at the Hong Kong ministerial in December 2005, of agreeing to a specific blueprint for the Doha Round. At the same time, EU Trade Commissioner Peter Mandelson announced that the Hong Kong goals would have to be lowered given the large substantive differences among members. See "US, EU Officials Acknowledge They Will Miss Goals at Hong Kong," *Inside U.S. Trade* 23, no. 45, November 11, 2005.

20. The Global Services Coalition, a group of Australian, Chilean, European, Indian, Japanese, and US providers, met with WTO officials in Geneva on June 24, 2005, and circulated an alert titled "WTO Services Negotiations in Crisis; Political Will Must Be Mobilized Urgently."

21. See "NAMA Group Struggling to Readjust Goal for Hong Kong," *Inside U.S. Trade* 23, no. 45, November 11, 2005.

Bahrain. Several more are in various stages of discussion and negotiation. For its part, Pakistan has signed an FTA with Sri Lanka and is completing negotiations with Singapore and the Gulf Cooperation Council (made up of Bahrain, Kuwait, Oman, Qatar, Saudi Arabia, and the United Arab Emirates).[22] Pakistan has also entered into a preferential trade agreement with China as a step toward signing an FTA. In addition, Pakistan belongs to the South Asian Association for Regional Cooperation (SAARC). This group of countries—Bangladesh, Bhutan, India, Maldives, Nepal, Pakistan, and Sri Lanka—established the SAARC Preferential Trading Arrangement (SAPTA) in 1993 and the South Asian Free Trade Area (SAFTA) in 2004.[23]

So far, none of the US or Pakistan free trade pacts have been found in violation of GATT Article 24, even though some of them cover much less than "substantially all trade." The simple reason that they have not been found wanting is that GATT/WTO reviews of Article 24 compatibility either say nothing or convey only bland misgivings (Schott 2004). Indeed, only one review group (for the Czech-Slovak pact) reached an affirmative consensus (Sutherland et al. 2004).[24] Nevertheless, it is reasonable to state that US FTAs come fairly close to the Article 24 ideal of eliminating barriers on substantially all the merchandise trade of the partners. The major shortcomings of the US FTAs are the inadequate coverage of agricultural barriers (as in the US-Canada FTA signed in 1989) or very long phaseouts and even exclusions for sensitive agricultural products (a conspicuous fault of the US-Australia FTA, at US insistence). In contrast to their agricultural shortcomings, the FTAs agreed by the United States liberalize services and investment, areas that the GATT/WTO system barely touches.

Under the Enabling Clause of the GATT,[25] exceptions from most favored nation (MFN) treatment are allowed either in the form of differential and more favorable treatment of a developing country by a developed country, or in regional or global arrangements among developing countries (such as SAFTA). This clause could permit the United States to stop far short of liberalizing substantially all imports from Pakistan and yet not run afoul of Article 24. However, the United States is not disposed to rely on the Enabling Clause in its FTA pacts with developing countries.

---

22. See "Pakistan to Sign FTA with GCC Soon," *Daily Times*, Islamabad, October 25, 2005.

23. Afghanistan was admitted as the eighth full member of SAARC in the Dhaka Declaration of the 13th SAARC Summit, adopted on November 13, 2005.

24. Even when an FTA is fully consistent with Article 24, one or both parties may still owe "compensation" to other WTO members for trade diversion. Usually such claims are settled in the context of larger trade negotiations, such as the Tokyo Round, the Uruguay Round, and now the Doha Round.

25. GATT Decision of November 28, 1979, on Differential and More Favorable Treatment; see GATT, 26th Supplement, Basic Instruments and Selected Documents (BISD) 203 (1980).

If Pakistan and the United States reach an FTA, it should come close to the Article 24 ideal. While long phaseouts and special safeguards may be necessary on both sides for sensitive agricultural products, the coverage should otherwise be comprehensive and the elimination of barriers rapid.

Pakistan's Place in the Queue

As mentioned, the United States is currently engaged in free trade talks with many potential partners, most of them developing countries, although three belong to the Organization for Economic Cooperation and Development (OECD)—Switzerland, New Zealand, and South Korea. Given the relatively long list of potential FTA partners, the new US Trade Representative, Ambassador Susan Schwab, will inevitably establish priorities. These will depend on a variety of considerations, such as political alliances, prospective economic payoff, likely speed and ease of negotiation, and quality of results. Most of these considerations cannot be quantified, but available data do shed light on the strength of trade and investment ties between the United States and its prospective partners, the extent of protective barriers, and the degree of social similarity, measured by corruption, economic freedom, and labor and environmental standards.

In 2003 the United States and Pakistan signed a trade and investment framework agreement (TIFA) that established a Joint Council designed to facilitate the discussion of bilateral issues. In 2004, following the recommendations of the council, the United States and Pakistan began to negotiate a bilateral investment treaty (BIT). Recent negotiations have stalled due to disagreement over appropriate dispute resolution clauses.[26] Nevertheless, developments in US trade policy, global politics, the US-Pakistan relationship, and Pakistani domestic policies all enhance the prospects both for concluding the BIT and opening talks on an FTA.

We now turn to an array of quantitative and qualitative indicators that enable a comparison of Pakistan and other current and prospective US FTA partners. The quantitative indicators consist of inward and outward foreign direct investment (FDI) stocks, two-way US merchandise trade, two-way US services trade, and the average MFN tariff rates for

---

26. The United States wants to include a clause that stipulates, in the event of arbitration, that only the Washington-based International Center for Settlement of Investment Disputes (ICSID) should be used as a forum. Pakistan agrees to an arbitration clause, but calls for dispute resolution by the United Nations Commission on International Trade Law (Uncitral), based in Vienna, Austria. Pakistan has also declined to accept a clause that would provide retroactive coverage for investments made by US firms prior to the date when the BIT enters into force. See Ihtashamul Haque, "US-Pakistan Differences over BIT Persist," *Dawn*, August 19, 2005, available at www.dawn.com (accessed October 25, 2005).

agricultural and nonagricultural products. The qualitative indicators include a corruption index, two economic freedom indexes, and indexes for labor and environmental standards.

Based on these indicators, appendix tables 1A.1 through 1A.7 compare Pakistan with current and potential US FTA partners. The current partners include Israel (1986), Canada (1989), Mexico (1993), Jordan (2001), Chile (2003), Singapore (2004), Australia (2004), Morocco (2004), CAFTA-DR (2005), and Bahrain (2006). Prospective US FTA partners are divided into three groups:

- partners for which an FTA has been negotiated but not yet ratified: Oman, Peru, and Colombia (in the final drafting stage)

- partners in the process of negotiation: Ecuador, Panama, SACU countries, South Korea, Thailand, and the United Arab Emirates

- partners under consideration: Bangladesh, Bolivia, the Caribbean Community (Caricom), Egypt, Indonesia, Malaysia, New Zealand, Pakistan, Philippines, Qatar, and Taiwan.

Quantitative Indicators

Table 1A.1 shows that Pakistan's two-way FDI stocks with the United States rank 24th out of the 32 current and prospective US partners. If a BIT and an FTA are both concluded, US multinational enterprises (MNEs) as well as European and Asian MNEs may take a more favorable view toward expanding stakes in Pakistan.

Table 1A.2 depicts US merchandise trade with current and potential FTA partners. When two countries have an important base of merchandise trade, not only do business firms have a tangible reason to support an FTA but also the prospects are much better for a substantial dollar increase in bilateral commerce. Pakistan ranks 23rd among 32 current and prospective US partners, with a dollar figure in 2003 of about $5 billion in two-way merchandise trade. This figure is obviously far behind NAFTA partners Mexico and Canada (whose two-way trade with the United States totals $356 billion), but it easily exceeds the two-way trade of three current Muslim partners: Jordan, Morocco, and Bahrain. Compared with other prospective partners, Pakistan's two-way merchandise trade with the United States is similar in magnitude to that of Egypt and New Zealand.

Table 1A.3 presents two-way trade in services between current and potential US FTA partners. The logic of this indicator parallels that for merchandise trade. While data on services trade do not exist for many countries, and are thus missing for several of the current and prospective FTA partners, tentative conclusions can be drawn from the available figures. Based on these data, Pakistan ranks ninth in two-way trade in services, around $2.3 billion annually. These flows exceed US services trade with Chile and are comparable to bilateral trade in this area with prospective partners in Southeast Asia and New Zealand.

Table 1A.4 presents recent MFN tariff rates for current and prospective FTA partners. The MFN figures are averages of applied tariff rates for agricultural and nonagricultural products. The rationale for this indicator is that it suggests whether commercial negotiations will be more or less difficult, in the sense of whether larger or smaller tariff cuts will be needed to reach the goal of free trade. An FTA, by definition, aims at eliminating tariffs and quotas, and achieving this goal is easier if the partner country already has low applied MFN tariff rates.

Pakistan has a high MFN average applied rate for nonagricultural products. At an applied average rate of 16.6 percent, Pakistan ranks 27th, just behind Thailand. Pakistan also has a high applied average MFN rate for agricultural products, ranking 24th on this indicator. It must be noted that Pakistan's bound tariff rates substantially exceed its applied rates. Pakistan's wall of actual (applied) and theoretical (bound) tariff protection implies difficult FTA negotiations. But looking on the bright side, the current high tariffs mean that the potential benefits to both countries of an FTA are substantial.

The United States has concluded FTAs with countries that had both high and low applied MFN tariffs. Canada, Singapore, Australia, and Chile had relatively low applied MFN tariff rates on both agricultural and nonagricultural products.[27] By contrast, Mexico, Jordan, Morocco, and Israel have much higher applied MFN rates. From this spectrum, one might conclude that the United States can negotiate with partners that have a wide range of MFN barriers, provided that high-barrier countries are prepared to make asymmetric cuts.

Qualitative Indicators

Table 1A.5 presents a comparative perspective of the degree of corruption among current and prospective FTA partners. The logic of this indicator is twofold. First, less corruption probably means less political influence by vested interests that seek to preserve the economic rents generated by trade and investment barriers. Second, less corruption definitely means a more desirable environment for foreign firms to expand their trade and investment contacts with the partner country.

Corruption can be a stumbling block to a successful agreement and subsequent implementation. Apart from Jordan, Mexico, and Morocco,

---

27. While the figures in table 1A.4 refer to the situation in 2004, at the time the FTAs were negotiated all these partners had comparatively low average MFN tariffs.

current US FTA partners have low levels of corruption. By contrast, several prospective partners have somewhat higher levels. With levels of corruption exceeded only by Bangladesh and Indonesia, Pakistan ranks 30th out of 32 current and prospective partners.

Table 1A.5 also presents two different indexes of economic freedom (Heritage Foundation and the World Economic Forum), covering trade policy, fiscal burdens, government intervention in the economy, monetary policies, capital flows and foreign direct investment, wages and prices, banking and finance, property rights, and overt and informal market regulation. The indexes suggest that Pakistan offers a less attractive business environment compared with all but two other prospective partners, ranking 27th out of 28 countries (data are not available to rank CAFTA, Caricom, Oman, and Qatar). While Pakistan's current score places it in the "mostly unfree" category from an economic standpoint, the Heritage Foundation does note improvements in the business environment due to reduced regulation and increased privatization.

Table 1A.6 presents the Environmental Sustainability Index (ESI) for current and prospective US FTA partners. The ESI assesses water and air pollution, protected areas, and environmental regulations and enforcement. Pakistan is on the lower end of the scale, at a disadvantageous position compared with other prospective partners. An FTA between the United States and Pakistan could raise environmental concerns in the US Congress. Because Pakistan may face criticism akin to what Central American countries faced over CAFTA-DR, a strong commitment from Pakistan to increase efforts to enforce its environmental laws will be necessary.

Table 1A.7 compares labor standards for current and prospective US FTA partners. The labor standard index is based on five indicators: the right of association (i.e., the right to form unions) and the related rights to bargain and strike; forced labor; child labor; working conditions; and the number of international labor treaties that have been ratified. The index rates each country as high, medium/high, medium, medium/low, or low in these five categories. The results show that this is another troublesome area for Pakistan and could mean that an agreement with Pakistan would face opposition in the US Congress. A credible assurance from Pakistan to adhere to the core labor standards will help to answer critics.

While Pakistan's relatively weak performance on some indicators gives the country a less favorable position in the US FTA queue, it is worth noting that Pakistan has made significant headway in the last decade. Moreover, President Musharraf has committed his government to dramatic political and economic reform, the effects of which should be reflected in future rankings.

A US-Pakistan FTA could help anchor existing commitments, enhance credibility, and hasten the reform process. It could also put economic relations between the two countries on a better footing, moving away from aid to trade. The US FTA with Jordan provides evidence that such agreements can work. In 1999 total US imports from Jordan amounted to a paltry $31 million dollars, US apparel imports from Jordan were negligible ($2 million), and the United States had a trade surplus with the country of $239 million. Just five years later, in 2004, US imports were almost $1.1 billion, of which $956 million was apparel, and US exports had almost doubled, from $270 million to $531 million. Jordan's bilateral merchandise trade balance with the United States shifted from a deficit of $239 million to a surplus of $562 million. The remarkable increase in Jordanian exports, which come mainly from a set of qualifying industrial zones (QIZs), demonstrates how rapidly a country can take advantage of trade preferences (Galal and Lawrence 2005).

While some US officials have taken the position that countries with weaker initial conditions, such as Jordan, Egypt, or Morocco, should undertake further reforms before FTA negotiations begin, this leaves open the question of how much reform is enough for the process to move forward. Indeed, while Pakistan has much to reform, the same can be said of other countries that are already US FTA partners. More importantly, such a hurdle would diminish one of the key benefits of the agreement, namely its value as a reform anchor. To avoid vagueness about what is required of Pakistan, and for the FTA to sustain and boost reform, the agreement can be constructed in such a way as to create monitoring mechanisms to ensure compliance.

Plan of the Report

Agriculture and foodstuffs are highly protected in both Pakistan and the United States, and so two-way trade in agricultural goods and foodstuffs represents only 7 percent of bilateral merchandise trade between the two countries. Chapter 2 addresses the agricultural barriers and sanitary and phytosanitary standards that reflect the sensitivity of the sector for both countries. The chapter concludes with recommendations for their gradual phaseout in the context of a bilateral FTA.

Chapter 3 addresses textiles and clothing, an area that is by far the dominant component of bilateral merchandise trade between the United States and Pakistan, amounting to about $2.7 billion annually. Historically, the US textile and clothing industry has been highly allergic to trade liberalization that does not take place on its own terms. Moreover, the industry faces intense pressure in the aftermath of the recent elimination of quotas that long restricted trade under the Multi-Fiber Arrangement. Indeed, the US textile and clothing industry has sought and obtained renewed protection in the form of safeguards on imports of Chinese goods. A US-Pakistan FTA, if negotiated and ratified, will be the first agreement between the United States and a country with a highly competitive textile and clothing industry. Chapter 3 presents a brief profile of the industries in each country and discusses the possible impact of a US-Pakistan FTA on trade flows. The chapter also addresses remaining barriers and past negotiating experiences of the United States and Pakistan in this area.

Chapter 4 turns to commerce in manufactures besides textiles and clothing, a category we call "other manufactures." Trade in this area is an integral part of US-Pakistan commercial relations, as more than 80 percent of US exports to Pakistan fall in the "other manufactures" product category (although Pakistan does not export large amounts of "other manufactures" to the United States). Despite serious efforts at liberalization, Pakistan still applies high tariffs and nontariff barriers on manufactured imports. The Pakistani MFN rate on manufactured imports—excluding textiles and clothing—is about 14 percent, while the corresponding US tariffs (with a few exceptions) are mostly low (the US MFN rate is just below 4 percent). In addition, some Pakistani firms already enjoy duty-free access to the US market through GSP or MFN rates. Hence, our discussion in chapter 4 focuses largely on Pakistan's manufacturing sector, though we also examine barriers that affect Pakistan's access to the US market.

Chapter 5 discusses how labor and environmental issues might be addressed in a US-Pakistan FTA. We review how these areas have been treated in other agreements and recap the arguments raised during the congressional ratification of CAFTA-DR.

Chapter 6 reviews government procurement, an area that has proven highly resistant to liberalization in the WTO and that evokes political sensitivities in both countries. The United States has selectively opened up its market on a reciprocal basis. We recommend that Pakistan join the WTO's Government Procurement Agreement (GPA) and that Pakistan and the United States extend to each other the best government procurement terms offered to any other country, either through the GPA or in bilateral FTAs (an unconditional MFN approach).

Direct and portfolio investment links between Pakistan and the United States, as well as the services sector, are taken up in chapter 7. The chapter identifies areas of FDI friction and provides an overview of current international investment agreements between the two countries. Turning to services, the chapter analyzes selected sectors in each country and concludes with recommendations for investment and priorities.

Chapter 8 provides estimates of potential US-Pakistan trade expansion, based on gravity and computable general equilibrium (CGE) models. The two models attempt to forecast the effect of a bilateral FTA on the volume of trade created between the two countries, the volume of trade diverted from third countries, and economic gains in the two partners.

Chapter 9 concludes with a review of the main points and recommendations of the previous chapters. While our book is essentially an economic analysis, we recognize that geopolitical forces will determine the course and outcome of FTA talks between Pakistan and the United States.

Appendix A takes a historical look at trade in the South Asian region and explores the most significant attempt at intraregional integration, the South Asian Free Trade Area (SAFTA). The appendix concludes that for Pakistan, a US-Pakistan FTA could complement SAFTA by increasing Pakistan's trade both within South Asia and with the rest of the world. Also, as countries reduce tariffs across the board, trade facilitation—customs procedures, transport, and standards—becomes increasingly important. A US-Pakistan FTA could spur the reform process in SAFTA in this key area.

Appendix 1A

Table 1A.1 Foreign direct investment stocks, 2003
(billions of US dollars)

Partner	Rank[a]	From United States	To United States	Two-way FDI
NAFTA				
Mexico	3	61.5	6.7	68.2
Canada	1	192.4	105.3	297.7
Other current				
Australia	4	41.0	24.7	65.6
CAFTA	18	3.4	0	3.4
Dominican Republic	25	0.9	0	0.9
Chile	12	10.0	0.1	10.0
Israel	13	6.2	3.8	10.0
Jordan	32	0.1	0	0
Morocco	30	0.3	0	0.3
Singapore	5	57.6	−0.2	57.4
To be ratified				
Bahrain	26	0.2	0.3	0.5
Colombia	20	2.8	−0.2	2.6
Oman	29	0.4	0	0.4
Peru[b]	21	2.7	−0.1	2.5
Under negotiation				
Ecuador	22	1.4	0	1.5
Panama	9	6.5	8.4	14.9
SACU-5	26	0.8	0.1	0.9
Thailand	15	7.4	0.2	7.6
United Arab Emirates	23	1.4	0	1.5
Under consideration				
Europe				
Switzerland	2	86.4	112.9	199.3
Middle East				
Egypt	7	19.0	0	18.9
Qatar	19	3.1	0	3.1
East Asia and Pacific				
Indonesia	11	10.4	0	10.4
Malaysia	14	7.6	0.2	7.8
New Zealand	17	3.8	0.6	4.5
Philippines	16	4.7	0	4.7
South Korea	8	13.3	2.3	15.7
Taiwan	10	11.0	2.7	13.7

(table continues next page)

Table 1A.1 *(continued)*

Partner	Rank[a]	From United States	To United States	Two-way FDI
Latin America				
Bolivia	28	0.4	0	0.4
Caricom	6	17.0	10.0	26.9
South Asia				
Bangladesh	31	0.2	0	0.2
Pakistan	24	1.1	0	1.1

CAFTA = Central American Free Trade Agreement
Caricom = Caribbean Community
NAFTA = North American Free Trade Agreement
SACU-5 = Southern African Customs Union (South Africa, Botswana, Lesotho, Namibia, and Swaziland)

Note: FDI stock is computed as direct investment position on a historical-cost basis.

a. Based on two-way FDI.
b. Data for 2001.

Source: BEA (2004a).

Table 1A.2 US merchandise trade, 2004 (billions of US dollars)

Partner	Rank[a]	US exports	US imports	Two-way trade
NAFTA				
Mexico	2	110.8	155.8	266.6
Canada	1	189.1	255.9	445.0
Other current partners				
Australia	10	14.3	7.5	21.8
CAFTA	7	15.7	17.7	33.4
Dominican Republic	17	4.3	4.5	8.9
Chile	18	3.6	4.7	8.4
Israel	9	9.2	14.5	23.7
Jordan	27	0.6	1.1	1.6
Morocco	28	0.5	0.5	1.0
Singapore	6	19.6	15.3	34.9
To be ratified				
Bahrain	31	0.3	0.4	0.7
Colombia	15	4.5	7.3	11.8
Oman	30	0.3	0.4	0.7
Peru	20	2.1	3.7	5.8
Under negotiation				
Ecuador	19	1.7	4.3	6.0
Panama	26	1.8	0.3	2.1
SACU-5	16	3.3	6.9	10.2
Thailand	8	6.4	17.6	23.9
United Arab Emirates	21	4.1	1.1	5.2
Under consideration				
Europe				
Switzerland	11	9.3	11.6	20.9
Middle East				
Egypt	24	3.1	1.3	4.4
Qatar	29	0.5	0.4	0.8
East Asia and Pacific				
Indonesia	13	2.7	10.8	13.5
Malaysia	5	10.9	28.2	39.1
New Zealand	22	2.1	3.0	5.0
Philippines	12	7.1	9.1	16.2
South Korea	3	26.3	46.2	72.5
Taiwan	4	21.7	34.6	56.3
Latin America				
Bolivia	32	0.2	0.3	0.5
Caricom	14	5.7	7.7	13.4

(table continues next page)

Table 1A.2 *(continued)*

Partner	Rank[a]	US exports	US imports	Two-way trade
South Asia				
Bangladesh	25	0.3	2.3	2.6
Pakistan	23	1.8	2.9	4.7

CAFTA = Central American Free Trade Agreement
Caricom = Caribbean Community
NAFTA = North American Free Trade Agreement
SACU-5 = Southern African Customs Union (South Africa, Botswana, Lesotho, Namibia, and Swaziland)

a. Ranking based on two-way trade.

Source: US Department of Commerce, TradeStats Express, http://tse.export.gov.

Table 1A.3 US trade in services, 2003 (billions of US dollars)

Partner	Rank[b]	US exports	US imports	Two-way trade
NAFTA				
Mexico	2	16.6	11.7	28.3
Canada	1	26.7	19.1	45.9
Other current partners				
Australia	6	5.8	3.2	9.0
CAFTA	n.a.	n.a.	n.a.	n.a.
Dominican Republic	n.a.	n.a.	n.a.	n.a.
Chile	14	1.0	0.7	1.7
Israel	7	2.3	1.8	4.1
Jordan	n.a.	n.a.	n.a.	n.a.
Morocco	n.a.	n.a.	n.a.	n.a.
Singapore	5	6.9	4.9	11.8
To be ratified				
Bahrain	n.a.	n.a.	n.a.	n.a.
Colombia	n.a.	n.a.	n.a.	n.a.
Oman	n.a.	n.a.	n.a.	n.a.
Peru	n.a.	n.a.	n.a.	n.a.
Under negotiation				
Ecuador	n.a.	n.a.	n.a.	n.a.
Panama	n.a.	n.a.	n.a.	n.a.
SACU-5[a]	10	1.2	1.0	2.2
Thailand	12	1.1	0.7	1.8
United Arab Emirates	n.a.	n.a.	n.a.	n.a.
Under consideration				
Europe				
Switzerland	3	8.0	8.3	16.4
Middle East				
Egypt	n.a.	n.a.	n.a.	n.a.
Qatar	n.a.	n.a.	n.a.	n.a.
East Asia and Pacific				
Indonesia	15	1.1	0.3	1.4
Malaysia	13	1.2	0.5	1.7
New Zealand	11	1.0	1.1	2.1
Philippines	8	1.4	1.4	2.8
South Korea	4	8.4	4.4	12.8
Taiwan	n.a.	n.a.	n.a.	n.a.
Latin America				
Bolivia	n.a.	n.a.	n.a.	n.a.
Caricom	n.a.	n.a.	n.a.	n.a.

(table continues next page)

Table 1A.3 *(continued)*

Partner	Rank[b]	US exports	US imports	Two-way trade
South Asia				
Bangladesh	n.a.	n.a.	n.a.	n.a.
Pakistan	9	0.7	1.7	2.3

n.a. = not available

CAFTA = Central American Free Trade Agreement

Caricom = Caribbean Community

NAFTA = North American Free Trade Agreement

SACU-5 = Southern African Customs Union (South Africa, Botswana, Lesotho, Namibia, and Swaziland)

a. Using data for South Africa.

b. Based on two-way trade; rank positions exclude countries for which information is not available.

Sources: US Department of Commerce, Bureau of Economic Analysis, www.bea.gov (accessed October 20, 2005); State Bank of Pakistan.

Table 1A.4 Average MFN tariff rates, 2003–04
(simple average ad valorem rates)

Partner	Agricultural			Nonagricultural		
	Bound	Applied	Rank[e]	Bound	Applied	Rank
NAFTA						
Mexico	35.1	24.5	27	34.9	17.1	28
Canada	3.5	3.1	5	5.3	4.2	6
Other current partners						
Australia	3.2	1.1	2	11.0	4.6	8
CAFTA[a]	42.3	10.5	14	38.2	5.7	11
Dominican Republic	39.6	13.0	16	34.2	7.8	18
Chile	26.0	6.0	7	25.0	5.9	13
Israel	73.0	15.9	19	9.2	4.0	4
Jordan	23.7	19.8	23	19.8	12.1	24
Morocco	54.5	48.6	30	39.2	27.5	31
Singapore	9.5	0	1	6.3	0	1
To be ratified						
Bahrain	37.5	9.0	10	35.1	7.6	17
Colombia	91.9	14.9	15	35.4	11.9	23
Oman	28.0	10.2	13	11.6	5.0	9
Peru	30.8	17.2	21	30.0	13.1	25
Under negotiation						
Ecuador	25.5	14.7	17	21.1	11.5	22
Panama	27.7	14.8	18	22.9	7.4	16
SACU-5[b]	39.2	9.1	11	15.8	5.3	10
Thailand	35.5	29.0	28	24.2	14.2	26
United Arab Emirates	25.4	n.a.	n.a.	13.1	n.a.	n.a.
Under consideration						
Europe						
Switzerland[c]	n.a.	36.2	29	n.a.	2.3	2
Middle East						
Egypt	95.3	22.8	26	28.3	19.4	30
Qatar	25.7	4.9	6	14.5	4.1	5
East Asia and Pacific						
Indonesia	47.0	8.2	9	35.6	6.7	14
Malaysia	12.2	2.1	4	14.9	8.1	19
New Zealand	5.7	1.7	3	11.0	3.5	3
Philippines	34.7	8.0	8	61.8	4.3	7
South Korea	52.9	52.1	31	10.2	7.0	15
Taiwan	15.3	16.3	20	4.8	5.5	12
Latin America						
Bolivia	40.0	10.0	12	40.0	9.3	20
Caricom[d]	98.0	18.4	22	51.2	11.1	21

(table continues next page)

Table 1A.4 *(continued)*

Partner	Agricultural			Nonagricultural		
	Bound	**Applied**	**Rank[e]**	**Bound**	**Applied**	**Rank**
South Asia						
Bangladesh	188.5	21.7	25	35.7	19.2	29
Pakistan	97.1	20.4	24	35.3	16.6	27
US comparison	6.9	5.1	7	3.2	3.7	4

CAFTA = Central American Free Trade Agreement
Caricom = Caribbean Community
n.a. = not available
MFN = most favored nation
NAFTA = North American Free Trade Agreement
SACU-5 = Southern African Customs Union (South Africa, Botswana, Lesotho, Namibia, and Swaziland)

a. Simple average of observations for Costa Rica, El Salvador, Guatemala, Honduras, and Nicaragua.
b. Using South Africa's average bound tariff. Tariff binding figures are based on simple averages of national averages reported by the World Trade Organization (WTO) and exclude Lesotho.
c. Using ad valorem equivalent (AVE). Switzerland has a 99.8 percent binding coverage, but bindings are in the form of specific tariffs.
d. Simple averages of observations reported by the WTO for each Caricom member.
e. Ranks based on applied rates and run from high to low.

Sources: World Trade Organization, *2004 World Report* and *Trade Profiles*.

Table 1A.5 Corruption and economic freedom
(index values)

Partner	Corruption, 2004[a]	Corruption rank	Economic freedom Heritage, 2005[b]	WEF, 2005[c]	Average rank
NAFTA					
Mexico	3.6	20	3.1	3.9	17
Canada	8.5	5	4.1	5.1	6
Other current partners					
Australia	8.8	4	4.2	5.2	5
CAFTA	3.2	23	n.a.	n.a.	n.a.
Dominican Republic	2.9	26	2.5	3.1	26
Chile	7.4	6	4.2	4.9	7
Israel	6.4	7	3.6	4.8	11
Jordan	5.3	12	3.2	4.3	14
Morocco	3.2	23	2.8	3.5	23
Singapore	9.3	2	4.4	5.5	1
To be ratified					
Bahrain	5.8	10	3.9	4.5	9
Colombia	3.8	19	2.8	3.8	20
Oman	6.1	8	3.2	n.a.	n.a.
Peru	3.5	22	3.2	3.7	19
Under negotiation					
Ecuador	2.4	28	2.5	3.0	28
Panama	3.7	18	3.3	3.6	18
SACU-5[d]	4.9	15	3.2	4.3	15
Thailand	3.6	20	3.0	4.5	16
United Arab Emirates	6.1	8	3.3	5.0	12
Under consideration					
Europe					
Switzerland	9.1	3	4.1	5.5	3
East Asia and Pacific					
Indonesia	2.0	31	2.5	3.5	25
Malaysia	5.0	14	3.0	4.9	13
New Zealand	9.6	1	4.3	5.1	4
Philippines	2.6	27	2.7	3.5	24
South Korea	4.5	16	3.4	5.1	10
Taiwan	5.6	11	3.7	5.6	8
Middle East					
Egypt	3.2	23	2.6	4.0	22
Qatar	5.2	13	2.9	n.a.	n.a.
Latin America					
Bolivia	2.2	29	3.3	3.1	21
Caricom	4.0	17	n.a.	n.a.	n.a.

(table continues next page)

Table 1A.5 *(continued)*

Partner	Corruption, 2004[a]	Corruption rank	Economic freedom Heritage, 2005[b]	WEF, 2005[c]	Average rank
South Asia					
Bangladesh	1.5	32	2.0	2.9	29
Pakistan	2.1	30	2.3	3.3	27
US comparison	7.5	6	4.1	5.8	2

n.a. = not available

CAFTA = Central American Free Trade Agreement

Caricom = Caribbean Community

NAFTA = North American Free Trade Agreement

SACU-5 = Southern African Customs Union (South Africa, Botswana, Lesotho, Namibia, and Swaziland)

WEF = World Economic Forum

a. Countries with a high score are the most transparent (i.e., a high score is better).

b. High score = economically more free. Heritage Index scores have been rescaled so that 5 = "economically free" and 1 = "economically unfree."

c. High score = economically more free.

d. Using data for South Africa.

Sources: Transparency International (2005); Heritage Foundation (2005); WEF (2005).

Table 1A.6 Environmental standards

Partner	ESI rank 2005[a]	ESI[b]	CO_2 emissions damage[c]	Protected areas[d]	Compliance[e]	Treaty[f]
NAFTA						
Mexico	19	46.2	High	Low	Medium	Medium/High
Canada	1	64.4	High	Low	High	High
Other current partners						
Australia	3	61.0	Medium	Medium	Medium	High
CAFTA	15	49.0	High	Medium	Low	Medium
Dominican Republic	25	43.7	Medium	High	Medium/Low	Medium
Chile	10	53.6	Medium	Medium	Medium/High	High
Israel	12	50.9	High	Medium	Medium	Medium
Jordan	18	47.8	Low	Medium	Medium/High	Medium
Morocco	20	44.8	Medium	Low	Medium/Low	High
Singapore	13	50.0	Medium	Low	High	Low
To be ratified						
Bahrain	n.a.	n.a.	Low	Low	n.a.	Low
Colombia	7	58.9	High	High	Medium	Medium/High
Oman	17	47.9	Medium	Medium	Medium/Low	Medium/Low
Peru	5	60.4	High	Medium	Low	Medium/High

Under negotiation

Ecuador	12	52.4	Low	High	Low	Medium/High
Panama	8	57.7	Medium	High	Med/Low	Medium/High
SACU-5	11	52.9	Medium	Medium	Medium	Medium/Low
Thailand	14	49.7	Low	Medium	Medium	Medium
United Arab Emirates	21	44.6	Low	Low	n.a.	Medium/Low

Under consideration

Europe						
Switzerland	2	63.7	High	High	High	High
Middle East						
Egypt	24	44.0	Low	Medium	Medium	High
Qatar	n.a.	n.a.	Low	Low	n.a.	Low
East Asia and Pacific						
Indonesia	16	48.8	Medium	Low	Medium/Low	Medium
Malaysia	9	54.0	Low	High	Medium/High	Medium
New Zealand	4	60.9	High	Medium	High	Medium/High
Philippines	22	44.3	Medium	Low	Low	Medium/High
South Korea	26	43.0	Medium	Low	Medium/High	Medium/High
Taiwan	29	32.7	Medium	Low	Medium/High	Low
Latin America						
Bolivia	6	59.5	Low	Medium	Low	Medium
Caricom	27	41.0	Medium	Low	Medium	Medium

(table continues next page)

Table 1A.6 Environmental standards (*continued*)

Partner	ESI rank 2005[a]	ESI[b]	CO$_2$ emissions damage[c]	Protected areas[d]	Compliance[e]	Treaty[f]
South Asia						
Bangladesh	23	44.1	High	Low	Low	Medium/Low
Pakistan	28	39.9	Low	Low	Low	Medium
US comparison	11	52.9	High	High	Medium	High

n.a. = not available

CAFTA = Central American Free Trade Agreement

Caricom = Caribbean Community

ESI = Environmental Sustainability Index

NAFTA = North American Free Trade Agreement

SACU-5 = Southern African Customs Union (South Africa, Botswana, Lesotho, Namibia, and Swaziland)

a. Low rank = poor environmental standards. Rank is inverse to score because high score indicates high environmental standards.

b. Countries with high ESI have high environmental standards.

c. High = CO$_2$ damage < 0.5 percent, medium = CO$_2$ damage > 0.5 and < 1 percent, low = CO$_2$ damage > 1 percent.

d. Ratio of protected area to total area: high = ratio > 0.2, medium = ratio > 0.1 and < 0.2, low = ratio.

e. High = compliance score > 5.8, medium/high = compliance < 5.8 and > 4.6, medium = compliance < 4.6 and > 4.0, medium/low = compliance > 3.6 and < 4.0, low = compliance < 3.6.

f. High = more than 120 treaties, medium/high = between 80 and 120, medium = 60 to 80, medium/low = between 50 and 60, low = less than 50.

Sources: 2004 Environmental Sustainability Index of the Environmental Performance Measurement Project (Yale University, Columbia University, and World Economic Forum); World Bank (2004b); UN Environmental Statistics for Protected Areas; Globalis Human Impact 2002; Environmental Treaties and Resource Indicators (ENTRI) for Treaties Participation.

Table 1A.7 Labor standards

Partner	Rank (ca. 2004)	Index[a]	Right of association	Forced labor	Child labor	Working conditions	Conventions ratified[b]
NAFTA							
Mexico	8	3.6	High	Medium	Medium	Medium	High
Canada	4	4.4	High	Medium/High	High	High	Medium
Other current partners							
Australia	2	4.8	High	High	High	Medium/High	High
CAFTA	8	3.6	Medium	Medium/High	Medium/High	Medium	Medium/High
Dominican Republic	24	2.0	Medium/Low	Medium	Low	Low	Medium
Chile	4	4.4	Medium/High	High	Medium/High	Medium/High	High
Israel	6	4.0	Medium	High	High	Medium	Medium/High
Jordan	13	3.0	Medium	Medium	Medium/High	Medium/Low	Medium
Morocco	19	2.6	Medium/Low	Medium	Medium	Low	Medium/High
Singapore	7	3.8	Medium	High	Medium/High	Medium/High	Medium
To be ratified							
Bahrain	19	2.6	Medium	Medium	Medium	Medium	Low
Colombia	13	3.0	Medium/Low	Medium/High	Medium/Low	Medium/Low	High
Oman	22	2.2	Medium	Medium	High	Medium	Low
Peru	13	3.0	Medium	Medium	Medium/Low	Medium/Low	High
Under negotiation							
Ecuador	16	2.8	Medium/Low	Medium	Medium/Low	Medium/Low	High
Panama	12	3.2	Medium	Medium	Medium/Low	Medium	High
SACU-5	27	1.8	Low	Medium	Low	Low	Medium
Thailand	30	1.4	Medium/Low	Low	Low	Medium/Low	Low
United Arab Emirates	22	2.2	Medium	Medium	Medium/High	Medium	Low

(table continues next page)

Table 1A.7 Labor standards *(continued)*

Partner	Rank (ca. 2004)	Index[a]	Right of association	Forced labor	Child labor	Working conditions	Conventions ratified[b]
Under consideration							
Europe							
Switzerland	1	5.0	High	High	High	High	High
Middle East							
Egypt	16	2.8	Medium/Low	Medium	Low	Medium	High
Qatar	27	1.8	Low	Medium/Low	Medium/High	Low	Low
East Asia and Pacific							
Indonesia	24	2.0	Medium	Medium/Low	Low	Medium	Low
Malaysia	19	2.6	Medium/Low	Medium/Low	Medium	Medium	Medium
New Zealand	2	4.8	Medium/High	High	High	High	High
Philippines	29	1.6	Medium	Low	Low	Medium/Low	Medium
South Korea	11	3.4	Medium	Medium/High	Medium/High	Medium	Medium
Taiwan	16	2.8	Medium/Low	Medium	Medium/High	Medium/Low	Medium
Latin America							
Bolivia	24	2.0	Medium/Low	Low	Low	Medium/Low	Medium/High
Caricom	8	3.6	Medium/High	High	Medium/High	Medium/High	Medium
South Asia							
Bangladesh	30	1.4	Medium/Low	Low	Low	Low	Medium
Pakistan	30	1.4	Medium/Low	Low	Low	Low	Medium
US comparison	5	4.2	High	High	High	High	Low

n.a. = not available

CAFTA = Central American Free Trade Agreement

Caricom = Caribbean Community

NAFTA = North American Free Trade Agreement

SACU-5 = Southern African Customs Union (South Africa, Botswana, Lesotho, Namibia, and Swaziland)

Note: Methodology for labor indicators

1. *Collective bargaining, right of association, and labor strikes*
   Low: Collective bargaining, strikes, and right of association all prohibited.
   Medium/Low: Some prohibited or government approval needed.
   Medium: Not prohibited and no requirement to seek authorization prior to forming unions, but labor rights are not really enforced or widespread antiunion discrimination exists.
   Medium/High: Not prohibited and labor rights are enforced most of the time.
   High: All allowed and labor rights enforced.

2. *Forced labor.*
   Low: Pervasive forced labor.
   Medium/Low: Law prohibits forced labor but certain foreigners and local groups are consistently subject to forced labor.
   Medium: Forced labor is prohibited but some cases are reported.
   Medium/High: Rare cases of forced labor reported
   High: No cases of forced labor reported.

3. *Child labor*
   Low: Pervasive (child labor exceeds 8 percent of the age group).
   Medium/Low: Prohibited but many cases reported in different sectors of the economy (child labor represents 2 to 8 percent of the age group).
   Medium: Prohibited but some cases are reported in the informal sector (child labor 0 to 2 percent of the age group).
   Medium/High: Prohibited but rare cases of child labor are reported.
   High: No child labor reported.

4. *Working conditions*
   Low: Low or no negotiations possible with employer, low or no protection, working standards not "enforced, substandard living conditions, lack of protections, abuse, and labor law violations."
   Medium/Low: Labor laws exist but not well enforced regarding protection, safety and health standards, and working hours.
   Medium: Working conditions acceptable, usually with acceptable safety and health standards, and premium for working longer hours.
   Medium/High: Most working conditions are satisfied.
   High: All working conditions are satisfied.

a. Low rank = low labor standards. Rank is inverse to score because higher score indicates better labor standards. Index based on average of the 5 indicators: high = 5, medium/high = 4, medium = 3, medium/low = 2, low = 1.
b. ILO conventions ratified: high = ratified conventions > 50, medium/high = ratified conventions > 40 and < 50, medium = ratified conventions > 20 and < 40, low = ratified conventions < 20.

Sources: World Trade Organization; US Department of State (2002, 2004, 2005); World Bank (2004b); ILO database.

2

Agricultural Market Access and Related Issues

Agriculture will challenge negotiators of a US-Pakistan FTA. Pakistan will want to protect a key sector that provides employment and sustenance for the majority of its population, and US producers will want maximum access to a market with high growth potential. But empirical studies suggest that commerce stimulated by bilateral free trade will not displace major segments of agriculture in Pakistan. Trade expansion will affect some commodities that are accustomed to high protection, but long phaseout periods should allow adequate time for adjustment in truly sensitive items. Pakistan will emphasize assistance to build its capacity to ensure clean and safe agricultural shipments.

A US-Pakistan FTA could result in a solid relationship that fosters agricultural trade by eventually eliminating tariffs and tariff-rate quotas (TRQs) and reducing uncertainties and risks. Following the established US approach to other FTAs, subsidies will not be part of the negotiation. To be sure, US agricultural subsidies have a major impact on world trade and commodity prices, and are a legitimate concern to trading partners. However, US doctrine insists that subsidies can only be negotiated multilaterally.

Agricultural aspects of the negotiations for a US-Pakistan FTA are considered in three sections in this chapter. The first presents a brief discussion of Pakistan's agricultural sector and bilateral trade patterns. The second examines tariffs, TRQs, agricultural subsidies, and other barriers. The third section addresses sanitary and phytosanitary (SPS) matters. We conclude with our recommendations for the negotiations in these areas.

Pakistan's Agricultural Sector and Bilateral Trade

With more than 65 percent of its population living in rural areas, Pakistan remains an agrarian society. Agriculture accounts for nearly 23 percent of the country's GDP and employs 42 percent of its labor force. Pakistan's agricultural sector is also composed largely of small farm and livestock units. In fact, farms of fewer than 49 acres constitute about 80 percent of the farm area, while the median herd has just a few animals (table 2.1a).[1]

While these features underscore the economic importance of agriculture in Pakistan, the sector's special sensitivity results from the high incidence of poverty in rural areas. According to 2002 World Bank data, 72 percent of Pakistan's poor live in rural areas.[2] Agriculture provides, directly or indirectly, their main source of income. Milk, butter, and wheat are especially sensitive, as they furnish the livelihood of most people.

Livestock (including byproducts such as meats, milk, and eggs) contributes almost half of all value added in agriculture. The largest numbers of livestock are buffalo and cattle, although poultry flocks have grown rapidly in recent years (table 2.1b). Livestock production faces daunting development problems: lack of commercial farms, low productivity due to poor animal nutrition, weak infrastructure, lack of financing, and recently, avian flu. For these reasons, dairy items and poultry meats are the most sensitive animal products in Pakistan. Yet despite these problems, Pakistan is mostly self-sufficient in animal products.

A few major crops—sugarcane, wheat, cotton, and rice (table 2.1b)—contribute most of the remaining value added (some 34 percent) to the country's total agricultural GDP. Pakistan is the world's fourth-largest producer of cotton, the fifth in sugarcane, and the twelfth in paddy rice. The country's top exports (e.g., textiles and clothing, rice, and sugar) are based on these crops, but it also imports large quantities of cotton and nondurum wheat.[3] As the leading food staple and an important source of farm income, wheat is the most sensitive crop in Pakistan and benefits from specific governmental support (e.g., state purchases). Other "minor crops" are produced in Pakistan, but their contribution is declining. Notable exceptions are fruits, dates, and corn. In fact, Pakistan is among the top 10 world producers of mangoes, apricots, tropical fruit, dates, onions,

---

1. Conversely, in the United States all farmland is controlled by farm units well over 50 acres—the median size is over 2,000 acres—while most of the livestock is held in large herds of well over 50 animals (table 2.1a).

2. In 2002, about 47 million Pakistanis lived below the national poverty line, of which 34 million lived in rural areas (World Bank 2004a).

3. Pakistan is emerging, however, as a wheat exporter, particularly of wheat flour.

Table 2.1a Agricultural profile of the United States and Pakistan (percent distribution)

Type of farm or herd	Pakistan			United States		
	Share of total farms	Share of farm area	Livestock[a]	Share of total farms	Share of farm area	Livestock[b]
0–10 acres or heads[c]	86	43	76	8	0	2
10–49 acres or heads[c]	13	35	21	26	0	16
More than 50 acres or heads	2	21	3	65	100	82
Total	100	100	100	100	100	100
Median	3 to 5 acres	12 to 25 acres	5 to 6 heads	70 to 99 acres	2,000 to 5,000 acres	200 to 499 heads

a. Cattle and buffalo only.
b. Cattle of all kinds.
c. For Pakistan's farm sizes, the categories used are 0 to 12.5 acres and 12.6 to 49 acres.

Sources: Government of Pakistan (2000); USDA (2002b).

Table 2.1b Pakistan's agricultural production

Product	2000–2001	2004–05
Selected livestock population (millions of heads)[a]		
Buffalo	23.3	26.3
Cattle	22.4	24.2
Goats	49.2	56.7
Poultry	292.4	366.0
Sheep	24.2	24.9
Animal products (millions of metric tons)		
All meats[b]	2.0	2.3
Milk	26.2	29.4
Major crops (millions of metric tons)		
Sugarcane	43.6	45.3
Wheat	19.0	21.1
Cotton (bales)	10.7	14.6
Rice	4.8	5.0
Corn	1.6	2.8

a. Ranked according to the Food and Agriculture Organization's (FAO) livestock unit conversion factors: cattle and buffalo (0.50); sheep and goats (0.10); and poultry (0.01).
b. Beef, mutton, and poultry.

Sources: FAO (2005); Government of Pakistan (2005a).

peas, and pulses (Food and Agriculture Organization's FAOSTAT database, 2005).

Pakistan's food processing industry (food, beverages, and tobacco) contributes 4 percent of GDP and employs 2 percent of the country's labor force.[4] While these sectors are relatively large components of the nation's manufacturing base (comprising 22 percent of manufacturing value added and 13 percent of the manufacturing labor force), they face important development challenges, such as the absence of a sophisticated canning and packaging industry, coupled with weak transportation and storage facilities. Pakistan has welcomed joint ventures with foreign firms to raise standards. EU and Swiss investors have strengthened Pakistan production of poultry, cereals, biscuits, breads, fruit juices, and dairy. US firms dominate Pakistan's small soft drink and fast foods sectors and have a stake in soups, noodles, mayonnaise, and canola and sunflower oil. Pakistan's imports of processed foods are small and limited to a few supermarkets that cater to the country's elite and the armed forces (Promopak 2001).

---

4. The government retains a small role in the food processing sector (i.e., vegetable ghee and breakfast cereal production), while sugar production is "almost entirely owned by politicians operating a cartel" (*The Economist,* 2006, 5).

Exports

For decades, Pakistan's agriculture has suffered development policies that established unfavorable relative prices and reduced investment incentives. In addition, geopolitical tensions effectively cut off agricultural exports to the Indian market. But priorities are now shifting. The government believes that the revitalization of agriculture can play a major role in raising the incomes of the poor and in diversifying national exports. Pakistan's total agricultural exports have increased rapidly in recent years, particularly in value terms (table 2.2). Export volume increased significantly during 1996–2000, but gains were small in 2000–2004.

Pakistan is strategically placed in a net food-importing region. About 54 percent of its agricultural exports are shipped to the Persian Gulf countries and Afghanistan (table 2.2).[5] Other important markets include the United Kingdom, India, some eastern African countries, China, and the Association for Southeast Asian Nations (ASEAN) (table 2.2). Progress in bilateral and regional negotiations could create new opportunities for Pakistani farmers in these and other regional markets.

Agricultural exports to the United States are very small—$38 million in 2004 (table 2.3), or just under 3 percent of Pakistan's total agricultural exports (table 2.2). Table 2.4 lists the principal product categories: rice, vegetable saps, sugars, spices, and dates. While total export values to the US market are barely significant, some commodities have performed well. Rice exports have doubled in volume and value; but fresh fruits (mangoes, tangerines, guava, and apricots) and shrimp perform rather poorly in the US market compared with Canada and the United Kingdom.[6]

Imports

While Pakistan is a significant producer of many agricultural products, the size of its domestic market creates substantial import needs for specific products, with the result that, on balance, Pakistan is a net agricultural importer. In 2004 Pakistan exported $1.3 billion in agricultural products and imported about $2.5 billion. The import figure is low in

---

5. Agricultural exports represent almost 30 percent of Pakistan's exports to Saudi Arabia, the United Arab Emirates, and Kuwait. The share of agriculture in total Pakistan exports is only 8 percent.

6. Shrimp exports (not technically an agricultural product) were the object of trade litigation with environmental overtones. In 1996 the government of Pakistan challenged in the WTO a US import ban on the importation of shrimp. The US import ban reflected US regulation requiring devices and measures that reduce the mortality of sea turtles. After some modifications to the original provisions, the WTO Appellate Body sustained the US regulation under Article XX of the GATT 1994.

Table 2.2 Pakistan's total agricultural exports
(millions of US dollars)

Country/region	1996	2000	2004
Middle East[a]	255	320	462
United Arab Emirates	119	151	236
Saudi Arabia	63	62	73
Economic Cooperation Organization[b]	60	89	249
Afghanistan	6	78	203
Iran	49	9	45
EU-15[c]	122	147	166
United Kingdom	36	62	56
Netherlands	53	38	31
Africa[d]	147	141	157
SAFTA[e]	72	107	89
India	29	47	43
North Asia[f]	68	59	76
China and Hong Kong	26	26	37
ASEAN[g]	31	41	59
Other partners	80	60	64
Total	835	964	1,322

ASEAN = Association of Southeast Asian Nations
SAFTA = South Asian Free Trade Area

a. Middle East includes Bahrain, Egypt, Iraq, Jordan, Kuwait, Lebanon, Oman, Qatar, Saudi Arabia, Syria, United Arab Emirates, and Yemen.
b. The Economic Cooperation Organization comprises Afghanistan, Azerbaijan, Iran, Kazakhstan, Kyrgyz Republic, Tajikistan, Turkey, Turkmenistan, and Uzbekistan.
c. European Union excluding the 10 new members.
d. All African countries excluding Egypt.
e. SAFTA comprises Bangladesh, Bhutan, India, Maldives, Nepal, and Sri Lanka.
f. North Asia comprises China, Hong Kong, Japan, North and South Korea, and Taiwan.
g. ASEAN includes Brunei Darussalam, Cambodia, Indonesia, Laos, Malaysia, Myanmar, Philippines, Singapore, Thailand, and Vietnam.

Note: Agriculture is defined as sections 0, 1, 2 (2.2 only), and 4 of the Standard International Trade Classification (SITC) Rev. 3. Includes commodities and food, beverages and tobacco, and oils of animal and vegetable origin.

Source: UN Statistics Division (2005).

relation to the total population: Pakistanis spent only $15 per capita per year in foreign foods and fibers (including raw cotton). Trade barriers undoubtedly depressed imports, but consumer preferences for fresh foods, the relatively small urban population, and low income levels are important factors in the equation.

Table 2.3 Agricultural and total trade between the United States and Pakistan

Category	1996	1998	2000	2002	2004
Agricultural trade (millions of US dollars)					
US exports	345	188	56	194	300
US imports	43	29	32	31	38
Trade balance	302	159	24	163	261
Total trade (millions of US dollars)					
US exports	1,277	726	462	694	1,811
US imports	1,266	1,691	2,167	2,305	2,874
Trade balance	11	−965	−1,705	−1,611	−1,063
Shares of agriculture (percent)					
In total bilateral trade	15	9	3	7	7
In US exports to Pakistan	27	26	12	28	17
In US imports from Pakistan	3	2	1	1	1

Source: USITC (2005a).

Pakistan's agricultural imports are highly concentrated in a few products and countries. Animal and vegetable oils, raw cotton, oilseeds, cereals, and tea account for more than 85 percent of the country's imports (table 2.5). Malaysia, the United States, Indonesia, and Australia provide the bulk of Pakistan's imports (table 2.6). The country's current rapid GDP growth rates—if sustained—will expand import demand, especially for animal protein and packaged foods.[7]

Current levels of US agricultural exports to Pakistan, about one-sixth of total US exports to the country, total around $300 million,[8] and as table 2.5 illustrates, are highly concentrated in primary commodities or semiprocessed products, namely cotton and cereals.

The United States remains the leading supplier of high-quality cotton. The United States is the main corn supplier to Pakistan, and has traditionally been the main wheat supplier as well, although Australian wheat has successfully challenged US wheat over the past decade.[9] In

---

7. The UN Food and Agriculture Organization (FAO 2003) projects almost a doubling in consumption of milk, meats, and eggs between 2000 and 2015. It also estimates that, in 2015, domestic production of these products will match or exceed domestic consumption.

8. Estimates of bilateral trade differ substantially across sources. While the USITC estimates 2004 US exports to Pakistan at $300 million, UN Comtrade reports $400 million. Differences result from conflicting estimates of trade in cereals and animal and vegetable oils. Table 2.5 presents trade estimates from each source.

9. According to the Commerce Department, Australian wheat has made inroads into the market through "predatory pricing, cheap freight and credit, and other non-market tactics" (US Commercial Service 2001). As indicated in the text, political factors may have damaged the reputation of US producers as reliable suppliers.

Table 2.4 Pakistan's top agricultural exports to the United States
(millions of US dollars)

HS category	Description	Exports, 2004	Share, 2004	Average MFN tariff, 2002 (percent)	Under GSP
HS 10	Rice (HS 1006)	12	.32	4.2[a]	0
1006.30.90	Long grain rice	7	.17	11.2[b]	0
1006.20.20	Basmati rice	5	.13	1.1[c]	0
HS 13	Vegetable saps and extracts (HS 1302)	9	.24	1.1[a]	1
1302.32.00	Mucilages and thickeners	8	.21	Free	0
1302.12.00	Vegetable saps	1	.03	3.8	1
HS 17	Sugars and sugar confectionery	4	.12	13[a]	4
1703.10.50	Other molasses	3	.09	0[d]	3
HS 19-22	Prepared foodstuff	4	.09	9.6[a]	4
2106.90.99	Food preparation nesoi	1	.03	6.4	1
HS 09	Spices	3	.09	0.9[a]	2
091.50.00	Curry	1	.04	Free	0
091.91.00	Other mixed spices	1	.03	1.9	1
HS 08	Dates	2	.05	4.2[a]	0
0804.10.60	Dates without pit	2	.05	3.5[e]	0
	Other commodities	4	.10	n.a.	0
	Total	38	1.00	8.7[f]	11

GSP = generalized system of preferences
HS = Harmonized Schedule
MFN = most favored nation
n.a. = not applicable
nesoi = not elsewhere specified or included

a. Simple average of all tariff lines, including ad valorem equivalents (AVEs), for the corresponding HS category.
b. The value reported corresponds to the most recent AVE (2002). The actual value of the 2005 tariff is 1.4 cents/kg.
c. The value reported corresponds to the most recent AVE (2002). The actual value of the 2005 tariff is 0.83 cents/kg.
d. The value reported corresponds to the most recent AVE (2002). The actual value of the 2005 tariff is 0.01 cents/kg of total sugar.
e. The value reported corresponds to the most recent AVE (2002). The actual value of the 2005 tariff is 2.8 cents/kg.
f. Average estimated based on customs duties paid by Pakistan's agricultural exports.

Source: USITC (2005a, 2005b).

Table 2.5 Pakistan's agricultural imports from the world and the United States, 2004 (millions of US dollars)

HS chapter	Description	From world	From United States Comtrade	From United States USITC	US share in Pakistan imports[a] (percent)
15	Fats, animal and vegetable	798	46	26	6
52[b]	Cotton	591	196	181	33
12	Oilseeds	269	8	8	3
10	Cereals	254	140	68	55
09	Coffee, tea, spices	251	0	0	0
07	Edible vegetables	106	1	1	1
08	Edible fruit, nuts	50	1	1	1
23	Residues, wastes	27	0	0	0
19	Cereal, flour, starch	26	1	1	2
41[a]	Raw hides and skins	26	1	0	2
04	Dairy products	17	2	6	10
21	Miscellaneous edible preparations	15	3	3	18
11	Milling products	14	8	0	53
	Other agricultural chapters	108	4	4	3
	Of which, processed food products[c]	1,301	61	37	5
	Total	2,552	408	305	16

USITC = US International Trade Commission

a. Based on UN Comtrade database.
b. Tariff lines corresponding to agricultural products only.
c. Food products includes dairy products; fruits, vegetables, or spices; products of cereal and flours; preparations of vegetables, fruits, or nuts; vegetable and animal oils; miscellaneous edible preparations; and beverages.

Source: UN Statistics Division (2005).

vegetable oils—the largest agricultural import of Pakistan—US exports trail far behind palm oil exporters from Malaysia and Indonesia. Australian and EU firms outsell US oilseed producers.

Foreign policy decisions have often affected bilateral trade since US food aid programs have been used to exercise pressure on Pakistan to comply with US security concerns. In 1998–99, US agricultural exports to

Table 2.6 Pakistan's total agricultural imports, selected sources
(millions of US dollars)

Source country	1996	2000	2004
Malaysia	583	346	454
United States	437	71	405
Indonesia	71	62	282
Australia	101	227	241
Brazil, Canada, and Argentina	125	125	162
Kenya	105	144	146
India and Sri Lanka	172	115	118
Total	1,946	1,656	2,552

Note: Agriculture is defined as sections 0, 1, 2 (2.1, 2.2, 2.3, and 2.6.3 only), and 4 of SITC Rev. 3.

Source: UN Statistics Division (2005).

Pakistan, particularly exports of wheat, were sharply curtailed when the United States sanctioned both India and Pakistan after they detonated nuclear bombs (table 2.3).[10] The US reputation as a reliable source—particularly for wheat—was damaged in this episode.

Historically, Pakistan has been a prominent recipient of agricultural exports under US food aid programs, but such exports have declined since 2002. US food aid shipments to Pakistan in 2004 were only $24 million—about a third of average values recorded in earlier years and only 8 percent of total US agricultural exports to Pakistan that year (table 2.7).[11] Eligible food and commodities vary year to year, but vegetable oils have accounted for the largest share of shipments to Pakistan in recent years.

Impact of a US-Pakistan FTA: The CGE Model

The computable general equilibrium (CGE) and gravity models provide a reassuring view of the political feasibility of the US-Pakistan FTA negoti-

---

10. The United States imposed sanctions on India on May 13, 1998, and on Pakistan on May 30, 1998, pursuant to section 102 of the Arms Export Control Act (also known as the Glenn Amendment). In 1996 Pakistan was the top 25th export market for US agricultural exports; when the full effect of sanctions was felt in 1999, the country dropped to the 62nd position.

11. US food aid shipments to Pakistan were large between 2000 and 2002, partly on account of a drought that curtailed Pakistani agricultural production.

Table 2.7 Food aid in US agricultural exports to Pakistan
(average, millions of US dollars)

Category	1999–2000	2001–02	2003–04
US agricultural exports to Pakistan	72	164	266
US food aid to Pakistan	54	88	21
Vegetable oils	n.a.	63	8
Wheat	n.a.	1	2
Other commodities[a]	n.a.	24	12
Ratio of food aid to US exports (percent)	75	54	8

n.a. = not available

a. Other commodities include soybeans, dry milk, lentils, tallow, and peas.

Source: USDA (2005b).

ations, predicting, among other things, significant growth (nearly 40 percent) in two-way agricultural trade.

Additionally, the CGE model predicts that nearly all of these gains will accrue to US agricultural exports to Pakistan, with strong performances of US exports of grains and processed foods. For a net food importing country such as Pakistan, this could have important benefits for some segments of the population, particularly urban dwellers (who would, for example, enjoy a richer and more varied diet and access to cheaper foods).

On the other hand, the CGE model also predicts that a US-Pakistan FTA would not lead to higher agricultural exports overall from Pakistan to the United States. While the CGE estimates are too conservative, they reflect the fact that a number of Pakistan's agricultural exports already have duty-free access to the US market. The agreement should, however, help surmount SPS obstacles that currently limit Pakistan's exports, particularly in certain fruits and vegetables where the country could become a competitive supplier. As shown in table 2.8, over the four-year period 1999–2002, US producer prices for a wide range of fruits and vegetables averaged well above Pakistani levels. Gains could also be facilitated by the presence of large South Asian ethnic communities in the United States.[12]

A US-Pakistan FTA should not lead to large displacements in Pakistan's rural areas: Calculations suggest only a 1 percent fall in production by volume for the declining subsectors in agriculture. However, the

---

12. According to the latest census data, nearly 225,000 Pakistanis (by birth regardless of citizenship status) live in the United States, compared with 340,000 in the United Kingdom. The Pakistani-born US population has a higher median per capita income and better educational attainments than the Pakistani-born population in the United Kingdom.

Table 2.8 Ratio of average producer prices, 1999–2002
(based on prices in US dollars per ton;
Pakistan price = 100)

Product	India	United States
Fruits and vegetables		
Bananas	79	498
Dates	n.a.	348
Fruits, fresh nes	84	381
Grapes	55	74
Lemons	62	92
Mangoes[a]	111	227
Oranges	357	161
Tangerines	n.a.	326
Potatoes	115	108
Onions, dry	94	208
Major crops		
Corn	82	55
Cotton lint[b]	215	173
Rice, paddy	82	70
Soybeans	81	67
Sugar cane	96	151
Tobacco	86	666
Wheat	103	74
Animal products (live weight)		
Cattle meat	n.a.	68
Chicken meat	125	96
Sheep meat	295	356
Milk and other animal products		
Cow milk, whole fresh	72	104
Hen eggs	65	110
Wool	155	157

n.a. = not applicable
nes = not elsewhere specified

a. US price corresponds to import unit price.
b. Quality differences distinguish all farm products, but in the case of cotton, the quality difference between US fiber and Pakistan fiber is sharp. Hence the higher US price index is a misleading indicator of bilateral comparative advantage.

Note: FAOSTAT producer prices refer to the national average prices of individual commodities comprising all grades, kinds, and varieties received by farmers when they participate in their capacity as sellers of their own products at the farm gate or first point of sale. Pakistan, however, reported wholesale prices.

Source: FAO (2005).

impact could be noticeable in the food processing sector, where the CGE calculations indicate a 5 percent decline. The drop might be mitigated by increased foreign investment and joint ventures.

Tariffs, TRQs, and Other Barriers

This section examines the principal trade policy measures that limit agricultural imports in both countries. The analysis for Pakistan centers on tariffs for two reasons: They are the country's principal trade policy instrument (WTO 2002a), and they are the focus of all US negotiating efforts with developing countries. US protection entails instruments besides tariffs, such as TRQs, antidumping measures, SPS measures, and subsidies.

Pakistan

In recent years, Pakistan has made significant efforts to lower and simplify its tariff structure (WTO 2002a). The simple average tariff for agricultural imports, using the WTO definition, dropped from 44 to 19 percent between 1996 and 2006. In overall terms, Pakistan's level of tariff protection for agricultural products is similar to that for manufactured products. While the government does not apply TRQs, it maintains import bans on imports from India and Israel.

The extent of tariff dispersion in agriculture was simplified by assigning nearly all products to one of five duty categories: 5, 10, 15, 20, and 25 percent. About half of all agricultural tariff lines fall in the first two categories (5 and 10 percent tariffs). However, tariffs of 25 percent affect close to a third of tariff lines in agriculture.[13] The *2002 WTO Trade Policy Review* identifies tariff escalation as a feature of the Pakistani tariff schedule (WTO 2002a). Table 2.9 shows that 2005 applied tariffs are particularly high for dairy products (HS 4); fruits (HS 8); certain food preparations based on meat (HS 16); and processed foods such as fruit juices, soups and broths, pasta, sauces and condiments, foods from roasted cereals, and honey (HS 19–22). Poultry meats and some instances exported final products (e.g., dates, fruits, and spices) also obtain above-average protection.[14]

---

13. We define agricultural products to mean HS chapters 1 through 24, plus selected lines in HS chapters corresponding to hides, wool, and cotton (HS 41, 50, 52). Fish and forestry products were excluded.

14. The following reassurance was extended by Minister of Finance Omar Ayub Khan in the 2005–06 budget speech: "[The] Agriculture Sector enjoys primary importance in our economy. Therefore we have proposed reduction[s] in many tariff lines pertaining to agriculture. At the same time it has been ensured that such reductions do not adversely affect the existing protections available to our developing dairy, poultry, and fish farming sectors."

Table 2.9 Pakistan's applied MFN tariffs for agricultural products, 2005

HS chapter	Item	Number of lines Ad valorem	Non ad valorem	Simple average tariff (percent)[a]	Standard deviation (percent)
01	Live animals	32	0	6.9	5.9
02	Meat, edible offal	58	0	15.8	8.4
04	Dairy products	31	0	21.6	7.0
05	Animal products nes	23	0	7.6	6.9
06	Live trees, plants	14	0	9.3	6.2
07	Edible vegetables	67	0	8.6	4.5
08	Edible fruit, nuts	61	0	20.2	7.9
09	Coffee, tea, spices	38	0	9.1	4.2
10	Cereals	17	0	7.1	2.5
11	Milling products	30	0	14.3	3.4
12	Oilseed	49	0	5.8	3.1
13	Lac, gums, resins,	15	0	17.0	4.1
14	Vegetable plaiting	11	1	15.0	7.1
15	Fats, animal and vegetable	17	38	14.1	7.3
16	Meat, fish, preparations	28	0	20.5	1.6
17	Sugars	26	0	13.3	6.3
18	Cocoa and cocoa preparations	12	0	15.0	10.4
19	Cereal, flour, starch	20	0	22.1	3.3
20	Vegetable, fruit, preparations	52	0	22.7	4.0
21	Miscellaneous edible preparations	24	0	19.4	7.0
22	Beverages, vinegar	23	0	76.0	31.0
23	Residues, wastes	26	0	11.3	4.6
24	Tobacco	10	0	19.0	9.7
41[b]	Raw hides and skins	14	0	6.3	5.2
43[b]	Furskins	6	0	5.0	.0
50[b]	Silk	5	0	5.0	.0
51[b]	Wool, animal hair	17	0	5.0	.0
52[b]	Cotton	7	0	7.1	2.7
53[b]	Vegetable textile	6	0	5.0	.0
	Totals and averages	739	39	15.6	6.0

MFN = most favored nation
nes = not elsewhere specified

a. Ad valorem tariff lines only.
b. Tariff lines corresponding to agricultural products only.

Source: Pakistan Central Board of Revenue (2005a).

Two product categories are highly sensitive in Pakistan and consequently are granted differential treatment: animal and vegetable oils and alcoholic beverages. The government applies specific duties and surcharges on imports of vegetable and animal oil (HS 15)—its top agricultural import from the world and an important US export to Pakistan (table 2.5).[15] For religious reasons, imports of beer, wine, and spirits face tariff peaks ranging from 50 to 100 percent (table 2.10).[16] As a Muslim country, Pakistan bans the consumption of alcoholic beverages; however, the *Census of Manufacturing Industries 2000/01* reports the existence of a limited number of local breweries. Elimination of the high tariffs on vegetable oils and alcoholic beverages could in part explain the significant expansion in US exports of processed foods predicted by the CGE model.

Almost 90 percent of US agricultural exports to Pakistan are subject to tariffs below 10 percent.[17] The bulk of US exports to Pakistan are concentrated in three products—wheat, corn, and raw cotton (table 2.11)—that serve either as basic food staples or as inputs for manufactured exports. Though other factors also come into play to limit US exports—geographic distance, competitive suppliers, and income levels—high tariffs restrict specific US exports such as vegetable oils, poultry, and certain processed foods.

While applied tariffs are generally moderate, bound tariffs are another matter. The *2002 WTO Trade Policy Review* (WTO 2002a) reports that Pakistan has bound 90 percent of its agricultural tariff lines with a simple average of 97 percent. The gap between the average bound and average applied rates is nearly three times larger than the gap for manufactured products. Pakistani authorities argue that the gap permits necessary flexibility to deal with temporary imbalances. At the same time, the gap obviously introduces uncertainty for exporters.

Pakistan is actively pursuing bilateral negotiations that have involved, or will involve, the concession of preferential access for agricultural products. To date, only one FTA has been concluded, with Sri Lanka. A limited agreement with Iran and early harvest agreements with China and Malaysia may serve as preludes for true FTAs.[18] The latter

---

15. The *2002 WTO Trade Policy Review* states that no ad valorem equivalent was reported for those tariff lines. However, Pakistan tariffs on edible oil could reach as high as 40 percent.

16. According to the 2005/06 Import Policy Order, imports of wines and spirits (HS 2203–09) and brewing and distilling machinery are altogether prohibited in Pakistan, although the items are nevertheless subject to listed tariffs of 100 percent. Religious reasons are also cited in the case of the prohibition of imports of pork; however, listed tariff rates are much lower for pork products—around 25 percent.

17. However, wheat faces other charges such as regulatory duties. For the current year the regulatory duty for wheat imports was established at 415 rupees per 40 kilograms.

18. The early harvest agreement between Pakistan and China includes reciprocal duty-free treatment for a few agricultural products, mostly fruits and vegetables (HS chapters 7 and 8). The early harvest agreement between Pakistan and Malaysia reduces tariffs on palm nuts but not on palm oil.

Table 2.10 Pakistan's highest tariff peaks and specific tariffs in agriculture, 2005

HS 4-digit category	Description	Average tariff	Number of tariff lines[a]
Peaks above 25 percent			
2203	Beer made from malt	100	1
2204	Wine of fresh grapes, including fortified wines	100	4
2205	Vermouth and other wine flavored with plants or other substances	100	2
2206	Fermented beverages and mixtures nesoi	100	1
2207	Undenatured ethyl alcohol of more than 80 percent volume	75	2
2208	Undenatured ethyl alcohol of less than 80 percent volume	100	7
Specific tariffs			
1404	Vegetable products nesoi—betel leaves	Rs.150/Kg	1
1507	Soybean oil and its fractions	Rs. 9,625/ MT	2
1508	Groundnut oil and its fractions	Rs. 13,725/MT	2
1509	Olive oil and its fractions	Rs. 9,625/ MT	4
1510	Other oils and their fractions	Rs. 10,200/MT	1
1511	Palm oil and its fractions	Rs. 9,840/ MT	5
1512	Sunflower seed, safflower, or cotton seed oil and their fractions	Rs. 16,225/MT	4
1513	Coconut or babassu oil and their fractions	Rs. 10,150/ MT	4
1514	Rape, colza, or mustard oil and their fractions	Rs. 13,525/MT	4
1515	Other fixed vegetable fats and oils and their fractions	Rs. 11,925/ MT	8
1516	Animal or vegetable fats and oils and their fractions	Rs. 10,200/MT	3
1517	Margarine; edible mixtures of animal or vegetable fats or oils	Rs. 10,800/MT	2
1518	Animal or vegetable fats and oils and their fractions, nesoi	Rs. 10,800/MT	1

MT = metric tons
nesoi = not elsewhere specified or included
Rs. = Pakistan rupees

a. Number of tariff lines with high peaks (above 25 percent) or specific tariffs.

Source: Pakistan Central Board of Revenue (2005a).

Table 2.11 Top US agricultural exports to Pakistan
(millions of US dollars and percent)

HS 8-digit category	Description	2004 Exports	2004 Share	2005 tariff (percent)
HS 5201	**Raw cotton** (not carded or combed)	181	0.64	5.0[a]
5201.00.10	Cotton, staple length under 28.58 mm	135	0.48	5.0
5201.00.20	Other cotton, staple length < 34.9 mm	20	0.07	5.0
5201.00.90	Other cotton, staple length > 34.9 mm	16	0.06	5.0
5201.00.10	Raw cotton, staple length under 25.4 mm	10	0.03	5.0
HS 10	**Cereals**	64	0.23	7.1[b]
1001.90.20	White wheat	54	0.19	10.0
1005.10.00	Yellow corn	10	0.03	5.0
HS 15	**Oils and fats**	26	0.09	14.1[b]
1515.90.80	Other vegetable fats and oils	16	0.06	Rs.10,800/ton
1502.00.00	Animal fat, inedible tallow	8	0.03	10.0
1507.10.00	Soybean oil, crude	2	0.01	Rs. 9,050/ton
	Other commodities	13	0.05	n.a.
	Total	283	1.00	7.8[c]

n.a. = not applicable
Rs. = Pakistan rupees

a. Simple average of all tariff lines for the corresponding HS category.
b. Excludes lines with specific tariffs.
c. Trade-weighted average for US exports based on values reported in this table. For tariff lines with specific duties we assumed an ad valorem equivalent equal to the highest ad valorem duty applied by Pakistan in agricultural products (25 percent). For other commodities, we assumed a value equivalent to Pakistan's MFN average tariff for agricultural products (15.6 percent).

Sources: USITC (2005a, 2005b); Pakistan Central Board of Revenue (2005a).

two agreements provide substantial preferential access for a number of highly protected products such as vegetables and fruits.

In recent years, Pakistan and India have also taken steps to normalize trading relations and increase bilateral trade. India has granted Pakistan most favored nation (MFN) status unilaterally. Pakistan has not reciprocated, but has allowed increased imports, some of which (live animals, garlic, onions, potatoes, and tomatoes) enjoy duty-free access.[19] In December 2004, both countries agreed to normalize trade relations in the context of the South Asian Free Trade Area (SAFTA) initiative. A strong SAFTA could lead to interregional specialization in agricultural products (e.g., cotton, rice, sugars, fruits and vegetables, and processed foods), and would surely alter Pakistan's import patterns for the better.

The government of Pakistan also restricts certain exports as a way of managing the price level for key products, including agricultural inputs used in manufactured exports. Export restrictions currently in force target cotton and wheat, while hides face export taxes. Restrictions on wheat exports aim in principle to ensure food security, as wheat is a central staple of the population. However, in recent years, Pakistan has become an exporter of wheat products. Cotton exports are regulated on the basis of types and grades. In addition to the export taxes on hides, exports of livestock must meet certain procedures and conditions. Previous US bilateral FTAs have typically addressed export controls and taxes and state trading organizations with a view to curtailing their role.

The Trading Corporation of Pakistan (TCP) is responsible for stabilizing the prices of certain commodities (e.g., cotton and sugarcane) at the lower end in the local market, although other government bodies also attempt to fix prices (e.g., provincial governments have a role in pricing sugar cane). TCP interventions are announced on the basis of minimum prices to provide a "fair return to growers" (Akhatar 2005). However, the TCP's role in actual procurement varies from commodity to commodity. For example, the TCP's 2001–02 and 2004–05 interventions in the cotton market failed to sustain the price announced by the government, but still had a positive impact on market sentiment (Orden et al. 2006). The TCP may also leverage its power as a buyer to ensure the production of contamination-free cotton. TCP authorities view a stable cotton market as a precondition to increased production of better grades and staple lengths, which may eventually translate into greater foreign earnings from cotton exports.

The TCP also plays a role in the imports of other sensitive commodities (e.g., sugar and wheat) by encouraging production through the operation of procurement depots that buy and sell at administered prices.[20] Through these depots, the government intervenes in the market and holds large wheat stocks. At moments of low stock, the TCP may import

---

19. Appendix G of the Import Policy Order 2004/2005 lists all importable items from India. Notable exclusions in agriculture are all meats (HS 2), fish (HS 3), dairy items (HS 4), fresh fruits (HS 8), and most processed foods (HS 19–24).

20. USDA GAIN Report PK5017 mentions that the government increased its procurement price to reach a target of 22 million tons of production.

wheat from the United States or Australia.[21] The government also sets minimum procurement prices and quality checks for basmati rice.

Reports by different US agencies raise other specific concerns about the Pakistani trade regime. A US Trade Representative report makes claims of misconduct in customs valuation procedures (USTR 2005a). The US Department of Agriculture (USDA) mentions that the difficulty of collecting sales and income taxes from domestic firms, contrasted with the ease of imposing them on imports, makes these taxes "tantamount to placing a differential tax on imports."

United States

Agriculture remains the most highly protected sector in the United States. Certain products enjoy exceptional levels of protection through high tariffs, TRQs, and other instruments, such as antidumping measures and safeguards. Foreign reports also frequently cite US export subsidies for agricultural products.

High US tariffs and strict TRQs are compounded by the application of specific tariffs on more than 700 agricultural tariff lines (table 2.12). According to the *2004 WTO Trade Policy Review* (WTO 2004a), the US simple average applied MFN tariff in 2002, including ad valorem equivalents, was 5.2 percent on all merchandise but 9.8 percent on agricultural products. Tariff dispersion is very high in selected agricultural chapters and tariff escalation is clearly a feature for certain agricultural products. US tariff peaks are evident on agricultural products that undergo a greater extent of transformation; table 2.13 shows that some of the highest US tariff peaks are found on tobacco, peanuts, sugars and sugar confectionery, dairy products, and food products (HS 18–21). Phaseout schedules in US bilateral FTAs prolong the incidence of tariff escalation, because many of the highest tariff peaks enjoy the longest phaseout periods. Pakistani officials have a record of attacking tariff escalation, and in a US-Pakistan negotiation they will raise specific grievances, such as the high tariffs on dates.[22]

---

21. US producers have complained that the TCP's tender specifications placed US farmers at a disadvantage vis-à-vis Australian competitors. In a recent trip to the United States, the chair of the TCP pledged to review these specifications ("Pakistan Officials in US on Wheat Trade Visit," Kansas Wheat Commission News Archive, www.kswheat.com [accessed July 2006]).

22. Pakistani views on tariff escalation are laid out in the statement discussing an early EU proposal on agriculture in WTO Doha negotiations (WTO document G/AG/NG/W/90). The ad valorem equivalent for US MFN tariffs on imports of fresh or dried dates is about 4 percent on average and does not exceed 8 percent. The US MFN tariff on prepared or preserved dates, however, is 22.4 percent. In the US-Australia FTA, most tariffs on fresh dates were phased out either immediately or over four years. But preserved dates will only reach duty-free treatment 18 years after the agreement entered into force. The pattern is seen in other US FTAs but the differential margins in the phaseout schedules are narrower (e.g., five years in the US-Morocco FTA).

Table 2.12 US applied MFN tariffs for agricultural products, 2002

HS chapter	Product description	Number of lines Ad valorem	Number of lines Non ad valorem	Simple average tariff (percent)[a]	Standard deviation (percent)
01	Live animals	20	8	1.1	2.0
02	Meat, edible offal	54	45	6.1	8.1
04	Dairy products	125	126	12.4	5.0
05	Animal products nes	20	1	0.6	1.4
06	Live trees, plants	20	8	2.9	2.5
07	Edible vegetables	78	89	9.0	7.4
08	Edible fruits, nuts	55	63	5.3	7.7
09	Coffee, tea, spices	40	7	0.7	1.7
10	Cereals	7	14	2.2	4.1
11	Milling products	19	19	4.2	4.2
12	Oilseed	37	24	8.2	34.0
13	Lac, gums, resins	14	1	0.7	1.3
14	Vegetable plaiting	11	2	1.1	1.6
15	Fats, animal and vegetable	37	31	3.6	5.3
16	Meat, fish, preparations	81	9	4.2	5.5
17	Sugars	32	34	6.4	2.9
18	Cocoa and cocoa preparations	44	34	5.8	3.6
19	Cereal, flour, starch	52	18	9.0	5.9
20	Vegetable, fruit, preparations	106	77	11.1	21.5
21	Miscellaneous edible preparations	50	39	7.8	5.4
22	Beverages, vinegar	37	36	1.5	4.8
23	Residues, wastes	24	13	1.8	2.7
24	Tobacco	27	29	90.7	156.3
41[b]	Raw hides and skins	122	n.a.	2.4	1.6
43[b]	Furskins	22	n.a.	2.3	2.1
50[b]	Silk	13	n.a.	1.5	1.6
51[b]	Wool, animal hair	73	26	6.1	8.0
52[b]	Cotton	221	12	9.0	3.7
	Totals and averages	1,441	765	9.8	9.4

MFN = most favored nation
n.a. = not available

a. Includes ad valorem equivalents.
b. All lines considered, including agricultural and nonagricultural products.

Table 2.13 US tariff peaks in agriculture, 2002

HS chapter	Product description	Number of tariff lines above 15 percent	Average peak[a] (percent)
52	Cotton (HS 5201–5203 only)	3	34.5
24	Tobacco and manufactured tobacco substitutes	14	187.5
23	Residues and prepared animal feed	1	17.0
22	Beverages, spirits, and vinegar	7	25.3
21	Miscellaneous edible preparations	23	33.8
20	Preparations of vegetables, fruit, nuts, or other	24	36.2
19	Preparations of cereals, flour, starch, or milk	24	32.2
18	Cocoa and cocoa preparations	16	31.7
17	Sugar and sugar confectionery	12	49.0
16	Preparations of meat, fish, crustaceans, or other	5	36.5
15	Animal or vegetable fats, oils, and waxes	3	18.7
12	Oilseeds and oleaginous fruits and other	2	147.8
8	Edible fruit and nuts; peel of citrus fruit or melons	7	23.8
7	Edible vegetables and certain roots and tubers	16	22.1
4	Dairy items	117	35.6
	Of which:		
	Cheese	83	33.4
	Milk and cream	14	30.9
	Other dairy	20	47.8
3	Fish, crustaceans, mollusks, and other	2	15.0
2	Meat and edible meat offal	7	25.0

a. Average of all tariff lines above 15 percent within 4-digit category, based on ad valorem equivalents.

Note: Tariff peaks are defined as tariffs above 15 percent on an ad valorem equivalent basis.

Source: USITC (2005a, 2005b).

Certain Pakistani agricultural exports, particularly spices, certain sugars, and processed foods, do however benefit from generalized system of preferences (GSP) duty-free access. About 30 to 40 percent of Pakistan's agricultural exports to the United States entered through the GSP between 1999 and 2003. Apart from GSP benefits, other Pakistani exports, such as curry and certain vegetable saps, also enjoy duty-free MFN access to the United States. Overall, just over 60 percent of existing Pakistani agricultural exports already enjoy duty-free access to the US market.

US tariffs remain an immediate obstacle for existing exports of Pakistani rice (specific tariffs have an ad valorem equivalent (AVE) as high as 11 percent) and dates (table 2.4). These products and tobacco are the largest contributors to the US Treasury among Pakistan's limited agricultural exports.

Rice accounts for nearly 50 percent of Pakistan's total agricultural exports to the world, but the United States remains an elusive market: In 2004, less than 2 percent of Pakistan's exports of rice were destined to the United States, mostly to supply ethnic communities. Securing preferential market access for rice exports will be an important objective for Pakistan in its negotiation with the United States, but other concerns, such as the ongoing dispute over the patenting of the basmati name, will arise as well.[23]

US tariffs are also applied on imports of certain fresh and processed fruits such as cantaloupes, tangerines, oranges, apricots, and dried mangoes (although for Pakistan SPS barriers are probably more important in the case of fresh fruits). Tariff escalation is quite strong in both fruits and vegetables. Harvest periods in Pakistan for a few fruits and vegetables coincide with seasonal high tariffs in the United States; for example, watermelons are harvested in March through June, a period when the US tariff jumps from 9 to 17 percent. Many preparations based on fruits and vegetables (HS 20, excluding items based on peanuts) face two-digit tariffs and selective GSP access (typically granted to least-developed countries and not to Pakistan). High US tariffs also restrict US imports of fruit juices, jams, pastes, jellies, purées, and fruits and vegetables otherwise preserved.

The highest US tariffs on agricultural imports are generally levied under US Section 22 TRQs (table 2.14). Certain out-of-quota tariffs are prohibitive, such as those on tobacco (350 percent), peanuts (140 percent), peanut butter and paste (132 percent), and butter oil and substitutes (98 percent). Table 2.15 lists US TRQs. Pakistan has been granted special

---

23. Pakistan and US rice producers from Texas have an ongoing dispute over the patenting of "basmati." So far Pakistan is winning: The US Patent and Trademark Office ruled that US producers had not proven that their rice qualities were significantly different from "prior art" and hence rejected 13 out of 16 claims.

Table 2.14 US tariff-rate quotas, 2002 (tons unless otherwise stated)

Product description	Average out-of-quota tariff rate (percent)[a]	Bound import quota	Fill ratio (percent)[b]
Beef: Fresh, chilled, or frozen	26.4	696,621	83
Cream (hectolitres)	26.8	6,695	65
Evaporated/condensed milk	26.6	6,857	87
Nonfat dried milk	52.6	5,261	98
Dried whole milk	53.8	3,321	96
Dried whey/buttermilk	6.8	296	22
Butter	59.5	6,977	98
Butter oil and substitutes	98.0	6,080	100
Dairy mixtures	37.0	4,105	100
Blue cheese	39.0	2,911	97
Cheddar cheese	30.5	13,256	98
American-type cheese	58.4	3,523	99
Edam and Gouda cheese	50.3	6,816	98
Italian-type cheese	48.1	13,481	99
Swiss/Emmenthal cheese	42.4	34,475	83
Gruyere cheese	46.7	7,855	86
Other cheese	35.7	48,628	99
Lowfat cheese	32.9	5,475	65
Peanuts	139.8	52,906	100
Chocolate crumbs	15.1	26,168	79
Infant formula containing oligosaccharides	64.8	100	100
Place-packed stuffed olives	2.0	2,700	31
Green olives, other	2.7	550	69
Green whole olives	4.3	4,400	19
Mandarin oranges (Satsuma)	0.4	40,000	100
Peanut butter and paste[c]	131.8	20,000	78
Ice cream (hectolitres)	30.4	5,668	57
Raw cane sugar	48.8	1,117,000	81
Other cane or beet sugars or syrups	49.8	22,000	151
Other mixtures over 10 percent sugar	19.6	64,709	99

(table continues next page)

Table 2.14 US tariff peaks in agriculture, 2002 *(continued)*

Product description	Average out-of-quota tariff rate (percent)[a]	Bound import quota	Fill ratio (percent)[b]
Sweetened cocoa powder	18.8	2,313	15
Mixes and doughs	25.8	5,398	100
Mixed condiments and seasonings	13.1	689	45
Tobacco	350.0	150,700	75
Long staple cotton[d]	3.0	40,100	13
Cotton, processed but not spun[d]	29.0	3	100

a. Average based on ad valorem rates or on ad valorem equivalents provided by the authorities.
b. Calculated as the ratio of actual import volumes to the bound import quota.
c. Pakistan and other countries listed on US note 6 to the 2005 US Tariff Schedule are jointly allocated 8 percent of the bound import quota.
d. The bound import quotas have been increased in recent years. India and Pakistan jointly benefit from 35 and 3 percent of the 2005 bound quotas on staple cotton and processed but not spun cotton respectively. The bound values for these tariff-rate quotas are nearly 2.6 million and 1 million respectively.

Note: Table lists tariffs with 2002 fill ratios above 10 percent. Quotas with 2002 fill ratios below 10 percent applied to dried cream, low-fat chocolate, green olives, animal feed containing milk, and four types of cotton.

access under the US TRQs on peanuts and cotton, although the TRQ on peanuts might not be important as this product is not a major export of Pakistan; likewise, the TRQs on raw cotton might not be at issue since Pakistan itself restricts exports of cotton, on the basis of types and grades, to favor domestic producers. Additionally, US TRQs have not prevented Pakistani out-of-quota exports of cotton waste (HS 5202.99) to the United States.

Pakistan counts as a large producer of sugar cane and is a net exporter of sugars and molasses, including to the United States. In 2004 Pakistan's sugar exports to the United States amounted to less than $10 million (table 2.4), which is far below its exports to the United Kingdom. The United States applies low tariffs on molasses, and the majority of Pakistani sugar-related exports to the United States enter through the GSP program. Still, US TRQs affect some exports of sugar confectionery (HS 1704) and sugar-based products. Pakistan's total exports of molasses and confectionery to the world have increased (both in value and quantity) in recent years, reaching nearly $100 million combined. Pakistan is also a large producer of tobacco leaves, but current exports to the world were barely $10 million in 2004, and exports to the United States, where tobacco is a sensitive and highly protected product, are negligible.

Table 2.15 FTA maximum phaseout terms for selected agricultural products

Product	NAFTA: United States–Mexico	United States–Australia	United States–Bahrain	CAFTA-DR[a]	United States–Chile	United States–Morocco	United States–Jordan
Beef	Mexico: IMM US: IMM Except Mexico: Beef offal	Australia: IMM US: TRQ → 18y WTO TRQ and preferential TRQ SFG >> 18y (US)	Bahrain: IMM US: TRQ → 10y	CAFTA-6: Tariffs → 15y US: TRQs → 15y Except DR: TRQs → 15y	Chile: TRQ → 4y US: TRQ → 4y	Morocco: TRQ >> 18y US: TRQ → 15y	Jordan: Tariffs → 10y US: Tariffs → 10y
Poultry	Mexico: TRQ → 10y US: IMM	Australia: Zero US: Tariffs → 4y	Bahrain: IMM US: Tariffs → 5y	CAFTA-6: TRQ → 20y US: Zero SFG (CAFTA-6)	Chile: TRQ → 10y US: TRQ → 10y SFG (Chile)	Morocco: TRQ → 25y US: Tariffs → 10y SFG (Morocco)	Jordan: Tariffs → 10y US: Tariffs → 5y
Turkey	Mexico: TRQ → 10y US: IMM	Australia: Zero US: Tariffs → 4y	Bahrain: IMM US: Tariffs → 5y	CAFTA-6: Tariffs → 10y US: Zero	Chile: TRQ → 10y US: TRQ → 10y SFG (US, Chile)	Morocco: TRQ → 19y US: Tariffs → 10y SFG (Morocco)	Jordan: Tariffs → 10y US: Tariffs → 10y
Pork	Mexico: TRQ → 10y US: IMM SFG (Mexico)	Australia: Zero US: IMM	Bahrain: IMM[b] US: IMM	CAFTA-6: TRQ → 15y US: IMM SFG (CAFTA-6)	Chile: IMM US: IMM	n.a.	Jordan: Tariffs → 10y US: IMM
Corn	Mexico: TRQ → 15y US: IMM	Australia: Zero US: IMM	Bahrain: Zero US: IMM	CAFTA-6: TRQs >> 15y US: Zero SFG (CAFTA-6)	Chile: Tariffs → 4y US: IMM	Morocco: Tariffs → 5y US: IMM	Jordan: IMM US: IMM
Soybeans, meal, and flour	Mexico: Tariffs → 10y US: IMM	Australia: IMM US: IMM	Bahrain: Zero US: IMM	CAFTA-6: IMM US: Zero	Chile: IMM US: IMM	Morocco: Tariffs → 5y US: IMM	Jordan: Tariffs → 5y US: IMM
Soybean oils	Mexico: Tariffs → 10y US: Tariffs → 4y	Australia: IMM US: Tariffs → 10y	Bahrain: IMM US: Tariffs → 10y	CAFTA-6: Tariffs → 15y US: Zero SFG: (CAFTA-6)	Chile: Tariffs → 12y US: Tariffs → 12y	Morocco: Tariffs → 10y US: Tariffs → 10y	Jordan: Tariffs → 10y US: Tariffs → 5y

(table continues next page)

Table 2.15 FTA maximum phaseout terms for selected agricultural products (continued)

Product	NAFTA: United States–Mexico	United States–Australia	United States–Bahrain	CAFTA–DR	United States–Chile	United States–Morocco	United States–Jordan
Wheat	Mexico: Tariffs → 10y US: Tariffs → 10y	Australia: Zero US: IMM	Bahrain: Zero US: IMM	CAFTA-6: Zero US: Zero Except CAFTA-6: Wheat flour tariffs → 15y	Chile: IMM US: IMM Chile: Price band →12y Wheat flour tariffs → 12y SFG (Chile)	Morocco: TRQs >> 15y US: IMM	Jordan: IMM US: IMM
Rice	Mexico: Tariffs → 10y US: Tariffs → 10y	Australia: Zero US: IMM Except parboiled rice (US) tariffs → 4y	Bahrain: Zero US: IMM	CAFTA-6: TRQ →18-20y US: Zero SFG (CAFTA-6)	Chile: Tariffs → 12y US: IMM SFG (Chile)	Morocco: Tariffs → 10y US: IMM	Jordan: IMM US: Tariffs → 5y
Other grains	Mexico: TRQ → 10y US: IMM	Australia: Zero US: IMM	Bahrain: IMM US: IMM	CAFTA-6: Tariffs → 15y US: Zero	Chile: IMM US: IMM	Morocco: Tariffs → 15 y US: IMM	Jordan: Tariffs → 4y US: IMM
Nuts	Mexico: IMM US: IMM	Australia: Zero US: Tariffs → 4y	Bahrain: IMM US: IMM Except US: almonds Tariffs → 10y	CAFTA-6: Tariffs → 10y US: Zero	Chile: IMM US: Tariffs → 4y	Morocco: Tariffs → 5y US: Tariffs → 10y Except Morocco: TRQ almonds (15y) SFG (Morocco)	Jordan: Tariffs → 10y US: Tariffs → 4y
Peanuts and peanut butter	Mexico: Zero US: TRQ → 15y	Australia: IMM US: TRQ → 18y	Bahrain: Zero US: TRQ → 10y	CAFTA-6: IMM US: TRQ → 15y Except Guatemala and Nicaragua Tariffs → 5-10y SFG (US)	Chile: Tariffs → 8y US: Tariffs → 12y	Morocco: Tariffs → 10y US: TRQ → 15y	Jordan: Tariffs → 10y US: TRQ → 10y
Raw cotton	Mexico: Tariffs → 10y US: TRQ → 10y	Australia: Zero US: TRQ → 18y	Bahrain: IMM US: TRQ → 10y	CAFTA-6: IMM US: Tariffs → 15y	Chile: IMM US: Tariffs → 12y	Morocco: IMM US: TRQ → 15y	US: TRQ → 10y

	Mexico	Australia	Bahrain	CAFTA-6	Chile	Morocco	Jordan
Milk and creams	Mexico: TRQ → 10y US: TRQ → 10y	Australia: IMM US: TRQ >> 18y, Same tariffs	Bahrain: IMM US: TRQ → 10y	CAFTA-6: TRQ → 20y US: TRQ → 20y SFG (all parties)	Chile: Tariffs → 8y US: TRQ → 12y	Morocco: Tariffs → 15y US: TRQ → 15y	Jordan: Tariffs → 10y US: TRQ → 10y
Cheese	Mexico: TRQ → 10y US: TRQ → 10y	Australia: IMM US: TRQ >> 18y, Same tariffs	Bahrain: IMM US: TRQ → 10y	CAFTA-6: TRQ → 20y US: TRQ → 20y SFG (all parties)	Chile: Tariffs → 4y US: TRQ → 12y	Morocco: Tariffs → 10y US: TRQ → 15y	Jordan: Tariffs → 5y US: TRQ → 10y
Butter	Mexico: n.a. US: n.a.	Australia: IMM US: TRQ >> 18y, Same tariffs	Bahrain: IMM US: TRQ → 10y	CAFTA-6: TRQ → 20y US: TRQ → 20y SFG (all parties)	Chile: Tariffs → 4y US: TRQ → 12y	Morocco: Tariffs → 8y US: TRQ → 15y	Jordan: IMM US: TRQ → 10y
Fruits	Mexico: Tariffs → 10y US: TRQs → 10y Except Mexico: TRQ apples SFG (US, Mexico)	Australia: Zero US: Tariffs → 18y SFG (US)	Bahrain: IMM US: Tariffs → 10y	CAFTA-6: Tariffs → 15y US: Zero	Chile: IMM US: Tariffs → 12y	Morocco: Tariffs → 10y US: Tariffs → 18y Except Morocco: TRQ apples	Jordan: Tariffs → 10y US: Tariffs → 10y
Fruit juices	Mexico: TRQ → 15y US: TRQ → 15y	Australia: IMM US: Tariffs → 18y Exceptions (US) SFG (US)	Bahrain: IMM US: Tariffs → 10y	CAFTA-6: Tariffs → 15y US: Zero	Chile: IMM US: Tariffs → 12y Exceptions (US) SFG (US)	Morocco: Tariffs → 10y US: Tariffs → 15y SFG (US)	Jordan: Tariffs → 10y US: Tariffs → 10y
Vegetables	Mexico: Tariffs → 10y US: TRQs → 10y Except Mexico: TRQ potatoes SFG (US, Mexico)	Australia: Zero US: Tariffs → 18y Except US: TRQ avocados SFG (US)	Bahrain: IMM US: Tariffs → 10y	CAFTA-6: Tariffs → 15y US: Zero Except Costa Rica TRQs >> 20y (onions, potatoes)	Chile: Tariffs → 12y US: Tariffs → 12y Except US: TRQ avocados SFG (US)	Morocco: Tariffs → 15y US: Tariffs → 18y Except US: TRQ onions, garlic, tomato products (15y) SFG (US, Morocco)	Jordan: Tariffs → 10y US: Tariffs → 10y
Sugar and sugar products	Mexico: TRQ → 15y US: TRQ → 15y	Australia: IMM US: No change	Bahrain: IMM US: TRQ → 10y	CAFTA-6: TRQ >> 15y US: TRQ >> 15y	Chile: Tariffs → 12y US: TRQ → 12y	Morocco: Tariffs → 18y US: TRQ → 15y	Jordan: Tariffs → 10y US: TRQ → 10y

(table continues next page)

Table 2.15 FTA maximum phaseout terms for selected agricultural products *(continued)*

Product	NAFTA: United States–Mexico	United States–Australia	United States–Bahrain	CAFTA-DR	United States–Chile	United States–Morocco	United States–Jordan
Tobacco	Mexico: Tariffs → 10y; US: Tariffs → 10y	Australia: Zero; US: TRQ → 18y	Bahrain: Tariffs → 10y; US: TRQ → 10y	CAFTA-6: Tariffs → 15y; US: TRQ → 15y	Chile: IMM; US: TRQ → 12y	Morocco: Tariffs → 10y; US: TRQ → 15y	Jordan: Excluded; US: Excluded
Distilled spirits and beer	Mexico: Tariffs → 8y; US: Tariffs → 10y	Australia: IMM; US: Tariffs → 18y	Bahrain: Tariffs → 10y; US: Tariffs → 5y	CAFTA-6: Tariffs → 10y; US: Zero	Chile: Tariffs → 2y; US: Tariffs → 12y	Morocco: Tariffs → 15y; US: Tariffs → 15y	US: Tariffs → 10y
Wine	Mexico: Tariffs → 10y; US: Tariffs → 10y	Australia: IMM; US: Tariffs → 11y	Bahrain: Tariffs → 10y; US: Tariffs → 5y	CAFTA-6: Tariffs → 5y; US: Zero	Chile: Tariffs → 12y; US: Tariffs → 12y	Morocco: Tariffs → 10y; US: Tariffs → 11y	US: Tariffs → 10y

CAFTA-DR = Central American Free Trade Agreement–Dominican Republic
Except = Product exception to the phaseout.
IMM = Immediate duty-free treatment
n.a. = not available
Same T = In-quota tariff will remain at its pre-FTA rate.
Same TRQ = Tariff-rate quota will remain at its pre-FTA level.
SFG = Country retains right to invoke special safeguards on this product.
Tariffs → 8y = Tariffs to be phased out in 8 years.
TRQs → 4y/5y/10y/15y/18y/20y = Tariff rate quotas will be eliminated in 4, 5, 10, 15, 18, 20 years.
TRQ, SFG, Tariffs >> 15y/18y/20y = TRQs (or special safeguards or tariffs) will outlive the 15-year/18-year/20-year phaseout period.
Zero = Zero duty before the FTA.

a. US "zero" duty for CAFTA products reflects preferences granted in US unilateral programs.
b. Bahrain will continue to prohibit the importation of live swines provided that such prohibition is not inconsistent with the terms of this agreement or the WTO agreement.

Note: This table does not reflect the "standard phaseout" treatment of each commodity but rather identifies the maximum phaseout allowed by the United States or any of its partners.

Pakistan's agricultural exports have not been targeted by US antidumping or safeguard measures in recent years, although other countries have voiced concern over US licensing systems, invoice requirements, customs fees, and other charges. More recently, foreign governments have objected to higher transaction costs and delays associated with the Homeland Security Act of 2002.

With the noteworthy exceptions of the Mexican and Chilean FTA pacts, most US bilateral FTAs do not promise full elimination of agricultural barriers. In recent FTA negotiations with developing countries, the United States has granted and requested notable exceptions to the free trade benchmark. For example, Morocco's TRQs on certain US beef, wheat and certain pasta products, and poultry will generally extend beyond 20 years, and will last indefinitely for some specific tariff lines. Similarly, the Central American Free Trade Agreement–Dominican Republic (CAFTA-DR) includes virtually permanent exceptions to free trade on sugar and ethanol for imports by the United States, fresh potatoes and onions for imports by Costa Rica, and white corn for imports by the other Central American countries. Table 2.15 illustrates some of the maximum phaseouts allowed in selected US FTAs. However, it should be emphasized that the average US preferential agricultural tariffs, both in unilateral preference schemes and in bilateral FTAs, are significantly lower than the MFN rates (table 2.16).

Pakistan already benefits from preferential access to the US market through the GSP. However, GSP margins of preference for agricultural products are narrower than those in bilateral FTAs.[24] A few simple averages help illustrate this point. In 2002, for agriculture only, the simple average US MFN tariff stood at 9.6 percent, while the figure for GSP was 8.4 percent, and the figure for the North American Free Trade Agreement (US-Mexico) was 2.7 percent.

As developing countries—including Pakistan—have abandoned policies that deliberately imposed an antiagricultural bias in their economies, they have become more aware of the harmful impact of Organization for Economic Cooperation and Development (OECD) subsidy programs. Such programs, especially those maintained by the United States and the European Union, have become a justified target not only for developing countries but also for NGOs and the world community at large. US, EU, and Chinese support policies jointly depress world prices for many commodities produced in Pakistan, most importantly cotton, followed by corn, rice, and wheat. Agricultural subsidy programs thus constitute an important irritant in relations between the United States and Pakistan (see box 2.1 on page 74). In previous FTAs, however, the United States has not accepted terms that might limit its agricultural subsidy programs,

---

24. GSP rates are also less stable, as they are subject to renewal as well as compliance with labor standards and other requirements.

Table 2.16 US average MFN and preferential tariffs by partner country or group, 2002 (percent)

Country/group	All products	Agriculture	Nonagriculture[a]
Canada	0.7	4.3	0.0
Mexico	0.6	2.7	0.2
Jordan	2.7	6.2	2.1
Israel	0.7	4.4	0.0
AGOA[b]	2.4	6.0	1.8
ATPDEA	2.6	6.0	1.9
CBERA	2.4	5.9	1.8
CBTPA	2.3	5.9	1.6
LDC	2.7	6.2	2.1
GSP	3.7	8.4	2.8
MFN	5.1	9.8	4.2

AGOA = Africa Growth and Opportunity Act
ATPDEA = Andean Trade Promotion and Drug Eradication Act
CBERA = Caribbean Basin Economic Recovery Act
CBTPA = Caribbean Basin Trade Partnership Act of 2000
GSP = generalized system of preferences
LDC = less developed countries
MFN = most favored nation

a. Excludes petroleum products.
b. The calculations were made for LDC AGOA beneficiaries, as they constitute the majority of beneficiaries.

Note: If a tariff line is not eligible for the preferential program, the rate used in the calculation of averages is the GSP or MFN rate.

Source: WTO (2004a).

apart from provisions on export subsidies, and it seems most unlikely that a US-Pakistan FTA would depart from this pattern.

While US trade officials recognize the need to reduce US agricultural subsidies, they also contend that subsidies are best handled in the framework of the WTO Doha Round talks. US negotiators stress the need to reach a balanced outcome—which is possible only in the context of the multilateral Doha Round—and they recall that Uruguay Round commitments allowed comparatively high ceilings on European and Japanese subsidy programs. Hence, the United States has proposed a 60 percent cut in its bound ceiling for domestic subsidies, provided that the European Union and Japan correspond with higher cuts of about 83 percent. This negotiating stance gives the United States a rationale for excluding subsidies from the bilateral FTAs.

Table 2.17 US production, consumption, and support of the agricultural sector, 2004

Indicator	Billions of US dollars
Total value of production (at farm gate)	225.4
Total value of agricultural exports[a]	61.4
Total value of agricultural imports[a]	54.0
Total support estimate	108.7
	(48)[b]
Producer support estimate	46.5
	(21)
Of which, market price supports	16.2
	(5)
General services support estimate	34.1
	(15)
Transfers to consumers from taxpayers	28.0
	(12)

a. 2003 cost, insurance, and freight (c.i.f.) import values.
b. Percent share of production in parentheses.

Source: OECD PSE/CSE database, 2004.

With respect to subsidies, the OECD (2003) concludes, "Agricultural policy in the United States is characterized by levels of support below the OECD average." The OECD also notes a long-term tendency toward reduced support payments. However, support under the Farm Act of 2002 is higher, and the extent of market orientation is lower, than when the Farm Act of 1996 was in force.

The producer support estimate (PSE) indicators measure the price-raising effect of border barriers as well as government subsidies. After two years of substantial decline, the PSE increased sharply in 2004 to a level of about $46 billion (mainly because of higher direct subsidies), but still below the record levels of 1999 and 2000 (table 2.17).

The US government's export subsidy programs are frequently mentioned in foreign reports. However, in 2002, the latest figures reported by the WTO, the United States distributed only $32 million, much lower than the $594 million cap agreed under the WTO agreement. Reported export subsidy figures, however, do not include US export finance, insurance, and guarantee programs, which also play a role in promoting exports. US agricultural exports to Pakistan have obtained, and still qualify for, support under some of these programs.[25] According to the *2004 WTO Trade*

25. According to the USDA, allocations of guaranteed export credit under the GSM-102 program amounted to $92 million for Pakistan in 2004. The total value of officially supported export credits for agricultural shipments was $3.4 billion in 2002.

Policy Review (WTO 2004a, 111), "Government-guaranteed export financing confers an export advantage, because the interest rate charged does not reflect the actual risk of the transaction, but rather the credit rating of the underlying guarantee."

Sanitary and Phytosanitary Measures

SPS measures are sometimes viewed as behind-the-border trade barriers. While not necessarily imposed with protectionist intent, SPS standards can become effective barriers to exports for countries, such as Pakistan, that lack the capacity to ensure compliance. The *2004 WTO Trade Policy Review* (WTO 2004a, 47), for example, cites "actions targeted to safeguard consumer health [as] one of the most frequent reasons behind most US quantitative restriction and controls on trade." The *2002 WTO Trade Policy Review* (WTO 2002a) mentions that some Pakistani measures have likewise led to "occasional discrimination" against foreign products.

Approaches to SPS Issues in Other FTAs

SPS issues have received secondary attention in US FTA negotiations with developing countries.[26] The United States has concentrated on outstanding SPS issues rather than raising new issues related to rights and obligations that go beyond the WTO SPS agreement. By contrast, US partners, particularly those that already benefit from duty-free access under a unilateral preferential scheme, often put a higher priority on SPS issues.

Negotiators often deal with outstanding SPS issues before submitting the pact for legislative approval. The US-Chile FTA and CAFTA-DR present valuable precedents of progress in removing barriers in this area that allow for an optimistic assessment of the potential accomplishments of a US-Pakistan FTA. Certain institutional issues were tackled during CAFTA-DR negotiations, and the United States pledged technical assistance from the relevant US agencies. That scenario could be repeated, especially since Pakistan has a record of requesting technical cooperation with respect to the application of WTO SPS measures, as well as to dealing with specific issues such as fruit fly and aflatoxin as SPS problems affecting key Pakistani agricultural exports, namely fruits (citrus and mango) and rice respectively.[27]

---

26. However, a major stumbling block to CAFTA's implementation is whether Central American countries will accept USDA certification of meat products to satisfy local SPS standards.

27. Two irradiation plants were established in November 2005. Governmental agencies are designing a strategy for the dairy sector.

Studies by the International Trade Center (2001) and US Commercial Service (2001) claim that the lack of modern food processing, preservation and distribution systems, and the lack of grading and inspection services constitute serious obstacles to the marketing of Pakistan's poultry, milk, fruits, and vegetables. These deficiencies damage more than a quarter of total fruit production. Progress is under way. The 2003–04 trade policy of Pakistan announced programs for fruit and vegetable treatment and processing plants (apples, potatoes, onions, and dates), and the establishment of a national certification program for organic products. Foreign cooperation has facilitated access to food processing (vapor treatment plants) and packaging technology.

Outstanding SPS Issues for the US-Pakistan FTA

US agencies do not currently identify specific concerns about Pakistani SPS measures, and Pakistan has notified very few SPS measures to the WTO Sanitary and Phytosanitary Committee. From a US perspective, the most recent bilateral SPS issue of relevance was successfully resolved in 2002, when Pakistan eliminated SPS-related barriers that limited US exports of apples and cotton (USDA 2002a). US exports of cotton to Pakistan subsequently boomed.

Pakistan import bans on beef and poultry from countries that reported infections of BSE (or avian influenza) do no affect imports from the United States. However, recognition of US inspection systems for fruits, meats and dairy items exported to Pakistan will be an important US interest. Another area that could attract US interest is labeling requirements.

Products derived from biotechnology do not face hurdles in Pakistan. Genetically modified (GM) soybean and soybean oil are currently imported into Pakistan, and the USDA (2005) does not report specific biotechnology-related trade barriers. Pakistan currently does not grow biotech crops (James 2005), but it expects to increase its reliance on GM seeds.

No US SPS measure notified to the WTO has attracted a response from Pakistan. Still, cargo rejection reports show that some Pakistan agricultural exports fail to meet US requirements. Pakistan's agricultural exports have been rejected (among other reasons) for failure to comply with labeling requirements; salmonella and filthy conditions; and the use of color additives or pesticides prohibited in the United States.[28] Rejected products included citrus, mango, rice, and processed foods such as fruit juices and biscuits.

---

28. Neither the United States nor the European Union systematically tracks the volume or value of rejected cargo. The value estimated by Jaffe and Henson (2005) is low, but these authors also argue that border rejections represent only a small part of the constraints on trade associated with food safety and agricultural health measures.

In April 2005 the United States expanded import eligibility for certain fruits and vegetables. Pakistan was not listed among the countries that benefited from the legislation. The legislation applied principles of regionalization to zones free of fruit flies and established treatment conditions that would serve to qualify certain imports. Similar issues should be of interest to Pakistan. As of December 2005, the USDA Animal and Plant Health Inspection Service (APHIS) was conducting pest-risk assessments on mango and tangerine imports from Pakistan. The trade policy speech of 2003–04 announced a number of policy measures aimed at promoting the export of fresh fruits and vegetables, including the establishment of a national certification for organic products. But while exports of fruits have expanded rapidly since 1990, surpassing $100 million in 2004, exports of vegetables have not shown much improvement.

Recommendations

In previous FTAs with developing countries, the United States has recognized the special sensitivity of agriculture and strived for a balance between development needs and free trade principles. A US-Pakistan FTA will undoubtedly follow the same pattern. Properly managed adjustment, with long phaseout periods for sensitive products, should be feasible. Our recommendations follow.

For Sensitive Products

■ A US-Pakistan FTA should expand market access for Pakistani refined sugar and confectionery producers, on roughly similar conditions as granted under CAFTA-DR to Costa Rica, the Dominican Republic, or Honduras. Pakistan may establish a reciprocal duty-free TRQ for US sugar, high fructose corn syrup (HFCS), and confectionery.

■ Pakistan should grant duty-free TRQ access for US poultry meats. After an 18-year transition period, all imports should be free. Wheat and corn should qualify for linear tariff elimination within 10 years, and parallel elimination of other charges. However, during the transition period the TCP should retain its ability to set procurement prices and restrict exports of these sensitive commodities. The United States should eliminate immediately its tariffs on these products.

■ With regards to the dairy products, US producers will want to establish the "right precedent" for other negotiations and Pakistan will want to protect sensitive items such as milk and butter. The United States and Pakistan should establish large initial duty-free TRQs, with a linear expansion and free trade at the end of a 15-year transition period.

- Beyond the dairy complex, standard US negotiating approach involves TRQs on raw cotton and tobacco. Peanuts, dried onions or tomato paste—products that occasionally qualify for TRQs—should instead qualify for 10-year linear phaseouts. Pakistan should provide immediate duty-free access on raw cotton and commit to a full deregulation of the market within a reasonable period. As highlighted in box 2.1, cotton is an important cash crop and has important implications in poverty reduction.[29] Pakistan should eliminate tariffs on tobacco over 15 years. It may reciprocate on other products.

- US requests for extending TRQ protection for its sensitive products should be balanced with Pakistan's requests for extended protection for vegetable oils. Pakistan should grant significant initial preferences (e.g., initial 50 percent tariff cut), particularly on soybean oils.

Other Products

- While the list of sensitive items is by no means exhaustive, both countries should strive to eliminate their remaining tariffs within 10 years. Vegetables, fruits and nuts, and spices are areas of considerable interest to Pakistan, with different sensitivities on both sides. With few exceptions, the United States should eliminate tariffs on fruits, vegetables, and spices immediately. Pakistan should reciprocate, but it may request 10-year phaseout periods for some processed items (e.g., fresh fruits, jams, juices, and prepared vegetables), but US beef should qualify for immediate duty-free access in Pakistan.

- Pakistan should eliminate tariff peaks established for religious reasons but retain the right to establish regulatory measures that are consistent with the WTO agreement.

- For all other products, regulatory duties and other customs charges should be reviewed and streamlined.

SPS Issues

- The United States should accelerate regulatory changes to allow the importation of fruits and vegetables from Pakistan. Meanwhile, Pakistan should recognize USDA certification for animal products, including beef, poultry products, and dairy items.

- The United States should extend to Pakistan targeted technical assistance to upgrade its domestic SPS regulatory framework. The CAFTA-DR framework should provide the model.

---

29. Tariffs should not be an obstacle since Pakistan has liberalized cotton imports unilaterally. Tackling the role of the TCP will be more difficult.

Box 2.1 US cotton subsidies

Unlike many agricultural products, cotton generally faces low tariff barriers; therefore, most of the gains from liberalization for cotton producers are crucially related to the elimination of subsidies. EU, US, and Chinese cotton producers receive the bulk of world cotton subsidies. Mid-range estimates suggest that worldwide subsidies and other barriers drive down world cotton prices by 10 to 20 percent.[1] There is however considerable debate as to each country's role in distorting world cotton prices. Estimates depend on the assumptions built into each model. Some models conclude that US subsidies, by virtue of being the largest in absolute dollar terms, are particularly damaging. Other models assume fragmented world markets and conclude that EU cotton subsidies—the highest in the world per unit of cotton production—more directly affect producers in poor African countries.

In September 2004 a WTO panel determined that certain US support policies for cotton were inconsistent with US WTO obligations and that they adversely affect the world price of cotton.[2] Furthermore, the panel rejected the US categorization of certain subsidy programs as "minimally trade-distorting." The *US-Brazil Upland Cotton* dispute was closely followed in Islamabad, and Pakistan participated as a third party in the dispute. World cotton prices affect the supply decisions of Pakistan's textile industry, which increasingly relies on US cotton. The mills push back low world cotton prices to Pakistani farmers, particularly sharecroppers and cotton pickers, with adverse implications for the government's poverty reduction efforts and price support mechanisms.[3]

Anderson and Valenzuela (2006) found that Pakistan's cotton production and exports could increase 5 and 60 percent respectively as a result of a successful conclusion of the WTO Doha Round and full US compliance with the WTO panel. Orden et al. (2006) estimate that a 20 percent increase in real cotton prices would lift almost two million Pakistanis out of poverty and reduce the poverty rate among Pakistan's sharecropper households that produce cotton by 40 to 60 percent.[4] The findings in these two reports illustrate some of the real benefits awaiting a successful conclusion of the WTO Doha Round, keeping in mind of course that other market forces—including world demand for cotton and synthetic fibers, and the rupee/dollar exchange rate—play a larger role in price determination.[5]

The *Upland* cotton case reminded US congress members that inaction on subsidies will come at a price: poor prospects for the WTO Doha Round and strong prospects of further litigation in Geneva. Uruguay, for example, is already considering the establishment of a panel to review the impact of US subsidy programs on rice. Hence, the US Congress is currently under pressure to reassess the terms of many subsidy programs, and eliminate those that cause "serious prejudice" to other WTO members (Schnepf 2005).[6]

(box continues on next page)

Box 2.1 *(continued)*

The United States has stated its commitment to comply with the ruling on the *Upland* cotton case. Administrative changes on export credit guarantee programs were announced in June 2005, and a week later the United States proposed legislation relating to the export credit guarantee and step 2 programs. In February 2006 the US Congress repealed two parts of the Step 2 program. Ensuring full compliance with the ruling will demand further congressional action in 2006, but the largest repercussions of the case will be seen when the 2007 farm bill is drafted. Brazilian authorities, however, have expressed doubts about the United States' full compliance with the ruling.

---

[1] Orden et al. (2006) conduct a literature review of studies that estimate the impact of subsidies on world cotton prices.

[2] These findings apply to subsidy programs contingent on market prices for the years 1999–2002. However, the panel reported no numeric estimate of the impact.

[3] Note that US and Pakistani cotton participate in differentiated markets due to dissimilar qualities. Cotlook "A" and "B" cotton price indexes have moved in tandem but price differentials have expanded in recent years. However, Gillson et al. (2004) list Pakistan among the group of countries that stand to gain from full elimination of cotton subsidies.

[4] The overall impact for Pakistan's agriculture could be much larger than suggested by those estimates. According to Food and Agriculture Organization estimates, 7 million rural Pakistani households were involved in cotton production in 2001. However, Anderson and Valenzuela (2006) calculate a negative net welfare effect for Pakistan as a whole from the elimination of cotton subsidies.

[5] Likewise other factors could contribute to improving the situation of poor cotton farmers in Pakistan. The introduction (and local adaptation) of genetically modified cotton—increasingly a preferred choice of American, Australian, Chinese, and Indian cotton farmers but still not available in Pakistan—is one prominent example. Aksoy and Beghin (2004) report that the majority of benefits from growing Bt cotton in China went to farmers; and while these findings are not replicated by similar studies in the other producing countries, Anderson and Valenzuela (2006) find large welfare gains for Pakistan as a whole from adoption of genetically modified cotton.

[6] These include mostly wheat, corn, barley, cotton, rice, soybeans, and peanuts.

Source: Baily and Lawrence (2004).

3

Textiles and Clothing

Access to the US textiles and clothing (T&C) market may well present the toughest challenge in the negotiation for a US-Pakistan FTA. Historically the US T&C market has been highly allergic to trade liberalization, and it is currently under intense pressure following the termination of the Multi-Fiber Arrangement (MFA) in January 2005. In FTA talks, it is predictable that Pakistan will strive for maximum market access for T&C, its leading export sector. Such access implies a rapid reduction of US tariffs, liberal rules of origin, and no new quotas. A US-Pakistan FTA should strive to reach these goals. At the same time, Pakistan must dismantle its own barriers to US T&C exports. By eliminating barriers in both countries, and by introducing reasonable rules of origin, the agreement will promote the vertical integration of T&C production between the United States and Pakistan, thereby creating new market opportunities for producers in both countries.[1]

This chapter is structured in four sections. The first section provides a brief account of the industries in both countries and the trends in bilateral trade. The second section reviews trade barriers that persist since the MFA quota system was dismantled in January 2005. The second section also reviews the partial resurrection of quotas with respect to Chinese

---

1. Throughout this chapter, the words "textiles" and "clothing" correspond with the WTO product classifications. Textiles include inputs used in the clothing sector, such as yarn and synthetic fibers, as well as various items for household use, such as bed and bathroom linens and carpets. The abbreviation T&C thus refers to the entire textile and clothing industry.

T&C exports in the fall of 2005. The third section describes the T&C negotiating experiences of both countries in prior FTAs, focusing on phase-out periods, rules of origin, and safeguards. Finally, in the fourth section, we present our recommendations for a US-Pakistan FTA.

Textile and Clothing Production and Bilateral Trade

Pakistan and the United States are both major world producers, exporters, and importers of T&C. The United States is a leading textile exporter and one of the largest importers of T&C (20 percent of world imports).[2] Accordingly, US trade policy has important effects on world T&C trade (WTO 2004a), particularly in finished clothing, which accounts for 80 percent of US imports. With an export share of 2 percent of world T&C trade, Pakistan is a second-tier supplier of total T&C products, although it is a leading world producer and exporter of cotton-based products, particularly textiles.[3]

The importance of the domestic T&C industry for each national economy is quite different. Based on US Census Bureau (2004) data, the contribution of T&C manufacturing to the US economy is quite modest, in terms of both output (3 percent of manufacturing value added and just under 0.5 percent of total GDP) and employment (5 percent of employment in manufacturing and 0.7 percent of total employment). Moreover, the T&C industry has been declining in relative terms since at least 1980 (table 3.1).[4] By contrast, T&C is the leading manufacturing sector in Pakistan (9 percent of total GDP), the largest employer outside of agriculture (35 percent of the nonagricultural labor force), and the principal source of foreign exchange earnings (67 percent of merchandise export sales) (Government of Pakistan 2005a, World Bank 2004b).

---

2. In 2004, US imports ($96 billion) were significantly higher than extra-EU imports of the European Union ($40 billion). However, the relation changes if intra-EU imports ($169 billion) are considered. If the European Union and China/Hong Kong are regarded as unified trading blocs, the United States is also the third largest world exporter of T&C products ($16 billion), mainly textiles (WTO 2005b).

3. Pakistan has the world's third largest installed capacity of short-staple spindles for spun cotton yarn (USITC 2004a). In 2004 Pakistan supplied nearly 30 percent of world cotton yarn exports and 8 percent of world exports of cotton products. WTO statistics rank Pakistan as the 9th world exporter of textiles (Government of Pakistan 2005a).

4. The relative importance of the US T&C industry is also slightly lower than it is in the European Union, where it accounts for 4 percent of manufacturing value added and 7 percent of manufacturing employment (Nordas 2004). The decline of the US T&C industry accelerated after 1995, particularly in terms of employment.

Table 3.1 Long-term trends in the US textile and clothing industries, 1980–2002 (billions of US dollars)

Indicator	1980	1983	1986	1989	1990	1993	1995	1998	2000	2002
Manufacturing GDP	581	683	832	966	1,040	1,131	1,289	1,344	1,426	1,352
Textile and clothing value added	37	38	41	45	47	53	52	53	52	46
Share of textiles and clothing in manufacturing GDP (percent)	6.4	5.6	4.9	4.7	4.6	4.7	4.0	4.0	3.6	3.4
Imports and exports of textiles and clothing										
Exports	5	3	4	7	8	11	14	18	20	17
Imports	11	14	25	32	34	44	52	69	83	84
Net imports	4	10	21	26	26	33	38	51	64	67
Net imports to textile and clothing value added (percent)	12	27	51	57	55	63	73	96	123	146
Textile and clothing productivity and employment										
Value added in constant 2002 dollars (billions)	16	20	25	31	34	43	36	48	49	46
Number of employees (thousands)[a]	n.a.	1,906	1,753	n.a.	1,630	n.a.	1,502	1,172	1,091	846
Value added per employee in constant 2002 dollars[b]	n.a.	10,500	14,100	n.a.	20,700	n.a.	24,000	41,200	45,000	54,400

n.a. = not available

a. Values correspond to data for nearest available year when data for column year were not available. Years used: 1982 for 1983; 1987 for 1986; 1991 for 1990; and 1997 for 1998.

b. Figures rounded to the nearest hundred.

Note: Figures may not add to line totals due to rounding. US import and export figures differ slightly from values in tables 3.3, 3.4, and 3.6 as data is based on different sources.

Sources: US Census Bureau (1990, 1993, 2001, and 2004); WTO (2005b).

The long-term decline of the US T&C industry has been particularly felt by US clothing firms. As a result, textiles have become the largest subsector in the industry, in terms of both shipments and employment. The US textile sector still supplies the bulk of US domestic demand, as indicated by the fact that, in 2002, imports amounted to only 20 percent of domestic textile shipments.

Despite high tariffs and quota protection, US imports of T&C have experienced sustained growth since the early 1980s (table 3.1), at a much faster rate than overall US imports of manufactures.[5] Rising imports of clothing are associated with the emergence of powerful retailing firms with strong connections to foreign suppliers.[6] Two other stylized factors provide the bedrock for import growth: the relaxation and eventual elimination of MFA quotas, and the vertical integration of the T&C industry, especially in the Western Hemisphere.

Until 1994, world trade in T&C was rigidly channeled by the MFA, which allowed developed countries to protect their domestic industries through detailed line item quotas.[7] These quotas limited the overall growth of imports and distributed shares in the US market between competing foreign suppliers. The result in practice was to severely limit market access for the most competitive foreign producers such as China, India, and Pakistan. For example, in 1996 Pakistan shipped only 9 percent of its total textile exports to the US market (table 3.2). China and India faced a similar situation. Correspondingly, the quota system created an incentive for firms to establish production in a wide range of countries that were not particularly competitive but were also not constrained by their assigned quota levels. In 1994 the WTO Agreement on Textiles and Clothing (ATC)—the successor to the MFA that was negotiated in the Uruguay Round—mandated an eventual end to the quota system, following a 10-year transition period. However, the ATC allowed backloaded phaseout schedules; consequently, the highly restrictive effects of textile quotas on the most competitive sup-

---

5. The ratio of net imports to domestic T&C value added jumped from 12 percent in the early 1980s to 63 percent in 1993, and approached 150 percent in 2002, when the ratio of net imports of all manufactures to all manufacturing value added was around 30 percent (Council of Economic Advisers 2004, 63–64).

6. Gereffi and Memedovic (2003, 7) define this phenomenon as the rise of "vertical retailing, whereby a diverse array of national department stores (e.g., JC Penney and Sears), discount chains (e.g., Wal-Mart and Kmart) and specialty retailers (e.g., Gap, Limited Inc., and Benetton) have taken on manufacturing responsibilities to produce private-label or store-brand lines. Today's retailers' overseas offices go well beyond their original buying functions, and they are actively engaged in product design, fabric selection and procurement and monitoring contracted sewing." This tendency is also recorded in EU countries.

7. For a general description of the MFA quota system, see Hoekman and Kostecki (1995). For a specific discussion of the implications of MFA provisions for the United States in the 1990s, see Hufbauer and Elliott (1994).

**Table 3.2 Composition of Pakistan's exports of textiles
and clothing** (millions of US dollars or percent)

Exports	1996	2000	2004
To the United States			
Textiles	444	915	1,394
Clothing	631	1,016	1,217
Textiles and clothing	1,075	1,931	2,611
Share of textiles	41	47	53
Share of clothing	59	53	47
To the rest of the world (excluding the United States)			
Textiles	4,475	3,617	4,731
Clothing	1,241	1,128	1,809
Textiles and clothing	5,716	4,745	6,539
Share of textiles	78	76	72
Share of clothing	22	24	28
Share of the US market in Pakistan textile and clothing exports			
Textiles	9	20	23
Clothing	34	47	40

a. Exports to the United States as percentage of total Pakistani exports.

Note: Textiles and clothing are defined as divisions 65 and 84 of Standard International Trade Classification (SITC) Rev. 3. Therefore, table excludes fibers (raw cotton, man-made, and synthetic fibers) in division 26 of SITC Rev. 3.

Sources: UN Statistics Division (2005); USITC (2005a).

pliers (including Pakistan) were felt until December 2004, and the consequences of the quota removal are still being played out in 2006.

While the quota system was being phased out, US T&C firms relocated their most labor-intensive lines (mainly clothing) to regional partners with lower wages.[8] US imports began to reflect the emergence of a vertically integrated T&C industry throughout North America, Central America, and the Caribbean. The US government promoted integration through a number of initiatives, ranging from the North American Free Trade Agreement (NAFTA), which eliminated tariffs and quotas on Mexican exports, to the

8. Table 3.1 shows that value added per worker in the T&C industry has grown significantly since the 1980s. In the United States, production-sharing programs preceded NAFTA by allowing duty-free treatment for the US components of imported products. While many manufactured products benefited from these programs, clothing was prominent. Vertical integration is not exclusive to North America; it is also observed between EU partners and nonmember Mediterranean countries as well as in East Asia (Gereffi 2001).

Caribbean Basin Initiative (CBI), with similar provisions, and subsequently the Central American Free Trade Agreement–Dominican Republic (CAFTA-DR). T&C imports from NAFTA and CAFTA-DR partners showed remarkable growth during the 1996–2000 period (tables 3.3 and 3.4). Partner countries thus benefited from increased exports and new employment in their T&C industries.

At the same time, rules of origin embedded in these agreements were seen as a means to defend US producers and US jobs (USITC 1998). The so-called yarn-forward rules in NAFTA and other FTAs ensured that the US textile industry would supply a large share of yarn and fabrics used to make clothing that would ultimately be sold in the US market.[9] At the same time, US clothing manufacturers focused on high value added segments, such as fashion clothing, product design, and marketing.

In recent years, the gradual elimination of T&C quotas has triggered a reshuffling of supply, allowing Pakistan and other Asian producers to compete more effectively in the US market. Table 3.3 shows that most market gains for US clothing imports have accrued to China and a few East Asian countries (such as Vietnam and Cambodia), with some displacement of NAFTA and North Asian suppliers. Table 3.4 shows a similar picture for textiles. Large gains appear for Chinese and South Asian textile imports, but in this subsector EU and NAFTA imports fared much better than in clothing sector exports.[10]

In keeping with these broad trends, the gradual elimination of MFA quotas has prompted the rapid growth of Pakistan's T&C exports to the United States (table 3.5). As a result, the United States has become a more important trading partner for Pakistan, not only in T&C but also in overall terms (table 3.5).[11]

Thus today textiles lie at the heart of the US-Pakistan trading relationship, at least from Pakistan's point of view.[12] In 2004, the United

---

9. "Yarn-forward" is a concept that applies to a large number of different rules of origin that mandate that the yarn used in "originating clothing" must be spun or extruded in the territory defined under the agreement. In practice, since most partners lack competitive ginning and spinning sectors, they are constrained to rely on US inputs. In the third section of this chapter we present a deeper discussion of rules of origin in US FTAs.

10. Many elements besides labor costs are involved in purchasing decisions. According to an official submission of the United States Association of Importers of Textiles and Apparel, "factors such as cost, logistics, infrastructure, supply chain management, social and government stability, human rights, plant efficiency, reliability and relationships, and vertical integration capabilities will influence sourcing decisions after 2005" (USITC 2004a, 4–13).

11. The relative strengthening of textiles in Pakistan's trade with the United States coincided with a period of solid performance in Pakistan's nontextile exports (table 3.5).

12. Pakistan is increasingly specializing in specific cotton textiles (towels and bed linen). According to a review of the Pakistani T&C sector (USITC 2004a), the firms producing these textile items are large and equipped with new technology (which is not always the case in other areas of the textile industry).

Table 3.3 US imports of textiles, 1996–2004
(millions of US dollars or percent)

Country/region	1996	2000	2004	Percent growth 1996–2000	Percent growth 2000–2004
NAFTA[a] partners	2,158	3,461	3,687	60	7
Share of US imports	0.21	0.23	0.19		
Other FTA partners[b]	259	388	562	50	45
Share of US imports	0.03	0.03	0.03		
EU-25[c]	2,338	2,710	3,000	16	11
Share of US imports	0.23	0.18	0.15		
China	1,047	1,823	4,254	74	133
Share of US imports	0.10	0.12	0.22		
East Asia[d]	468	742	790	59	6
Share of US imports	0.05	0.05	0.04		
North Asia[e]	2,075	2,493	2,267	20	–9
Share of US imports	0.20	0.16	0.12		
South Asia[f]	1,205	2,243	3,211	86	43
India	636	1,119	1,659	76	48
Share of US imports	0.06	0.07	0.09		
Pakistan	444	915	1,394	106	52
Share of US imports	0.04	0.06	0.07		
Other countries	679	1,264	1,721	86	36
Share of US imports	0.07	0.08	0.09		
Total	10,248	15,175	19,505	48	29

FTA = free trade agreement
NAFTA = North American Free Trade Agreement

a. Canada and Mexico.
b. Australia, Bahrain, CAFTA partners, Chile, Dominican Republic, Israel, Jordan, Morocco, and Singapore.
c. EU-15, Cyprus, Czech Republic, Estonia, Hungary, Latvia, Lithuania, Malta, Poland, Slovakia, and Slovenia.
d. Cambodia, Indonesia, Malaysia, Philippines, Thailand, and Vietnam.
e. Hong Kong, Japan, Macao, South Korea, and Taiwan.
f. Bangladesh, India, Pakistan, and Sri Lanka.

Note: Textiles are defined as division 65 of SITC Rev. 3.

Source: USITC (2005a).

Table 3.4 US imports of clothing, 1996–2004
(millions of US dollars or percent)

Country/region	1996	2000	2004	Percent growth 1996–2000	Percent growth 2000–2004
NAFTA[a] partners	4,933	10,643	8,637	116	−19
Share of US imports	0.12	0.17	0.12		
CAFTA-DR[b]	5,397	9,138	9,608	69	5
Share of US imports	0.13	0.14	0.13		
Other FTA partners[c]	834	1,320	2,007	58	52
Share of US imports	0.02	0.02	0.03		
China	6,307	8,483	13,607	35	60
Share of US imports	0.15	0.13	0.19		
Other East Asia[d]	5,466	8,412	11,714	54	39
Share of US imports	0.13	0.13	0.16		
North Asia[e]	8,438	10,473	9,264	24	−12
Share of US imports	0.20	0.16	0.13		
South Asia[f]	4,163	6,644	7,169	60	8
India	1,349	2,002	2,378	48	19
Share of US imports	0.03	0.03	0.03		
Pakistan	631	1,016	1,217	61	20
Share of US imports	0.02	0.02	0.02		
Other countries	6,002	8,870	10,628	48	20
Share of US imports	0.14	0.14	0.15		
Total	41,559	64,296	72,311	55	12

a. Canada and Mexico.
b. Costa Rica, Dominican Republic, El Salvador, Honduras, Guatemala, and Nicaragua.
c. Australia, Bahrain, Chile, Israel, Jordan, Morocco, and Singapore.
d. Cambodia, Indonesia, Malaysia, Philippines, and Vietnam.
e. Hong Kong, Japan, Macao, South Korea, and Taiwan.
f. Bangladesh, India, Pakistan, and Sri Lanka.

Note: Clothing is defined as division 84 of SITC Rev. 3.

Source: USITC (2005a).

States purchased 23 percent of total Pakistani textile exports, up from only 9 percent in 1996 (table 3.2). As a result of the gradual elimination of textile quotas, Pakistan's share of the US import market in textiles jumped from 4 percent in 1996 to 7 percent in 2004. Few other countries experienced such a rapid surge in market share over that period (table 3.4).

Table 3.5 Pakistan's exports of textiles and clothing versus all other products (millions of US dollars or percent)

Country/region	1996	2000	2004
To the United States	1,266	2,167	2,874
Textiles and clothing	1,075	1,931	2,611
All other products	191	236	263
Share of textiles and clothing	85	89	91
Share of all other products	15	11	9
All other markets (excluding the United States)	8,056	7,034	10,505
Textiles and clothing	5,716	4,745	6,539
All other products	2,340	2,289	3,966
Share of textiles and clothing	71	67	62
Share of all other products	29	33	38
US share of total Pakistan exports			
Textiles and clothing	16	29	29
All other products	8	9	6

Note: Textiles and clothing are defined as divisions 65 and 84 of SITC Rev. 3. Therefore table excludes fibers (raw cotton, man-made, and synthetic) in division 26 of SITC Rev. 3.

Sources: UN Statistics Division (2005); USITC (2005a).

Pakistan's clothing exports to the United States—for the most part, men's cotton garments—also increased during the phaseout of MFA quotas (table 3.2). Growth not only exceeded the overall growth rate of US clothing imports but also surpassed two regional competitors, India and Bangladesh (table 3.3). However, table 3.3 shows that the high growth in Pakistani clothing exports has not translated into gains in terms of US market share.[13] Moreover, the first few months of 2005 do not show Pakistan among the main beneficiaries of the last phase of MFA quota elimination (which occurred in January 2005). Though US safeguards on Chinese clothing could provide a temporary helping hand to Pakistani clothing exports, a US-Pakistan FTA would provide stronger and more durable incentives for US retailers to consider Pakistan as an alternative supplier for the US market.

While clothing exports have been overshadowed by textile exports, clothing remains an important component of Pakistan's export portfolio. Strengthening the performance of clothing exports will therefore rank among Pakistan's important objectives in FTA talks.

---

13. While the Pakistani share of US textile imports consistently increased between 1983 and 2000, the country's share of US clothing imports remained stable at about 2 percent.

Many US firms regard Pakistan as a competitive alternative to China, particularly for men's apparel (USITC 2004a). Conditions that make Pakistan an attractive source include low wages, a local supply of raw cotton, established firms, and an improving business environment. But other features weaken Pakistan's competitiveness: the irregular quality of domestic raw cotton (due to leaf curl virus), outdated machinery in critical stages of the supply chain (e.g., ginning), low competitiveness on finer-count yarns, the possibility of corruption, nonexistent or poorly enforced labor standards, personal safety risks for foreign business executives, and missing expertise in the advanced stages of the supply chain (marketing and design).[14]

Probably the most pressing issue at the moment is to improve relations between Pakistani producers and US manufacturers and retailers. Speaking about the challenges faced by Pakistan, Commerce Minister Humayun Akhtar Khan stressed in his 2005–06 trade policy speech the vital need "to improve Pakistan's image as a reliable and efficient supplier."[15] Pakistan may seek to build business relations with US clothing manufacturers in conjunction with Chinese firms.[16] In the *Economic Survey of Pakistan 2004–05*, the Pakistani government welcomed the prospects of joint venture agreements between US (or EU) and Pakistani firms that would bring a transfer of technology and know-how.[17] A US-Pakistan FTA could further this prospect.

At the same time, a US-Pakistan FTA would have to reflect the forces that informed previous US bilateral FTAs. This means that the new FTA would have to respect the concerns of US textile producers and include provisions that preserve their role as major input suppliers for finished T&C sold both in the United States and Pakistan (the yarn-forward con-

---

14. Additionally, some US retailers have refused to purchase from private mills not funded by World Bank loans, fearing that the finances of these mills may be tainted by illegal money laundering (USITC 2004a).

15. The speech is available at the Web site of the Export Promotion Bureau of Pakistan, www.epb.gov.pk (accessed November 2005).

16. The possibility of Chinese support in upgrading Pakistan's T&C industry has been explored by the government of Pakistan. In addition to its early harvest agreement with China, which contains bilateral concessions on T&C, Pakistan has purchased textile machinery on credit from China. According to the All Pakistan Textile Mills Association (APTMA), high officials of the Chinese textile producers association conducted a visit during the first semester of 2005 to explore investment opportunities in Pakistan.

17. In his 2005–06 trade policy speech, Commerce Minister Khan announced concrete measures designed to attract firms to Pakistan, including partial payment of relocation costs, the provision of infrastructure, and financial credits for firms established in garment cities. The Export Promotion Bureau of Pakistan (2005a) has also published measures favoring the relocation of T&C industries.

Table 3.6 US exports of textiles and clothing (millions of US dollars)

Category	1996	2000	2004
US textile exports	8,008	10,952	11,989
Selected bilateral FTA partners	4,170	7,523	8,770
Pakistan	6	4	10
US clothing exports	7,511	8,629	5,059
Selected bilateral FTA partners	4,780	6,964	3,771
Pakistan	0	1	2
Total US textiles and clothing exports	15,520	19,581	17,049
Selected bilateral FTA partners	8,950	14,487	12,542
Pakistan	7	5	11
US fiber exports	4,389	3,187	5,660
Selected bilateral FTA partners	780	1,074	1,149
Pakistan	28	34	184

Note: Fibers are defined as division 26 of SITC Rev. 3, textiles as division 65, and clothing as division 84 of SITC Rev. 3. Selected FTA partners include Israel, Jordan, NAFTA, and CAFTA-DR partners. Numbers may not add up due to rounding.

Sources: UN Statistics Division (2005).

cept). The FTA should also include strong provisions for the enforcement of intellectual property in T&C designs and trademarks.

Table 3.6 shows that US T&C exports to Pakistan, excluding raw cotton, are very small ($11 million in 2004); moreover, table 3.7 shows that Pakistan's textile imports from the world are also quite low ($310 million in 2004).[18] Countries with vertically integrated T&C industries, such as Pakistan, China, and India, tend to have a low share of foreign value added embodied in their exports (Nordas 2004).[19] This is changing as Pakistani firms adapt to the model of global input sourcing: Table 3.7 shows that Pakistani textile imports have grown rapidly in recent years, and that China and other Asian neighbors are becoming important sources. A US-Pakistan FTA could help US textile firms gain access to segments of Pakistan's market.

---

18. Pakistan's total imports of clothing stood at only $13 million in 2004 and so are not detailed in table 3.7.

19. This does not mean that Pakistan's T&C production is fully done at home; in fact, T&C production creates a direct import demand for cotton, chemicals and plastics, and machinery. Many US chemical imports supply the needs of Pakistan's T&C sector.

Table 3.7 Pakistan's textile imports, 1996–2004
(millions of US dollars or percent)

Country/region	1996	2000[a]	2004	Percent growth 1996– 2000	Percent growth 2000– 2004
China	3	14	64	454	347
Share of Pakistan's imports	0.02	0.11	0.21		
East and South Asia	18	25	88	36	256
Share of Pakistan's imports	0.16	0.19	0.28		
North Asia	48	50	62	4	24
Share of Pakistan's imports	0.43	0.38	0.20		
EU-25	22	16	19	−25	16
Share of Pakistan's imports	0.20	0.12	0.06		
United States	7	5	9	−31	100
Share of Pakistan's imports	0.06	0.04	0.03		
All other countries[b]	14	20	69	47	244
Share of Pakistan's imports	0.12	0.15	0.22		
Total	111	130	310	17	140

Note: Textiles are defined as division 65 of SITC Rev. 3. Values of imports may differ from estimates based on HS classification. We present Pakistan's imports based on alternative classifications in table 3.13. Pakistan's total imports of clothing stood at $13 million in 2004; thus they are not detailed here.

a. Between 2000 and 2002, the government of Pakistan eliminated all import prohibitions on textiles and clothing.
b. Includes countries with exports exceeding $500,000 only.

Source: UN Statistics Division (2005).

Impact of a US-Pakistan FTA: The CGE Model

The computed general equilibrium (CGE) model predicts T&C export gains for producers in both countries.[20] While the projected gains for US textile and clothing producers are large in relative terms (200 and 450 percent, respectively), the gains are less significant in absolute terms, possibly $20 million to $30 million. We believe, however, that the predicted expansion of US exports is understated, as the model does not take into

20. Chapter 8 presents a full discussion of results for simulations of the potential impact of a US-Pakistan FTA using two techniques, the CGE and gravity models. In this chapter we discuss only the latter's results as the former does not disaggregate T&C from the manufacturing category.

account the boost in bilateral trade stemming from the phaseout of restrictive rules of origin. On the other hand, the CGE model predicts that Pakistan's T&C exports will increase between 30 and 50 percent, implying an expansion of roughly $1 billion. This magnitude seems plausible.

Bilateral Barriers to T&C Trade

This section identifies the principal trade policy measures that limit textile and clothing imports in Pakistan and the United States. The analysis centers on tariffs, antidumping (AD) measures, and safeguards. We also examine the elimination of the last stage of MFA quotas and its preliminary effect on Pakistan.

United States

The T&C industry ranks first in the US list of import-sensitive manufactures.[21] This sensitivity can be traced both to the industry's long decline and the concentration of production in areas where alternative jobs for unskilled workers are scarce (Nordas 2004). T&C provides an important source of wages and employment in South Atlantic states such as Georgia and the Carolinas and to a lesser extent in Virginia. In 2003 almost 40 percent of all US T&C jobs were concentrated in those four states, accounting for 17 percent of their aggregate employment in manufacturing. The industry in these states focuses on textiles, and accounts for 55 percent of US textile production and 60 percent of US textile employment. Clothing production is much more dispersed, with clusters in California, New York, and other large states.

The US T&C industry has historically been protected through a variety of trade policy instruments: quotas, high tariffs, and other measures. This section discusses US reliance on each instrument, focusing on its relevance for Pakistan. T&C provisions in other FTAs are addressed in the next section.

Quotas

Following the ATC, quotas on T&C produced in WTO member countries were phased out and finally eliminated in January 2005. However, the

---

21. Protection of the US T&C industry dates back to the 1950s, when major Asian producers, including Pakistan, agreed to restrain their T&C exports to the United States. During the 1960s, trade in T&C products was regulated by the Long-Term Agreement Regarding International Trade in Cotton Textiles (LTA). The LTA was replaced in 1974 by the MFA, which was renegotiated several times and expired in 1994. The ATC established a 10-year transition period for the full integration of textiles into the principles of the multilateral system.

United States still applies quantitative restrictions on imports of T&C from non-WTO members: Belarus, Russia, Ukraine, and Vietnam. Moreover, in November 2005 the United States negotiated a new set of quantitative limits on imports from China. Also, as discussed in chapter 2 on agriculture, the United States applies WTO and preferential tariff-rate quotas (TRQs) on imports of raw cotton.[22]

The United States delayed the elimination of quotas on its most sensitive products to the last stage of the ATC transition period (USITC 2004b). As late as 2002, the United States still applied quotas to 45 countries, including Pakistan. Thus about 48 percent of US clothing imports and 24 percent of US textile imports were subject to quantitative restraints in 2002 (WTO 2004a). Table 3.8 lists the Pakistani T&C export lines that filled at least 90 percent of their import quota in 2004. It is worth noting that some Pakistani T&C exports, not listed in table 3.9, filled less than 10 percent of their quota limits. Excluding quotas on raw cotton, all US quotas on T&C imports from Pakistan have now been eliminated.

Table 3.9 shows recent trends in US T&C imports, based on monthly data for 2005. While the growth of imports from Pakistan of certain finished textile products (e.g., rugs and carpets, bed and bath linens) is remarkable, the performance of Pakistan's clothing exports is well below the experience of leading competitors.

The full impact of MFA quota elimination will not be apparent for several years, as suppliers find their niches of comparative advantage and as market shares shift in response to competitive pressure, especially from Chinese exports. For the moment, US safeguards on Chinese T&C exports are slowing the adjustment process. But while the end of the MFA era eliminates the most obvious instrument of protection, other barriers remain in place.

Tariffs

The United States applies high most favored nation (MFN) tariffs on T&C imports. The simple average MFN tariff on T&C (HS section 11) for 2002 was 9.6 percent, one of the highest averages in the US schedule outside agriculture (WTO 2004a).[23] The trade weighted average, based only on

---

22. Pakistan's allocated import limit is aggregated with imports from India. The quantities allowed are 32,000 kilograms for cotton card strips with staple length under 30 millimeters, and 909,000 kilograms for cotton not carded or combed with staple length under 28.5 millimeters.

23. Apart from agricultural products, only tariffs on footwear and headwear (at 13.5 percent average, HS section 12) are higher than simple average tariffs on T&C.

Table 3.8 Selected US textile and clothing quotas for Pakistan, 2004

Quota no.	Product	Unit	2004 limit (thousands)	Percent growth 2005[a]
334/634	Men's coats, other	Dozen	791	33[b]
338	Men's shirts, not knit	Dozen	9,801	23
347/348	Men's trousers, breeches, and shorts	Dozen	1,976	68[c]
351/651	Nightwear and pajamas	Dozen	930	34[c]
352/652	Underwear	Dozen	2,022	n.a.
360	Pillow cases	Number of	10,504	471
361	Sheets	Number of	11,557	481
363	Terry and other pile towels	Number of	74,329	131
369-S	Shop towels[d]	Kilograms	1,427	6
666	Other synthetic fiber furnishings	Kilograms	8,487	−26

n.a. = not available

a. Change is measured by quantities based on a comparison of imports, January–October 2004 versus January–October 2005.
b. Category 334 only.
c. Simple average growth of both categories.
d. A US countervailing order affecting imports of cotton shop towels from Pakistan was revoked in February 2005.

Note: US quotas with more than 90 percent fill rate by Pakistan's imports.

Source: US Customs and Border Protection (2004a).

dutiable imports (i.e., excluding duty-free imports under preferential arrangements such as NAFTA) was 15.8 percent for clothing, 9.3 for textile mill articles (e.g., yarn, thread), and 13.0 percent for textiles (USITC 2004b). The US tariff profile for T&C reflects a high incidence of tariff escalation; table 3.10 confirms that most US peaks apply to clothing imports (HS chapters 61 and 62). However, in general, cotton-based textile and clothing products face lower duties than similar products based on synthetic fibers.

Pakistan's T&C exports to the United States face, on a trade-weighted basis, slightly lower duties than the averages reported by the US International Trade Commission (USITC). Because most Pakistani clothing exports are cotton-based, they do not face the highest tariffs applied to

Table 3.9 US textile and clothing imports, 2005 (millions of US dollars)

NAICS category	Pakistan		India		China		Total US imports	
	Value	Percent growth	Value	Percent growth	Value	Percent growth	Value	Percent growth
Textile mill goods[a]	417	−23	299	10	962	40	7,625	0
Other textile products[b]	1,200	33	1,640	16	5,513	29	13,298	16
Clothing[c]	1,271	8	3,224	32	20,142	63	74,246	8
Total	2,888	10	5,162	25	26,616	53	95,168	9

NAICS = North American Industry Classification System

a. Corresponds to NAICS code 313 and includes yarn, thread, and fabric mill goods.
b. Corresponds to NAICS code 314 and includes carpets and rugs, bed and bath linens, canvas products, and other textile products.
c. Corresponds to NAICS code 315.

Note: Annualized figures based on January–August data. Percent growth is measured by import quantity, January–August 2005 versus January–August 2004.

Source: USITC (2005a).

Table 3.10 US tariff schedule 2005: Textile and clothing chapters

HS chapter	Product description	Total number of tariff lines	Specific tariff lines[a]	Peak tariff lines[b]	Average tariff rate (percent)[c]
50	Silk	13	0	0	0.9
51	Wool, animal hair; horsehair yarn and woven fabric	101	19	12	6.7
52	Cotton	233	8	15	9.2
53	Other vegetable textile fibers; paper yarn	41	1	3	2.0
54	Synthetic filaments	120	21	35	11.6
55	Synthetic staple fibers	131	7	40	11.8
56	Wadding; nonwovens; special yarns, cordage, and other	60	4	0	5.4
57	Carpets and other textile floor coverings	42	1	0	3.4
58	Woven and tufted fabrics; tapestries; trimmings; and other	67	0	10	7.8
59	Impregnated, coated, covered or laminated fabrics	59	0	0	3.7
60	Knitted or crocheted fabrics	77	0	4	10.5
61	Articles of apparel and clothing accessories, knitted or crocheted	230	14	92	12.4
62	Articles of apparel and clothing accessories, knitted or crocheted	301	28	96	11.3
63	Other textile articles; worn clothing and rags	100	3	5	7.3
	Textiles and clothing[d]	1,575	106	312	9.4
	All manufacturing[e]	8,755	368	369	3.9

a. Includes specific tariffs and tariffs with other special rates.
b. Tariff peaks are defined as tariffs above 15 percent on an ad valorem basis. For the purposes of calculating tariff peaks, specific tariffs are evaluated based on their 2002 ad valorem equivalents.
c. The average tariff rate includes ad valorem equivalents of specific tariffs. When specific tariffs are present, the average tariff rate corresponds to 2002.
d. Comprises all HS chapters 50 through 63.
e. Comprises all HS chapters 25 through 97.

Source: USITC (2005a).

synthetic apparel products. Still, the average on Pakistan's clothing exports is similar to the simple average for the corresponding chapters. As shown in table 3.11, US tariffs on imports of Pakistani clothing are high, as are tariffs on imports of certain Pakistani textile-mill products (yarns and fabrics). On the other hand, Pakistan's best-performing textile

Table 3.11 US tariffs on selected textile and clothing imports from Pakistan

HS 8-digit category	Product description	Imports, 2005[a] (millions of US dollars)	Tariff, 2005 (percent)	GSP?
Textile mill goods				
5208.19.20	Satin or twill weave fabrics of cotton	165	8[b]	No
5210.19.80	Woven fabrics of cotton, nesoi, below 85 percent cotton by weight	40	8	No
5205.22.00	Single cotton yarn, above 85 percent cotton by weight	34	10	No
5210.19.60	Woven fabrics of cotton, nesoi, above 85 percent cotton by weight	28	7	No
5205.12.10	Single cotton yarn, above 85 percent cotton	25	9	No
5208.19.80	Woven fabrics of cotton, nesoi, above 85 percent cotton by weight	22	5	No
		16	11	No
Other textile products				
6302.60.00	Toilet linen and kitchen linen of cotton, of terry toweling	1,057	7[b]	No
6302.31.90	Bed linen of cotton, not kn./cr, not printed or embroided	256	9	No
5701.10.40	Textile floor coverings, of wool or fine animal hair	164	7	No
6307.10.10	Dustcloths, mop cloths, and polishing cloths of cotton	108	Free	No
6302.21.90	Bed linen of cotton, not kn./cr., printed, not embroided	100	4	No
6302.10.00	Bed linen, kn./cr.	99	7	No
6303.91.00	Curtains and valances of cotton, not kn./cr.	74	6	No
6304.92.00	Furnishing articles of cotton, not kn./cr.	41	10	No
6302.22.20	Bed linen of synthetic fibers, not kn./cr, printed, nesoi	35	6	No
6302.31.50	Bed linen of cotton, not kn./cr. with embroidery	31	11	No
6302.21.70	Bed linen of cotton, not kn./cr., printed	28	21	No
6301.30.00	Blankets and traveling rugs of cotton	23	3	No
6307.90.98	National flags and other textile materials, nesoi	21	8	No
6302.31.70	Bed linen of cotton, not kn./cr.	21	7	Yes
6307.10.20	Floor cloths, dishcloths, and similar cleaning cloths	20	4	No
6302.91.00	Toilet and kitchen linen of cotton, not terry toweling	20	5	No
		16	9	No

Clothing, cotton

HS code	Description	Value	GSP	Preference
6110.20.20	Sweaters, pullovers, and similar articles, kn./cr.	986	16[b]	No
6105.10.00	Men's shirts, kn./cr.	296	17	No
6203.42.40	Men's trousers and shorts, not kn./cr.	190	20	No
6109.10.00	T-shirts, tank tops, and similar garments, kn./cr.	102	17	No
6115.92.90	Stockings and socks nesoi, kn./cr.	82	17	No
6204.62.40	Women's trousers and shorts, not kn./cr.	76	14	No
6101.20.00	Men's overcoats, anoraks, and similar articles, kn./cr.	60	17	No
6211.42.00	Women's track suits or other garments nesoi, not kn./cr.	40	16	No
6107.11.00	Men's underpants and briefs, kni./cr.	26	8	No
6205.20.20	Men's shirts nesoi, not kn./cr.	21	7	No
6106.10.00	Women's blouses and shirts, kn./cr.	21	20	No
6108.31.00	Women's nightdresses and pajamas, kn./cr.	19	20	No
6103.42.10	Men's trousers and shorts, kn./cr.	17	9	No
6102.20.00	Women's overcoats, anoraks, and similar articles, kn./cr.	17	16	No
		17	16	No
	Subtotal	2,207	11[b]	
	Total US textile and clothing imports from Pakistan	2,888	10[c]	

GSP = generalized system of preferences

kn./cr. = knitted or crocheted

nesoi = not elsewhere specified or included

a. Annualized figures based on January–August data.

b. Trade-weighted average based on obsevations in this table.

c. Average based on calculated duties over total US imports from Pakistan.

Sources: USITC (2005a, 2005b)

exports (e.g., bed and bath linens, carpets, and rugs) face comparatively low US tariffs.[24]

Very few Pakistani T&C exports benefit from generalized system of preferences (GSP) duty-free access to the US market. The GSP coverage in 2004 for T&C imports was only $24 million (about 1 percent of US imports of T&C products from Pakistan).[25]

Antidumping Measures and Countervailing Duties

During the MFA era, the United States was an infrequent user of AD and countervailing duty (CVD) measures against T&C imports. Between 1995 and 2005, the United States notified to the WTO only five AD measures targeting T&C imports. In contrast, other WTO members—principally India, the European Union, Turkey, South Africa, and Argentina—imposed 120 AD measures against T&C imports over the same period.[26] Of these 120, only seven investigations and five final measures were targeted against Pakistani T&C exporters, and targeted cotton yarn (Japan), cotton bed linen (the European Union and South Africa), and various cotton fabrics (the European Union) (WTO 2005c, 2005d).[27]

No Pakistani T&C export to the United States is currently the subject of AD measures. US CVDs, however, have limited Pakistani exports of cotton shop towels. The Department of Commerce issued the countervailing order in 1984, and a first sunset review in 2000 extended the measure.[28] A second sunset review finally revoked the order in February 2005, along with AD measures targeting similar products originating in China and Bangladesh.[29]

---

24. The average trade-weighted tariff for Pakistani exports of textile products was 6.8 percent, whereas the US trade-weighted average for all textile dutiable imports was 13 percent.

25. Five textile products were disqualified from GSP benefits after 1996, because of US objections to labor practices in Pakistan. GSP benefits were restored in December 2004.

26. Over that period, the United States initiated eight AD investigations on T&C imports, while all other WTO members combined reported the initiation of 180 AD investigations, some of which were terminated without the imposition of measures.

27. Countries more frequently targeted include Korea, China, Taiwan, Thailand, and India (in that order).

28. During the first review in 2000, one commissioner dissented from the decision to renew the measures. This commissioner argued that Pakistani and Bangladeshi exports were not likely to lead to the recurrence of material injury, and she also noted that an asymmetry of information favored domestic producers (USITC 2000).

29. In revoking the order, the Department of Commerce observed that "no domestic interested party responded to the sunset review notice of initiation by the applicable deadline" (US Department of Commerce 2005a). For more information, see USITC Investigations 701-TA-202, 731-TA-103, and 731-TA-514 (Second Review). Imports of cotton shop towels from Pakistan and other targeted countries were subject to MFA quotas at the same time that they were targeted by AD and CVD measures (table 3.8).

Now that the MFA has passed into history, it seems likely that AD and CVD measures will be invoked more frequently against T&C imports to the US market. In the MFA era, potential trade injury was generally averted by line item quotas, and so the injury component of AD and CVD petitions could rarely be demonstrated. Now that quotas are eliminated, the possibility of trade injury is quite real, and if "less than fair value" sales—the dumping price standard—or subsidized sales (the CVD standard) can be shown, trade remedy cases are likely to be launched.[30]

Safeguards

Since 1995, the United States has invoked safeguards on T&C imports, both under the ATC and under the transitional mechanism established in Paragraph 242 of the Report of the Working Party on the Accession of China to the WTO.[31]

The US invocation of safeguards under the ATC in March 1999, on combed cotton yarn from Pakistan, led to the establishment of a WTO dispute settlement panel. The panel and the Appellate Body found against the United States, and safeguards were terminated in November 2001 (WTO 2001a). Before this incident, the United States had also invoked safeguards under the ATC on India (WTO 1996).

Since 2001, the United States has also invoked safeguards on T&C imports from China, following the procedures agreed in paragraph 242 of the Report of the Working Party on the Accession of China to the WTO. These safeguards, which are renewed annually, take the form of quantitative restrictions with a mandated growth rate of 7.5 percent annually (WTO 2001b, 46). Products subject to US safeguard quotas as of November 2005 included combed cotton yarn, socks, trousers, shirts, brassieres, underwear, and synthetic fiber (table 3.12a).[32] US safeguards affect one-quarter of US T&C imports from China (IMF 2005, 48). In 2005 the US T&C industry filed several safeguard requests covering additional Chinese cotton-based T&C products; however, the Committee for the Implementation of Textile Agreements (CITA) decided on November 24, 2005,

---

30. Additionally, it is possible that Pakistan's tax and duty exemptions on textile exports might be the subject of a CVD investigation. The Pakistani government has recently faced pressure to increase duty exemptions for its textile producers, as several have threatened to expand in Bangladesh. Pakistani textile producers point out that Bangladesh offers better tax collection conditions and that Bangladesh faces no AD measures in the European Union. Moreover, they stress that the European Union has granted Bangladesh better unilateral preferences.

31. Paragraph 242 was originally numbered paragraph 238 in the draft accession agreement and is still often referred to as such.

32. Pakistan is a direct competitor of China in most of these products.

**Table 3.12a US textile and clothing quotas on China,
as of November 30, 2005** (percent)

Quota no.	Product category	Fill rate
301	Combed cotton yarn	60
332/432/632	Cotton, wool, and man-made fiber socks	96
338/339	Men's cotton shirts and blouses	100
340/640	Men's cotton and synthetic fiber shirts	100
347/348	Men's cotton trousers, breeches, and shorts	100
349/649	Cotton and synthetic fiber brassieres	55
352/652	Cotton and synthetic fiber underwear	100
620	Other synthetic fiber fabric	100
638/639	Synthetic fiber blouses	100
647/648	Synthetic fiber trousers	100

Source: US Customs and Border Protection (2005b).

"to end further consideration of 24 requests for safeguard action on imports from China" (US Department of Commerce 2005b).[33]

The requests were terminated because, on November 8, 2005, the United States and China reached an umbrella agreement on the permitted growth rate for the 2006–08 period for quotas invoked under paragraph 242. The Memorandum of Understanding between the Governments of the United States of America and the People's Republic of China Concerning Trade in Textile and Apparel Products aims to provide the T&C industries in the United States and China with "a stable and predictable trading environment" and to resolve trade concerns through consultations, as provided under paragraph 242 (USTR 2005b).

Annex I of the memorandum of understanding (MoU) between China and the United States lists the products covered by the agreement and establishes the quota limits for 2006–08 (table 3.12b). The US Trade

---

33. The list of Chinese products that had been considered included many that are typically exported by Pakistan, such as towels, curtains, and items of cotton apparel. The full list of products seeking protection under the China Textile Safeguard Action in 2005 is available at the Office of Textiles and Apparel (OTEXA) Web site, http://otexa.ita.doc.gov. The CITA press release states, "The agreement [US-China MoU on textiles and apparel products] establishes conditions on trade in the vast majority of products covered by these cases and provides a general framework for textile trade between the United States and China. Based on these considerations, CITA has ended further consideration of all pending textile safeguard petitions" (US Department of Commerce 2005b, 1).

Table 3.12b US textile and clothing quotas on China, 2006–08

Quota no.	Product category	Unit	Quota limit (millions)[a]		
			2006	2007	2008
200/301	Sewing thread or combed cotton yarn	Kilograms	7.5	8.7	10.1
222	Knit fabric	Kilograms	16.0	18.4	21.5
229	Special purpose fabric	Kilograms	33.2	38.5	45.0
332/432/632-T	Cotton, wool, and synthetic fiber socks	Dozen pairs	64.4	74.0	85.1
332/432/632-B	Cotton, wool, and synthetic fiber socks	Dozen pairs	61.1	70.3	80.9
338/339	Cotton knit shirts	Dozen	20.8	23.4	26.9
340/640	Men's and boys' woven shirts	Dozen	6.7	7.6	8.7
345/645/646	Sweaters	Dozen	8.2	9.2	10.7
347/348	Cotton trousers	Dozen	19.7	22.1	25.4
349/649	Brassieres	Dozen	22.8	25.6	29.5
352/652	Underwear	Dozen	18.9	21.3	24.5
359S/659S	Swimwear	Kilograms	4.6	5.2	6.0
363	Pile towels	Number of	103.3	116.2	134.8
666	Window blinds or shades	Kilograms	1.0	1.1	1.3
443	Wool suits, men's and boys'	Number of	1.3	1.5	1.8
447	Wool trousers, men's and boys'	Dozen	0.2	0.2	0.3
619	Polyester filament	M2	55.3	62.2	72.1
620	Other synthetic filaments	M2	80.2	90.2	103.8
622	Glass fabric	M2	32.3	37.1	43.4
638/639	Synthetic fiber knit shirts	Dozen	8.1	9.1	10.4
647/648	Synthetic fiber trousers	Dozen	8.0	9.0	10.3
847	Silk blend and vegetable fiber trousers	Dozen	17.6	19.9	23.0

M2 = squared meter

a. Figures are rounded.

Source: USTR (2005a).

Representative (USTR) analysis of the agreement distinguishes between results for "core" and "other" products (USTR 2005b).[34] Core clothing products include trousers and knit shirts of cotton and synthetic fiber, woven shirts, brassieres, and underwear. China's quota limits for core clothing products will expand to 5.5 percent in 2006, 7.8 percent in 2007, and 10.3 percent in 2008. In 2006 quota growth for "core" products will thus fall below the rate of 7.5 percent established under the WTO accession documents in 2006 but will surpass that benchmark in 2007 and 2008.[35] Many of Pakistan's clothing exports to the United States belong to the core category and thus over the next two years will face a more predictable scenario and less competition from China in the US market. Limits on other categories (i.e., noncore products) will increase 10 to 16 percent annually between 2006 and 2008.

The United States pledged in the MoU not to request consultations for products listed under Annex I, but committed only to "exercise restraint" concerning the application of safeguards on products not subject to the agreement (USTR 2005b).

Textile Procurement Provisions

The "Buy American Act" and the Berry amendment mandate US-origin products for US government and Defense Department procurement.[36] T&C items are considered vital to military readiness and therefore US forces are required to comply with these origin requirements. To the chagrin of foreign producers, previous FTAs have not opened the US defense procurement market.[37]

Pakistan

Pakistan has a vertically integrated textile and clothing industry that is oriented toward cotton-based products (homegrown cotton, cotton yarn and cloth, made-up textiles). Most T&C production in Pakistan relies on domestic inputs, and T&C imports—largely raw materials and fibers—

---

34. The distinction between core and other products is not contemplated in the agreement but appears in the USTR press release.

35. China's WTO accession protocol established a maximum 7.5 percent growth of shipments above the amount entered during the first 12 months of the most recent 14 months preceding the month in which the request for consultations had been made.

36. Government procurement practices are covered more extensively in chapter 6. For a recent discussion of the Berry amendment, see the Congressional Research Service report for Congress, *The Berry Amendment: Requiring Defense Procurement to Come from Domestic Sources* (order code RL31236).

37. By contrast, US producers of both T&C specifically commended the USTR for preserving the Berry amendment (USTR 2004a, 4–5).

represent just 5 percent of total imports. For many years the industry's growth has been tied to the local cotton crop and its competitiveness retarded by bottlenecks and inefficiencies in the value chain.

Cotton accounts for 70 percent of the industry's fiber consumption, while synthetic fibers (polyester, acrylic, and viscose) contribute the remainder (USITC 2004a). Pakistan ranks among the largest producers of cotton and cotton yarn in the world. However, the quality of its cotton is irregular and most yarn production consists of coarse and medium counts (70 percent) or polyester/cotton blends (24 percent). Domestic clothing firms have therefore supplemented domestic cotton supplies with finer-count imported yarn, other synthetic fibers (e.g., acrylic, rayon), and blended or high-tenacity yarns (e.g., polyester/viscose, nylon) in an effort to reach the global market for noncotton fabrics in higher value added niches of cotton-based textiles.[38]

The T&C industry has long been the object of special protection in Pakistan, starting in the era of import substitution industrialization. In recent years, the government has charted a new course, eliminating import prohibitions and relaxing protection in an effort to improve export competitiveness. Yet protection is still high and limits trade: In 2004 Pakistan's imports of items in HS chapters 58 through 63 were under $30 million. Tariffs are the principal instrument, but export promotion schemes and AD measures have also been used.

Tariffs

In 2005 Pakistan's domestic T&C industry received average tariff protection of 18.6 percent, exceeding the 14.2 percent average tariff for all manufacturing products. These averages, however, are lower than their 2002 values (26 and 20.2 percent, respectively), marking the continuation of progressive liberalization.[39] Still, the Pakistan Customs Tariff 2005–06 contains a very large number of tariff peaks in the T&C section (Pakistan Central Board of Revenue 2005a). Almost 60 percent of the T&C tariff lines (HS 50-63) list duties of 25 percent (table 3.13).[40] Pakistan has bound nearly all tariff lines in the T&C category (WTO 2002a).

Tariff escalation is a feature of the Pakistani customs schedule. Inputs receive lower protection than final T&C items: With the exception of cotton yarn, other yarn and fiber imports pay tariffs that are half the level prevailing on finished T&C products (table 3.13). Moreover, the lower-tariff products were subject to the largest cuts in protection during

---

38. For in-depth studies, see USITC (2004a) and Government of Pakistan (2005c).

39. The largest cuts in T&C tariffs took place between 1997 and 2000. In 1996 the average tariff on T&C exceeded 50 percent.

40. Twenty-five percent is the highest duty applied in HS section 11 of the 2005–06 Pakistan Customs Tariff.

Table 3.13 Pakistan's tariffs on textile and clothing imports, 2005

HS chapter	Product description	Total tariff lines	Tariff peaks[a]	Average tariff rate (percent)	Percentage point tariff reduction, 2002–05[b]
Textile mill goods and other textile products		662	281	16	–8
50	Silk	10	0	8	–8
51	Wool, animal hair; horsehair yarn and woven fabric	37	0	8	–6
52	Cotton	136	51	15	–7
53	Other vegetable textile fibers, paper yarn	21	7	10	–5
54	Synthetic filaments	69	0	10	–14
55	Synthetic staple fibers	119	0	11	–14
56	Wadding; nonwovens; special yarns, cordage, and other	37	19	19	–8
57	Carpets and other textile floor coverings	32	23	21	–5
58	Woven and tufted fabrics, tapestries, trimmings, and other	45	45	25	–5
59	Impregnated, coated, covered or laminated fabrics	26	16	19	–3
60	Knitted or crocheted fabrics	44	44	25	–5
63	Other made-up textile articles; worn clothing and rags	86	78	24	–6
Clothing		242	240	25	–5
61	Articles of apparel and clothing accessories, kn./cr	119	119	25	–5
62	Articles of apparel and clothing accessories, not kn./cr	125	123	25	–5
	Textiles and clothing (HS 50–63)	906	521	19	–7
	All manufacturing (HS 25–97)	5,516	1,524	14	–6

kn./cr. = knitted or crocheted

a. Tariff peaks are defined as tariffs with rates equal to or above 25 percent. In 2005 the highest tariff rate applied in HS section 11 was 25 percent. All tariff peaks in HS section 11 take that value. Higher peaks apply to manufactured products in other categories.

b. The "average tariff reduction 2002–05" was obtained by comparing simple average tariff rates for the above reported categories in 2005 versus 2002. Averages for 2002 were obtained from the *WTO Trade Policy Review of Pakistan* (2002).

Source: Pakistan Board of Revenue (2005).

2002–05. For example, the average tariffs on synthetic filaments and staple fibers were cut by 14 percentage points, to current averages of 10 to 11 percent (table 3.14). In his 2005–06 trade policy speech, Commerce Minister Khan announced targeted customs tariff and sales tax elimination, aimed at imported raw materials.[41]

The progressive reduction of tariffs is correlated with rising imports. Blended yarns and synthetic fibers now account for the bulk of Pakistan's T&C imports, apart from raw cotton (table 3.14).[42] Conversely, imports of cloth—where tariffs remain very high—are still negligible. In recent years, China and Southeast Asian countries have become principal suppliers to Pakistan's T&C industry (table 3.7).

Antidumping Measures

Pakistan's experience with AD measures is relatively recent. The oldest measure currently in force dates from 2002, and as of June 2005 the country had only seven measures in force. Of these, only one targets textile products, namely AD measures on acrylic towel imports from Uzbekistan (imposed in August 2004). In December 2005 the government of Pakistan announced the imposition of provisional AD duties on imports of polyester filament yarn (PFY). Countries targeted by that measure are Indonesia, Korea, Malaysia, and Thailand (National Tariff Commission of Pakistan 2005).

Import Licensing, Customs Procedures, and Charges

All importers are required to pay, in addition to sales tax (15 percent), a 1 percent charge on the cost, insurance, and freight (c.i.f) value of imported goods and a 1 percent handling charge. Additionally, imports to Pakistan are subject to documentation requirements; for example, used clothing imports require certificates of cleanliness from accredited physicians (US Department of Commerce 2005a).[43]

---

41. Tariff elimination programs are applicable only for inputs used in the production of goods for export. The exemptions encompass imports of thread, polyester, woven cotton, synthetic lining, wadding, and interlining materials (US Department of Commerce 2005a).

42. In his 2005–06 trade policy speech, Commerce Minister Khan highlighted the new government policy toward synthetic fiber in the following way: "The government has now solved this long-standing problem and rationalized the tariff structure for man made fibre and synthetic textile chain. This would lead the major growth in this sector." See speech at the Web site of the Export Promotion Bureau of Pakistan, www.epb.gov.pk (accessed November 2005).

43. Pakistan used to apply quantitative restrictions on the import of textiles; however, all such restrictions were phased out by December 2001, in advance of the time frame stipulated under the agreement with the WTO Balance-of-Payments Committee. We address standards and labeling requirements more generally in chapter 5. For more information on documentation requirements, see the International Trade Association's Web pages on Pakistan: Import Procedures and Documentation at http://otexa.ita.doc.gov.

Table 3.14 Pakistan's textile and clothing tariff rates and imports from the world and the United States

HS 6-digit category	Product description	Imports, 2004 (millions of US dollars) World	United States	Tariff, 2005[a] (percent)
Selected raw materials		628	195	5[b]
5101.19	Wool, not carded/combed, greasy	7	0	5
5201.00	Cotton, not carded/combed	591	195[c]	5
5303.10	Jute and other textile bast fibers, raw/retted	30	0	5
Synthetic fibers and yarns		232	8	6[b]
5402.33	Textured yarn of polyesters	34	0	7
5402.43	Yarn other than high-B14 tenacity/textured yarn	27	0	7
5402.49	Synthetic filament yarn other than sewing thread	21	2	6
5403.31	Artificial filament yarn other than sewing thread	13	0	7
5501.30	Synthetic filament tow, acrylic/modacrylic	15	2	7
5502.00	Artificial filament tow	20	2	6
5503.20	Synthetic staple fibers for spinning, of polyester	15	1	7
5503.30	Synthetic staple fibers for spinning, of acrylic	9	1	7
5504.10	Artificial staple fibers for spinning, of viscose rayon	71	0	5

(table continues next page)

Textiles and Clothing in Other Bilateral FTAs

In this section we present a brief discussion of the treatment of T&C in other FTA negotiations that could serve as important references for a US-Pakistan FTA: US-Morocco, US-Australia, US-Singapore, and CAFTA-DR. We examine a selection of key provisions, but our focus is on tariff phaseout schedules and rules of origin.

United States

As mentioned earlier, the United States maintains high MFN tariffs on T&C imports. Parties to US bilateral agreements, however, enjoy impor-

Table 3.14 *(continued)*

HS 6-digit category	Product description	Imports, 2004 (millions of US dollars) World	United States	Tariff, 2005[a] (percent)
Woven fabrics		59	0	18[b]
5208.12	Woven fabrics, 85 percent or more by weight of cotton	17	0	25
5210.19	Woven fabrics, less than 85 percent by weight of cotton	6	0	14
5407.42	Woven fabrics, 85 percent or more by weight of filament	11	0	14
5407.94	Woven fabrics of synthetic filament yarn	5	0	14
5703.20	Textile floor coverings, tufted	5	0	8
5902.10	Tire cord fabric of high-tenacity yarn of nylon	8	0	5
5903.90	Other textile fabrics with plastics	7	0	25
Worn clothing		37	11	10[b]
6309.00	Worn clothing and other worn articles	37	11	10
	Subtotal	948	214	6[b]
	All other textile and clothing imports	178	6[d]	n.a.
	Total imports of textiles and clothing	1,126	220	18.6

n.a. = not applicable

a. Tariffs correspond to the duty rate listed in the Pakistan Customs Tariff 2005–06. Exclusions and special duty programs (e.g., export processing zones) are not considered. Figures are rounded up to the nearest unit. When several tariff lines apply to 6-digit category trade flow, we report the simple averages of those lines.
b. Trade-weighted average based on observations in this table.
c. This value is significantly larger than the value reported by the US International Trade Commission.
d. All other US exports include products with annual flows below $1 million.

Sources: UN Statistics Division (2005); Pakistan Board of Revenue (2005).

tant preference margins (table 3.15). Imports under preferential programs are quite significant and constitute a rising share of US imports of T&C goods. In 2004, 25 percent of US clothing imports and 18 percent of US textile imports, by value, enjoyed preferential access to the US market.[44]

---

44. There was a rapid increase in imports under preferential programs between 2000 and 2004. This might seem at odds with the low growth recorded by T&C exports from a number of countries that enjoy preferences (tables 3.3 and 3.4), but the surge reflects the inclusion of T&C items under the Africa Growth and Opportunity Act (AGOA), Caribbean Basin Trade Partnership Act of 2000 (CBTPA), and Andean Trade Promotion and Drug Eradication Act (ATPDEA) in the early 2000s.

Table 3.15 US tariff schedule: Average MFN and preferential tariff rates on textiles and clothing, 2005 (percent)

HS chapter	Product description	MFN[a]	Mexico[b]	Jordan[c]	Singapore[d]	Australia[e]	GSP[f]
50	Silk	0.9	0.0	0.0	0.0	0.0	0.3
51	Wool, animal hair; horsehair yarn and woven fabric	5.9	0.0	1.8	0.1	3.0	5.8
52	Cotton	8.2	0.0	0.4[g]	0.0[g]	5.4[g]	8.0
53	Other vegetable textile fibers, paper yarn	1.6	0.0	0.0	0.0	0.0	1.5
54	Synthetic filaments	10.4	0.0	1.0	0.0	5.1	10.3
55	Synthetic staple fibers	11.0	0.0	0.8	0.0	5.0	11.0
56	Wadding; nonwovens; special yarns, cordage, and other	4.5	0.0	0.0	0.0	2.0	1.7
57	Carpets and other textile floor coverings	3.3	0.0	0.0	0.0	1.9	2.5
58	Woven and tufted fabrics; tapestries; trimmings; and other	7.0	0.0	0.5	0.0	3.2	7.0
59	Impregnated, coated, covered or laminated fabrics	3.1	0.0	0.0	0.0	1.7	2.8
60	Knitted or crocheted fabrics	10.1	0.0	0.0	0.0	6.9	10.1
61	Articles of apparel and clothing accessories, kn./cr.	11.7	0.0	2.1	0.0	7.1	11.5
62	Articles of apparel and clothing accessories, not kn./cr.	10.7	0.0	1.9	0.0	7.4	10.6
63	Other made-up textile articles, worn clothing and rags	6.6	0.0	0.2	0.0	4.4	6.1
HS section 11 (chapters 50–63)		8.7	0.0	1.0	0.0	5.2	8.4

a. MFN: most favored nation. Base treatment granted to all WTO members.

b. Entered into force in January 1994, NAFTA eliminated all tariffs on textiles and clothing within 10 years.

c. Entered into force in January 2002, the US-Jordan FTA will eliminate all tariffs on textiles and clothing within 10 years.

d. Entered into force in January 2004, the US-Singapore immediately eliminated virtually all tariffs on textiles and clothing.

e. Entered into force in January 2005, the US-Australia FTA includes phaseouts of as long as 18 years in certain textiles tariff lines (e.g., raw cotton). However, most tariffs not subject to immediate eliminations will be completely eliminated within 10 to 15 years.

f. We present the maximum generalized system of preferences (GSP) margin; however, not all GSP participating countries may qualify for all of these preferential tariffs.

g. A few tariff lines, corresponding to raw cotton and not considered in these averages, are subject to quotas.

Note: Table excludes specific and other tariffs but includes the ad valorem component of composed tariffs.

Source: USITC (2005a).

Table 3.16 US imports of textiles and clothing under selected preferential programs (millions of US dollars)

Program	1996	2000	2004
Subject to MFN tariffs	46,530	67,832	70,251
Under preferential programs	6,337	11,994	21,478
NAFTA	5,410	10,462	10,339
CBTPA[a]	n.a.	159	6,489
AGOA	n.a.	355[b]	1,614
Andean Act (ATPA/ATPDEA)	4	6	1,161
West Bank and Gaza	n.a.	23	926
US-Israel	425	611	527
GSP	403	274	378
CBI	95	105	31
US-Jordan	n.a.	n.a.	13
Total US textile and clothing imports	52,867	79,471	91,729

AGOA = Africa Growth and Opportunity Act
ATPA/ATPDEA = Andean Trade Preference Act/Andean Trade Promotion and Drug Eradication Act
CBERA = Caribbean Basin Economic Recovery Act
CBI = Caribbean Basin Initiative
CBTPA = Caribbean Basin Trade Partnership Act of 2000
GSP = generalized system of preferences
n.a. = not available
NAFTA = North American Free Trade Agreement

a. Total imports entering under MFN tariff treatment. Values correspond to "No Program Claimed" in USITC Dataweb.
b. Value corresponds to 2001.

Source: USITC (2005a).

Table 3.16 shows that US FTA partners, rather than countries enjoying unilateral preferences, provide the bulk of imports, some 85 percent (including imports from CAFTA partners under the US-Caribbean Trade Partnership Act, CBTPA).[45]

US FTAs are the most stable and comprehensive preferential programs, but other preference programs have served as stepping-stones for FTA pacts. For example, the production sharing agreements (CBTPA) and the Andean Trade Promotion and Drug Eradication Act (ATPDEA) succeeded in stimulating imports from qualifying partners and paved the way for full-blown FTA negotiations. But most of these earlier programs

---

45. This figure would surpass 90 percent if one included imports under preference programs for the Andean countries (which are currently negotiating an FTA with the United States). Tariff elimination under CAFTA-DR is retroactive to 2004.

granted unilateral duty concessions subject to various conditions that limited the potential benefits to partner countries.

NAFTA and the US-Israel FTA represented the first permanent and fully reciprocal US preference agreements. NAFTA charted the basic model that was later applied in other negotiations. After the ratification of NAFTA in 1993, T&C trade volumes between Mexico and the United States grew rapidly, with Mexico importing US textile inputs, and the United States importing Mexican finished clothing and textiles.[46] In part, NAFTA rules of origin explain the resulting trade patterns, as the rules denied duty-free entry to T&C products with significant inputs from outside North America. However, NAFTA also allowed Mexico to move beyond mere assembly of imported fabrics to "full-package" production (Nordas 2004).[47]

After NAFTA, the United States concluded CAFTA-DR as well as bilateral FTAs with Jordan, Singapore, Chile, Morocco, Australia, and, most recently, Bahrain. None of these partners has the capacity to pose a serious competitive challenge to the US T&C industries, however. In this respect, a US-Pakistan FTA would be different. In the other agreements, rules of origin played a key role in answering the demands of the US T&C industries. It is unclear whether the standard yarn-forward rules would be equally satisfactory—from the standpoint of US firms—with a country that has a vertically integrated and highly competitive domestic T&C industry. On the other hand, Pakistan's vertical integration reflects very high protective barriers; as Pakistan's tariffs are reduced, rules of origin will play a more important role in shaping sources of supply.

During the negotiations, it seems likely that the US T&C industry will insist on longer transition periods (especially on certain cotton-based products) than those agreed in prior FTAs. But other elements of prior FTAs will be relevant in a US-Pakistan FTA. Reviewing past negotiations can therefore provide useful insights.

Tariff Elimination

The previous US bilateral FTAs considered in this section contemplate the eventual elimination, on a reciprocal basis, of all tariffs and quotas for T&C items that qualify under the rules of origin.[48] US FTAs eliminate the

---

46. Nordas (2004) also records important gains in employment in the Mexican T&C industry between 1995 and 2000, and other specialists have observed gains in investment.

47. Undoubtedly, the comprehensive and permanent nature of NAFTA gave Mexico an advantage over other T&C suppliers and contributed to an upgrade in Mexico's role.

48. The discussion on tariff elimination is based on the actual phaseout schedules in the agreements. The texts consulted are listed in the references as follows: US-Jordan FTA (USTR 2000), US-Singapore FTA (USTR 2003b), US-Chile FTA (USTR 2003c), CAFTA-DR (USTR 2004c), US-Morocco FTA (USTR 2004d), US-Australia FTA (USTR 2004e), and US-Bahrain FTA (USTR 2004f).

majority of tariffs on both sides within the first 6 years after implementation, and nearly all tariffs within 10 years.

Previous agreements contain tailored provisions for sensitive items; consequently, some reach full duty-free status sooner than others. The US-Singapore FTA, like the near contemporary US-Chile and US-Bahrain FTAs, granted immediate duty-free access for virtually all products on both sides.[49] CAFTA-DR even established retroactive reciprocal tariff elimination, one year before implementation, for nearly all textile tariffs.[50]

Other bilateral FTAs contain transition periods of up to 10 years after implementation. While NAFTA eliminated duties on 80 percent of bilateral T&C trade between Mexico and the United States within 6 years, it established 10-year phaseouts for sensitive T&C products (US Department of Commerce 2005d). The US-Jordan FTA also included phaseout periods of up to 10 years, but most tariff cuts took place within the first three years after implementation in 2002.

Tariff elimination in US bilateral FTAs is typically based on the principle of reciprocity. For example, tariff elimination in the US-Jordan FTA was geared to obtain reciprocal tariff treatment for items in similar tariff ranges: Tariffs above 20 percent will be eliminated in 10 years in both countries, while tariffs below 5 percent were eliminated immediately. With this approach, Jordan, which applied higher initial tariffs, retained somewhat longer protection than the United States.

Reciprocity was also the guiding principle to T&C market access in the US-Australia and US-Morocco FTAs. However, phaseouts under those FTAs were determined on an item-by-item basis, with longer US phaseouts closely correlated to the partner's sensitivities rather than US sensitivities.[51]

Under the US-Australia FTA, most Australian tariff peaks—tariffs above 15 percent—will be phased out in 10 years. Consequently, the US schedule likewise contemplates 10-year phaseout periods for the items subject to tariff peaks in the Australian schedule.[52] For example, about 70

---

49. Tariffs and quotas on a few tariff lines corresponding to wool and animal hair and cotton will be phased out over 10 to 12 years.

50. However, some duties in the US schedule were removed immediately, but not retroactively, in accordance with existing WTO duty elimination commitments (WTO Schedule XX for the United States). A similar situation applies to traditional handcrafted goods.

51. This is a rough characterization and there are exceptions. For example, the United States requested longer phaseouts or quotas for wool and cotton and, interestingly, these were not "reciprocated" by the partner. There are also instances where the United States and the partner country both decided to eliminate all barriers. But overall US phaseout periods seem closely correlated to peaks in the partner's tariff schedule.

52. There are two important exceptions: The United States did not retaliate against Australian protection on products that already enjoy MFN duty-free entry in the US market, and the United States eliminated "nuisance tariffs" (tariffs of less than 3 percent) immediately, regardless of the Australian tariff or phaseout period.

percent of US and Australian tariff lines on clothing (HS chapters 61 and 62) will be subject to 10-year backloaded phaseout schedules, even though the incidence of tariff peaks on clothing in the US tariff schedule is just 35 percent of tariff lines. US insistence on playing by its own rules of origin may have heightened Australian sensitivities.[53]

In any case, the resulting tariff elimination schedules did not please producers in either country. The Textile, Clothing and Footwear Union of Australia complained that tariff reductions would benefit only US producers.[54] Most industry representatives to the US Advisory Committee on Textiles and Apparel characterized the phaseout periods as "exceptionally" or "extremely" long and complained that long phaseouts would curtail their benefits from the agreement (USTR 2004a).[55] US clothing producers resented the lack of immediate duty-free access, as they noted that Australia already grants duty preferences to other partners (USTR 2004a).[56]

Tariff elimination for T&C items under the US-Morocco FTA follows the same principles as the US-Australia FTA, although in this negotiation the United States mirrored Morocco's requests for longer phaseouts even on items where the United States applies only nuisance tariffs.[57] Moreover, the US-Morocco FTA contains a distinctive feature: It is the only US agreement that established reciprocal TRQs for clothing products and certain made-up textiles (42 tariff lines defined at the 6-digit level in HS chapters 61–63, listed in Annex 4-B of the agreement). The selection of TRQ items appears to reflect Moroccan sensitivities. Morocco applied 50 percent tariffs on all TRQ items, while the United States applied much lower tariffs, ranging from 0.5 to 32.3 percent (USTR 2004d).[58] Total US

---

53. The Australian T&C industry has repeatedly claimed difficulties in meeting origin requirements established under US agreements, in part related to its increasing reliance on Chinese and East Asian textile imports. In 2002, Australian T&C exports represented around 0.3 percent of US T&C imports. In that same year, US T&C exports represented 7.0 percent of textile imports and 1.6 percent of Australian clothing imports. For more information see the next subsection on rules of origin.

54. See the Submission from the Textile, Clothing and Footwear Union of Australia to the Senate Select Committee on the Free Trade Agreement between Australia and the United States of America, available at www.aph.gov.au.

55. The Advisory Committee recommended that "US negotiators should continue to strive to level the playing field and achieve reciprocal tariff reductions on the part of negotiating partners" (USTR 2004a, 3).

56. They also resented the introduction (at the instigation of the US textile industry) of restrictive rules of origin.

57. See, for example, phaseouts for products under HS 5409–5411 in the schedule of each party.

58. The USTR fact sheet on the agreement states that TRQs "enabled the United States to obtain reciprocal access to Morocco's market" (USTR 2004g, 1).

T&C exports to Morocco on TRQ items were small in 2004 (less than $5 million), possibly reflecting the high tariffs applied by Morocco. Perhaps in a gesture of trade-restricting reciprocity, the selection of TRQ items under the agreement covered 85 percent of Morocco's total T&C exports to the United States in 2004.[59] Unlike long-lasting TRQs for sensitive agricultural products in US agreements, the T&C TRQs in the US-Morocco FTA will expire after six years. With a few exceptions, in-quota volumes for all textile TRQs will double between year one and year five.

Rules of Origin

Rules of origin in US bilateral FTAs have often reflected the pursuit of protectionist objectives. Nowhere is this more evident than in the T&C sector. In this section we offer a stylized account of the US approach to T&C rules of origin, explaining how those rules are designed to protect US domestic producers.[60]

Leaving aside products that are "wholly obtained" or "fully made" from material originating in the partner countries, the rules of origin for T&C items in US bilateral FTAs can be characterized in four different groups: fiber-forward, yarn-forward, fabric-forward, and cut and sewn (US CBP 2005a). Rules in each group require that origin be established at a common stage in the productive process for a given T&C item. For example, fiber-forward rules require that the fiber must be formed (and all subsequent actions performed) in the territory covered by the agreement, while fabric-forward rules require that the fabric must be knitted or woven in the territory of the parties. US agreements that follow the NAFTA pattern often use fiber-forward rules for yarns and yarn-forward rules from that point on (e.g., for fabrics and apparel). Of course there are numerous exceptions to these characterizations.[61]

The adoption of yarn-forward rules in US FTAs is associated with a conscious decision by the US government to ensure a supplying role for the US textile industry. US textile producers argue that the requirements are necessary to ensure that the bulk of value-added processes take place in the partner countries rather than in third countries (USTR 2004a).

---

59. According to data from USITC Dataweb, in 2004 the United States imported $76 million of T&C goods from Morocco, of which $65 million were in items that will be subject to a TRQ under the agreement. By contrast, in that same year, Morocco imported only $4.5 million of T&C goods from the United States, and very little in tariff lines subject to TRQs.

60. However, the complex nature of interest in the US T&C industry should be noted. Important domestic producers, mainly apparel producers, often disapprove of the US stance on textile rules of origin and find certain provisions "too restrictive."

61. For a general but quite informative presentation of rules of origin in US bilateral agreements, see the CBP publication *NAFTA (the North American Free Trade Agreement) for Textiles and Textile Articles—An Informed Compliance Publication*, available at www.cbp.gov.

Yarn-forward rules are often denounced by both US clothing firms and by partner-country producers. Foreign producers argue that such rules often force second-best sourcing options and favor the party with the relatively more competitive textile sector. Because the United States has, to date, negotiated with countries that had relatively less competitive textile sectors, the yarn-forward rules have often promoted US exports of textile products (fibers, yarns, and fabrics) to the partner country. For example, as a result of CAFTA-DR, more than 90 percent of all clothing made in CAFTA countries will utilize US yarns and fabrics (USTR 2005d). Tony Woolgar, national secretary of the Textile, Clothing and Footwear Union of Australia, complained to the Australian Senate Committee on the US-Australia FTA, "Given the failure to change the rules of origin this will be a one-way free trade agreement" (Woolgar 2004). His position was acknowledged by the Australian negotiators and also in the Australian Senate investigation (Parliament of Australia Senate 2004).[62]

US clothing producers have also publicly opposed yarn-forward rules. For example, representatives of the clothing sector, commenting on the US-Australia FTA, expressed extreme disappointment "that the principal rule of origin is overly restrictive and complicated and it continues a disturbing pattern in which a specific industry sector [apparel and textiles] is subject to minute restrictions that can only serve to assure that this sector will not participate in [the Australian] market" (USTR 2004a). The experience of the US-Australia FTA shows that rigid yarn-forward rules can be viewed adversely by many US firms, both for their direct impact and because they inspire counterclaims by firms in the partner country for longer phaseouts of high tariffs on clothing imports.

US agreements do contain exceptions to the standard rules of origin. One exception is the de minimis rule, which allows goods to claim origin even when their components fail to meet the required change of tariff heading, so long as the failure is less than a given percentage of the weight of the component that determines the classification (e.g., 7 percent under NAFTA and the US-Morocco and US-Australia FTAs, but 10 percent under CAFTA-DR and the US-Singapore FTA). Other exceptions are introduced through tariff preference levels (TPLs), which allow a set quantity of products to qualify for preferential duty rates under the agreement even if the goods are nonoriginating. TPLs were established in recent US FTAs, except for the US-Australia FTA and CAFTA-DR.[63] Unlike TPLs in

62. Stephen Deady, Australian chief negotiator, stated to the Australian Senate Commission on the US-Australia FTA: "With the support of Australian industry, the Government also sought to have the latter approach applied to the T&C sector rather than the special 'yarn-forward' rule proposed by the United States side, but was unable to persuade the US to move from this position" (Parliament of Australia Senate 2004).

63. Only Nicaragua obtained a TPL that phases out over 10 years.

earlier agreements such as NAFTA, the TPLs in recent FTAs, such as the US-Bahrain FTA, are valid during the transition period only (usually 10 years).[64]

Textile Safeguards

Recourse to special textile safeguards is a standard feature of US FTAs.[65] The provisions establishing special safeguards share similarities across US agreements, but there are also important differences among them.

Similarities include notification requirements, the strength and length of measures (e.g., restoration of MFN duties for two to three years), the requirement of compensation and the ultimate option of recourse to retaliation, standards for determining serious damage, the transitional nature of the safeguard mechanism, and a prohibition against targeting a particular product twice.

However, there are important differences. First and foremost, agreements have different provisions as to the duration of special safeguards. Some agreements (e.g., the US-Australia, US-Bahrain, and US-Morocco FTAs) allow the invocation of special T&C safeguards for as long as 10 years after a tariff has been eliminated under the agreement. Others, such as CAFTA-DR and the US-Singapore FTA, limit the invocation of special safeguards to the transition period while tariffs are being eliminated (e.g., five years in the CAFTA-DR pact).[66] Second, not all agreements contemplate the renewal of a special safeguard measure. The US-Australia, US-Morocco, and US-Singapore FTAs allow the renewal of a measure under certain conditions, but CAFTA-DR and the US-Bahrain FTA do not expressly contemplate renewal. Another important difference lies in the requirement of an investigation before applying special safeguards. CAFTA-DR and the US-Bahrain and US-Morocco FTAs require a prior investigation; the US-Australia FTA permits safeguards without an investigation, under special conditions; and the US-Singapore FTA has no text on the issue.

---

64. The TPL under the US-Morocco FTA allowed for the largest quantities in relation to the partner's initial T&C exports to the United States (150 percent). TPLs under the US-Jordan, US-Israel, US-Chile, and US-Bahrain FTAs amount to 100 percent of the US partner country's T&C exports to the United States. Lower values were granted under the US-Singapore FTA (35 percent), NAFTA (16 percent), and CAFTA-DR (10 percent) (USTR 2005d).

65. US and foreign textile producers have noted that compensation mechanisms reduce the usefulness of the special safeguard mechanism. US apparel producers questioned the need for special textile safeguards in light of the establishment of strong origin requirements.

66. Large numbers of tariff lines will be phased out in 10 years under the US-Australia FTA, and consequently the special safeguards will be applicable for 20 years after implementation. The transition period in the US-Singapore FTA is defined as 10 years.

All agreements establish rules preventing the concurrent invocation of safeguards under the special textile mechanism and other mechanisms, such as the safeguard provisions of the WTO ATC, and Article XIX of GATT 1994.

Customs Enforcement of T&C Provisions

T&C customs procedures are largely designed to combat illegal transshipment of nonoriginating products, and enforcement is gaining greater prominence in T&C chapters. Evidence of smuggled products of Chinese origin, entering the United States under the NAFTA umbrella led US producers to insist on strict enforcement of T&C rules of origin.

CAFTA-DR and the US-Singapore FTA include the most extensive treatment of T&C customs procedures, and these agreements now serve as the models for other FTAs. The US-Singapore FTA requires that all Singaporean T&C companies register to claim benefits under the agreement (USTR 2003b). CAFTA-DR includes special verification procedures, such as unannounced factory visits, publication of the names of violators, and strong penalties such as jail time. CAFTA-DR also prohibits subsequent transformation outside the territory covered under the agreement.[67] None of these enforcement elements are present in NAFTA. The MoU between the United States and China concerning T&C trade, agreed in November 2005, mandates cooperation in preventing circumvention by transshipment, rerouting, and other means.[68]

T&C customs cooperation in bilateral FTAs has additional purposes beyond the prevention of illegal transshipment. CAFTA-DR and the US-Morocco FTA expressly note that parties will cooperate in enforcing their respective laws, regulations, and procedures (e.g., intellectual property protection and fire-retardant standards). A US-Pakistan FTA will likely cover these topics as well.

Pakistan

Obtaining better market access for its T&C exports has been a major Pakistani objective in previous trade agreements, but Pakistan has not always offered reciprocal access to the other party's T&C exports. Clothing items, synthetic filaments, and staple fibers are the most sensitive products for Pakistan, and therefore the products that retain long-lasting protection. In this section we discuss the Pakistan–Sri Lanka FTA, the early

---

67. For more information, see USTR publication *CAFTA Gets Tough on Illegal Transshipment*, available at www.ustr.gov.

68. The MoU also allows the subtraction from quota limits of an amount equal to any quantities that entered the United States in circumvention transactions.

harvest agreement between Pakistan and China, and the Economic Cooperation Organization Trade Agreement.[69]

Pakistan–Sri Lanka FTA

Implemented in June 2005, the Pakistan–Sri Lanka pact is the first bilateral FTA signed by Pakistan.[70] The agreement does not eliminate all tariffs: negative lists of items permanently excluded from tariff cuts cover 1,210 tariff lines at the six-digit level on both sides; in addition, partial concessions through TRQs cover another 30 tariff lines at the six-digit level; and 6 tariff lines at the six-digit level have preferential duty margins.[71] T&C account for a significant share of these exclusions and partial concessions. Excluded T&C products include nearly 205 tariff lines at the six-digit level, representing about 17 percent of all excluded tariff lines in the negative lists of both countries.

Aggregate numbers, however, mask the fact that Pakistan adopted a more defensive stance on clothing products than did Sri Lanka. The tariff structure of Sri Lanka reflected a liberal trade regime for T&C imports, both because the country is a competitive clothing supplier and because it relies heavily on imported raw materials.[72] However, Pakistan excluded about 170 tariff lines for clothing, almost 90 percent of its negative list for T&C items. The exclusion is quite important, as Pakistan has only 242 tariff lines for its clothing imports (HS chapters 61 and 62). Pakistani clothing producers are also protected through TRQs; in fact, the vast majority of Pakistan's TRQs under the agreement will apply to clothing trade (21 of 26 tariff lines). While Pakistan excluded most clothing items from the agreement, Sri Lanka did not include clothing products in its negative list, nor will it apply TRQs on these products.

Pakistan's textile exclusions also target mainly synthetic filaments and staple fibers (HS chapters 54 and 55), particularly items based on

---

69. Pakistan has also signed an early harvest agreement with Malaysia.

70. For this section we consulted the text of the Pakistan–Sri Lanka FTA, available at www.boi.lk.

71. Items in the TRQ list were also included in the negative lists.

72. According to data from the *WTO Trade Policy Review for Sri Lanka*, the average tariffs for Sri Lanka in 2003 were 4 percent for textiles and 11 percent for clothing. Pakistan's average tariffs currently stand at about 16 percent for textiles and almost 25 percent for clothing. Exports of T&C account for about 50 percent of Sri Lanka's total export earnings, and represent nearly 5 percent of GDP. A few large-scale manufacturers with strong marketing links to foreign buyers conduct clothing production and export in Sri Lanka. Almost 94 percent of exports are destined for the markets of the United States or European Union. While Sri Lanka imported textiles in the amount of $1.3 billion in 2002, the country's imports from Pakistan amounted to only $26 million (or 2 percent). Exports from Sri Lanka to Pakistan were less than half a million dollars in 2002 (WTO 2004b).

polyester.[73] Sri Lanka excluded several netting items, twines, certain vegetable fibers, and gauze. No TRQs were applied to textile products.

A few T&C items were included in the lists for immediate duty elimination, and tariffs on nearly all covered T&C products will be eliminated over three years in the case of Pakistan and over five years for Sri Lanka. Within three years of implementation, more than 95 percent of Pakistani textile tariffs will be eliminated, but less than 30 percent of Pakistani clothing tariffs will be eliminated, owing to multiple exclusions.

The agreement does not contemplate product-specific safeguards or special rules of origin. It does, however, incorporate general safeguards as well as a joint committee to oversee the application of the agreement. While the agreement allows the negotiation of "lower value added norms" for specific manufactured products, Annex C on rules of origin enumerates only general rules. The agreement also establishes consultation procedures in the event that rules of origin are circumvented.

Early Harvest Agreement Between China and Pakistan

Both China and Pakistan are net T&C exporters on a large scale, but T&C trade between the two countries is small, with T&C flows barely reaching 3 percent of total bilateral imports.[74] Nevertheless, T&C barriers were a prominent topic of negotiation in the early harvest agreement, which now grants full duty-free access for many textile products. Additionally, both countries will grant margins of duty preferences (by comparison with MFN rates) on several T&C tariff lines.

China granted full duty-free access to almost 470 textile tariff lines (HS 50–60 and 63), roughly 72 percent of all duty-free tariff lines granted to Pakistan under the agreement. Pakistan received duty-free treatment for yarns, fabrics, and fibers, and—importantly—for key exports of final textile products such as bath, bed, and table linens, tents and tarpaulins, curtains, and mattresses. Jerseys, pullovers, and ties are the only clothing items that qualify for duty-free treatment. The longest phaseout period for covered tariffs is two years. Furthermore, Pakistani exports will qualify for preferential tariff margins (versus MFN tariff rates) on about 400 Chinese T&C tariff lines. About half of these preferential margins will apply just to clothing exports (HS 61 and 62). The average tariff preference margin on T&C items (HS 50–63) is 24 percent of the MFN tariff rate.[75]

---

73. Targeted products also include bed linens and carpets.

74. For this section we consulted the text of the early harvest agreement between China and Pakistan, which was provided by the Embassy of Pakistan in Washington. The tariff schedules were obtained from the Chinese Ministry of Commerce, at http://english.mofcom.gov.cn.

75. In other words, if China's MFN tariff is 10 percent, Pakistan's exports would receive a preference of 2.4 percentage points, and pay a tariff of 7.6 percent. The highest preference margin on T&C products is 50 percent.

With the exception of a few wool-based products, Pakistan did not extend duty-free treatment to Chinese T&C exports, nor grant concessions on clothing products. Moreover, Pakistan will provide a lower preferential margin (with an average value of 15 percent) for a limited number of textile tariff lines (32 in total).[76] Pakistan did, however, grant duty-free treatment on imports of Chinese textile machinery. Additionally, Pakistan agreed in a separate MoU not to apply either Article 15 (third-country price comparability in determining subsidies and dumping) or Article 16 (the transitional product-specific safeguard mechanism) under China's Protocol of Accession to the WTO. Pakistan also renounced recourse to special transitional textile safeguards under paragraph 242 of the *Report of the Working Party on the Accession of China to the WTO.*

The early harvest agreement did not specify rules of origin for covered products. China and Pakistan agreed to negotiate a single set of rules of origin during their subsequent FTA talks, and not later than September 2005, three months before full implementation. During the first round of FTA negotiations between Pakistan and China, held August 16, 2005, the delegations agreed *ad referendum* on draft text on rules of origin (Commerce Division of the Embassy of Pakistan 2005).

Economic Cooperation Organization

Pakistan has negotiated trade preferences with Middle Eastern and Central Asian partners of the Economic Cooperation Organization (ECO).[77] The ECO Trade Agreement, signed in July 2003, establishes tariff preferences of 10 to 15 percent. The scope of coverage includes a positive list of all products actually traded among the parties as of the date of entry into force, as well as a negative list of exceptions that is limited to 1 percent of tariff lines at the six-digit level. Textile products (mainly raw cotton, cotton yarn, and fabrics) account for the vast majority of Pakistan's exports to the region, especially to Iran and Turkey. Pakistan expects that preference margins will convey a significant advantage vis-à-vis third countries—for example, in the Iranian market, as Iran is not a WTO member and applies high tariffs.[78] The maximum transition period contemplated by the agreement is eight years from implementation. The ECO agreement includes a pledge by parties to prepare a common set of rules that will guide the application of AD

---

76. The maximum tariff preference margin on textile and clothing products, excluding wool and fine animal hair, is 15 percent.

77. The ECO members are Afghanistan, Azerbaijan, Iran, Kazakhstan, Kyrgyz Republic, Pakistan, Tajikistan, Turkey, Turkmenistan, and Uzbekistan.

78. However, Iran has yet to ratify the agreement.

measures.[79] However, according to the Pakistan Ministry of Foreign Affairs, "For a variety of reasons ECO has not been able to make worthwhile progress on the crucial issue of economic integration of the region."[80]

Recommendations

In a sense, results from the CGE model state the obvious: Market access for T&C will be Pakistan's primary interest, while US commercial interests will focus on agriculture and durable manufactures. Hence, an opportunity exists for cross-sectoral concessions. However, the CGE model conveys a more subtle point: Without substantial US opening on T&C, a US-Pakistan FTA would be a lopsided bargain.

The prospect of a US-Pakistan FTA could create formidable opposition in Pakistan, among anti-Americans, industrialists in threatened sectors, antiglobalization NGOs, and farmers. Moreover, a US-Pakistan FTA might be perceived as a battleground for Pakistan's foreign policy. Reform leaders in Pakistan will need to advertise market access benefits and related employment creation in order to enlist support from a majority of domestic stakeholders. With these considerations in mind, we offer several recommendations for the negotiations affecting the T&C sector.

- Bilateral clothing trade should be liberalized more quickly than textile trade because relative trade volumes are much smaller in the US market. The United States should immediately liberalize at least 95 percent of Pakistan's current clothing exports.[81] The remaining tariffs on clothing should be phased out over six years.

- Likewise, Pakistan should provide immediate duty-free access for selected US clothing exports and streamline administrative rules on the importation of used clothing. Pakistan's tariffs on remaining clothing imports should be phased out in equal annual stages over six years.

- As a general rule, Pakistan and the United States should eliminate tariffs on yarns immediately, while tariffs on fabrics and finished textiles (e.g., bed, bathroom, and kitchen linens, curtains, blankets)

---

79. Turkey is also a frequent user of antidumping measures on T&C items, and it has a record of targeting products that compete with Pakistani textile exports. However, Pakistan has not been affected by measures imposed by Turkey.

80. In fact, Turkey imposed quantitative restrictions on Pakistani textile and clothing exports (Pakistan Ministry of Foreign Affairs 2004).

81. Table 3.11 shows that the United States could achieve that target by eliminating tariffs on the top 10 clothing items at the 8-digit level.

should be phased out within six years. A few exceptions for truly sensitive items should be allowed (e.g., synthetic filaments and fibers).

- Pakistan should accept the US yarn-forward rules of origin. However, the United States should allow for a large de minimis exception (e.g., 10 percent). Other exceptions should be evaluated through consultations in the joint committee under the agreement.

- The agreement should contain strong provisions of customs cooperation, including language and penalties on illegal transshipments and intellectual property violations. Recourse to special textile safeguards should be available, but only during the transition period before all tariffs are eliminated.

4

Other Manufactures

Trade in manufactures besides textiles and clothing, a category we call "other manufactures," forms an integral part of the US-Pakistan commercial relationship.[1] More than 80 percent of US exports to Pakistan fall in the other manufactures product category. Pakistan, however, does not export large amounts of other manufactures to the United States.

Despite serious efforts at liberalization, Pakistan still applies high tariffs on manufactured imports. Over the past decade, US exporters have conducted business in Pakistan in a setting with high political risk. While the business environment has improved in recent years, it is possible that US exporters of manufactured goods could find themselves at a disadvantage if Pakistan enters into FTAs with other partners. A US-Pakistan FTA would eliminate Pakistan's remaining tariffs and ensure an equal footing for US firms.

With a few exceptions, notably leather-based items and sporting goods, Pakistan's other manufactures are highly oriented toward the domestic market. US tariffs on other manufactures are mostly low, and some Pakistani firms already enjoy duty-free access to the US market through generalized system of preferences (GSP) or most favored nation (MFN) rates. Pakistan's commercial interest in an FTA will center on securing

---

1. We use the category of "other manufactures" throughout this chapter to refer to products included in HS chapters 25 through 97, excluding HS chapters 50 to 63. Thus the category includes traditional manufactures (e.g., chemicals, plastics, articles of metals, machinery, vehicles, instruments, etc.) and excludes textiles and clothing (discussed in chapter 3); food, beverages, and tobacco manufactures (discussed in chapter 2); and petroleum, gold, and silver.

permanent duty-free access and eliminating remaining US barriers. Equally important, a US-Pakistan FTA could encourage investment in Pakistan's manufacturing sector. However, a US-Pakistan FTA will require considerable adjustment in Pakistan's "other manufacturing" sector: The initial impact of a bilateral pact will be smaller production, as Pakistani firms close down high-cost, low-quality lines. Only as efficient techniques are adopted and new products are manufactured will output and employment increase.

This chapter is structured in two sections. The first section reviews production and trade patterns. The second section identifies barriers and issues that should be addressed in the negotiation. We conclude with recommendations for the US-Pakistan FTA negotiations.

Manufacturing Production and Bilateral Trade

After Pakistan's independence was established in 1947, the country's manufacturing sector occupied the central role in national development—it was considered the main engine of the economy and was expected to provide the primary avenue of new employment. However, despite years of targeted promotion policies, Pakistan's total industrial sector remains a relatively small part of the economy (only 18 percent of GDP in 2005).[2] Comparisons with other South and East Asian countries indicate that manufacturing GDP in Pakistan is not only small but also heavily concentrated in textiles and clothing, foods, beverages, and tobacco.[3]

Other manufactures account for roughly 8 percent of Pakistan's total GDP (and less than half of the country's total manufacturing GDP) and employ about 2 million workers (almost 35 percent of manufacturing employment, as shown in table 4.1).[4] The principal subsectors, in terms of both output and employment, are chemicals and basic metals (iron and steel) and their products (table 4.1). Examples of domestic industrial products include: caustic soda and soda ash; nitrogenous and phosphatic

---

2. Agriculture accounts for 23 percent of GDP, while the share of services is just below 60 percent.

3. According to UNIDO (2005), the share of the manufacturing sector in the GDP of all South and East Asian countries was roughly 33 percent, well above Pakistan's 18 percent. The same share for all developing countries averaged 23 percent, so Pakistan is even below the developing country average. The share of textiles and clothing and foods, beverages, and tobacco in the manufacturing sector in South and East Asian countries was roughly 9 and 13 percent respectively (UNIDO 2005). Table 4.1 shows that the shares of those sectors in Pakistan's manufacturing GDP are 29 and 22 percent respectively. Other sources present higher estimates for the share of textiles and clothing in Pakistan's manufacturing GDP.

4. These figures are rough estimates. The method of estimation is explained in the notes to table 4.1.

Table 4.1 Pakistan's manufacturing sector (millions of US dollars)

HS category	Value added, 2003–04[a]	As percent of total manufacturing value added, 2001	Thousands of workers, 2004[b]	Total exports, 2004[c]	Total imports, 2004[c]	Net exports, 2004	FDI inflows, 2002–05[d] United States	FDI inflows, 2002–05[d] Total
Foods, beverages, and tobacco	3,417	22	739	278	916	–638	15	40
Textiles and clothing[e]	4,490	29	3,170	8,790	518	8,273	47	101
Petroleum and fuels	867	6	22	362	3,903	–3,541	342	682
Total other manufactures	6,807	43	1,899	2,462	10,663	–8,201	69	344
Leather and leather products[f]	224	1	135	818	57	761	4	11
Paper, pulp, printing	316	2	123	16	283	–267	0	3
Chemicals and their products	2,505	16	440	162	2,708	–2,546	36	215
Plastic, rubber, and their products	189	1	79	173	932	–759	0	0
Nonmetallic mineral products[g]	884	6	169	43	125	–82	13	19
Basic metals and their products	1,097	7	306	128	1,168	–1,041	2	8
Machinery, electrical equipment, and precision instruments	844	5	322	311	3,522	–3,211	12	51
Transport equipment	531	3	173	378	1,547	–1,169	2	37
Sports goods	136	1	97	267	6	261	n.a.	n.a.
Remaining other manufactures	82	1	57	165	314	–150	n.a.	n.a.
All manufactures	15,681	100	5,830	11,893	15,994	–4,101	473	1,167

HS = Harmonized Schedule; n.a. = not available

a. Estimates based on aggregate data on manufacturing GDP reported by the *Pakistan Economic Survey 2004–05* and the sectoral shares of manufacturing GDP reported by the *Census of Manufacturing Industries 2000–01*.

b. Estimates based on aggregate data on manufacturing employment reported by the *Pakistan Economic Survey 2004–05*, and the sectoral shares of manufacturing employment reported by the *Census of Manufacturing Industries 2000–01*.

c. Values estimated based on UN Comtrade data at 5 digits in HS 2002 classification.

d. Accumulated inflow estimates based on reports of the Pakistan Board of Investment for the years 2002–03 through the first trimester of 2005–06.

e. Excludes silk, wool, and cotton in raw state. Trade data for this category include man-made fibers.

f. Includes leather-based footwear.

g. Excludes gold trade flows.

Sources: Pakistan Board of Investment (2005a); Pakistan Federal Census Bureau of Statistics (2005a); UNIDO (2005); UN Statistics Division (2005).

fertilizer; pharmaceuticals; soap and detergent; paints and varnishes; cement; motorcycles, vehicles, and parts;[5] paper and paperboard; agricultural and textile (sewing) machinery; electrical appliances (TV sets, fans, refrigerators, electric bulbs, and tubes); iron and steel products (razors; heating and cooking equipment); and leather products and sports goods.[6] Most of these products enjoy above average tariff protection.

New Realities

Pakistan's Poverty Reduction Strategy Paper highlights the fact that employment creation in the manufacturing sector is low in comparison to other sectors of the economy.[7] As a result, the industrial sector has ceased to be the centerpiece of the country's development strategy (Government of Pakistan 2003). The government's view for the industrial sector involves "pursuing technological transformation . . . to face the challenges of competitive environment" (Government of Pakistan 2003, 2–3). A transformed manufacturing sector could play a fundamental role in regaining lost ground with respect to emerging Asian economies.

As a sign of its commitment to market forces, the government is privatizing the remaining publicly owned industrial units. A large number of automotive, cement, chemical, and fertilizer plants were privatized between 1992 and 1996,[8] and in recent years the government put additional industrial plants on the market, including the Pakistan Steel Mills Corporation.[9]

Trade policy has reinforced the government's market-oriented agenda. Pakistan has pursued multitier trade liberalization that combines unilateral tariff reductions with active participation in bilateral and multilateral negotiations. Bilateral agreements with large partner countries are

---

5. Pakistan produces jeeps and cars, tractors, light commercial vehicles, and motorcycles. While motorcycles are the majority of vehicle units produced in Pakistan (45 percent), vehicles account for the largest contribution to value added. Pakistan also has a significant auto parts industry, with some limited export orientation.

6. For a complete listing of manufactures produced in Pakistan, see the *Pakistan Census of Manufacturing Industries 2000–01*, available at www.statpak.gov.pk.

7. Manufacturing employment elasticity with respect to GDP dropped from an average of 1.1 during the 1970s to practically zero during the 1990s. Other sectors experienced a less pronounced decline, as indicated by the fact that the overall employment elasticity for the national economy fell from 0.64 to 0.41 during that period. On the bright side, these figures indicate a restructuring of Pakistan's manufacturing toward greater efficiency.

8. The privatization program also covered ghee mills, textile mills, and rice and roti plants, but the proceeds from these sales were modest.

9. The Pakistan Steel Mills Corporation supplies about 25 percent of Pakistan's total demand for steel. The government intends to sell 51 to 75 percent of the shares, together with management control.

expected to improve the competitiveness of Pakistan's manufacturing sector by providing access to cheaper inputs and machinery and by introducing more competition in markets for final consumer products.

With the exception of leather products and sports goods, Pakistan's production of other manufactures is now heavily oriented toward domestic demand. In fact, the net imports to GDP ratios are high in most sectors, particularly for durable goods (table 4.1). Other manufactures contribute to only just above 20 percent of Pakistan's total exports.

Pakistani Imports of Other Manufactures

Imports of other manufactures account for the majority of Pakistan's merchandise imports (59 percent). Chemicals and durable goods are the largest components.

In 2004, the top sources of other manufactured imports were (in order) the European Union, China, the United States, Japan, and ASEAN countries (table 4.2). Since 1996, China, ASEAN, South Korea, Taiwan, and Hong Kong have increased their shares of Pakistan's manufactured imports.[10] Increases show up in both durable and nondurable goods (table 4.2), with the competitive pressure greatest in low- and medium-technology products.[11] In response, some domestic producers (e.g., of footwear) are seeking the imposition of safeguards and antidumping measures. In 2001 the US Commercial Service identified Chinese firms (including foreign firms based in China) as direct competitors of US producers for several Pakistani industrial imports: plastics; industrial chemicals; oil and gas machinery and supplies; textile machinery; pumps, valves, and compressors; and general industrial and office equipment and supplies (US Commercial Service 2001).[12] Table 4.3 shows that in 2004 Chinese firms were the leading suppliers of Pakistan's imports of many of these products, and surpassed US firms in all product categories except power generating machineries and aircraft (other transport equipment in table 4.3), fertilizers, and scientific equipment. Table 4.3 also

---

10. Saudi Arabia, United Arab Emirates, and Kuwait also increased their share of Pakistan's total imports, but petroleum accounted for nearly all of their exports.

11. As a very rough indicator, the unit values (values divided by units of machinery) for most items of machinery and equipment listed in table 4.3 tend to be lower for imports from China and ASEAN countries than for Japan, the United States, and the European Union.

12. The same source identified ASEAN firms, particularly Singaporean firms, as strong competitors for computers and oil and gas machinery. That source also identified Japan and the European Union as distinct competitors on certain telecom equipment, pharmaceuticals, agricultural chemicals, pollution control equipment, aircraft and other transportation equipment, and food processing and packaging equipment.

Table 4.2 Pakistan's imports of other manufactures, by top partners (millions of US dollars)

Partner	Nondurables^a		Durables^b		Total		Percent growth of other manufactures imports
	1996	2004	1996	2004	1996	2004	
China and Hong Kong	188	447	362	950	550	1,397	154
Share of total other manufactures	0.08	0.13	0.08	0.15	0.08	0.14	
ASEAN	176	445	169	379	344	825	139
Share of total other manufactures	0.08	0.13	0.04	0.06	0.05	0.08	
Korea and Taiwan	213	232	191	318	404	550	36
Share of total other manufactures	0.09	0.07	0.04	0.05	0.06	0.06	
Japan	137	97	1,048	1,029	1,185	1,126	–5
Share of total other manufactures	0.06	0.03	0.24	0.16	0.18	0.11	
United States	317	296	493	891	810	1,187	47
Share of total other manufactures	0.14	0.09	0.11	0.14	0.12	0.12	
EU-15	752	605	1,531	1,323	2,283	1,929	–16
Share of total other manufactures	0.33	0.18	0.35	0.21	0.34	0.20	
Other	518	1,296	612	1,538	1,130	2,834	151
Share of total other manufactures	0.23	0.38	0.14	0.24	0.17	0.29	
Subtotal	2,300	3,419	4,406	6,428	6,706	9,846	47
Total other manufactures	2,568	3,670	4,547	6,686	7,115	10,357	46

ASEAN = Association of Southeast Asian Nations

a. Nondurables include chemicals (SITC section 5); leather, rubber, cork, and paper (SITC section 6, chapters 6.1–6.4); and plumbing and lighting fixtures, travel goods, footwear (SITC section 8, chapters 8.1, 8.3 and 8.5).
b. Durables include minerals, metals, and their products (SITC section 6, chapters 6.6–6.9); machinery and transport equipment (SITC section 7); furniture, scientific equipment, photographic apparatus, and miscellaneous manufactures (SITC section 8, chapters 8.2 and 8.7–8.9).

Note: Textiles and clothing; foods, beverages, and tobacco; fuels; and gold are not included in this table. Shares are estimated with respect to the subtotal. They exclude other manufactures in raw state such as pulp and waste paper, crude fertilizer, crude rubber, hides, raw cork, and metalliferous scrap.

Source: UN Statistics Division (2005).

Table 4.3 Pakistan's imports of other manufactures, by selected products and countries, 2004 (millions of US dollars)

Product	China[a]	Japan	United States	EU-15	East Asian tigers[b]	Total	Share of tabulated countries
Chemicals	312	68	251	463	201	3,640	0.36
Organic and inorganic	138	32	97	183	100	1,476	0.37
Fertilizers	24	1	100	21	0	356	0.41
Miscellaneous	95	7	31	81	31	340	0.72
Plastics and rubber	79	39	42	87	169	932	0.45
Glass and ceramics	67	2	1	15	5	111	0.80
Basic metals and their products	81	77	56	212	132	1,174	0.48
Machinery and equipment	698	944	823	1,095	349	5,061	0.77
Power-generating mach nes	27	20	70	143	9	314	0.86
Special industrial machinery	168	255	72	433	69	1,250	0.80
Metalworking machinery	7	19	5	13	6	56	0.90
General industrial machinery nes	129	58	70	162	63	631	0.76
Office machines	47	6	36	26	51	229	0.73
Telecommunication and sound equipment	136	13	89	122	62	575	0.73
Electrical machinery	77	23	24	69	27	274	0.80
Road vehicles	47	523	9	33	34	743	0.87
Other transport equipment	40	0	417	33	2	779	0.63
Scientific equipment nes	11	11	30	58	20	162	0.80
Photographic apparatus	8	16	2	5	5	47	0.79

nes = not elsewhere specified

a. Does not include imports from Hong Kong.
b. Hong Kong, South Korea, Singapore, and Taiwan.

Source: UN Statistics Division (2005).

shows a strong supplying role for the East Asian tigers (Hong Kong, South Korea, Singapore, and Taiwan).

Despite a 47 percent increase in Pakistan's imports of foreign other manufactures between 1996 and 2004, imports from Japan and the European Union declined during that period (table 4.2). The US share of Pakistan's imports of other manufactures has remained stable at around 9 percent of total imports. In part, this reflects the fact that the United States is well positioned in high-tech products, chiefly aircraft. However, table 4.4 shows large swings in US exports over the past decade. Political decisions, notably the US imposition of sanctions on Pakistan and India, affected US exports to Pakistan in 1998. In 2004 US exports bounced back, surpassing their 1996 level, with a particularly strong performance by durable exports.[13]

The dynamic exports are fertilizers (HS 3100), electric generating sets (HS 8502), transmission apparatus for telephony and broadcasting (HS 8525), and medical instruments (HS 9018 and 9027). US exports to Pakistan of nearly all these products have at least doubled since 1996; moreover, export growth continued strong in 2005. But while certain US exports show impressive sustained growth, others have stagnated over the past decade (1996–2004). For example, exports of most organic chemicals (HS 29) and machinery (HS 84) remain below their 1996 levels. The early harvest agreement between China and Pakistan will increase Chinese pressure in these declining products.

Recent US FDI flows to Pakistan's other manufactures sector have been small (table 4.1). Figures for 2005 also show a sharp drop in US exports of aircraft.[14] In fact, similar to Japanese and EU exports, US exports of other manufactures will drop below their 1996 export level.

Pakistan's Exports of Other Manufactures

Pakistan's exports of other manufactures to the United States are small, about $220 million total (table 4.4), or 7 percent of Pakistan's exports to the US market. Moreover, Pakistani exports of other manufactures to the United States have declined in recent years. The principal products exported, listed according to their 2004 trade values, are leather, medical devices, sports goods (inflatable balls), cutlery, and jewelry (table 4.5). Most of these products enjoy duty-free access (through GSP or MFN rates); however, US tariffs may be an obstacle for Pakistani leather and footwear exporters. Pakistan is the fourth largest supplier of US imports

---

13. Data for 2001–03 and 2005 indicate that 2004 was in fact an exceptional year for US manufactured exports to Pakistan.

14. However, in years to come Pakistan's aircraft purchases could increase if the country completes the planned opening of the airline industry.

**Table 4.4 Other manufactures trade between the United States
and Pakistan** (millions of US dollars)

	1996	2000	2004	2005[a]
Other manufactures				
US exports to Pakistan	925	401	1,373	890
US imports from Pakistan	177	256	215	220
US trade balance	748	145	1,158	670
Total trade				
US exports to Pakistan	1,277	462	1,811	1,159
US imports from Pakistan	1,266	2,167	2,874	3,202
US trade balance	11	−1,705	−1,063	−2,042
Share of other manufactures (percent)				
In total bilateral trade	43	25	34	25
In US exports to Pakistan	72	87	76	77
In US imports from Pakistan	14	12	7	7

a. Preliminary figures: annualized January–October data.

Note: Table excludes textiles and clothing products; food, tobacco, and beverages; petroleum and fuels; and gold. Values may differ from those reported in other tables as this table reports US export data (f.o.b), while other tables report Pakistan's import data (c.i.f). Moreover, Pakistan records statistics on budget-year basis (July–June) rather than the calendar year as the USITC does. Another reason for the difference is that Pakistan does not include military goods (e.g., aircraft) in its trade statistics.

Source: USITC (2005).

of leather clothing (gloves and jackets), but imports from Pakistan account for only 4 percent of US imports, while China supplies almost 70 percent.

Many of the leading Pakistani exports of other manufactures to the US market have declined since 2000 (table 4.6). While Pakistan's export performance for the same items in the European market has been slightly better, the 2004 export values remain below the 1996 levels (table 4.6). Indeed, table 4.6 shows that the combined share of the US and EU markets in Pakistan's exports of other manufactures dropped from 71 percent to 56 percent between 1996 and 2004. In contrast, Pakistan's exports of other manufactures to other markets have increased rapidly, indicating that the best export prospects for Pakistan's manufacturing sector probably lie outside the US and EU markets.

The Export Promotion Bureau of Pakistan considers leather products, sports goods, and surgical instruments core export products; and some of them, chiefly leather-based goods, receive export incentives. Chemicals, certain "engineering goods," and jewelry are also considered products where Pakistan "currently enjoys, or can achieve, a strong competitive edge" (Export Promotion Bureau of Pakistan 2005b).

Table 4.5 Pakistan's exports of other manufactures to the United States and to the world, 2004 (millions of US dollars)

Product description	United States		World	Share of US market in Pakistan's exports to the world
	Total[a]	Under GSP		
Hides, leathers, and furskins (HS section VIII)	93	4	783	0.12
Articles of leather; saddlery and harness, travel equipment (ch. 42)	90	2	497	0.18
Other hides, leathers, and furskins (ch. 41 and 43)	3	2	286	0.01
Construction and precious stones; glass (HS sections XIII-XIV)	29	24	72	0.40
Articles of stone, plaster, cement, or similar materials (ch. 68)	12	9	22	0.54
Pearls, precious or semiprecious stones (ch. 71)	17	15	29	0.58
Other stones or glass (ch. 69–70)	0	0	21	0.02
Base metals and articles thereof (HS section XV)	27	18	128	0.21
Tools, cutlery, silverware, of base metal (ch. 82)	22	16	44	0.51
Other metals or articles thereof (ch. 72–81; 83)	5	2	84	0.05
All remaining other manufactures	96	12	1,842	0.05
Medical devices (ch. 90)	34	0	163	0.21
Sports goods (ch. 95)	25	1	268	0.09
Remaining other manufactures	37	11	1,410	0.03
Total	245[b]	59	2,825	0.09

GSP = generalized system of preferences
HS = Harmonized Schedule

a. Includes exports under preferential (GSP) and nonpreferential access programs.
b. The value is different from the one reported in table 4.4. The difference is explained in the notes to that table.

Note: Excludes textile and clothing products; food, tobacco, and beverages; petroleum and fuels; and gold.

Sources: UN Statistics Division (2005); USITC (2005).

Table 4.6 Pakistan's leading exports of other manufactures, 1996–2004
(millions of US dollars)

Category	1996	2000	2004	Percent change 1996–2000	Percent change 2000–2004
United States	183	215	180	17	−16
Cutlery (SITC 696)	10	16	12		
Leather (SITC 611, 612, and 8481)[a]	59	86	82		
Leather footwear (SITC 8514)	0	0	1		
Medical instruments (SITC 872)	59	46	44		
Sporting goods (SITC 8947)	56	67	40		
European Union	597	485	559	−19	15
Cutlery (SITC 696)	5	5	7		
Leather (SITC 611, 612, and 8481)[a]	371	312	315		
Leather footwear (SITC 8514)	1	1	27		
Medical instruments (SITC 872)	49	44	60		
Sporting goods (SITC 8947)	172	124	150		
World	1,093	1,050	1,312	−4	25
Cutlery (SITC 696)	20	27	31		
Leather (SITC 611, 612, and 8481)[a]	641	614			
Leather footwear (SITC 8514)	3	2	81		
Medical instruments (SITC 872)	138	125	157		
Sporting goods (SITC 8947)	291	282	315		
US and EU share of Pakistan's total exports	0.71	0.67	0.56		

SITC = Standard International Trade Classification

a. These values are lower than those reported in table 4.1, which are based on the Harmonized Schedule classification.

Source: UN Statistics Division (2005).

Impact of a US-Pakistan FTA: The CGE Model

The computable general equilibrium (CGE) model predicts large gains for US exports of other manufactures, roughly a 170 percent increase.[15] While exports of all product categories are expected to at least double, the most significant absolute gains will accrue to sales of chemicals and

---

15. The gravity model predicts a 75 percent increase in bilateral trade in manufactured products. Unlike the CGE model, however, it does not provide insights as to the composition or direction of these gains. We discuss the full results of both models in chapter 8.

machinery and equipment (other than transport and electronic equipment). US gains in other transport equipment (not including motor vehicles) and electronic machinery could also be important. Additional product categories may expand rapidly, but starting from very low levels. Some caveats are in order, however: These projections could be overstated, and the model ignores preferences that Pakistan could grant to other competitors (China, India, or ASEAN countries) that would cut into the calculated US export gains.

According to the CGE model, with an FTA, Pakistan's exports of other manufactures to the United States and to the rest of the world will both decline about 25 percent. Specifically, the model predicts lower production of leather items (a 25 percent decrease), miscellaneous manufactures such as medical instruments (which will decline by almost 10 percent), and chemical production (which will contract by about 7 percent). We are skeptical of these results for two reasons. In the first place, the underlying CGE assumption that labor and capital resources are fixed in total quantity may give too little credit to the ability of firms to mobilize underutilized workers and idle plants. In the second place, large efficiency gains should enable firms to produce more with the same inputs. On balance, it seems implausible that Pakistan's exporters of manufactured goods will surrender foreign markets in the wake of an FTA with the United States. More likely they will adapt and expand.

The CGE model generates mixed results with respect to the impact of the FTA on customs revenue. According to the model, Pakistan could experience a decline of about $152 million annually. Of this amount $84 million is a direct loss, resulting from lower tariffs on imports from the United States; the remaining $68 is an indirect loss, reflecting import diversion from third sources (in both cases, mainly imports of other manufactures).[16] The calculated loss represents about 2 percent of Pakistan's total tax revenues. However, the CGE model predicts that, over the long term, the positive income effect of an FTA will increase Pakistan's imports from all sources, not just the United States, and the increased imports could mitigate the loss of revenue from lower tariff rates. Moreover, a US-Pakistan FTA will not lead to elimination of tariffs overnight, so the government of Pakistan will have time to balance its fiscal books by closing loopholes or raising other taxes.

---

16. In 2004 US exports of other manufactures contributed between $63 million and $84 million to Pakistan's treasury—in other words, most of the direct loss of revenue projected by the CGE model. The upper bound estimate (for 2004) assumes the simple average tariff on other manufactures in the Pakistan schedule (13.2 percent) and no SRO exceptions for 33 percent of US exports. The lower bound estimate assumes instead the trade-weighted average on US exports to Pakistan reported in table 4.7 (8.2 percent).

Tariffs and Other Barriers

Pakistan

Like many developing countries, in the late 1980s Pakistan started on a path of unilateral trade liberalization. But despite increased liberalization, Pakistan's domestic industry is still highly protected. Protectionist interests, however, are not the only reason for Pakistan's high duties on imports of other manufactures; revenue considerations also play a role. The Pakistani tariff system has a clear proindustrial bias: Higher rates are applied on luxury and nonessential items while raw materials and industrial plants and machinery imports pay lower rates (Burki and Akbar 2005). Pakistan applies no quantitative restrictions.[17]

While tariffs are the principal instrument of trade policy in Pakistan, other instruments are also used. The number and restrictiveness of nontariff barriers have decreased significantly over the past decade (Burki and Akbar 2005), but Pakistan still maintains noteworthy obstacles such as charges and taxes, licensing and procedural requirements, and import bans. The United States has not officially questioned Pakistan's import requirements and procedures in the WTO Committee on Import Licensing, but past negotiating experience demonstrates that these issues will be prominent in the US agenda.

Tariffs

The simple average applied tariff for all manufactured products, which surpassed 100 percent in the 1980s, declined to 21 percent in 2001(WTO 2002a). Estimates based on the Pakistan Customs Tariff 2005–06 indicate a further reduction to about 14 percent in 2005.[18] The average tariff on other manufactures in 2005 was just above 13 percent. But US exports of other manufactures, because of their sectoral composition, pay significantly lower tariffs than suggested by these figures: In 2004 the trade-weighted average applied tariff for Pakistan's imports of other manufactures from the United States was about 8 percent (tables 4.7 and 4.8).[19]

---

17. According to the *Pakistan Economic Survey 2004–05*, there are exceptions for phasing out chlorofluorocarbon gases (CFCs) and a few WTO-compatible tariff quotas allowed to member countries of the South Asian Association for Regional Cooperation (SAARC).

18. While Pakistan's average MFN tariffs have declined below South Asian averages, they are still higher than the average tariffs of most emerging markets in East Asia, Latin America, and Eastern Europe, particularly for manufactured products.

19. This figure is based on customs rates listed in the Pakistan Customs Tariff 2005–06. If exemptions are considered, the simple average paid by the top 30 exports is even lower: 3.6 percent.

Table 4.7 Pakistan's top 30 imports of other manufactures from the United States, 2004 (millions of US dollars and approximate applied tariff)

HS 6-digit category	Product description	Import value	Share	Applied tariff (percent)	Tariff exempt?
8802.40	Airplanes and other aircraft of an unladen weight under 15tn	364	0.30	5.0	Yes[a]
3105.30	Diammonium hydrogenortho-phosphate	67	0.05	5.0	No
8803.30	Other parts of airplanes/helicopters	50	0.04	5.0	Yes[b]
8525.10	Transmission apparatus for telephony and broadcasting	45	0.04	10.0	No
8502.13	Electric generating sets	32	0.03	13.3	No
2902.43	p-Xylene	32	0.03	5.0	Yes[c]
8525.20	Transmission apparatus for telephony and broadcasting	20	0.02	6.3	Yes[d]
3105.90	Mineral and chemical fertilizers with nitrogen	19	0.02	5.0	No
2926.10	Acrylonitrile	15	0.01	5.0	Yes[d]
3808.10	Insecticides (mosquito coils, mats, and the like)	14	0.01	25.0	No
8411.99	Parts of other gas turbines of 8411.81 & 8411.82	13	0.01	5.0	No
8414.80	Air pumps, air and other gas compressors and fans	11	0.01	20.0	No
8419.89	Machinery, plant, and laboratory equipment	11	0.01	25.0	No
8471.30	Portable digital automatic data processing machines	10	0.01	5.0	Yes[d]
3104.30	Potassium sulphate	10	0.01	5.0	No
8471.60	Input/output units of automatic data processing machines	9	0.01	8.6	Yes[e]
7210.49	Flat-rolled products of iron nonalloy steel	9	0.01	17.5	Yes[d]
3907.20	Polyethers other than polyacetals, in primary forms	9	0.01	5.0	No
8411.91	Parts of the turbojets and turbopropellers	7	0.01	5.0	No

(table continues next page)

The trade-weighted tariff averages and estimates of actual duties paid on current imports both understate the level of distortion induced by Pakistan's tariff policy. Calculations of average tariffs do not entirely reflect the effect of prohibitive peaks, tariff escalation, and targeted duty exemptions. Additionally, Pakistan continues to avoid commitments for the

Table 4.7 *(continued)*

HS 6-digit category	Product description	Import value	Share	Applied tariff (percent)	Tariff exempt?
8431.43	Parts suitable for machinery of 8430.41	7	0.01	5.0	No
8517.50	Apparatus for carrier-current line or digital line systems	7	0.01	25.0	No
3902.10	Polypropylene, in primary forms	7	0.01	5.0	No
8529.90	Parts suitable for appliances of 85.25-85.28	7	0.01	12.5	Yes[f]
9018.90	Instruments used in medical, surgical, and veterinary sciences	6	0.01	5.0	Yes[g]
3905.30	Polyvinyl alcohol	6	0.01	5.0	No
8446.30	Weaving machines (looms)	6	0.00	5.0	No
8517.90	Parts of the appliances and equipment of 85.17	6	0.00	10.0	No
8451.80	Machinery for washing, cleaning, wringing, and finishing textiles	6	0.00	5.0	No
8473.30	Parts and accessories	6	0.00	5.0	No
4703.21	Chemical wood pulp, soda, and sulphate	6	0.00	5.0	No
2941.50	Erythromycin and its derivates and salts thereof	6	0.00	10.0	No
	Subtotal	818	0.67	6.7[h]	3.5[i]
	Total	1223	1.00	8.2[j]	

a. Duty-free according to SRO 567. Exemption valid only if imported by commercial airline.
b. Exempted by budget 2005–06.
c. Duty-free according to SRO 567. Valid if imported by Pakistan PTA Limited for the manufacture of pure terephthalic acid (PTA).
d. Duty-free according to SRO 567.
e. 10 percent duty according to SRO 565.
f. 5 or 10 percent according to SRO 565.
g. Duty-free according to SRO 575.
h. Trade-weigted average based on duty listed in this column.
i. Trade-weighted average incorporating exemptions or duty reductions.
j. Trade-weighted average based on Pakistan's imports from the United States exceeding $1 million in 2004 (or 87 percent of total).

Sources: Pakistan Customs Revenue Board (2005b, 2005c, 2005d); UN Statistics Division (2005).

binding of tariffs. About 50 percent of tariff lines (some 2,730 lines) for manufactured products are not bound (WTO 2005e). Moreover, while Pakistan has bound the covered manufactures tariffs at a significantly lower average rate than its bound agricultural lines (35 percent versus 97 percent), authorities still retain considerable room for maneuver between bound and applied tariffs, even for manufactured products.

Table 4.8 Pakistan's tariffs on imports of other manufactures, selected chapters, 2005–06 (millions of US dollars)

Product description	Number of tariff lines	Number of peaks[a]	Simple average tariff rate	US exports to Pakistan (millions of dollars)	Weighted average tariff on imports from United States[b]
Chemicals and plastics (HS sections VI–VII)	1,356	349	10.4	293	6.7
Fertilizers (ch. 31)	26	0	5.0	100	5.0
Organic chemicals (ch. 29)	477	28	6.7	94	6.2
Miscellaneous chemical products (ch. 38)	96	37	13.4	37	14.5
Plastics and articles thereof (ch. 39)	154	101	16.5	31	5.9
Base metals and articles thereof (HS section XV)	714	308	14.3	56	16.9
Iron and steel (ch. 72)	241	78	12.6	34	16.6
Articles of iron or steel (ch. 73)	144	105	19.4	14	20.8
Machinery and equipment (HS section XVI)	1,054	331	12.0	360	11.1
Machinery and mechanical appliances (ch. 84)	680	142	10.1	212	10.7
Electrical machinery and equipment (ch. 85)	374	189	15.4	148	11.8
Transport equipment (HS section XVII)	162	100	33.0	426	5.9
Aircraft and spacecraft (ch. 88)	14	0	5.0	414	5.0
Other transport equipment (ch. 86–87; 89)	148	100	35.8	12	57.8
All remaining "other manufactures"	1,114	577	15.1	77	7.1
Photographic and medical precision instruments (ch. 90)	201	21	7.6	39	6.6
Pulp and paper; articles thereof (ch. 47–48)	157	120	18.8	19	8.7
Total	4,400	1,665	13.4	1,215	8.2

a. Peaks are defined as tariffs equal to or above 20 percent.

b. Analysis performed considering only tariff lines at the 6-digit level for which Pakistan's imports from the United States exceeded $1 million in 2004 (roughly 87 percent of actual trade in this category considered).

Note: "Other manufactures" are defined as all tariff lines in HS chapters 25–97, except chapters 50–63 and 94 (textiles and clothing).

Source: UN Statistics Division (2005).

Tariff peaks are the norm rather than the exception in Pakistan's tariff schedule. Almost 40 percent of all tariff lines on other manufactures are subject to tariffs equal to or above 20 percent (table 4.8).[20] High average tariffs are applied to chapters such as automobiles, trucks, and motorcycles (HS 87);[21] articles of iron and steel (HS 73); tools, implements, cutlery, and miscellaneous articles of base metal (HS 82–83); pulp and paper (HS 47–48); plastics (HS 39); and electrical machinery and equipment (HS 85). In these chapters, the incidence of tariff peaks exceeds 60 percent of tariff lines (table 4.8). Table 4.8 shows that tariff peaks are also important in products such as miscellaneous chemicals (HS 38) as well as mechanical machinery and equipment (HS 84).

As shown in table 4.7, 5 of the top 30 US exports of other manufactures to Pakistan could be subject to tariff peaks.[22] However, some of the top 30 benefit from exceptions and others simply face lower tariffs. Table 4.8 shows that existing US exports of other manufactures pay less than Pakistan's average tariffs on manufactured imports in all product categories except base metals and vehicles, where trade is small.[23] Table 4.7 confirms these results.[24] Nevertheless, tariff elimination under a US-Pakistan FTA is clearly important. For one thing, Pakistan still applies very high tariffs on nearly all HS chapters of interest to US manufacturers (with the exception of fertilizers and aircraft), and a substantial number of tariff peaks probably stifle trade. Moreover, small and medium-sized US firms may be adversely affected by the influence of lobbies in the design of Pakistan's tariff schedule and duty exceptions.[25]

Domestic Pakistani firms further benefit from tariff escalation and targeted duty exemption on raw materials and machinery not produced in the

---

20. Tariff peaks are defined as tariffs above 15 percent. Eight tariff lines in the other manufactures category are subject to specific tariffs. We classified these lines as peaks although no ad valorem equivalents were available. These specific tariffs are applied on petroleum and oils other than crude (HS 2710), gold and silver (HS 7106–08), and one chemical product (HS 2815.12).

21. The worst peaks in chapters 84 and 85 correspond to parts for motor vehicles covered in chapter 87. Chapter 84 contains more than 100 tariff lines with peaks.

22. Since trade flows in the UN Comtrade database are recorded at the 6-digit level, this calculation is approximate.

23. Only those items for which trade flows exceeded $1 million were considered; this covers 87 percent of US exports by value.

24. Table 4.7 also shows that some US exports of base metals qualify for duty-free access under statutory regulatory orders (SROs).

25. For example, SRO 559 grants customs duty and sales tax exemptions on specified goods if imported by British Airways. According to the National Association of Manufacturers, 95 percent of US exporters of manufactured goods are small companies and account for 30 percent of total US manufactured exports. These firms often have a hard time working the political system of foreign markets.

country (WTO 2002a). Despite recent tariff reductions, the highest tariffs are still assessed on fully processed products rather than products in the elementary stages of production. Tariff escalation is an important factor for imports of wood and furniture, leather, rubbers and plastics, paper and printed books, chemicals, iron and steel, other metals, and nonmetallic mineral products. The Pakistan Customs Tariff 2005–06 shows large variations between HS chapters 28–29 and chapters 33, 35, and 38 (chemicals); chapter 72 and chapter 73 (iron and steel); HS 4000–03 and HS 4004–17 (rubber); HS 3901–03 and HS 3904–26 (plastics). Within each family of products, items in a raw state or elementary form often are subject to 5 percent tariffs, while those in a more elaborated form are mostly subject to tariffs above 10 percent.

Pakistan's statutory regulatory orders (SROs) are used to either reduce duties (in order to provide relief to certain sectors) or to enhance them. SROs 565 and 567 of June 2005 listed dozens of products that benefit from duty-free or reduced duty access if imported as inputs for domestic manufacturing,[26] SRO 453 grants exemptions specifically targeted for the motor vehicle industry, and SRO 575 lists targeted customs duty and sales tax exemptions. The impact of these programs on the top 30 US exports of other manufactures to Pakistan is quite important. Table 4.7 shows that 70 percent of current US exports by value are subject to an average tariff of only 3.5 percent (taking into account the SRO exemptions). Note, however, that eligibility conditions sometimes impose additional costs. For example, imports of parts for vehicles and tractors not manufactured domestically qualify for duty-free treatment if they meet the following criteria: Imports are in completely knocked down condition (CKD) and used for further transformation in Pakistan; manufacturing firms conform to specified input/output ratios; parts are consumed within one year; and the manufacturer notifies the use of imported items to Pakistan Customs in writing and within a specified period.

In light of Pakistan's overall tariff policy, the country's bilateral FTAs will grant substantial margins of preferential access. Pakistan's negotiations with China, Malaysia, Singapore, and other regional partners could be a matter of concern for US manufacturers, given the rapid penetration of Chinese and ASEAN other manufactured products into the Pakistani market even without the benefit of preferential access (table 4.2).

Pakistan's early harvest agreement with China will provide, as of January 2007, certain Chinese manufacturers with an advantage over foreign competitors, including some US firms.[27] The advantage will be important

---

26. Exemptions are often granted as long as the product is not produced domestically.

27. We report the results of the early harvest agreement with China because that agreement represents Pakistan's most extensive commitments to date with a major trading nation. Pakistan's concessions under its early harvest agreement with Malaysia were much more limited and focused on agricultural, textile, office, and other machinery (HS 84), and to a lesser degree on chemicals and rubbers, wood products, and electrical equipment.

for organic chemicals (HS 29) and certain machinery and mechanical equipment (HS 84), two leading import categories of Pakistan and important areas of Chinese interest (table 4.3). The agreement contains important concessions on organic chemicals, which are also of interest to some US firms as they constitute the second most important category of US chemical exports to Pakistan. The principal US exports of organic chemicals (for the most part inputs for production of textiles and clothing or paints and varnishes) benefit from duty-free access (table 4.7). While the early harvest agreement leaves most peaks on organic chemicals untouched—28 according to table 4.8—it grants duty-free access, effective January 2007, on nearly 118 tariff lines (out of 477 total tariff lines in the chapter in Pakistan's tariff schedule). Pakistan currently applies 5 percent tariffs to about 90 percent of these lines.[28]

Pakistan also will grant China duty-free access—again, for the most part effective in January 2007—on 40 percent of all tariff lines in HS chapter 84 on machinery and mechanical equipment.[29] Pakistan's concessions on machinery correspond to tariff lines subject to low tariffs (5 percent); however, a few lines might correspond to top US exports.[30] Only 17 tariff lines granted in HS chapter 84 are subject to tariffs above 10 percent, and most of them correspond to textile machinery. The share of textile machinery in Pakistani imports under HS chapter 84 is large (36 percent), but this product category is not among the main areas of interest to US exporters.[31]

Additionally, some other products (e.g., selected items in HS 85 and 90) will receive margins of preference ranging between 5 and 20 percent under applied MFN rates. Pakistan's extension of preferential access to Chinese exporters does not cover the peak tariff lines, and in some instances involves tariff lines that already receive MFN duty-free access through SROs. In other cases, preferences apply to tariff lines where Chinese exports are currently small. It is also important to note that the Early Harvest Agreement is not a final arrangement but rather a steppingstone to a full FTA; hence, the margins of preference are likely to expand with the conclusion of a Pakistan-China FTA.

---

28. The agreement eliminates duties on only two peak tariff lines (these will be phased out by January 2008). Additionally, under the early harvest agreement, some 20 tariff lines corresponding to organic chemicals will be granted margins of preference ranging from 5 to 15 percent by comparison with MFN rates.

29. Some 40 extra tariff lines in chapter 84 will qualify for margins of preference ranging from 5 to 20 percent by comparison with MFN rates.

30. One example is parts of turbo propellers or gas turbines.

31. Under its Textile Vision 2005, the Government of Pakistan pledged to grant duty-free treatment for textile machinery not produced domestically, provided that it is imported as an input for textile exports (Government of Pakistan 2005c).

Nontariff Barriers

Pakistan applies various import charges and taxes, such as landing, clearing, forwarding, and bank charges. According to the US Commercial Service (2001), these charges may increase the import price by 7 percent over the c.i.f price. Advance payment of sales and income taxes puts an additional differential burden on imported products, since many domestic producers evade taxes. Pakistani sales tax exemption programs create further advantages for domestic producers; for example, exemptions are not available to pharmaceuticals subject to tariffs above 10 percent (e.g., eyedrops, first-aid boxes and kits, and bandages and adhesives for medical use).[32]

Certain commodities can be imported into Pakistan only by approved entities that hold a valid license from the concerned government agency. Possibly of US interest will be licenses that affect the pharmaceutical industry (e.g., on nonbanned narcotic drugs and psychotropic substances, blood, disinfectants, and certain raw materials); transmission apparatus (with the exception of fax machines and mobile phones); certain chemicals used as inputs or ingredients for pesticides, insecticides, and fungicides; and licenses for CKD vehicles and tractors issued to support "progressive local manufacturing" (Government of Pakistan 2005b). Apart from reviewing some of these licensing systems, a US-Pakistan FTA could address other procedural impositions such as registration requirements for the import of drugs and medicines. According to the US Trade Representative (USTR 2005a), delays in the registration process—often one to two years—exacerbate patent theft.[33] Exports of fertilizers, certain chemicals, and some metals are restricted through special regulations, which should be reviewed as they may retard promising exports.

Pakistan enforces a few import prohibitions that are for the most part defensible on the basis of Articles XX (general exceptions) and XXI (security exceptions) of GATT 1994, although some are in direct conflict with the basic principles of the multilateral trading system. The government allows imports only of specific products from India (the "positive list" approach) and maintains a full ban of imports from Israel.[34] Possi-

---

32. Most pharmaceuticals, however, are subject to tariffs not higher than 10 percent.

33. Patent theft and other intellectual property violations are also a matter of urgent concern to US pharmaceutical producers. The USTR states that "Pakistan fails to protect against unfair commercial use of test or other data. In addition, the government has authorized the sale of pharmaceuticals without requiring checks confirming that another firm does not hold an active patent on the compound. Although courts have issued injunction orders against firms licensed by the Ministry of Health that sell drugs in violation of patent holder rights, such orders are not consistently enforced" (USTR 2005a, 5).

34. In both cases, the prohibitions apply to goods from India or Israel as well as to goods of Indian or Israeli origin.

bly more relevant for US firms, Pakistan prohibits, with a clear protectionist intent, imports of used or secondhand commodities as well as factory rejects and job lots or stock lots.[35] Products targeted include consumer machinery (boilers, compressors, air conditioners, refrigerators, hand tools, household machinery, parts); industrial machinery (for sugar, brewery, cement, oil refinery, thermal power, and other plants); electrical machinery (HS chapter 85); auto and auto parts including retreaded and used pneumatic tires (HS 40, 84, 85, 87, and 90); and apparatus and appliances (HS 90).[36] Although there are many exceptions (e.g., relocation schemes; oil, mining, and construction machinery; and other programs), the prohibitions coincide with many current or potential US exports. In previous FTAs, some US firms have expressed concern about similar barriers.[37]

To date, Pakistan has not applied safeguard measures on manufactured imports. In 2005 the country's National Tariff Commission conducted an investigation concerning imports of footwear from all sources (principally from China), but the investigation was concluded with no safeguard measures imposed (WTO 2005f). Pakistan does, however, apply antidumping measures on five products: urea from China, sorbitol from France and Indonesia, and glacial acid from Taiwan (chemicals); PVC resin from Iran and Korea (plastics); and tin plate from South Africa (metals). The National Tariff Commission is conducting an investigation against alleged dumping of tin plate from the United States and other sources. According to specialized news reports, Pakistan's Central Board of Revenue is considering launching an antidumping investigation on imports of office furniture and toys from East Asian countries (World Trade Review 2005). Taken together, these events show a tendency in Pakistan toward greater reliance on antidumping measures.

---

35. Pakistan's Customs General Order No. 12 (2002) defines a job lot as a collection of odds and ends (different specifications, color schemes, etc.) for sale as one lot. After selling a portion of the goods to a few buyers, the supplier is left with an assortment of goods with slight differences, and these remainders are generally sold as a job lot at a low price. The same source defines a stock lot as "goods which are kept in stock unsold because of change in tastes." Again, such goods can be sold at a low price.

36. Pakistan's import prohibitions cover more products than those listed above. For a full treatment, see the 2002 WTO Trade Policy Review for Pakistan (WTO 2002a) and the Import Policy Order 2005–06 by the Government of Pakistan (available at www.cbr.gov.pk).

37. Barriers to the importation of used goods were issues of interest in the US-Chile and the US-Morocco FTAs. The US-Chile FTA eliminated Chile's 50 percent surcharge on used goods (Vargo 2003). Under the US-Morocco FTA, Morocco committed to phase out its tariffs on used goods including tires, machinery, and vehicles (USTR 2004d). In all recent FTAs, the United States has insisted on language in the rules of origin so that remanufactured products are considered to originate in an FTA partner.

United States

In 2004 nearly 25 percent of Pakistan's exports of other manufactures qualified for GSP benefits. While Pakistan's exports under the US GSP program were small, the affected products represented 40 to 55 percent of the country's exports to the world. Table 4.5 disaggregates Pakistan's exports under GSP by HS chapter of relevance and shows that GSP access has benefited nontraditional Pakistani exports such as jewelry, cutlery, and articles of stone or plaster. Additionally, the United States applies zero MFN rates on medical devices (HS 9018.90) and football and soccer balls (HS 9506.62.40), two important export categories for Pakistan (table 4.9).

However, Pakistan's leading exports of other manufactures—namely leather gloves and jackets—have not qualified for GSP benefits and are still subject to relatively high duties, some of them above 10 percent (table 4.9).[38] Pakistan's exports of these products to the European Union expanded after the country qualified for duty-free access (table 4.6); thus it is possible that a US-Pakistan FTA would render Pakistan's leather exports (including leather footwear) more competitive vis-à-vis China and other suppliers. Addressing these market access concerns should be feasible: In recent years US leather manufacturers have moved away from leather clothing to specialize in other items.[39] (While some US tariffs on rubber footwear are exceptionally high—almost 50 percent—these ultrasensitive products are not exported by Pakistan.)[40]

According to WTO statistics, the United States does not currently apply antidumping duties on manufactured imports from Pakistan. However, other countries have voiced concern over US licensing systems, invoice requirements, customs fees, and other nontariff barriers. Foreign governments have also objected to higher transaction costs and delays associated with the Homeland Security Act of 2002. A US-Pakistan FTA should facilitate trade in ways that would ease some of these concerns. For example, the United States and Pakistan should extend the Container Security Initiative (CSI) to the port of Karachi.[41] In addition, the United

---

38. High US tariffs on existing Pakistani exports to the United States are mostly concentrated in HS 4203 (leather clothing such as jackets and gloves). Moderate tariffs on leather footwear could be a relevant barrier for Pakistani exporters.

39. The Industry Sector Advisory Committee for Footwear, Leather, and Leather Products states that most leather tanneries in the United States have "survived by specializing in high-end automotive and furniture upholstery leather." By contrast, Pakistan's leather exports are concentrated in gloves and jackets.

40. Pakistan is not among the top 20 sources of US imports of rubber footwear. Pakistan is also a minor player in travel goods. US producers of nonrubber footwear have embraced free trade.

41. Currently, Colombo (Sri Lanka) is the only South Asian operational port in the CSI system, but ports in other developing countries are participating in the CSI, such as Buenos Aires, Laem Chabang, Port Klang, and Santos. The minimum standards for CSI participation are explained on the US Customs Web site, www.customs.gov.

Table 4.9 Pakistan's top 30 exports of other manufactures to the United States, 2004 (millions of US dollars)

HS 6-digit category	Description	Import value[a]	Share	MFN tariff (percent)	GSP?
4203.10.40	Anoraks, coats, and jackets of leather or composition leather	47	0.22	6.0	No
9018.90.80	Medical or surgical instruments, nesoi	27	0.13	Free	n.a.
9506.62.40	Soccer balls	16	0.08	Free	n.a.
7113.19.50	Gold or platinum jewelry, nesoi	11	0.05	5.0	Yes
4203.29.30	Gloves and mittens of leather,nesoi	10	0.05	14.0	No
4203.21.80	Gloves specially designed for use in sports, nesoi	8	0.04	4.9	No
8214.20.30	Manicure or pedicure instruments	7	0.03	4.0	Yes
9307.00.00	Swords, cutlasses, bayonets, lances, and similar arms	5	0.02	2.7	Yes
4202.92.15	Travel, sports, and similar bags, outer surface of cotton	4	0.02	6.3	No
6802.91.15	Marble, other than slabs	4	0.02	4.9	Yes
8213.00.90	Other scissors, tailors, and similar shears	3	0.02	3.0¢ each	No
6802.92.00	Other calcareous stone, nesoi	3	0.01	4.9	Yes
8203.20.20	Tweezers base metal	3	0.01	4.0	Yes
8541.40.20	Photosensitive semiconductor devices, light-emitting diodes	3	0.01	Free	n.a.
9018.90.30	Anesthetic instruments and parts and accessories	3	0.01	Free	n.a.
4203.29.18	Horse or cowhide leather gloves, not wholly of leather, nesoi	2	0.01	14.0	No
9706.00.00	Antiques of age exceeding 100 years, nesoi	2	0.01	Free	n.a.
8203.20.60	Pliers except slip joint, base metal	2	0.01	12¢ per dozen + 5.5	Yes
4203.29.08	Horse or cowhide leather gloves, wholly of leather, nesoi	2	0.01	14.0	No
9018.49.80	Dental hand instruments and parts and accessories	1	0.01	Free	n.a.
8211.92.90	Sheath-type knives with fixed blades	1	0.01	0.4¢ each + 6.1	
4203.21.20	Batting gloves	1	0.01	3.0	No
7103.10.20	Rubies, sapphires, emeralds, and rock crystals	1	0.01	Free	n.a.

(table continues next page)

Table 4.9 Pakistan's top 30 exports of other manufactures
to the United States, 2004 (millions of US dollars) *(continued)*

HS 6-digit category	Description	Import value[a]	Share	MFN tariff (percent)	GSP?
6802.91.05	Marble slabs	1	0.01	2.5	Yes
9603.90.80	Brooms, brushes, squeegees, etc., nesoi	1	0.01	2.8	Yes
4203.30.00	Belts and bandoliers with or without buckles	1	0.01	2.7	Yes
9506.99.20	Football, soccer, and polo equipment, except balls	1	0.01	Free	n.a.
4203.29.40	Gloves and mittens, of leather, nesoi	1	0.01	12.6	No
9506.99.60	Equipment for gymnastics, outdoor games, other sports	1	0.01	4.0	Yes
7113.19.21	Gold rope necklaces and neck chains	1	0	5.0	Yes
	Total	215	1.00	3.2[a]	

GSP = generalized system of preferences
HS = Harmonized Schedule
n.a. = not applicable
nesoi = not elsewhere specified or included

a. Value calculated as ratio of collected duties to value of imports; hence it includes preferences under the GSP.

Source: USITC (2005a).

States and Pakistan might improve the tracking systems designed to combat illegal transshipments.

US imports of other manufactures from Pakistan are small and declining, despite an important degree of duty-free access. With the notable exception of leather items and footwear, US tariffs on Pakistani exports are low. While Pakistan will want to secure an equal standing with other FTA partners, and obtain margins of preference with respect to Chinese and other competitive producers, it is foreseeable that other manufactures will not be the principal concern of Pakistan in the negotiation of an FTA, nor will the category be particularly sensitive for the United States.

Recommendations

US negotiations with other developing countries have aimed to provide access based on reciprocity while recognizing development concerns (Allgeier 2004). The principal preoccupation for US negotiators in the other manufactures sector has been to obtain rapid and binding commitment to eliminate *all* tariffs. Previous US agreements resulted in immediate duty-free access on the order of 80 to 95 percent of existing two-way trade.

In light of the abundance of tariff peaks in Pakistan's tariff schedule, not all products that Pakistan regards as sensitive can be shielded through long phaseout periods. In the past, the United States has accepted long phaseouts for truly sensitive products when confronted with urgent requests from an FTA partner. The US-Morocco FTA is the prime example: In the agreement as signed, Morocco will liberalize less than two-thirds of its tariff lines on other manufactures within five years, while the remaining tariff lines in the category were allowed nine-year phaseout periods. The United States, on the other hand, offered Morocco immediate duty-free access, except in a few tariff lines.[42]

The CGE model predicts that a complete elimination of tariffs in a US-Pakistan FTA would lead to the largest gains in US exports (in both relative and absolute terms) in sensitive product categories, including chemicals and plastics, metals and their products, machinery and electrical equipment, and motor vehicles. With these considerations in mind, we offer the following recommendations:

- A US-Pakistan FTA should achieve reciprocal duty-free entry for all items in the other manufactures category after a 10-year transition period.

- Both parties should agree to an ambitious target of immediate liberalization of 95 percent of existing two-way trade (by value, not by tariff lines) in other manufactured products. This will entail a larger effort in Pakistan, but will balance US concessions on textiles and clothing, while maintaining room for longer phaseouts for sensitive items.[43]

United States

- With a few exceptions, the United States should grant immediate duty-free access to all existing imports of other manufactures from Pakistan. They present no real threat to US industry, and so the United States should not aim for sector reciprocity in this category. Leather goods should obtain immediate duty-free entry, provided that Pakistan eliminates its export taxes on hides. Tariffs on sensitive US

---

42. The United States retained phaseouts for a limited number of tariff lines in organic chemicals, plastics, paper, trunks and travel goods, headwear and footwear, and ceramics.

43. Pakistan could go a long way toward liberalizing bilateral trade by eliminating tariffs in the 5 to 10 percent range (e.g., fertilizer, plastics, medical and precision instruments, and most pharmaceuticals). Achieving that target will require eliminating a few tariffs above the 10 percent level.

products (i.e., travel goods, rubber footwear, and ceramics) should be phased out over 5 to 10 years. Pakistan could acquiesce to these terms, as its exports in these categories are for the most part negligible.

Pakistan

- Pakistan should grant immediate duty-free access on manufactures that are not produced domestically or that currently enjoy duty-free treatment not reflected on the tariff schedule (e.g., aircraft and parts thereof). Pakistan should also grant immediate equal footing for US firms in areas that compete directly with firms from third countries that already benefit from preferential access to Pakistan (e.g., in organic chemicals and some types of machinery and mechanical equipment).

- Pakistan's most sensitive items (i.e., construction materials, plastics and tires, articles and tools of base metal, transport equipment in CKD condition, bicycles, and soda in aqueous solution) should qualify for a 10-year phaseout period. However, a US-Pakistan FTA should also immediately relax licensing requirements, particularly those mandating progressive local manufacturing, and allow the import of used goods in the transport equipment sector.

- Domestically produced machinery and electrical equipment (some trade on HS 84 and nearly all trade on HS 85 excluding auto parts) will be a difficult area of negotiation. US interest is strong, and Pakistani tariff peaks and nontariff barriers abound. Pakistan should immediately eliminate nontariff barriers in these sectors and facilitate the import of new and used goods and parts. Tariffs on sensitive items should qualify for 10-year phaseouts.

- A more vigorous approach should be tried for the remaining peaks in chemicals (e.g., tanning products, soaps and cosmetics, pharmaceuticals, miscellaneous chemicals), rubbers, and pulp and paper. The phaseout periods should generally be shorter than 10 years. Pakistani licensing and registration requirements for chemicals and pharmaceuticals should likewise be reviewed and streamlined.

5

Environmental and Labor
Issues in Pakistan

Efforts to insert environmental and labor standards into trade agreements have proven quite controversial. As Ahmed Galal and Robert Lawrence (2005) observe about environmental standards, the scope of governance should normally match the scope of the problem. For that reason, national rather than international rules are best suited to address most environmental issues, as international spillover effects are the exception, not the rule. Even so, many nongovernmental organizations (NGOs) and legislators in America and Europe yearn for the inclusion of common standards in trade pacts. But countries at disparate levels of economic development often wish to make different environmental choices. Hence, built-in tension exists between the ideals of common standards and national sovereignty.

Greenhouse gases, global warming, and endangered species attract media attention and properly require international action. But while preservation of old growth timber, pristine wilderness, and rare fauna may well have top priority in a rich country, local air and water pollution frequently demand more urgent attention in a poor country. The harmonization of standards to the highest level could unfairly penalize countries with limited means. And when environmental problems have a truly international or global scope, they may be better addressed through an explicit environmental agreement, such as the Montreal Protocol, rather than through bilateral or multilateral trade agreements.

Labor standards are even more contentious than environmental standards, partly because "race to the bottom" and "social dumping" metaphors are more apt to apply to labor than to the environment. Nevertheless, it may be better to leave the determination of most labor standards to national processes, particularly when the standards primarily affect workers in nontraded goods and services. Moreover, it can be argued that fundamental labor standards that are akin to human rights are better addressed through the mechanisms of the International Labor Organization (ILO) rather than the World Trade Organization (WTO) or bilateral FTAs.

In 1998 the ILO approved a Declaration on Fundamental Principles and Rights at Work, which identified and provided a consensus definition of four core labor standards. These four standards, which have become the centerpiece of the global standards movement, are: freedom of association and the effective recognition of the right to collective bargaining; elimination of all forms of forced and compulsory labor; abolition of child labor; and elimination of discrimination in the workplace.

Eight ILO conventions have been identified as embodying these core standards.[1] Of these, Pakistan has ratified every one except Convention 138 concerning the Minimum Age for Employment—and according to a report by the ILO, "the [Pakistan] Government is taking further steps to ratify the Minimum Age Convention" (ILO 2005a). The United States has ratified only two: Convention 105 (Abolition of Forced Labor) and Convention 182 (Prohibition and Elimination of Worst Forms of Child Labor). The US approach has been to ratify only those conventions with which US law is already in accord. It has not been a high priority to ratify conventions that would require any modification or amendment of existing US legislation.[2] The US Congress holds an unstated view that US norms are already superior to ILO conventions, and that nothing would be gained by ratifying conventions that might muddy the obligations articulated in US labor law.

However, many members of Congress have tried since the early 1980s to link labor rights with trade pacts, with two purposes in mind. The first is to help "level the playing field" by protecting US jobs and US wage levels from what they consider unfair competition from low-standard, low-wage foreign producers. The second is to help improve working con-

---

1. The eight conventions are Convention 29 Concerning Forced Labor of 1930; Convention 87 Concerning Freedom of Association and Protection of the Right to Organize of 1948; Convention 98 Concerning the Application of the Principles of the Right to Organize and Bargain Collectively of 1949; Convention 100 Concerning Equal Remuneration for Men and Women Workers for Work of Equal Value of 1951; Convention 105 Concerning the Abolition of Forced Labor of 1957; Convention 111 Concerning Discrimination in Respect of Employment and Occupation of 1958; Convention 138 Concerning Minimum Age for Admission to Employment of 1973; and Convention 182 Concerning the Prohibition and Immediate Action for the Elimination of the Worst Forms of Child Labor of 1999.

2. For example, the Office of International Labor Affairs of the US Department of State "seeks ratification of ILO Convention 111 on non-discrimination in employment" as part of its mission statement, but this has yet to gain congressional approval. See www.state.gov/g/drl/lbr/ (accessed January 4, 2006).

ditions in developing countries. In a 1984 amendment to the generalized system of preferences (GSP), Congress prohibited GSP concessions to developing countries that were "not taking steps to afford their workers internationally recognized worker rights." Congress defined "internationally recognized worker rights" to include the following basic protections:[3] the right to associate, form unions, and bargain collectively; no forced or prison labor; rules against child labor; and minimum standards for wages, hours, and occupational safety and health.

This chapter first describes current labor and environmental conditions in Pakistan. Then it examines how labor and environmental issues have been addressed in existing US FTAs. The arguments raised during the congressional ratification of the Central American Free Trade Agreement-Dominican Republic (CAFTA-DR) are particularly important and so are considered separately. The last two sections present our recommendations for dealing with labor and environmental rules in the context of a prospective US-Pakistan FTA.

Labor Standards in Pakistan

The US Department of State (2005) examined human rights practices in Pakistan in its 2004 country report. The study concludes that, despite improvements in several areas, serious problems remain. Specifically, unions are discouraged, child labor is still widespread, and forced labor from indebted workers remains a problem. In addition, a worker's right to quit may be curtailed, and dismissed workers have no recourse to the labor courts (US Department of State 2004). We review here Pakistan's standing with respect to each of the ILO core labor standards.

The Right of Association

Pakistan's Industrial Relations Ordinance (IRO) of 2002 ensures industrial workers the right to form trade unions. According to estimates by the Pakistani government, union members were approximately 10 percent of the industrial labor force and 3 percent of the total estimated workforce in 2004[4] (US Department of State 2005). But workers in many sectors are not covered by the IRO 2002 and can be barred from forming unions or bargaining collectively. Moreover, the law does not apply to companies that employ fewer than 50 people, and the International Confederation of Free Trade Unions (ICFTU) reports that companies sometimes

---

3. See GSP Sec. 502(a)(4) at the USTR's Web site, www.ustr.gov.

4. Unions, however, claimed that the number of union members was underestimated (US Department of State 2005).

subdivide their workforces into artificial subsidiaries, while keeping them all on the same premises, in order to evade compliance with the IRO (ICFTU 2004).

Union organization and bargaining rights are further curtailed in several sectors by the Essential Services Maintenance Act (ESMA) of 1952, which covers state administration, government services to the public, and state enterprises. Thus security forces, most of the civil service, health care workers, and safety and security personnel at petroleum companies, airports, and seaports all fall under the ESMA. In these sectors, the act is often invoked to limit or ban strikes or curtail collective bargaining. In addition, under the ESMA, agricultural workers, nonprofit workers, and teachers (among others) are not permitted to form unions (US Department of State 2005). In a positive development, the government lifted a ban on union activity in the Water and Power Development Authority (WAPDA), which employs 130,000 workers, through a presidential ordinance issued in July 2000 (ICFTU 2002).

Pakistan's Civil Servants Act (CSA) of 1973 prohibits senior civil servants from forming trade unions and bargaining collectively, and denies them access to labor courts and the National Industrial Relations Commission (NIRC). The ILO Committee of Experts on the Application of Conventions and Recommendations (CEACR) has repeatedly advised Pakistan to amend this legislation to ensure that it is limited to senior officials, that these senior officials maintain their right to form an organization of their own choosing, and that the legislation does not restrict the rights of an excessive number of civil servants (ICFTU 2002).

The ILO has stated time and again that the law and practice of Pakistan violate the government's commitments under ILO Convention 87. The ILO has also expressed concern about the practice of artificial promotions that exclude workers from the purview of Convention 111 (US Department of State 2004). A complaint was brought before the ILO Committee on Freedom of Association by three trade union federations in 2002. Consequently, in April 2003, the ILO CEACR recommended many changes to bring Pakistan's legislation in line with international standards (ICFTU 2004). In response to a government request, the ILO has provided technical assistance to help conform Pakistan's labor laws with the ILO conventions, although as yet no legislative action has been taken (US Department of State 2004). However, at a meeting in September 2005, Prime Minister Shaukat Aziz informed national trade union officials that the government is considering amendments to the IRO (ICFTU 2005).

The Right to Organize and Bargain Collectively

In sectors covered by the IRO, unions are allowed to conduct certain activities. The IRO protects the right to collective bargaining (subject to restrictions), but limits the right to strike. It permits only one union to serve as the collective bargaining agent in a given establishment, group of establishments, or industry. When more than one union exists, the IRO establishes a secret balloting procedure to determine which union will be registered with the NIRC as the sole agent.

Legally required conciliation proceedings and cooling-off periods constrain the right to strike, and the government may ban strikes that cause serious hardship to the community, jeopardize the national interest, or that have continued for 30 days. The ESMA calls for up to one year of imprisonment for contravening the ban. Under the IRO, the government can prohibit strikes against public utility services, and it has invoked this power. The government regards as illegal any strike conducted by workers who are not members of a legally registered union. While the law prohibits employers from seeking retribution against leaders of a legal strike (and stipulates fines for offenders), it does not protect leaders of illegal strikes, as was evident when several small strikes occurred during 2004. In October 2004 workers' unions at the Pakistan Telecommunication Company Limited (PTCL) held intermittent brief strikes in various cities demanding higher wages and limits on the use of contract workers. The strikes ceased after the government termed them illegal.[5]

Under current laws, the Pakistani government must review collective bargaining agreements in "designated sectors" twice a year and may decide at any time to suspend this right. When collective bargaining is prohibited for a particular sector, as in the case of sectors subject to the ESMA, special wage boards decide wage levels. Such boards are established at the provincial level[6] and are composed of representatives from industry, labor, and the provincial labor ministry. More often than not, despite the presence of labor representatives, unions are dissatisfied with the determinations issued by these boards (US Department of State 2005). Appeals are adjudicated before the NIRC.[7]

---

5. The government claimed that the strikes were illegal because there was no union or collective bargaining agent in the company. Workers' representatives challenged this claim, citing a referendum that had been held in the PTCL on March 16, 2004, which the government-backed union lost. See "PTCL Workers' Strike Termed Illegal," *Dawn*, October 13, 2004, www.dawn.com (accessed December 19, 2005).

6. The four provinces of Pakistan are Baluchistan, the North-West Frontier Province (NWFP), Punjab, and Sindh. There are also the Islamabad Capital Territory and the Federally Administered Tribal Areas. The Pakistani-administered portion of the disputed Jammu and Kashmir region includes Azad Kashmir and the northern areas.

7. There was only one judge working in the NIRC during the PTCL strikes. This fact, in addition to the reluctance of the government to appoint additional members to the NIRC, was cited by workers' representatives as an obstacle to the resolution of the dispute. See "PTCL Workers' Strike Termed Illegal," *Dawn*, October 13, 2004, www.dawn.com (accessed December 19, 2005).

The estimated 12,500 employees working in Pakistan's three export processing zones (EPZs) are exempted by the ESMA from the right to form trade unions under the IRO. Instead, the Export Processing Zones Authority drafts its own labor laws for the EPZs. Trade unions claim that EPZ workers have no protection against antiunion rules (ICFTU 2004). In 1994, Pakistan stated that its exemption of EPZs from certain labor laws reflected a bargain made with foreign investors that had invested in the zones partly on the basis of such exemptions (Elliott and Freeman 2003).

Prohibition of Forced or Compulsory Labor

Pakistan's Constitution, reinforced by specific statutes, prohibits forced or bonded labor, including by children. In its 2005 report, *A Global Alliance Against Forced Labour,* the ILO commended Pakistan for developing one of the first national action plans against forced and bonded labor (ILO 2005b). The country's federal cabinet approved in 2001 a National Policy and Plan of Action for the Abolition of Bonded Labor and Rehabilitation of Freed Bonded Laborers (NPPA). The policy clearly states the government's commitment to this goal as well as the components of a national strategy to achieve it and an action plan that specifies the activities, time frame, and roles and responsibilities of partner organizations. Pakistan's laws include a detailed definition of bonded labor and bonded labor systems, penal provisions for the offense of exacting bonded labor, and modalities for enforcement. The Bonded Labor System (Abolition) Act (BLAA) of 1992 outlaws bonded labor, cancels all existing bonded debts, and forbids lawsuits for the recovery of such debts. The act makes bonded labor by children punishable by up to five years in prison and up to $843 (Rs. 50,000) in fines.

As with similar legislation in other developing countries, implementation of the NPPA has been slow, and the BLAA and related laws are not always enforced. Conservative estimates put the number of bonded workers in Pakistan at several million (US Department of State 2005). Bonded labor is said to be common in the brick, glass, carpet, and fishing industries and has also been found among agricultural and construction workers in rural areas.[8]

The correlation between poverty and bonded labor is high. There is broad consensus in the academic literature that workers often enter into bonded labor contracts as a means to avert acute poverty or even starvation. However, ILO data show that bonded laborers are usually unable to determine just when their debts are fully paid and that they remain in poverty while bonded (ILO 2005b). Those who escape frequently face retaliation from former employers or, once freed, return to their former sta-

---

8. For a sectoral analysis of bonded labor, see ILO (2005b, 33–35).

tus because of a lack of alternative livelihoods (US Department of State 2005).

Although the police do arrest violators of the law against bonded labor, miscreant "employers" often evade justice by paying bribes. In one report of an extreme case, human rights groups claim that a landlord in rural Sindh maintained as many as 50 private jails housing some 4,500 bonded laborers (US Department of State 2005). Ties between such landlords and influential politicians hamper the effective elimination of bonded labor.

Although pressure on the government from civil society groups and activists to eliminate bonded labor remains intense (ILO 2005b), there are no available data on prosecutions. According to data compiled by the Human Rights Commission of Pakistan's Special Task Force for Sindh Province, nearly 19,000 bonded sharecroppers were released from bondage in the period between January 2000 and June 2004 (HRCP 2005b). But the vast majority reportedly escaped through their own devices, while only a minority were released with the assistance of the high court or district administration.[9]

Effective law enforcement has also been impeded by jurisdictional conflicts between the federal and provincial courts. In January 2002, for example, justices of the Sindh high court dismissed 94 petitions of bonded sharecroppers against illegal arrest and detention by the landowner, on the grounds that the disputes should be handled under the Sindh Tenancy Act.[10] A recent positive development has been the official establishment, in 2004, of six district vigilance committees (DVCs) in Sindh Province. The DVCs have primary responsibility, at the local level, for the identification, release, and rehabilitation of bonded laborers. These committees are intended to lay the groundwork for more effective prosecution and punishment of the employers of bonded labor (ILO 2005b). In Punjab Province, a capacity-building program was held for all DVCs in early 2005, led by the provincial department of labor with ILO support (ILO 2005b).

Prohibition of Child Labor and Minimum Age Requirement for Employment

The principle of the effective abolition of child labor is recognized in Pakistan's Constitution and legislation. In addition, the country has ratified ILO Convention 182, one of the two core conventions on child labor. Under the Follow-up to the ILO Declaration on Fundamental Principles

---

9. Legal releases peaked in 2000 and 2001 and appear to have declined since, with no sharecroppers released through the Sindh high court in 2003, and only 30 through the district administration (ILO 2005b).

10. Constitutional Petition No. D35 of 2000, High Court of Sindh, Circuit Court, Hyderabad (para. 36(c) of judgment).

and Rights at Work, issued in 2002, Pakistan was among the 27 countries to establish a national policy and action plan aimed at ensuring the effective abolition of child labor (ILO 2002). The three principal goals of the national policy and action plan are to eradicate immediately the worst forms of child labor, to eliminate progressively all remaining forms of child labor, and to ensure at least primary education and vocational training for the targeted children (US Department of State 2002).

The Employment of Children Act of 1991 prohibits the employment of children under age 14 in factories, mines, and other hazardous occupations, and regulates their conditions of work in other occupations. No child is allowed to work overtime or at night. However, as with labor laws more generally, there are few child labor inspectors, and they often have insufficient resources and are susceptible to corruption. By law, inspectors may not inspect facilities that employ fewer than 10 persons, and most child labor occurs in these small-scale establishments. Hundreds of convictions have been obtained for violators of child labor laws, but the low fines levied by the courts—ranging from an average of $6 (Rs. 364) in the North-West Frontier Province (NWFP) to an average of $123 (Rs. 7,280) in Baluchistan—are not a significant deterrent. In fact, penalties are often not imposed on violators of child labor laws, even though the Employment of Children Act allows for fines of up to $337 (Rs. 20,000).

Child labor is particularly insidious in agricultural employment. It is estimated that approximately two-thirds of child laborers work in agriculture, way above the share of agricultural employment in the national economy (about 40 percent). The rest work in informal urban activities and various types of manufacturing, such as stitching, surgical instruments, brick kilns, and carpet making. Pakistan's widespread child labor goes hand in hand with very low attendance rates in primary education. The International Confederation of Free Trade Unions (ICFTU), in a 2002 report for the WTO General Council Review of Trade Policies of Pakistan, notes that estimates vary as to the exact degree of school attendance; government figures claim more than 70 percent, while independent surveys of Karachi suggest about 25 percent. Virtually all sources give higher attendance rates for boys than for girls (ICFTU 2002).

The International Labor Organization International Program on the Elimination of Child Labor (ILO IPEC) has ongoing programs to eliminate child labor in the carpet weaving, surgical instrument, rag picking, and deep-sea fishing industries. Working with industries and the government, the ILO IPEC uses a combination of monitoring, educational access, rehabilitation, and family member employment to transition children out of these industries.[11] An ILO IPEC program to eliminate

---

11. Among the largest recipients of IPEC assistance in 2002–03 were Bangladesh ($11 million), India ($15 million), and Pakistan ($3 million). Central American countries received another $10 million (Elliott and Freeman 2003).

child labor in the soccer ball manufacturing industry was completed in 2000 and deemed a success, with more than 17,000 children benefiting from the education program and IPEC monitoring production in 1,800 stitching centers (ILO 2002, 2005a).[12] The government of Pakistan reports that, in line with the National Education Policy (1998–2010), Education Sector Reform (2001–05), and National Plan of Action on Education for All (2001–15), the number of educational institutions and enrollments is increasing every year, as financial resources permit (ILO 2005a).

Acceptable Conditions of Work

The national minimum wage for unskilled workers in Pakistan is $42 (Rs. 2,500) per month, but this figure applies only to industrial and commercial establishments with 50 or more workers. Benefits required by the Federal Labor Code include official government holidays, overtime pay, annual and sick leave, health care, education for workers' children, social security, old age benefits, and a workers' welfare fund. Even with benefits, the national minimum wage is only marginally above a poverty line of $2 per person per day, and cannot provide a decent standard of living for workers and their families (US Department of State 2005).

Federal law in Pakistan establishes a maximum workweek of 48 hours (54 hours for seasonal factories), with rest periods during the day and paid annual holidays. These regulations do not apply, however, to agricultural workers, workers in factories with fewer than 10 employees, domestic workers, and contractors. Moreover, many workers are unaware of their rights (US Department of State 2005).

Health and safety standards are generally poor, and there is a serious lack of adherence to mine safety and health protocols in particular; for example, mines often have only one opening for entry, egress, and ventilation. Workers cannot leave dangerous working conditions without risking the loss of their jobs (US Department of State 2005).

Provincial governments have primary responsibility for enforcing all labor regulations, but enforcement has been ineffective due to limited resources, corruption, and inadequate regulatory structures (US Department of State 2005). Although organized labor groups press for improvements, government efforts to enforce existing legal provisions are weak (US Department of State 2004).

---

12. See Elliott and Freeman (2003, chapter 6) for a detailed account of the campaign to end child labor in the Pakistani soccer ball manufacturing industry.

Environmental Standards in Pakistan

Pakistan is ranked 131 out of 146 nations in the 2005 Environmental Sustainability Index (ESI) report,[13] which evaluates five broad areas:

- *quality of environmental systems:* measured by air quality, biodiversity, land, water quantity and water quality;

- *extent of environmental stress:* measured by air pollution, ecosystem stress, population stress, waste and consumption pressures, water stress, and natural resource management;

- *human vulnerability:* indexed by human sustenance and vulnerability to environment-related natural disasters;

- *social and institutional capacity:* including private-sector responsiveness, environmental governance, and the level of science and technology education and industry; and

- *global stewardship:* determined by international collaborative efforts, greenhouse gas emissions, and transboundary environmental pressures.

The ESI report places Pakistan in a cluster of countries with similar conditions, including current US FTA partners such as the Dominican Republic, Jordan, Mexico, and Morocco, and prospective FTA partners such as Egypt, Indonesia, South Africa, and Thailand. The report draws attention to current problems in Pakistan, such as water pollution from raw sewage, industrial waste, agricultural runoff, and limited freshwater resources. Other sources confirm that a majority of the population does not have access to potable water (CIA 2006). In a report released in 2004, the Pakistan Council for Research on Water Reservoirs (PCRWR) stated that industrial and domestic pollution contaminates drinking water in 21 major cities and that in most areas of these cities the drinking water is unfit for human consumption, capable of causing hepatitis, cholera, typhoid, and other potentially fatal diseases (HRCP 2005a).[14]

---

13. The report is a joint effort of the Yale University Center for Environmental Law and Policy and the Center for International Earth Science Information Network at Columbia University, in collaboration with the World Economic Forum and the European Commission's Joint Research Center. See www.yale.edu/esi.

14. The 21 cities where water was found to be unsafe were Bahawalpur, Faisalabad, Gujranwala, Gujrat, Hyderabad, Islamabad, Karachi, Kasur, Khuzdar, Lahore, Loralai, Mardan, Mingora, Multan, Peshawar, Quetta, Rawalpindi, Sheikhupura, Sialkot, Sukkur, and Ziarat.

The coastal waters of the Indus River and the Arabian Sea, as well as most other rivers and lakes, also suffer from pollution (ADB 2002). While adequate control measures exist for the production, processing, and import of fertilizers, pesticides, and other chemicals, no legal regimes govern their disposal, registration, and other aspects of quality control. Forests, which cover fewer than 5 million of the country's 85 million hectares, are shrinking at one of the highest rates in the world, 2.4 to 3.1 percent per year, resulting in severely reduced biological diversity (ADB 2002). Finally, since more than 50 percent of Pakistan is desert, soil erosion and the spread of desertification are urgent concerns (CIA 2006). Pakistan is trying to correct this record, and has earned higher ESI scores for capacity and stewardship because it is party to several international environmental agreements (including the Kyoto Protocol). But while basic policies and institutional and legislative frameworks covering environmental issues are in place, much needs to be done to develop and enforce specific rules and regulations. Pakistan's Environmental Protection Act (EPA) of 1997 is not being implemented, as procedural laws on hazardous waste, regulation of motor vehicles, and administrative penalties are not in place (HRCP 2005a). Environmental tribunals set up under the EPA are often nonfunctional (HRCP 2005a). Enforcement of existing legislation remains weak, and the institutional and technical capacity needed to deal with infringements of environmental regulations needs to be strengthened (ADB 2002). Despite growing evidence that environmental degradation is of great concern in both rural and urban areas, the government routinely allocates a mere 0.4 percent of the public-sector development budget for environmental initiatives (approximately $3.2 million in 2004). The Human Rights Commission of Pakistan (HRCP) recommends that this sum be increased and more resources allocated to the provincial environmental protection agencies (HRCP 2005a).

There are nonetheless encouraging signs of judicial activism on the environmental front. In July 2003, the Pakistan Ministry of Environment announced that it would launch a drive against vehicle pollution in five major cities. The move followed a *suo moto* notice by the Supreme Court of increased environmental degradation, particularly in Punjab, and a judicial order that the departments dealing with traffic, the environment, and transportation coordinate efforts to prevent a worsening of the situation (HRCP 2004). The chief justice also ordered that a report on the effectiveness of the measures taken be presented to the court before the end of the year. In response to this action, the federal government developed a detailed plan to clean up air pollution.

More recently, in September 2005, the chief justice of the Supreme Court took *suo moto* action based on newspaper articles and reports questioning, on environmental grounds, a Punjab government plan to construct a tourist resort in a protected forest near Murree.[15] This was followed by the court's ordering a halt to the planned construction of luxury villas in the Margalla Hills, also because of environmental concerns.[16] In addition, the bench directed the attorney general of Pakistan to take steps to formulate legislation pertaining to housing schemes. The Supreme Court said that the case was important particularly in light of the earthquake that had devastated the northern parts of the country.

Labor and Environment in US FTAs

Many voices in the United States, both in Congress and the broader public, urge the inclusion of labor and environmental rules in bilateral FTAs. These voices are now dominant in the US political debate, despite the misgivings of commentators who argue that labor and environmental matters should be addressed either at a national level or internationally by specialized organizations or protocols (e.g., the ILO and the Montreal Protocol). Given these pressures, which first erupted in the North American Free Trade Agreement (NAFTA) debate of 1993, it is useful to summarize how labor and the environment have been addressed in existing US FTAs.

None of the agreements negotiated by the United States require adherence to new and detailed environmental and labor standards. Instead, the agreements commit countries to promote workers' rights and protect the environment generally, proclaiming that each government should enforce its own domestic environmental and labor laws and not weaken laws or reduce domestic labor protection in a "race to the bottom" to en-

---

15. A five-member bench hearing on the New Murree Project on the *suo moto* notice directed the Pakistan Environmental Protection Agency to prepare an environmental impact assessment to be reviewed by public hearing. New Murree Development Authority representatives assured the court that no work would commence on the project until all requirements under the Environmental Protection Act of 1997 are met. Critics of the project cite the potential loss of 1 percent of the total tree population and adverse effects on the average annual rainfall. See "Court Assured New Murree Project Not to Harm Forest," *Dawn*, September 30, 2005, www.dawn.com (accessed January 24, 2006), and "SC Seeks PEPA Report on Effects," *Daily Times*, September 30, 2005, www.dailytimes.com.pk (accessed January 24, 2006).

16. On October 14, 2005, a three-member Supreme Court bench ordered authorities to halt construction work at the Islamabad Chalets housing development. The order was issued on the basis of a report by Justice Javed Iqbal stating that the Margalla Hills National Park is an integral part of the scenic and environmental beauty of Islamabad and that the housing scheme, only kilometers away from the park, threatened the ecology of the area. The site of the development also falls in the catchments of the Khanpur Dam, which is one of the main supply sources of potable water for Islamabad and Rawalpindi. See "'Islamabad Chalets' Housing Scheme: SC Takes Suo Moto Notice," *Daily Times*, October 12, 2005, and "SC Halts Construction Work on 'Islamabad Chalets' Scheme," *Daily Times*, October 14, 2005, www.dailytimes.com.pk (accessed January 24, 2006).

courage exports or foreign investment. The US FTAs with Chile and Singapore reaffirm each party's existing commitment to the core labor standards set forth in the ILO's Declaration on Fundamental Principles and Rights at Work and also "recognize that it is inappropriate to encourage trade or investment by weakening or reducing the protections afforded in domestic labor laws" (Elliott 2004).

NAFTA was the first trade agreement linked to worker rights provisions in a major way. Its companion side agreement, the North American Agreement on Labor Cooperation (NAALC), went into effect with NAFTA on January 1, 1994. Through the NAALC, the NAFTA signatories agree to enforce their own labor laws and standards while promoting 11 labor principles over the long run. These principles are divided into three tiers. Access to remedies for inadequate enforcement of domestic law varies according to the tier. Under the NAALC, monetary penalties and, theoretically, sanctions as an enforcement tool are applicable to only three of the 11 principles, those in the third tier: domestic law standards on minimum wages, child labor, and occupational safety and health (Hufbauer and Schott 2005).[17]

The main function of the NAALC is to provide a forum for cooperation. In principle, instances of noncompliance can be investigated following a citizen's complaint or a party's request. To this end, the Commission for Labor Cooperation (CLC) Secretariat was created to oversee implementation and promote cooperation (Hufbauer and Schott 2005).[18] The NAALC has been criticized, however, for its limited scope. While it does provide a mechanism for consultation and cooperation as well as a constrained dispute settlement arrangement, it does not provide effective remedies for workers whose rights are violated (Hufbauer and Schott 2005).

The environmental side agreement, the North American Agreement on Environmental Cooperation (NAAEC), was similarly designed to encourage cooperative initiatives, to ensure appropriate implementation of

---

17. By contrast, offenses under the first tier are susceptible only to review and ministerial oversight. No committee of experts is called to evaluate the enforcement of labor principles in the first tier and no penalties are provided for noncompliance. The first tier applies to matters concerning freedom of association, collective bargaining, and the right to strike. In the second tier are principles subject to review by the National Administrative Office (NAO), ministerial consultations, and evaluation by a committee of experts—but without arbitration of disputes and without penalties for noncompliance. The second tier covers principles concerning forced labor, minimum employment standards pertaining to overtime pay, gender pay equity, employment discrimination, compensation in case of injury or illness, and protection of migrant labor (Hufbauer and Schott 2005).

18. Since the CLC does not have the power to develop factual records (unlike the Commission for Environmental Cooperation), submissions have to be filed with the NAO of each country. Citizens wishing to bring a case against their own country must file with another country.

environmental legislation, and to mediate environmental disputes. The North American Commission for Environmental Cooperation (CEC) is the institutional structure created to achieve all three goals (Hufbauer and Schott 2005). The NAAEC has two major shortcomings. First, it deceives those who identified this mechanism as the "teeth" of the side agreement. Second, NAFTA governments have not given adequate funding and support to the CEC. These weaknesses have been addressed, to some degree, in subsequent US FTAs.

The US-Jordan FTA incorporated provisions from both the NAALC and the "fast-track" authorization bills debated in the 105th Congress (CRS 2001). The agreement established a precedent by including in the main text a section on labor that is subject to the same dispute settlement procedures as other provisions in the agreement. However, letters exchanged by the US and Jordanian governments vowed to resolve differences under the agreement without resorting to sanctions. Similar to the NAALC, the US-Jordan FTA provides that "a party shall not fail to effectively enforce its [own] laws" (Article 6(4)(a) [USTR 2000]). In addition, Article 6(2) of the agreement provides that "each Party shall strive to ensure that it does not waive or otherwise derogate from, or offer to derogate from, [domestic labor laws] as an encouragement for trade with the other Party."[19]

The labor language in the US-Jordan FTA was not particularly intended to exert upward pressure on standards and therefore does not provide procedural guarantees ensuring impartial tribunals for the adjudication of labor matters.[20] Nor is a labor-related institutional mechanism created by the agreement.[21] Moreover, the dispute settlement procedures in the agreement leave considerable discretion to each government in deciding whether and how hard to push enforcement actions on labor, environment, and other matters.[22] So far, no such actions have been brought under the US-Jordan FTA.

The next two US FTAs, with Chile and Singapore, followed the US-Jordan standard by including worker rights provisions in the body of the

---

19. CAFTA-DR and the US-Chile, US-Singapore, and US-Morocco FTAs expanded upon the Jordan language to make it clear that weakening or reducing labor protections should not be done to encourage trade or investment. They also define what is meant by a "derogation" that should not occur (USTR 2005e).

20. The procedural guarantees that were later written into CAFTA-DR and the US-Morocco FTA are based on those contained in the NAALC (USTR 2005e).

21. Both the CAFTA-DR and the US-Morocco FTA have annexes to the labor chapter detailing labor cooperation and capacity-building activities. The US-Jordan FTA has no such annex (USTR 2005e).

22. If the sequence of steps—consultations, a dispute settlement panel, and finally a hearing by the joint committee—do not resolve a dispute, the complaining party is authorized "to take any appropriate and commensurate measure" (Elliott and Freeman 2003).

agreement and making violations subject to the same dispute settlement procedures as commercial disputes. In contrast to the NAALC under NAFTA, there is no distinction among tiers of applicable labor standards. However, the US-Chile and US-Singapore FTAs follow the practice of basing labor obligations on the effective enforcement of each country's own laws in trade-related sectors. The US-Singapore FTA states, for example, that the parties "shall strive to ensure" that their own labor laws are enforced and are consistent with the right of association, the right to organize and bargain collectively, the prohibition of forced labor, a minimum age of employment, and acceptable work conditions (USTR 2003b). However, in a step back from the US-Jordan framework, while recognizing that it is inappropriate to encourage trade or investment by weakening or reducing the protections afforded in domestic laws, these agreements explicitly exclude such derogations from the dispute settlement provisions (Elliott and Freeman 2003).

Like the NAALC, and in a departure from the US-Jordan FTA, the US-Chile and US-Singapore agreements limit enforcement measures in labor disputes to monetary fines, with the possibility of suspending tariff concessions if necessary to collect such fines (fines are explicitly not a trade sanction). Unlike NAFTA, the fines accrue annually if a problem remains unresolved. In commercial disputes, the country in violation of the agreement can choose to pay a fine, but traditional trade retaliation remains an option. The US Trade Representative (USTR) argues that, while not "mirror images," the mechanisms for enforcement of labor and commercial disputes would be equally effective and therefore meet the congressional standard of equivalence (Elliott and Freeman 2003).

Labor and Environment in CAFTA-DR

CAFTA-DR is the eighth US FTA to include labor protections.[23] During the CAFTA-DR debates, Democrats in Congress argued that the labor frameworks in the Chile, Jordan, and Singapore FTAs were inadequate to address the severe labor problems of Central America and that Central American countries simply could not be relied upon to carry out meaningful enforcement. US promises to implement a cooperation program to promote compliance with labor standards proved insufficient to sway Democratic votes—partly because of the weak implementation record of the labor and environmental side agreements in NAFTA (Hufbauer and Schott 2005). While the labor and environmental provisions in Chapters 16 and 17 of CAFTA-DR pushed the frontier, they did not go far enough

---

23. The first seven are (in chronological order) NAFTA and the six US bilateral trade agreements with Jordan, Chile, Singapore, Australia, Morocco, and Bahrain. Subsequent to CAFTA-DR, US FTAs with Oman and Peru also contained labor provisions.

to satisfy critics, especially Democratic members of Congress. Yet, in a close congressional vote along highly partisan lines, CAFTA-DR was ratified (217-215) by the House of Representatives on July 28, 2005.

Chapter 16: Labor

Chapter 16 of CAFTA-DR requires consultations if a party believes that another party is not complying with one of the core labor standards. Under the agreement, only a partner government (i.e., not a union, individual worker, or group of workers) has standing to invoke consultations and subsequent enforcement measures. If the matter concerns a party's obligation to effectively enforce its labor laws, the complaining party may, after an initial 60-day consultation period, invoke the provisions of Chapter 20 (dispute settlement). These provisions entail additional consultations or a meeting of the CAFTA-DR cabinet-level Free Trade Commission. If the commission is unable to resolve the dispute, it may be referred to a dispute settlement panel. The parties maintain a roster of experts to serve on such panels.

To build institutional capacity for handling labor and environmental issues, $20 million in US government assistance has been allocated under CAFTA-DR. The Bush administration also supports a request for $40 million for fiscal 2006 and will propose similar funding levels through fiscal 2009, with the exact form and level of assistance to be decided on a country-specific basis.

Along with the money, Chapter 16 creates mechanisms to strengthen each adherent country's institutional capacity. The mechanisms assist the parties to establish priorities for, and carry out initiatives on, such topics as the effective application of fundamental labor rights, legislation and practice relating to ILO Convention 182 dealing with the worst forms of child labor, stronger labor inspection systems and labor tribunals, compliance with regulations pertaining to working conditions, and the elimination of gender discrimination in employment.

Chapter 16 establishes a cabinet-level Labor Affairs Council to oversee the chapter's implementation and to provide a forum for consultations and cooperation. Each country must designate a contact point for communications with the other parties and the public, and the contact point must provide transparent procedures for the submission, receipt, and consideration of communications from the public.

Chapter 17: Environment

Chapter 17 establishes a cabinet-level Environmental Affairs Council to oversee implementation and to provide opportunities at council meetings for members of the public to express their views. The parties also agree, under Chapter 17, to consult on WTO negotiations regarding multilateral environmental agreements. The Environmental Cooperation Agreement (ECA),[24] established under Article 17.5 of CAFTA-DR, provides for benchmarking to establish short-, medium-, and long-term goals for improving environmental protection and for outside monitoring by organizations such as the United Nations Environmental Program (UNEP) and the Inter-American Development Bank (IDB).

Although CAFTA-DR's Chapter 17 draws on the NAAEC of 1994 and on the environmental provisions of other US FTAs, it goes further: It is the first US FTA to provide a public submission process on environmental enforcement matters in the body of the FTA. Modeled on Articles 14 and 15 of the NAAEC, the submission mechanism creates a new avenue for citizens to raise specific problems associated with enforcement of environmental laws, subject to review by an independent secretariat.[25] The CAFTA-DR mechanism goes beyond NAFTA in these respects:

- It is easier for a meritorious case to move forward to the development of a detailed "factual record" (at the request of a single member of the Environmental Affairs Council, whereas NAFTA requires the assent of two of the three parties).

- There are modest provisions for acting on the findings of the "factual record"; for example, the joint Environmental Affairs Council can make recommendations to the Environmental Cooperation Commission. This provision represents an innovation to the NAAEC, which contains no such provision for follow-through.

- CAFTA-DR contains express provisions for including environmental expertise in the resolution of disputes.

- If a party does not comply with a dispute panel's finding that the party is failing to enforce its environmental laws, CAFTA-DR allows for monetary assessments to address the underlying enforcement problem.

---

24. The ECA was negotiated in parallel with CAFTA-DR. The agreement builds on the US Agency for International Development's (USAID) long-term environmental planning in the region and is specifically linked to activities under the Central American–US Joint Accord.

25. The CAFTA-DR public submissions procedure is not available to US citizens wishing to raise concerns with US enforcement of its environmental laws (such persons already have recourse to other remedies, including procedures under Articles 14 and 15 of the NAAEC). However, citizens of other CAFTA-DR parties may raise concerns with US enforcement under the CAFTA-DR provisions. The FTA governments agree to establish a new unit in the Secretariat for Central American Economic Integration (SIECA) to serve as the "secretariat or other appropriate body" to undertake the functions set out in Articles 17.7 and 17.8 of the agreement (USTR 2004c).

Equivalent compliance procedures apply to disputes over labor and environmental enforcement. If a panel determines that a party has not met its enforcement obligations, and if the disputing parties cannot agree on how to resolve the dispute, or the complaining party believes that the defending party has failed to implement an agreed resolution, the complaining party may ask the panel to determine an annual monetary assessment to be imposed on the defending party. The panel will establish the amount of the assessment, subject to a $15 million annual cap, taking into account relevant factors both trade related and otherwise. The assessment will be paid into a fund established by the commission for appropriate labor and environmental initiatives. If the defending party fails to pay the assessment, the complaining party may take other appropriate steps, such as suspension of tariff benefits, as necessary to collect the assessment.

Although the CAFTA-DR provisions seem amenable to the establishment of panels and the imposition of monetary fines, the absence of serious funding provisions in the pact is glaring. Funds to build institutions (even $40 million annually) will not make a meaningful difference when much heavier lifting is required for adequate sanitation, clean water, paved roads, and reforestation. On the other hand, the labor dispute settlement provisions seem promising—if the new measures focus on a limited number of core labor standards (child labor, discrimination, etc.) and come down hard in documented cases of abuse.

Recommendations

For Labor Provisions

The per capita income in Pakistan is $2,200 on a purchasing power parity basis.[26] This is approximately half that of current US FTA partners in the developing world—Jordan ($4,500), Morocco ($4,200), and the CAFTA-DR countries ($5,000)[27]—and a prospective US FTA partner, Egypt ($4,200). While higher labor standards alone cannot effectively raise a national average wage level,[28] they can be used to eradicate the

---

26. 2004 estimate from the *CIA World Factbook*, www.cia.gov (accessed December 27, 2005).

27. The CAFTA-DR figure is the simple average per capita income of the signatory countries: Costa Rica ($9,600), the Dominican Republic ($6,300), El Salvador ($4,900), Guatemala ($4,200), Honduras ($2,800), and Nicaragua ($2,300). A weighted average figure would be less, because Honduras and Nicaragua together have a relatively large population in the CAFTA-DR group.

28. Average wages are far more dependent on the national productivity level than on specific legislation aimed at labor abuses. National productivity is determined by an array of factors, of which labor legislation is a comparatively small component.

worst forms of labor abuse. With that goal in mind, we offer the following recommendations.

- A US-Pakistan FTA should adopt the basic labor and dispute settlement framework of the CAFTA-DR pact, as laid out in Chapter 16 and Chapter 20 of the agreement.

- The progression of labor chapters in US FTAs is toward stronger enforcement measures and higher standards. In light of that evolution, the Pakistani federal government should amend the Industrial Relations Ordinance (IRO) so that it conforms with the ILO conventions that Pakistan has ratified.

- Provincial governments should undertake more vigorous enforcement of existing labor legislation, such as the Employment of Children Act of 1991 and the Bonded Labor System (Abolition) Act (BLAA) of 1992. The provinces should commit to periodic independent audits of their accomplishments, for example by the ILO.

- Pakistan is a member of the International Organization for Standardization (ISO).[29] Just as businesses in Pakistan have adopted the voluntary quality standards developed by the ISO, firms that export to the United States should adopt codes of conduct for labor, based on the ILO Declaration on Fundamental Principles and Rights at Work. Companies should self-certify their compliance, and randomly selected companies (say, 10 percent per year) should submit to an independent audit to ensure that they observe the codes.

For Environmental Provisions

- Chapter 17 of the CAFTA-DR provides a good framework for environmental provisions in a US-Pakistan FTA. For violations with a direct trade impact, monetary assessments subject to approximately the same annual cap ($15 million) are appropriate.

- Initiatives should be adopted to strengthen the institutional and technical capacity needed to deal with infringements of environmental regulations. In addition, mechanisms should be established for external monitoring, such as those promoted by the Asian Development Bank (ADB 2002).

---

29. A member of the ISO is the national body "most representative of standardization in its country." Only one such body for each country is accepted for membership in the ISO. Member bodies are entitled to participate and exercise full voting rights on any technical committee and policy committee of the ISO. See www.iso.org (accessed January 3, 2006).

■ The United States should provide support at or above the CAFTA-DR level ($40 million annually), on a matching basis with Pakistan, to strengthen labor and environmental institutions. In addition, the United States should urge the World Bank to launch a major program specifically for water and sewer projects. We have not attempted to estimate the scope, but the funding required for such a program could reach several billion dollars over a decade.

6

Government Procurement

Buy-national procurement rules or other restrictions exist at the federal and subfederal levels in both Pakistan and the United States, and Pakistan is not yet a signatory to the World Trade Organization (WTO) Government Procurement Agreement (GPA). A US-Pakistan FTA would enable less fettered competition for government purchases and thus could deliver considerable benefits to both countries.

This chapter considers the ramifications of a US-Pakistan FTA for government procurement requirements. The first two sections review the regulatory environment and recent developments in the United States and in Pakistan. The third section outlines our recommendations for liberalizing government procurement in the context of a prospective US-Pakistan FTA.

The United States

Regulatory Environment

The United States signed the WTO GPA in 1996 along with 28 other nations. Thus US procurement rules, at the federal level and in most states, are generally applied in keeping with GPA obligations. The agreement, however, does not cover all US federal or state government procurement but only scheduled entities, and even then only for goods and services above certain threshold values. Coverage under the agreement is further restricted by exceptions listed in general notes to the schedules.

At the federal level, US public procurement takes place through various departments supervised by the Office of Management and Budget

(OMB) and two acquisition regulatory councils, the Defense Acquisition Regulations Council and the Civilian Agency Acquisition Council (WTO 2004a). The Federal Acquisition Regulation (FAR) establishes umbrella regulation for all federal entities, but permits them to follow their own internal guidelines (WTO 2004a).[1] Under the FAR, federal entities are obligated to publish their procurement requirements on a Web site known as FedBizOpps when the procurement exceeds $25,000. The proposed contract must be published at least 15 days before bids begin; thereafter, prospective bidders must be given at least 30 days to place their bids (WTO 2004a).[2]

At the subfederal level, state and local governments regulate procurement contracts, which are subject to threshold values and other provisions specific to each state. While some states grant preferences to local suppliers and impose local-content requirements, 37 states have adopted the GPA provisions[3] and are thus obligated to publish tender invitations on the FedBizOpps Web site for GPA-covered sectors.

The Buy American Act

The Buy American Act (BAA) of 1933 (as amended) is the core document governing US procurement of goods at the federal level. The act establishes discriminatory measures, also known as Buy American restrictions, for government-funded purchases, including supply and construction contracts (European Commission 2004). These restrictive measures can take several forms—prohibiting government entities from purchasing foreign goods and services, requiring a certain amount of local content, and preferring domestic suppliers when evaluating bid prices.

The United States maintains a number of Buy American procurement restrictions that are not covered by the GPA, the North American Free Trade Agreement (NAFTA), the WTO Agreement on Trade in Civil Aircraft, or bilateral procurement agreements with Australia, Chile, Israel, and Singapore (WTO 2004a). BAA requirements apply to goods, not services, and require federal entities to procure only US-mined or US-produced unprocessed goods as well as manufactured articles with at least 50 percent local content (European Commission 2004).

---

1. The FAR was amended in 2001 to change aspects of electronic procurement and preferential access for small businesses, improve transparency of procedures, and alter bidding processes and thresholds. Part 25 of the FAR deals with policies and procedures to acquire foreign supplies, services, and construction materials (WTO 2004a).

2. Exceptions are made for purchases of perishable supplies when the delayed publication could be damaging (WTO 2004a).

3. The 37 states are listed in Annex 2 of the US GPA schedule (WTO 2002b).

Executive Order 10582 of 1954 goes beyond the scope of the BAA by carving out special status for procurement contracts with small businesses and firms in areas with labor surpluses. The order also allows government entities to reject bids by foreign firms for national interest or security reasons (European Commission 2004).

The Berry Amendment

Like the BAA, the Berry amendment of 1941 provides strict guidelines that require the Department of Defense to prefer US producers when making procurement decisions. It is more stringent than the BAA, however, as it requires 100 percent domestic origin (as opposed to 50 percent under the BAA) and is not limited to contracts in the United States. Some interest groups have lobbied for the extension of the Berry amendment to other US government agencies (such as the Department of Homeland Security), but its provisions currently govern procurement only by the Department of Defense.[4]

As a US ally in the war against terrorism, Pakistan might request, during FTA negotiations, a limited role in Defense Department procurement of textile and clothing. In 2002, the US armed forces purchases of textiles and clothing were estimated at $2 billion, of which only $4 million were supplied directly by foreign firms (US Department of Commerce 2003).[5]

The Balance of Payments Program

The Balance of Payments Program is a nonstatutory program that potentially restricts the purchases of supplies by government entities and contracts for the construction, alteration, or repair of any public building outside the United States, such as a US embassy (WTO 2004a). Since 2001, this program no longer applies to civilian agency acquisitions, but it still applies to the Department of Defense for purchases of end products that are used abroad and exceed $100,000 in cost (WTO 2004a).

---

4. The Berry amendment has been a subject of debate in recent years. Critics point to the supposed gap between the legislative requirements of the amendment and US productive capacity, particularly in the textile and clothing sector. However, representatives of US textile and clothing firms consistently support the amendment as written.

5. However, the sensitivity of government procurement questions, including the Berry amendment, must be recognized. In the Central American Free Trade Agreement–Dominican Republic (CAFTA-DR) ratification debate, the USTR prominently advertised that the pact made no change in federal or state procurement laws, beyond extending to the new partners procurement opportunities already open to other foreign countries (USTR 2005f).

The Trade Agreements Act of 1979

The Trade Agreements Act of 1979 implemented the General Agreement on Tariffs and Trade (GATT) Government Procurement Code signed in the Tokyo Round. Essentially, it overrides the BAA and related legislation by ensuring national treatment for signatories of the code with respect to scheduled entities and above-threshold contracts (USITC 2004b). Thus, for designated parties the act gives up BAA preferences for civil aircraft and related articles[6] as well as other end products.[7]

Exemptions and Waivers

Exemptions and waivers to the BAA and Balance of Payments Program are granted if it can be shown that domestic preferences are inconsistent with national interests, and if the supply of a particular material is either unavailable or too expensive in the United States (WTO 2004a).[8] BAA restrictions have also been waived in acquisitions of defense equipment that originates from countries with which the United States has a reciprocal procurement agreement.[9]

Subchapters VIII and X of Chapter 98 of the BAA list goods that are not subject to customs duties when purchased for use in government contracts. Other supplies may also be eligible for duty-free entry if the contract price is reduced by the amount of duty that would prevail if the supplies did not enter duty free (WTO 2004a). Finally, excepting equipment, supplies destined for government-operated vessels or aircraft are eligible to enter the United States duty free (WTO 2004a).

The WTO GPA and US Bilateral Agreements

As of 2004, the threshold values of procurement contracts covered under the GPA remained at their 1996 levels (WTO 2004a). Table 6.1 shows the

---

6. Related articles are those that "meet the substantial transformation test of the Act and originate in countries that are parties to the WTO Agreement on Trade in Civil Aircraft" (WTO 2004a).

7. Similar preferences are extended unilaterally to eligible countries through the GPA, NAFTA, other bilateral procurement agreements, and to least-developed countries (WTO 2004a). For example, end products that are granted duty-free entry under the Caribbean Basin Economic Recovery Act (CBERA) are eligible for government contracts.

8. A domestic offer is judged too expensive if the foreign product is priced "below the lowest domestic offer when this offer is from a large business concern" (including import duty and a 6 percent added margin) (WTO 2004a). If the offer is from a small business, the added margin is 12 percent, and for defense-related purchases the price difference has to be a minimum of 50 percent.

9. However, the secretary of defense retains the right to restrict or reject an offer from a qualifying country for national defense reasons.

**Table 6.1 Threshold values of procurement contracts,
WTO GPA and selected US FTAs** (dollars)

Agreement	Supplies	Services	Construction
WTO GPA	169,000	169,000	6,481,000
Canada	25,000	56,190	7,304,733
Mexico	56,190	56,190	7,304,733
Chile	56,190	56,190	6,481,000
Singapore	56,190	56,190	6,481,000

FTA = free trade agreement
WTO GPA = World Trade Organization Government Procurement Agreement

Source: WTO (2004a).

threshold values set by the United States in the WTO GPA schedule, NAFTA, and the US FTAs with Singapore and Chile. Table 6.2 lists the services that the United States has chosen to exclude from the GPA and in selected bilateral FTAs.

The US-Chile and US-Singapore FTAs opened additional state and federal agencies to foreign bids (Schott 2004a). Local procurement is not covered under either the GPA or the two FTAs. Under the US-Singapore FTA, state-level obligations do not extend beyond the sector obligations already committed under the GPA. Under the US-Chile FTA, the 37 US states that have agreed to GPA provisions treat Chilean suppliers in essentially the same manner (USTR 2003c). Finally, the US-Chile and US-Singapore FTAs specify high threshold values, and exclude state set-aside programs for small and minority businesses (Salazar-Xirinachs and Granados 2004).[10]

Effect of Restrictions

US government expenditures amounted to $1.98 trillion in 2002, or 19 percent of GDP. Defense-related expenditures were the largest component, some $400 billion. Most federal expenditures, however, represent salaries and transfer payments.

---

10. Government procurement was a source of concern in the CAFTA-DR debate. Congressman Benjamin Cardin (D-MD) attempted to withdraw Maryland from the list of states subject to government procurement rules in the FTA package. However, Deputy US Trade Representative Peter Allgeier ultimately informed Cardin that Maryland "will have to remain on the list of states subject to government procurement rules" in CAFTA-DR. See "Maryland to Remain on Government Procurement Annex for CAFTA," *Inside U.S. Trade,* July 1, 2005, 5.

Table 6.2 Services excluded or included by the United States in the WTO GPA and selected US FTAs

Service	WTO	NAFTA/Chile	Singapore	Australia/Morocco
Purchase of military services overseas	Excluded	Excluded	Excluded	Excluded
Automatic data processing, telecom, and transmission	Excluded	Excluded	Included	Included
Telecom network, automated news services, data services	Excluded	Excluded	Included	Included
Basic telecommunications network services	Included	Included	Excluded	Excluded
Dredging	Excluded	Excluded	Excluded	Excluded
Federally funded research and development centers	Excluded	Included	Excluded	Included
Department of Defense, Energy, Aeronautics/Space facilities	Included	Excluded	Included	Excluded
Research and development	Excluded	Excluded	Excluded	Excluded
Transportation services	Excluded	Excluded	Excluded	Excluded
Utility services	Excluded	Excluded	Excluded	Excluded
Maintenance, repair, rebuilding, installation of equipment related to ships, including nonnuclear ship repair	Included	Excluded	Included	Excluded

FTA = free trade agreement
NAFTA = North American Free Trade Agreement
WTO GPA = World Trade Organization Government Procurement Agreement

Source: Integrated Acquisition Environment, Federal Acquisition Regulation, www.arnet.gov/far.

The European Commission has estimated that BAA restrictions each year affect approximately $25 billion of public contracts, most noticeably in mass transport and airport improvements (European Commission 2004).[11] Restrictions under the BAA and the Berry amendment would discourage Pakistani firms from participating in US procurement of goods such as textiles and clothing or medical devices.[12]

US public procurement restrictions are implemented on three levels: federal restrictions on procurement by federal entities, state restrictions on state and local procurement contracts, and federal restrictions on the use of federal grant money by state and local governments (USITC 2004b). At the federal level, the major restrictions relate to defense procurement contracts and small and minority-owned business contracts. At the state level, federal regulations (mostly BAA restrictions) prohibit the use of federal grant money in transportation and food assistance projects (USITC 2004b).

Public Transportation

Federal aid to state and local governments for public transportation is distributed by the Department of Transportation under the Highway Administration Act, the Urban Mass Transit Act, and the Airports Improvements Act. The federal government may fund 40 to 80 percent of a project while the state funds the rest. Regardless of the percentage of federal funding, all public transportation projects are subject to local content requirements of 60 percent (or, if they fall short of that minimum, a penalty of up to 25 percent of the price) (European Commission 2004).

Highway Construction

Federal assistance for highway projects amounted to $46 billion in 2002, while federal grants to state and local governments for highway construction totaled $26 billion (USITC 2004b). Under the BAA, highways must be constructed with domestically produced iron and steel. A waiver is possible but is rarely granted.

Airport Construction

The Federal Aviation Administration monitors BAA restrictions on state and local public procurement for airport construction projects. Some 80

---

11. This figure is expected to increase to $35 billion in 2005 (European Commission 2004).

12. According to the latest US notification of government procurement statistics to the WTO, total US federal government procurement of textiles and clothing in 1999, subject to GPA provisions, was around $70 million. That same source reported expenditures on medical appliances and precision and optical instruments, subject to GPA provisions, of about $1 billion (WTO document GPA/40/Add.4).

to 90 percent of airport construction spending comes from the federal government. Airport construction projects are obligated to use domestically produced steel and manufactured goods unless a waiver is invoked.

Food Assistance

Many food assistance procurement programs are monitored by the US Department of Agriculture and other federal entities (e.g., the Department of Health and Human Services). These programs, such as the National School Lunch Program and the Child and Adult Care food program, give preferences to local food suppliers. Even donated commodities must be of domestic origin. Some programs require that school food authorities buy domestic commodities to the maximum extent possible (USITC 2004b). However, under NAFTA and the Uruguay Round agreement, the United States retained the right to exempt from its national treatment obligations the "procurement of agricultural goods made in furtherance of agricultural support programs or human feeding programs" (USITC 2004b).

Small Business Set-Asides

Federal grants and subcontracts awarded to small business firms are governed by the Small Business Act of 1958 (SBA) (as amended), which establishes certain targets for the procurement of goods and services: 23 percent of prime contracts must be awarded to small businesses, 5 percent of prime and subcontracts to minority-owned businesses, 5 percent to woman-owned businesses, 3 percent to service-disabled veteran-owned businesses, and prime contracts for Historically Underutilized Business Zone (HUBZone) firms were phased in from 1 percent in fiscal 1999 to 2.5 percent in fiscal 2002 and 3 percent in fiscal 2003 (USITC 2004b). The SBA requires that all owners of small businesses be US citizens to qualify for preferential procurement. Because SBA regulations require that receipts of all domestic and foreign affiliates of the business be counted in determining whether the firm qualifies as a small business, US affiliates of foreign-owned corporations usually cannot obtain small business status. Most federal purchases under the SBA programs face BAA restrictions, although a general waiver may be granted for federal purchases of less than $2,500 (USITC 2004b).

Defense Procurement

The BAA governs domestic sourcing requirements for defense procurement. In addition, the Defense Federal Acquisition Regulations System (DFARS) covers defense-related procurement of specific products such as food, clothing and fibers, vessels, and anchor chain (USITC 2004b). DFARS is also intended to ensure that government procurement contracts comply with the memorandum of understanding (MoU) between the Department of Defense and SBA with respect to the small-business goals mentioned above (USITC 2004b). The North Atlantic Treaty Organization (NATO) countries that have ratified the MoU can obtain a waiver from the Department of Defense's domestic preferences (USITC 2004b).

State and Local Government Procurement

States impose procurement restrictions over and above the restrictions imposed by federal rules. So far, all negotiated US trade agreements have given states the choice to retain their state procurement rules or accede to the agreement; 37 of the 50 states have chosen to accept the GPA provisions in the WTO, and the same states have generally accepted similar FTA provisions. According to the most recent data reported by the United States to the WTO, in 1999 total procurement by all states that had acceded to GPA provisions reached $306 billion (WTO document GPA/40/Add.4). For the US FTA partner, the benefits of state accession include the opportunity to transcend the large number and diverse nature of state programs (USITC 2004b). As of 2005, Georgia, Indiana, New Jersey, Ohio, and Virginia were among the important holdout states.

Subfederal Selective Purchasing Laws

Selective purchasing laws at the subfederal level often block transactions with foreign firms that have links to "offensive" third countries, such as Burma. Penalty laws have been adopted by Massachusetts as well as 20 cities and local authorities (European Commission 2004). While the Supreme Court ruled that a Massachusetts law was preempted by federal legislation (*Crosby et al.* v. *National Foreign Trade Council*, U.S. Sup. Ct., No. 99-474, June 19, 2000), the holding had a narrow legal focus. Hence municipal selective purchases on foreign policy grounds can still be a problem. For example, in 2001, New York attempted to apply selective purchasing legislation based on the so-called MacBride principles, which are a code of conduct developed in Northern Ireland to address the problem of workplace religious discrimination (European Commission 2004). The proposal was dropped, but it flagged a continuing concern.

Services

While the BAA is not supposed to apply to procurement of services, the offshore outsourcing debate has inspired new legislative forays, mainly at the state level. In 2002, New Jersey (followed by Michigan in 2004) enacted legislation stating that "only citizens of the United States and persons authorized to work in the United States pursuant to federal law may be employed in the performance of services [funded by the state]" (European Commission 2004). Connecticut, Florida, Maryland, Missouri, and Wisconsin have announced the implementation of similar provisions (European Commission 2004). The aim of this legislation is to discourage the establishment of "call centers" and data processing services abroad (European Commission 2004).

Recent Developments

Recent initiatives have attempted to improve the efficiency of federal government procurement. The E-Government Act of 2002 led to the creation of an Internet portal for government procurement known as the Integrated Acquisition Environment initiative. In addition, the General Services Administration (GSA) has promoted two new programs. GSA Global Supply identifies an array of goods and services that conform to government acquisition policies and socioeconomic regulations (WTO 2004a). GSA Advantage is an Internet program that allows interested parties to communicate with authorized contractors online; under this program, 5,298 contracting foreign firms registered online in 2004 (WTO 2004a).

Pakistan

Pakistan's total government procurement market for goods and services in 2004–05 was roughly estimated at Rs. 224 billion ($3.8 billion) or 5 percent of GDP (Government of Pakistan 2005a, IMF 2003). However, Pakistan is not a signatory of the GPA and has not made a commitment to begin accession negotiations. Political influence on procurement decisions, charges of official corruption, and long delays in bureaucratic decision making have been noted. Investors have also reported instances of the government using the lowest bid as a basis for further negotiations rather than accepting it under the established tender rules. Occasionally the government has "disqualified" experienced and technically proficient bidders that were qualified under tender specifications (USTR 2005d). Reducing corruption in the civil service, particularly at the provincial and local levels, is a major challenge for Pakistan,[13] and procurement practices are on the front line of this battle.

Pakistan's National Accountability Bureau has a mandate to investigate alleged corruption. Its efforts are complemented by individual re-

---

13. Pakistan ranks 144 out of 158 nations in Transparency International's 2005 Corruption Perceptions Index.

gional accountability bureaus in each of the country's four provincial capitals and one in the federal area. If effective, these accountability bodies will help reduce corruption in public procurement.

Domestic legislation on government procurement dates back to 1972, and was amended most recently when the Pakistani government established the Public Procurement Regulatory Authority (PPRA) in May 2002 to strengthen procurement practices through increased transparency, accountability, and governance. In June 2004, the authority published detailed public procurement rules that are compatible with international best practices and that cover all agencies owned or controlled by the federal government, except those related to national security or the defense forces (PPRA 2004).

In accordance with the PPRA rules, work performed for federal agencies, including the purchase of imported equipment and services, is now customarily awarded through tenders that are publicly announced or issued to registered suppliers. The procurement of services is generally subject to the same procedures as the procurement of goods, although additional technical negotiations are required for services. Sole source contracting using company-specific specifications has been eliminated (USTR 2005d). All procurement opportunities over Rs. 40,000 ($675) must be published on the PPRA's Web site, and opportunities exceeding Rs. 1 million ($16,860) must also be published in the print media. In addition, an "integrity pact" must be signed between the procuring agency and the suppliers or contractors for procurements exceeding Rs. 10 million ($168,600) (ADB/OECD 2004).

While Pakistan has no "buy national" policies, the government does not invite private tenders for the transportation of crude oil. All transport of crude oil must be conducted by the state-owned Pakistan National Shipping Corporation.

Transparency International has monitored the enforcement of Pakistan's public procurement rules 2004 and has been consulted in connection with procurement contracts awarded by various bodies—the City of Karachi, Pakistan Steel, Pakistan Telecommunication Company Ltd., and the Ministry of Irrigation and Power of Sindh Province. Transparency International's findings indicate better governance, with the prospect of sustained improvement (Transparency International 2005).

Recommendations

Practices that impede competition in public procurement cannot be abolished overnight. Nevertheless, the US-Pakistan FTA should be ambitious and forward-looking. For budget reasons alone, public authorities in both countries should welcome greater competition. In addition, Pakistan should welcome the salutary impact of open procurement rules in its anticorruption campaign. With those goals in mind, we offer the following recommendations.

For the United States

■ The US-Pakistan FTA should grant Pakistani firms the best terms enjoyed both under the GPA and by the NAFTA partners, Australia, Chile, Singapore, and future US bilateral FTA partners (i.e., an unconditional most favored nation [MFN] provision). The MFN provision should apply to both federal and state procurement.

■ Without undercutting the thrust of the BAA or the Berry amendment, the United States should work toward extending its procurement coverage for Pakistani exports such as textiles and clothing and medical instruments. For example, negotiators of a US-Pakistan FTA should explore the possibility of relaxing origin requirements to facilitate procurement of Pakistani goods by US firms that supply the Department of Defense, particularly in overseas contracts.

■ The USTR should seek to include two or three "holdout" states (in addition to states that have previously agreed to GPA or FTA procurement provisions). Likely candidates might be Georgia, New Jersey, and Virginia.

For Pakistan

■ Pakistan should commit to accede to the GPA, in the context of the Doha Round. Accession will help Pakistan rationalize its own public procurement system and ensure the continued progress of domestic reform.

■ In the proposed FTA, Pakistan should schedule the same type of procurement obligations (allowing for similar reservations) as the United States has scheduled in the GPA and in its FTAs. Pakistan's commitments should mirror those stipulated by the GPA for developing countries and those of Central American Free Trade Agreement-Dominican Republic (CAFTA-DR) for US partners.

■ The FTA should grant US firms the best terms enjoyed under the GPA as well as by Pakistan's current and future bilateral FTA partners (i.e., an unconditional MFN provision). The unconditional MFN provision should apply to both federal and provincial procurement.

7

Investment and Services

Pakistan now ranks, along with India and China, among the fastest growing economies in Asia, with a growth rate of more than 6 percent annually. However, despite Pakistan's impressive growth, foreign direct investment (FDI) is well below levels attracted by countries with similar high growth records. A US-Pakistan FTA could address some concerns of foreign investors and lead to higher inflows.

This chapter addresses questions relating to direct and portfolio investment as well as the services sector, and highlights connections between service and investment issues. After exploring some of the characteristics of FDI in both Pakistan and the United States, areas of FDI friction will be identified. An overview of current international investment agreements between the two countries comes next, followed by an analysis of portfolio investment and remittances to Pakistan. The chapter then turns to the service sectors of both countries, and concludes with observations about the treatment of ser-vices and investment in other FTAs as well as recommendations for these areas in the context of a possible US-Pakistan FTA.

FDI Overview and Main Characteristics

Pakistan's total inward FDI stock grew from about 3 percent of the country's GDP in 1980 to about 11 percent (approximately $10 billion) by 2003. In other words, inward investment became more important to the economy over the two-decade period (UNCTAD 2004).[1] Inward FDI flows in recent years (1998–2003) have on average accounted for about 8 percent of gross fixed capital formation in Pakistan.[2]

However, Pakistan's outward FDI stock remains below 1 percent of GDP, despite an increasingly liberal approach to capital outflows. This is well below the 14 percent of GDP represented by the outward FDI stock of all developing countries (UNCTAD 2004).

Table 7.1 presents an overview of inward FDI stocks in Pakistan by country of origin since 2000. These estimates differ somewhat from parallel figures from other sources because the underlying calculations require some guesswork: The Pakistani government does not compile stock estimates of FDI, and so the figures in table 7.1 are assembled from indirect sources. Nonetheless, these estimates suggest that, in 2004, US firms were responsible for about 37 percent of the total FDI stock in Pakistan. In order of their importance, other source countries include the United Kingdom with 20 percent, the United Arab Emirates with 8 percent, followed by Saudi Arabia and Japan.

The figures in table 7.1 indicate fairly modest growth in Pakistan's inward FDI stock in recent years. Various explanations can be offered: inadequate infrastructure, political instability coupled with law and order difficulties, and unresolved disputes between foreign investors and the Pakistani government. Moreover, Pakistan's Board of Investment has been criticized for its weak leadership.[3]

Sectoral and Company Perspective

Table 7.2 offers a perspective on the sectoral breakdown of FDI stocks in Pakistan. Foreign investment is concentrated in relatively few sectors, the largest of which is mining, quarrying, and oil exploration, accounting for 25 percent of the total in 2004. Next in line comes the transportation, storage, and communications sector with a 15 percent share, followed by the power sector with 14 percent. Other important sectors include the combined chemical, pharmaceutical, and fertilizer industries with 10 percent, and financial services with about 9 percent.

---

1. Nonetheless, while the ratio of FDI to GDP is higher than for most of South Asia, with the exception of Sri Lanka, it is well below the average for other developing Asian or Latin American countries. According to UNCTAD (2004), inward FDI stocks represented 28 percent of the GDP of all developing economies in 2004.

2. Focusing on percentages ignores the fact that gross fixed capital formation in Pakistan (at around 17 percent of GDP) is lower than in many developing countries, particularly those that have grown rapidly for a decade or longer.

3. This viewpoint is drawn from research conducted by the US Commercial Service in an article titled "Pakistan Investment Climate Statement," available at www.buyusa.gov.

Table 7.1 Inward FDI stock in Pakistan by source country, 2004

Country	Percentage share
United States	37
United Kingdom	20
United Arab Emirates	8
Saudi Arabia	5
Japan	4
Germany	2
Netherlands	2
Hong Kong	1
Korea	1
France	0
Canada	0
Italy	0
Others	21
Total stock (millions of dollars)	7,596

Note: Calculated based on yearly UNCTAD stock totals and an average of flows between 1997 and 2004, as provided by the Pakistan Board of Investment. The flow figures do not include reinvested earnings, which lead to an understatement of FDI stocks.

Source: UNCTAD 2005 Country Fact Sheet for Pakistan, Pakistan Board of Investment, www.pakboi.gov.pk.

Table 7.3 provides a sectoral breakdown of FDI stocks held by US firms located abroad. Parallel figures are not available for FDI in Pakistan; however, from table 7.3 it is clear that US FDI abroad spans a wide range of sectors, with manufacturing and finance among the largest, accounting for shares of 21 and 18 percent respectively.

The most significant sectors for US investors in Pakistan appear to be transportation, storage, and communications, mostly telecommunications and information technology. Following the example set by India, Pakistan's current efforts to build up its human resources should lead to further foreign investment in its information technology sector. Oil and gas exploration, chemicals, pharmaceuticals, and fertilizers are other sectors with US investment.

Table 7.2 Inward FDI stock in Pakistan by industry, 2004

Industry	Percentage share
Mining and quarrying, oil exploration	25
Transport, storage, and communications	15
Power	14
Chemicals, pharmaceuticals, and fertilizer	10
Financial business	9
Food, beverages, and tobacco	4
Trade	4
Construction	3
Petrochemicals and refining	3
Textiles	3
Electronics	1
Electrical machinery	1
Machinery other than electrical	0
Other	9
Total stock (millions of dollars)	7,596

Note: Calculated based on yearly UNCTAD stock totals and an average of flows between 1997 and 2004, as provided by the Pakistan Board of Investment. The flow figures do not include reinvested earnings, which led to an understatement of FDI stocks.

Source: UNCTAD 2005 Country Fact Sheet for Pakistan, Pakistan Board of Investment, www.pakboi.gov.pk.

The Pakistan Board of Investment identified 15 major companies that attracted some of the largest FDI inflows from the United States in 2003–04. Three of the largest companies are in the oil and gas exploration sector. Other significant sectors include petroleum refining, telecommunications, and pharmaceuticals.

Areas of FDI Friction

Since the 1980s, Pakistan aimed to attract foreign investors through the establishment of Export Processing Zones Authority (for details, see www.pakboi.gov.pk). In fact, a major new port with export processing facilities is currently under construction at Gwadar, near the Iranian border (for details, see www.gwadarnews.com). While successful governance of

Table 7.3 US FDI stock abroad by industry, 2004

Industry	Billions of US dollars	Percent of total FDI
Manufacturing	428.2	21
Finance (except banks) and insurance	371.0	18
Wholesale trade	136.9	7
Mining	101.4	5
Depository institutions (banks)	68.1	3
Information	56.4	3
Professional, scientific, and technical services	42.1	2
Utilities	18.9	1
Other industries[a]	841.0	40
Total all industries	2,064.0	100

n.a. = not available

a. Holding companies (except banks) accounted for 84 percent of the "other industries" share to the world.

Note: Data are on a historical-cost basis, year-end 2004.

Source: BEA (2005).

these export processing zones can significantly improve investment ties between the United States and Pakistan, other aspects of FDI cause friction. A US-Pakistan FTA provides a unique opportunity to deal with some long-standing concerns with the Pakistani business environment. We review topics that will attract the attention of negotiators.

Impediments to Competition

In Pakistan, the Monopolies and Restrictive Trade Practices Ordinance is enforced by the Monopoly Control Authority. However, state-owned firms are exempt from the ordinance; consequently, competition policy and foreign investment do not reach important sectors of the economy. Major examples of such exempt businesses include the state-owned Water and Power Development Authority and the Karachi Electric Supply Corporation. In the telecom sector, Pakistan Telecommunication Company Limited maintains exclusive control over land lines and switching (though other aspects of telecommunications have been deregulated). In the airline industry, the dominant carrier is the state-owned Pakistan International Airlines, though two private airlines also provide service.

Cartels also feature in the economy's cement and sugar industries, which are further buttressed by high import duties.[4]

Foreign Ownership Restrictions

Foreign investors, welcomed by the Foreign Private Investment (Promotion and Protection) Act of 1976 and the Economic Reforms Act of 1992, can establish and acquire business enterprises in nearly all sectors of the Pakistani economy.[5] License requirements have generally been abolished, except for petroleum-related ventures. The government's investment policy promises full repatriation of original capital, capital gains, dividends, and other profits—upon the approval of the State Bank of Pakistan. There are no restrictions on technology transfers into or out of the country. Pakistani law protects against expropriation, for example by ensuring compensation in the case of a public taking.

Tax Incentives

Pakistan grants significant tax and duty incentives to two categories of industries: "priority industries" (including tourism, housing, and construction) and "value-added export industries" (manufactured goods such as garments, bed linens, surgical instruments, and sporting goods).[6] For priority industries, the government has repealed minimum equity investment and national ownership requirements; it has also reduced the maximum customs duty from 25 to 10 percent on imported plant machinery and equipment. Value-added export industries enjoy even better incentives: zero duties on imported plant, machinery, and equipment, and a 50 percent first-year depreciation allowance. In return, Pakistan imposes export performance requirements on all industries that receive these incentives. Such obligations might, for example, require the export of 50 percent of production during the first 10 years of operation.

Pakistan is considering tax simplification by consolidating approximately 20 federal taxes into three major categories: sales tax, income tax, and customs duties. At the provincial level, the number of taxes has already been reduced from 29 to 8. Consolidation has clear advantages for taxpayers and the government, through both simplification and a reduction in the number of potential corruption encounters.

---

4. In the retail food sector, the government has a voice in the pricing of essential foodstuffs. For further information, see www.jang.com.pk.

5. There are four restricted areas: arms and munitions, high explosives, currency/mint operations, and radioactive substances.

6. Tax relief has also been provided for modernizing and replacing equipment in existing industries.

Pakistan's Central Board of Revenue is being restructured to improve tax administration. In addition, a universal self-assessment system was recently introduced, whereby returns submitted by taxpayers are provisionally accepted as settlement of their tax liabilities. Audits are focused on a random sample of returns.

The United States has expressed concern over the discriminatory application of internal sales taxes in the pharmaceutical industry. Imported raw materials used to make pharmaceuticals are taxed at 15 percent, while identical raw materials produced domestically are exempt from taxation. Another US tax issue is the very high tax rate of 30 percent on motion picture royalties paid for US films shown in Pakistani theaters.

Pakistan has signed treaties for the avoidance of double taxation with more than 52 countries, including the United States. However, the US-Pakistan treaty provides very little tax relief from statutory withholding rates (30 percent) on international income flows, apart from FDI earnings. Thus, the bilateral US-Pakistan withholding tax rates for interest and most royalties (including film royalties) are 30 percent in both directions. However, the rate for FDI dividends paid by a subsidiary firm to its parent (which owns more than 50 percent of the voting stock) is capped at 15 percent.[7]

Corruption

The International Monetary Fund (IMF) recently singled out corruption as the major obstacle in boosting foreign investment in Pakistan. Both domestic and foreign business firms face significant problems relating to the "enforcement of contracts, financial obligations, bankruptcy law, and the interpretation of tax laws. [The Pakistani government now appears to be] focusing on accountability, and is liberalizing policies and privatizing state entities to attract investment and boost the national economy."[8]

Pakistan's National Accountability Bureau, the Federal Investigation Agency, and the Provincial Anti-Corruption Departments, along with federal and provincial ombudsmen, are all responsible for combating corruption. Nevertheless, corruption remains widespread in government procurement, the awarding of international contracts, and tax administration. Speculative estimates suggest that 30 percent of the original costs of some projects may end up illicitly benefiting contractors and officials in the form of kickbacks and commissions.[9] As one step toward correcting

---

7. Derived from PricewaterhouseCoopers' *Worldwide Summaries on Corporate Taxes 2004–2005*, 901.

8. Viewpoint in "IMF Sees Hurdles in Investment in Pakistan," Islamic Republic News Agency, August 10, 2005.

9. This statement is based on research conducted by the US Commercial Service in an article titled "Pakistan Investment Climate Statement," available at www.buyusa.gov.

such problems, in June 2000 the Musharraf government fired some 1,000 officials in the Central Board of Revenue on charges of corruption and inefficiency.[10]

International Investments, Agreements, and Remittances

The United States and Pakistan signed a trade and investment framework agreement (TIFA) in 2003. The TIFA creates a joint council for considering a wide range of commercial issues and sets out basic principles that underpin bilateral trade and investment relationships.[11] The government of Pakistan has also substantially complied with its commitments concerning local content rules under the WTO Agreement on Trade-Related Investment Measures. In addition, a bilateral investment treaty (BIT) has been discussed but not yet agreed, although the conclusion of a BIT would be a logical companion to a US-Pakistan FTA.[12]

The United States has ratified BITs with some 39 countries worldwide. These provide protection for thousands of US-owned businesses and their US investors as well as for investors from the partner country. BITs ratified by the United States reflect international law standards and require prompt, adequate, and effective compensation if a country expropriates an investment made by the citizens of the partner country. BITs ensure that an investor may repatriate profits and capital, and they provide investors with the right to seek binding international arbitration of claims.[13] Responsibility for BIT policy and negotiations is shared between the US Trade Representative (USTR) and the Department of State, after which each BIT requires Senate approval before entering into force.

Pakistan has signed its own bilateral agreements for the promotion and protection of investment with 46 countries, including China, France, Germany, Iran, Japan, the Netherlands, Switzerland, the United Arab Emirates, and the United Kingdom, all of which include dispute settlement procedures. If a dispute cannot be settled informally, investors can

---

10. The cases involved misappropriation of government funds, money laundering, fraud committed in the purchase of project equipment, award of large projects and services contracts in violation of prescribed rules and regulations, sale of government lands at giveaway prices, allotment of residential lands to favorites, and failure to repay huge loans from nationalized commercial banks and financial institutions.

11. A draft for a Business Development Forum was prepared in 1996 to facilitate business development between both countries. However, this project remains on the drawing board.

12. In January 2006 the United States and Pakistan concluded a fourth round of talks on the BIT proposal. Details are available at www.bilaterals.org.

13. Details are available at the US State Department's Web site, www.state.gov.

take the case to a court in the host country, or to an ad hoc arbitration panel established under the UN Commission on International Trade Law, the International Center for Settlement of Investment Disputes, or the Court of Arbitration of the International Chamber of Commerce.[14]

In ongoing BIT negotiations between the United States and Pakistan, progress has been impeded by disagreements over intellectual property rights and specific dispute resolution clauses.[15] The differences are fairly technical, and may be resolved in the course of further talks.

Portfolio Investment

The index of share prices in Pakistan for September 2005, as reported by the IMF, stood at 292, well over twice the level reported in 2000 (IMF's *International Financial Statistics 2005*, 42). The robust stock market underlines the attractiveness of Pakistan's portfolio investment environment. In recent years the country's equity market has grown tremendously, both institutionally and in size—whether measured in terms of number of companies listed or market capitalization. The market capital value of listed equity shares recently set a new all-time record of Rs. 2.9 trillion, almost $50 billion (for further information, see www.dawn.com). According to the US State Department's 2005 report on Pakistan's investment climate, Pakistan's equity markets are among the world's best performing over the past three years, even if they remain relatively small and illiquid by global standards.[16] Of the three stock exchanges in Pakistan—Karachi, Lahore, and Islamabad—Karachi is the dominant exchange. It lists approximately 780 companies, and trading volume increased from around 1 million shares a day in 1990 to approximately 50 million shares a day in 2004.[17]

---

14. One recent case is a dispute regarding a contract between Pakistan International Airlines (PIA) and a US company to centralize PIA's reservation system. The new managing director of PIA accused the US company of irregularities and kickbacks. In an effort to restore the contract, negotiations ensued between the US company, PIA, and the Pakistani government. These negotiations are currently ongoing. For more information see www.buyusa.gov/pakistan.

15. The intellectual property rights (IPR) questions are raised in an article titled "BIT with US: Pakistan Opposes Inclusion of IPR," available at www.bilaterals.org. Dispute resolution is covered in an article titled "Pakistan-US Differences over BIT Persist," available at www.bilaterals.org.

16. For more information on the equity market, see *2005 Investment Climate Statement—Pakistan*, available at www.state.gov. In 1997 the Asian Development Bank provided Pakistan with a loan of $250 million for the purpose of developing the share markets. Evidently, this loan was used to good advantage.

17. The Karachi Stock Exchange has posted some of the "highest returns within the global emerging market universe over the past four years" (Shehryar Ahmad, "Karachi Stock Exchange Showcases a Booming Pakistani Equity Market," *DinarStandard*, October 20, 2005, www.dinarstandard.com).

The Securities and Exchange Commission of Pakistan and the Registrar of Companies share responsibility for public regulation of the securities markets. The regulatory authority of these bodies derives from the Securities and Exchange Ordinance of 1969, the Securities and Exchange Rules of 1981, and the Companies Ordinance of 1984. Pakistan's Securities and Exchange Commission recently launched reforms to check possible insider trading and market manipulation by big brokerage houses.[18]

In a major move to attract foreign portfolio investment, the government announced a new set of policies in 2000.[19] The policy package includes a capital gains tax exemption, an exemption of "bonus shares" from income tax,[20] the exemption of foreigners from withholding tax on certain interest payments, and a repeal of the turnover tax on sale of shares.[21]

Remittances by Pakistani Expatriates

Pakistan attracts significant remittances of foreign exchange from its expatriate citizens. According to the World Bank, remittances are now the second largest source of external finance for developing countries, after FDI (World Bank 2005). Foreign residents of the United States—the largest national source of workers' remittances to developing countries—paid global remittances of over $34 billion in 2003. As reported by the World Bank, these remittances tend to be stable and may directly benefit the poor.[22] Pakistan's remittances reached $4 billion in 2003, placing it fifth among remittance-receiving countries from all sources (the top four are India, Mexico, the Philippines, and China). Recent growth in recorded remittances can be partially explained by the fact that, since September 11, 2001, money has shifted away from informal (and unrecorded) money transfer systems to regular banks and wire services.

---

18. See "Police Guard Pakistan Stock Exchange," *Aljazeera*, March 25, 2005.

19. Further information can be found at www.buyusa.gov/pakistan.

20. "Bonus shares" are stock dividends that are paid in shares.

21. Pakistan's market for bonds and other fixed income securities has not developed as quickly. At around 14 percent of GDP, Pakistan's savings rate is the lowest among developing Asian economies, and this may contribute to the slow development of the bond market.

22. Living standards may improve, for example, when remittances finance better health care, nutrition, housing, and education. See the World Bank's feature article, "When Money Really Matters—Remittances Vital to South Asia," July 19, 2005, available at www.worldbank.org.pk.

Services

US Services and Trade Barriers

The United States is the premier producer and exporter of services, with its service sector constituting about 64 percent of GDP and about 30 percent of total US exports (BEA 2005). The main service exports are business, professional, and technical services, travel services, royalties and license fees, and financial services. The United States has the largest insurance market in the world, and its telecommunications market also is highly competitive, with mobile, fixed line, and cable services as well as voice over Internet protocol.

Although barriers to foreign entry prevail in several US service sectors—finance, telecommunications, transportation, and professional services—the USTR has affirmed US intentions to further liberalize these activities.

Key Pakistani Service Sectors and Barriers

Foreign investment in services is generally allowed in Pakistan, subject to a minimum initial capital stake (now $150,000, compared with a previous minimum of $300,000).[23] Policy reforms enacted in 2004 enable foreign investors to hold a 100 percent equity stake in service ventures, and permit repatriation of 100 percent of profits (the previous limit was 60 percent). With some limitations, foreign investors in the service sectors may remit technical fees and royalties. Table 7.4 indicates the share of each service sector in Pakistan's GDP.

Telecommunications

Pakistan recently deregulated the telecommunications sector in order to comply with WTO commitments, ending the exclusive right of the state-controlled Pakistan Telecommunication Company Limited to provide basic telephone services. The government has subsequently issued 12 licenses to long distance telephone companies, 90 licenses to local loop regional telephone companies, and 70 licenses to wireless local loop companies. The 2005 *Asian Development Outlook* forecasts fast expansion of Pakistan's telecom sector as the new firms launch their operations.

---

23. Investors in information technology services are not subject to the requirement of a minimum initial investment and may hold a 100 percent equity stake.

Table 7.4 Service sectors in Pakistan, 2004–05

Sector	Share in GDP (percent)
Wholesale and retail trade	19.1
Transport, storage, and communications	11.1
Services	9.6
Public administration and defense	6.0
Finance and insurance	3.7
Ownership of dwellings	2.9
Total	52.4

Source: Government of Pakistan (2005a).

Finance and Insurance

After the WTO Financial Services Agreement was signed in 1997, the government of Pakistan granted new rights to foreign banks and foreign securities firms, and the State Bank of Pakistan eliminated restrictions on the number of branches for foreign banks.[24] Liabilities to foreign holders, deposited in Pakistani banks, reached $475 million in September 2005. These deposits by foreign holders (mainly banks) reflect a degree of international activity.

As another financial sector reform, Pakistan opened the insurance market. Foreign investors are now entitled to hold a 51 percent equity share of companies operating in the life and general insurance sectors. As a condition of operation, they are required to bring in a minimum of $2 million in foreign capital and raise an equal amount of equity in the local market. Pakistan does not regulate insurance premiums; however, the government issued a new insurance law in 2000 that raised capital adequacy standards and enhanced policyholder protections.

Despite liberalization, market domination in the insurance sector may create a substantial barrier to entry. The state-owned State Life Insurance Company writes over 80 percent of Pakistan's life insurance policies, and five companies account for 78 percent of the general insurance market. The government of Pakistan permits only the National Insurance Company to insure public-sector firms, while private-sector firms are obliged to use the state-owned Pakistan Reinsurance Company for at least 10 percent of their reinsurance requirements.

---

24. Both foreign and local banks must submit an annual branch expansion plan to the State Bank of Pakistan for approval. Foreign brokers, like their Pakistani counterparts, must register with the Securities and Exchange Commission of Pakistan.

Other Services

In the professional service sector, foreign professionals can offer legal and engineering consultancy services with 100 percent equity participation (previous regulations required that Pakistanis hold 40 percent of the equity for five years). Minimal capital requirements for professional services have been reduced from $300,000 to $150,000 since the 2004 reforms. Today it is no longer necessary for a legal consultant to be licensed in order to offer legal advice in Pakistan. However, foreign lawyers cannot appear in court or formally litigate cases unless they are licensed in Pakistan. The Islamabad-based Pakistan Bar Council licenses attorneys in Pakistan, with no legal impediments to the admission of foreign lawyers. Likewise, foreign doctors must register with the Pakistan Medical and Dental Council, and foreign engineers with the Pakistan Engineering Council, in order to practice their professions.

With respect to entertainment services, the government of Pakistan prohibits the importation of all films that are considered inconsistent with local religious and cultural standards.

Recommendations

In addition to the factors discussed in this chapter, the US FTAs with both Chile and Singapore provide valuable insights on how to approach a US-Pakistan FTA for investment and service sector liberalization. In the US-Chile FTA, specific measures were aimed at both tax reform and improved governance, with the result that, in the case of telecommunications services, Chile has achieved a high degree of market competitiveness and openness. In its index of foreign restrictiveness as of May 2005, Chile was only 0.09 for telecommunications services (a lower value means a more open sector). By comparison, Singapore's score was 0.44 and Pakistan's 0.55 for comparable telecommunications services.[25] The US-Singapore FTA achieved significant liberalization with respect to professional services; box 7.1 provides a summary of the service sector provisions in this FTA.

The development of investment and service sector exchanges between Pakistan and the United States holds much potential. While friction levels are generally low with respect to investment in Pakistan, improving the confidence of foreign investors remains a paramount objective. The conditions described above suggest several possible recommendations.

---

25. For more information, see the Findlay and Warren Restrictiveness Index on Trade in Services, available at www.pc.gov.au.

Box 7.1 Selected provisions relating to services in the US-Singapore FTA

Item	Provision
Scope of measures	Measures by central, regional, or local government affecting cross-border trade in services (negative list).
Schedules	Annex 8A (measures) and 8B (sectors) list scheduled exceptions to national treatment and most favored nation (MFN) treatment; market access; local presence; performance requirements; or senior management and boards of directors.
Market access	Applies to all sectors unless otherwise specified in the agreement. Removes limitations on the number of services providers; the value of services transactions; the quantity of services output; the number of persons that may be employed in a particular sector; and measures which restrict or require specific types of of legal entity or joint venture.
Most favored nation treatment	Unconditional MFN treatment in like circumstances.
National treatment	National treatment, unless otherwise specified in Annexes 8A and 8B.
Local presence	A Party shall not require a service supplier of the other Party to establish or maintain a representative office or any form of enterprise, or to be resident, in its territory as a condition for the cross-border supply of a service.
Domestic regulations	Measures relating to qualification and licence requirements should be based on objective and transparent criteria, not more burderdensome than necessary to ensure the quality of the service, and should not themselves restrict the provision of the service.
Transparency measures	Mandates publication of laws, regulations, procedures, and administrative rulings affecting trade in services, or the reason for failure to comply with these mandates.
Entry of business persons	Secures temporary access for business visitors and investors for up to 90 days. Also grants, not subject to labor market tests, 5,400 US work visas for different categories of Singaporean professionals. This concession was reciprocated by Singapore.
Full set of provisions on services	Chapter 8 Trade in Services Chapter 9 Telecommunications Chapter 10 Financial Services Chapter 11 Temporary Entry of Business Persons Annexes to chapters 8, 10, and 11.

Sources: USTR (2003b); MTI (2003).

Investment

- Our first recommendation is to conclude the US-Pakistan BIT both for its symbolic value as a seal of "good investment practices" and for its specific provisions. The treaty would enhance the legal certainty for US-owned firms that choose to do business in Pakistan.

- As part of the BIT text, or as a separate codicil, treaty benefits should be denied to an investor (or investee) that engages in significant corrupt practices. This provision will put foreign firms on notice that, if they corruptly procure license rights or other benefits, they stand to lose the protection afforded by the bilateral investment treaty.

- Pakistan and the United States should renegotiate their bilateral income tax treaty, so as to reduce sharply the withholding rates on dividends, interest, and royalties (including film royalties). Pakistan should also consider a program of 10-year tax holidays in its export processing zones. Both measures could encourage inward foreign investment. However, special tax benefits should be subject to revocation in the event of significant corruption on the part of the foreign investor.

- Taxes on imported and domestically produced raw materials should be enforced at the same rate in order to avoid discrimination. Either comparable taxes should be collected on domestically produced raw materials, or taxes on imported materials should be abandoned.

- Increased competition would be desirable for state-owned firms that are exempt from the Monopolies and Restrictive Trade Practices Ordinance, such as the Water and Power Development Authority, Karachi Electric Supply Corporation, and Pakistan International Airlines. Competition could be created by privatizing all or parts of these companies and allowing foreign companies to bid for the assets.

Services

- Pakistan should consider privatizing the State Life Insurance Company, and allow US and other foreign firms to compete in the bidding. Pakistan should also review competitive conditions in the insurance market and allow foreign firms to write insurance and reinsurance policies on a comparable basis as incumbent domestic companies, and permit access to public-sector insurance markets.

- The US FTAs with Chile and Singapore can serve as models for a US-Pakistan FTA. In the case of Singapore, reciprocal provisions cover a wide range of service activities. For example, the agreement removed all limitations on the number of service providers, the value of service transactions, the quantity of services output, and the number of persons that may be employed per sector.

Estimates from Gravity and Computable General Equilibrium Models

DEAN DeROSA and JOHN P. GILBERT

Quantitative assessments of the trade expansion and income gains fostered by a US-Pakistan FTA require detailed consideration of the economic structure and multilateral trade patterns of both countries. To carry out this task, we use both gravity and computable general equilibrium (CGE) models. Our gravity model is an augmented version of Andrew Rose's (2004) framework. Whereas Rose analyzed total merchandise trade between multiple partner countries, we use the CGE model to examine disaggregated merchandise trade. We also incorporate more extensive information about regional trade agreements (RTAs) than Rose originally considered. Our CGE model is based on the comparative static framework of world trade and economic activity designed by the Global Trade Analysis Project (GTAP). The GTAP model disaggregates world merchandise trade by sectors and also (unlike the gravity model) covers world trade in services.

The reason for presenting estimates from two models is to increase our confidence in the general tenor of the results. Whereas the gravity model is grounded in the empirical tradition of trade analysis, the CGE model rests foremost on theoretical foundations. Thus each model serves as a check on the other. The basic features and results of our gravity and CGE models are described in the sections that follow. Appendix B provides technical details on the two models.

Dean DeRosa is a visiting fellow at the Institute for International Economics. John P. Gilbert is associate professor of economics in the Department of Economics, Utah State University, Logan, Utah.

Gravity Model: Construction and Results

With the proliferation of preferential trading arrangements in the 1990s, the gravity model has become a widely used tool for analyzing the consequences of bilateral and regional trade agreements.[1] The basic gravity model evaluates thousands of two-way bilateral trade flows, measured in a common currency (adjusted for inflation), against the gravitational "mass" of explanatory variables describing the characteristics of bilateral trading partners. The "core" variables are distance and joint real GDP.[2] Nearly all gravity models find that two-way trade between countries is significantly greater the larger the combined GDP and the shorter the distance between them. Additional explanatory variables are specified as well, and these are of greatest interest as they show how much two-way trade expands or contracts from the quantity predicted by the basic core variables on account of the partners' institutional or policy features. For instance, trading partners that share a common border, a common language, or a common currency are typically found to enjoy significantly greater mutual trade.

To analyze RTAs, a dichotomous (0, 1) explanatory variable—often called a "dummy" variable—is introduced to represent preferential arrangements, individually or on a combined basis. If the coefficient on the dummy variable is positive and significant, then the RTA is judged to expand trade between the partners. The extent of trade expansion is usually measured in percentage terms, which can be derived from the estimated coefficient on the dummy variable. Given the log-linear specification of the gravity model regression equation,[3] the impact of an FTA on bilateral trade can be computed in percentage terms as $100*[exp(b_{rta})-1.00]$. In this expression, b_{rta} is the estimated coefficient for the dummy variable representing the presence of an RTA, and $exp(b_{rta})$ is

---

1. Greenaway and Milner (2002) provide an excellent introduction to and review of the recent literature on the gravity model and its econometric applications for assessing the trade and other consequences of preferential trading arrangements among regional trading partners.

2. A third "core" variable is joint GDP per capita. A higher joint GDP per capita figure implies a smaller joint population figure (for a given joint GDP level). Less combined population tends to depress the bilateral level of trade; hence the coefficient on joint GDP per capita is frequently negative. However, some gravity model investigators consider joint GDP per capita to serve as a proxy for accumulated physical and human capital, with the expectation that the coefficient on this variable in the regression equation would be positive.

3. In a log-linear regression equation, the dependent variable (here, two-way bilateral trade) is expressed in logarithmic terms, whereas some independent variables (notably the discrete dummy variables) are expressed simply as linear numbers (e.g., 0 or 1), while others (notably the continuous variables, such as distance or joint GDP) are expressed in logarithmic terms.

the value of the natural number e raised to the exponent b_{rta}. For example, if the coefficient b_{rta} is 0.33, then the value of $exp(b_{rta})$ is 1.39, and the percentage expansion in trade is estimated as 100*[1.39–1.00], which equals 39 percent.

Analytical Framework

We investigate the potential for expansion of US-Pakistan trade under an FTA following the approach of Jeffrey Frankel (1997) and Inbom Choi and Jeffrey Schott (2001), among others, using the general framework of the Rose (2004) gravity model. Our approach represents the existing RTAs on a combined basis, circa 2000, as reported to the World Trade Organization (WTO). It also tries to account for the possibility that the existing level of US-Pakistan trade is significantly greater or smaller than the level predicted by the basic explanatory variables of the gravity model in the absence of an FTA. It does this in two ways described below.

Our econometric results are based on bilateral trade flows worldwide from 1962 to 1999, compiled by Robert Feenstra and colleagues (2005). Those data were disaggregated according to the 4-digit Standard International Trade Classification (SITC), whereas for the present analysis they were aggregated to the 1-digit SITC level and deflated by the US consumer price index. The data were then concorded, by year and country pair, to the extensive set of explanatory variables compiled for the Rose (2004) gravity model.[4] The "core" explanatory variables in the Rose dataset include distance between trading partners, joint real GDP, and joint real GDP per capita. The Rose dataset also includes a number of country-specific variables, such as landlocked or island status, language, colonization, and dates of independence. In all, the dataset constructed for the present analysis, using the augmented Rose gravity model, entails nearly 940,000 observations, covering bilateral trade for about 61,000 combinations of commodities and pairs of trading countries.[5]

To the core explanatory variables are added dummy variables representing bilateral, regional, and other preferential trading arrangements such as the generalized system of preferences (GSP).[6] Whereas Rose

---

4. The regression variables constructed from the Feenstra et al. and Rose datasets are described in appendix table B.1.

5. Notwithstanding its large size, the combined Feenstra et al. and Rose dataset has some gaps, and excludes Taiwan and some centrally planned economies because of holes in the two datasets.

6. Under the GSP, a number of advanced countries extend preferences to less developed countries on a nonreciprocal basis. The GSP programs of major industrial and other countries are monitored by the UN Conference on Trade and Development (UNCTAD), including through a series of manuals describing the individual programs. See UNCTAD (2004a).

(2004) treated RTAs on a combined basis, covering 10 largely multilateral RTAs around the world,[7] we utilize official information about trade agreements notified to the WTO (Crawford and Fiorentino 2005) to consider 60 bilateral and regional trade agreements spanning the gravity model estimation period 1962–99.[8] The RTAs are represented by three independent RTA variables covering: (1) the European Union itself and 8 RTAs to which it is a party, plus 2 RTAs to which the United States is a party (the US-Israel FTA and the North American Free Trade Agreement [NAFTA]); (2) 10 RTAs organized by other high-income countries (HICs); and (3) 39 RTAs organized solely among middle- and low-income countries (MICs and LICs).[9]

The treatment of recent bilateral and regional trade agreements enables estimation of different gravity model coefficients for the impact on bilateral trade, according to whether the European Union or the United States is a party, whether the pact includes other (smaller) high-income countries, or whether the pact is solely between middle- and/or low-income countries. There are two reasons for these distinctions: first, a pact that includes either of the two giant economies (the European Union or the United States) could plausibly inspire a bigger percentage change in trade than one that includes a smaller high-income economy, such as Australia or Sweden; second, a group that includes only middle- or low-income countries might have more emphasis on diplomatic accommodation than economic liberalization, and thus might exert a smaller percentage impact on trade.

In our calculations, two variables representing US-Pakistan trade integration and openness are specified in addition to Rose's set of explanatory variables. For the first variable, actual trade integration between Pakistan and the United States is captured by a dummy (0, 1) variable for trade between the two countries, as if an FTA were already in place. For the second variable, "openness" is measured by a separate dummy variable for each country that takes the value of 1 each time Pakistan (or the

---

7. The Rose dataset includes dummy variables with a value of 1 for 10 prominent RTAs: the Association of Southeast Asian Nations (ASEAN), European Union, US-Israel FTA, North American Free Trade Agreement (NAFTA), Caribbean Community (Caricom), Agreement on Trade and Commercial Relations between the Government of Australia and the Government of Papua New Guinea (Patcra), Australia–New Zealand Closer Economic Relations Trade Agreement (Anzcerta), Central American Common Market (CACM), South Pacific Regional Trade and Economic Cooperation Agreement (Sparteca), and the Southern Cone Common Market (Mercosur).

8. According to Schott (2004a), by May 2003 some 155 bilateral and regional trade agreements had been notified to the WTO under Article 24 of the General Agreement on Tariffs and Trade (GATT).

9. The majority of the agreements included in the third RTA variable are bilateral and regional trade agreements among small developing countries and among the newly independent states of Eastern Europe. See Crawford and Fiorentino (2005) and appendix B.

United States) is a trading partner with any other country. The estimated coefficients for the openness variables suggest the degree to which either country's trade with the world is greater or less than the norm established both by the "core" gravity model variables and by other variables on the right-hand side of the gravity equation.

Finally, in light of concerns about the adverse impact of corruption on commercial ties, we have added an explanatory variable representing the sentiments of foreign firms about doing business not only in Pakistan but also in up to 50 other countries worldwide, as published since 1995 by Transparency International (TI). Specifically, we have added a "joint corruption perceptions" (shown in tables 8A.1 and 8A.2 as "joint TI index") variable to the Rose gravity model dataset. This variable is formed by the product of logarithmic TI scores for business integrity in each country covered by the TI published data for 1995–99. In this formulation of the model, the greater the perceived integrity of business transactions in the two trading countries, as measured by a higher joint TI index of integrity rankings, the greater the expected level of their mutual trade.[10]

Results from the Gravity Model

Tables 8A.1 and 8A.2 present the regression results for overall trade (SITC 0 through 9) and for trade by major commodity categories—food, beverages, and tobacco (SITC 0 and 1); raw materials (SITC 2 and 4); mineral fuels and lubricants (SITC 3); and manufactures (SITC 5 through 8). Regression coefficients are presented for the overall period 1962–99 and for two subperiods, 1990–99 and 1995–99, which correspond to the decade of the 1990s and the post–Uruguay Round period respectively. Finally, the gravity model estimates are presented both with and without the US-Pakistan trade integration and openness explanatory variables. As it turns out, against the backdrop of bilateral trade flows worldwide, the presence or absence of these additional variables makes little difference to the other coefficients.

The regression results for both total and disaggregated trade mirror the widely reported empirical robustness of the gravity model. In particular, the core explanatory variables, led by distance, joint real GDP, and joint real GDP per capita, bear the anticipated signs and are generally significant at high levels. Thus, for instance, bilateral trade is positively

---

10. Given the limited number of countries covered by the Transparency International rankings, bringing the joint TI index as an explanatory variable into the Rose gravity model cuts in half the number of observations available for estimating the model's parameters for the subperiod 1995–99. As seen in tables 8.1 through 8.3, adding the joint TI index also requires dropping two explanatory variables (*common country* and *currency union*) from the estimating equation for 1995–99, because these variables are collinear in the reduced sample, and this creates econometric problems.

related to the joint GDP of the partner countries and negatively related to the distance between them. Similarly, countries sharing a common border tend to trade significantly more with one another, whereas landlocked countries tend to trade significantly less than other pairs of countries. The influence on bilateral trade of a higher joint TI index, showing greater integrity in both domestic and international business dealings, is widely found to be positive and significant.[11]

The overall explanatory power of our gravity model, using disaggregated bilateral trade data from the Feenstra et al. dataset (R-squared generally about 0.30–0.40), is appreciably lower than that found by Rose (2004) using aggregate bilateral trade data (R-squared 0.50–0.60). An exception, however, is the impressive explanatory power of the regression results in table 8A.2 for manufactures (R-squared 0.50 and higher).

Gravity model studies by Rose (2004) and previous investigators, using aggregate bilateral trade data, frequently report estimated coefficients near unity for RTA variables representing about 10 "strong" RTAs combined. By contrast, in our analysis the estimated coefficients for our three RTA variables (distinguished by the character of each partner country) are generally less than 0.50, except the coefficients for the RTAs in which the European Union and the United States are partners in the post–Uruguay Round period (1995–99). For the EU and US RTAs in the late 1990s, the estimated RTA coefficients substantially exceed 0.50, both for total trade and for trade in agricultural and manufactured goods (the coefficients are especially high for trade in manufactures). Interestingly, the coefficient estimates for the middle- and low-income country RTAs variable are widely negative and significant throughout the 1990s, suggesting that these agreements are not robust in economic terms. It is also worth noting that the estimated coefficients for EU and US RTAs are sometimes substantially higher than the estimated coefficients for the other HIC RTAs variable, especially for trade in manufactures in the post–Uruguay Round period.

Separate regression results (not reported) that include a variable for the US-Israel FTA and NAFTA find an estimated coefficient for these two RTAs that is substantially higher—by more than two to one—than the estimated coefficient for the EU RTAs variable.

The openness variable of the gravity model reports the extent to which Pakistan's actual trade deviates from the levels predicted by the standard variables in the gravity model for an imaginary country with almost identical conditions (e.g., the same GDP, the same distance from markets, the same common borders, etc.). The only difference is that the "imaginary Pakistan" trades with its partners to the average extent pre-

---

11. Mineral fuels are an exception, reflecting the strong cross-country correlation between oil wealth and corruption.

dicted by all the right-hand variables in the gravity equation except the openness term.

The openness term (–0.93 for the whole period) indicates that Pakistan's actual trade falls below the average benchmark established by the model both for total trade and for trade in individual sectors. This suggests that protection and other "trade resistance" factors are especially strong in Pakistan. The model indicates that Pakistan's total trade is 61 percent less than the average benchmark. The openness coefficient for individual sectors gives similar results. Put another way, if Pakistan were to achieve the average level of openness of all countries (a coefficient of 0.00), its commerce with the world would more than double. By contrast, the regression coefficients for the US openness variable are uniformly positive and statistically significant.

Estimated coefficients for the US-Pakistan trade integration variable on a sector-by-sector basis (table 8A.2) are significant mainly for manufactured products, indicating that bilateral trade may already exceed the international norm for this important trade category.[12] Further, Pakistan's negative openness term suggests that US exports to Pakistan would grow more rapidly than Pakistani exports to the United States under the market-opening influence of a US-Pakistan FTA. The trade integration coefficients also suggest that nonmanufactures, especially agricultural products and raw materials, would be prime candidates for trade expansion in both directions. Other evidence, reported below, suggests that there is also considerable room for expanded trade in manufactures between Pakistan and the United States.[13]

The implications of the highly significant estimates for the joint TI index deserve additional consideration. The mean value of this explanatory variable is substantially lower for bilateral trade involving Pakistan (2.34) than for trade involving other country pairs (3.19), implying that poor business practices in Pakistan significantly reduce its trade with the United States and other countries. Based on the joint TI index coefficient estimate of 0.41 for overall trade during 1995–99 (table 8A.1), the "integrity burden" on Pakistan's trade (compared with the world norm) can be calculated on the order of 35 percent [100*(0.41)*(3.19–2.34)]. In other words, Pakistan's poor business practices result in 35 percent lower trade for the country than would otherwise be the case. If the US-Pakistan FTA contributes to better business practices in Pakistan, ultimately raising

---

12. The evidence is mixed on this point, however, in that the US-Pakistan integration variable is positive but insignificant for trade in manufactures during the post–Uruguay Round period.

13. Results of the CGE model support this discussion, as they also project that a US-Pakistan FTA will lead to faster growth rates for bilateral agricultural trade as well as for US exports. However, unlike what is argued in this paragraph, results from the CGE model do not show that trade expansion in agriculture will occur in both directions.

Table 8.1 Bilateral trade expansion predicted by gravity model coefficients for EU and US RTAs (percent)

	1962–99	1990–1999	1995–99	Simple average
Total trade (SITC 0-9)	13	22	95	43
Disaggregated trade				
Agriculture (SITC 0 and 1)	17	13	84	38
Raw material (SITC 2 and 4)	6	23	60	30
Fuels (SITC 3)	0	0	0	0
Manufacturing goods (SITC 5-8)	26	40	156	74

them to the norm of other countries, then Pakistan might instead enjoy an "integrity dividend" of 35 percent in its trade—not only with the United States but also with other trading partners.

Table 8.1 reports the bilateral trade expansion effects implied by the significant coefficient estimates for the EU and US RTAs variable in tables 8A.1 and 8A.2.[14] The simple average column gives equal weight to the coefficients estimated for each of the overlapping periods. Based on the simple average percentage expansion for total trade and for the four sectors taken together, it appears that overall US-Pakistan merchandise trade might expand, under an FTA, by a central estimate of about 43 percent, holding all other factors constant. Two-way trade in agriculture and manufactures might expand by about 38 percent and 74 percent, respectively. Based on data for the post–Uruguay Round period (1995–99), the impact for Pakistan of an FTA with the United States or the European Union as a partner might be significantly larger: a 95 percent increase for total trade, an 84 percent gain for agricultural trade, and a boost of 156 percent for trade in manufactures.

If the estimation results cited previously—those incorporating the US RTAs variable independently as an additional explanatory variable—are to be believed, then the expansion of US-Pakistan trade in agriculture and especially in industrial and other manufactured goods would be well in excess of 100 percent. Such an expansion of US-Pakistan trade in manufactures may seem implausible, but the figure accords with the negative

---

14. The figures in table 8.1 are based on the regressions that include the dummy variables for US-Pakistan trade integration and openness. However, as mentioned, the dummy variables make very little difference to the RTA coefficients. In table 8.1, the highly implausible negative estimated values for the coefficients of the EU and US RTAs variable that occur in the regressions for trade in fuels are treated as zero.

openness term estimated for Pakistan. Moreover, a great deal of bilateral trade expansion could be induced by improved business practices and by a leap in bilateral foreign direct investment, as suggested in chapter 7.[15]

CGE Model: Construction and Results

CGE models, based on general equilibrium principles, are built with the objective of turning abstract theories into practical tools. A number of features distinguish CGE models from other widely used frameworks for trade policy analysis (especially gravity models). In particular, the actions of economic agents are modeled explicitly through utility and profit maximizing assumptions, while economywide resource and expenditure constraints are rigorously enforced. Because they link markets into a single system, CGE techniques effectively capture feedback and flow-through effects induced by policy changes. Economic distortions often have repercussions beyond the sector in which they occur and CGE models are designed to capture these indirect effects. The models are particularly well suited to the examination of free trade arrangements, where multisector liberalization is undertaken in at least two economies simultaneously and where adverse consequences of discriminatory preferences may well arise (Panagariya 2000).

Against these significant advantages, CGE models are highly data intensive and subject to several uncertainties: How should equations be specified, what parameters should be used, and how should the FTA experiment be designed? Because CGE simulation results are sensitive to these decisions, they should be viewed cautiously. Our CGE model is based on the GTAP framework, a publicly available model that is widely accepted and used. The GTAP model is a multiregion, multisector model that assumes perfect competition and constant returns to scale. Other CGE frameworks, sometimes characterized as "dynamic" models, assume that countries enjoy increasing returns to scale as they specialize, and that monopolistic markups are eroded by trade liberalization. They may also assume that freer trade spurs investment and productivity. These additional assumptions typically result in larger calculated trade and economic gains as a consequence of removing barriers. By contrast, the results reported here, using a comparative statics framework, are probably conservative.

---

15. Ignoring the other coefficients, and focusing on post–Uruguay Round estimation results, the model suggests that overall US-Pakistan trade might grow by 184 percent, led by expansion of trade in manufactures (232 percent) and agriculture (306 percent). Even these results are plausible in light of Pakistan's negative openness term.

Experimental Design

The proposed FTA between Pakistan and the United States is first simulated independently of the existence of other actual and potential FTAs. The results thus reflect the estimated effect of the proposal in isolation from any liberalization that occurred after the reference year for the GTAP6 database (2001) or that might be on the drawing boards.

We then consider an all-partners experiment, in which the proposed US-Pakistan FTA is implemented simultaneously with a selection of other "new" US FTAs (those ratified after the GTAP6 database was assembled) and prospective US FTAs that might be negotiated in 2006 and 2007. The "new" US FTAs considered in the model are Australia, the Central American Free Trade Agreement–Dominican Republic (CAFTA-DR), Chile, Morocco, and Singapore; the prospective FTAs (in addition to the US-Pakistan FTA) are Korea, Malaysia, the Southern African Customs Union (SACU), Switzerland, and Thailand.[16]

In all cases, the arrangements are assumed to be implemented "clean," meaning that all import tariffs are eventually reduced to zero by the participating economies, on a bilateral preferential basis. Services trade barriers are also eliminated.[17] However, all other tariffs and barriers (i.e., those applied to nonparticipating economies) are left in place. In other words, possible liberalization negotiated in the WTO Doha Development Round is not taken into consideration. Moreover, in the experiment with all free trade areas, it is assumed that the FTAs are implemented only with the United States; preferential liberalization among the proposed partner regions is not considered.

To provide a benchmark for the implications of bilateral free trade areas, we also consider unilateral trade reform scenarios for Pakistan and the United States. In these scenarios, each economy is assumed to unilaterally remove all tariffs on a nondiscriminatory basis.

All of the simulations are run as exercises in comparative statics. This entails "before" and "after" pictures, allowing all the agreed bilateral liberalization to take place and all industries to adjust, but with no attempt to profile the time frame of adjustment. The factor market "closure" conditions allow full mobility of capital and labor across domestic industries. In other words, all capital and labor (both skilled and unskilled) are assumed fully employed once the adjustment process is complete. The im-

---

16. The United States has also ratified an FTA with Jordan and has signed an FTA with Bahrain, which is pending ratification. The GTAP6 database does not separately identify these two countries. In September 2005 Ambassador Robert Portman mentioned Egypt, Korea, Malaysia, and Switzerland as possible FTA partners in the near term. Since the GTAP6 database does not separately identify Egypt, that country is not shown in our tables.

17. Estimates of the extent of barriers to services were obtained from Dee, Hanslow, and Phamduc (2003).

plicit time frame is the long run, typically regarded as an adjustment period of about 10 years, although the adjustment path is not directly modeled. Land is treated as imperfectly mobile across agricultural activities, while other natural resources are assumed committed to individual industries as specific factors.

Results from the CGE Model

Estimates of the overall effect of the proposed agreement are presented in table 8A.3. The model predicts dramatic increases in the volume of bilateral trade between the United States and Pakistan, with US exports of goods and services to Pakistan increasing by 89 percent, and Pakistani exports of goods and services to the United States increasing by approximately 36 percent. Although this seems to indicate a significant imbalance, it is worth remembering that US exports amount to only 8 percent of Pakistan's total import bill. Conversely, the United States buys almost 25 percent of Pakistan's exports. Therefore, if these estimates are correct, the US-Pakistan FTA will not impose much pressure on Pakistan's balance of payments. In fact, Pakistan will still enjoy a trade surplus with the United States.

From this perspective a doubling of Pakistan's imports from the United States does not look all that dramatic—although it could present challenges for specific sectors. It might be thought that the reason for the dramatic increase in predicted US exports is that Pakistan's imports from other countries would decline once US firms enjoy a preferential tariff structure, an effect known as "trade diversion." But trade diversion is not predicted to occur with Pakistan, because the relatively large welfare effect for the country results in greater income, which is spent on imports from all countries, including countries that are not parties to an FTA with Pakistan. This income effect is large enough to outweigh the price effects of tariff preferences.

The overall welfare effects of the agreement are estimated to be small and negative for the United States but positive and substantial for Pakistan.[18] The unilateral benchmark results give some indication of why the outcomes differ for Pakistan and the United States. The United States is already a very open economy, and hence has little to gain in terms of efficiency from further liberalization. However, in the static CGE framework, the United States loses in welfare terms (although by only a small fraction of GDP) from unilateral reform due to an adverse shift in the terms of trade. Because Pakistan's market is relatively small, there are limited

---

18. The welfare effects presented in table 8.3 are measured as the equivalent variation in income. This is essentially the change in household income that is equivalent to the estimated change in GDP, at constant consumer prices.

opportunities to counter an adverse terms-of-trade shift with increased market access. In a CGE model with "dynamic" features, positive income effects would likely overshadow the adverse terms-of-trade effects. Some of the dynamic features not included in our static CGE model are enhanced competition and reduced markup margins following the elimination of trade barriers, and induced productivity in the competing domestic industries.

The welfare effects of the US-Pakistan FTA are presented in more detail in table 8A.4, for all regions in the model. Many economies suffer very small welfare losses as a consequence of the agreement, including the Central American countries, South Korea, the Philippines, and, notably, the other economies of the South Asian region (India, Bangladesh, and Sri Lanka). In addition, "preference dilution"—the phenomenon by which other FTA partners lose the benefits of preferential access to the US market when Pakistan enters into free trade with the United States—does not seem to be a significant factor for US partners, although there is a slight effect for Mexico and CAFTA-DR members. As a proportion of regional GDP, all welfare effects on nonmembers are very minor (less than 0.1 percent of GDP). Under unilateral reform, by contrast, nonmembers generally benefit.

Table 8A.5 presents details on changes in patterns of overall trade by region. The effects of the US-Pakistan FTA on nonmember exports to the United States are very small and generally negative. For Pakistan, however, the effects are more significant and positive, especially for the economies of East and Southeast Asia. This seemingly paradoxical effect reflects income expansion, as discussed above.

The CGE model allows us to predict which sectors are most likely to be affected by the proposed agreement. Table 8A.6 presents the estimated changes in the total dollar value of bilateral and total exports by economic sector. The simulations predict very large gains in US exports of some major items—processed food, chemicals, machinery and equipment (including electronic equipment), and some transport equipment. Rapid trade growth, but from a small base, is also predicted for clothing, fabricated metal products, and motor vehicles. Several of these are accorded high levels of protection in Pakistan: The GTAP6 database records a 25 percent tariff on clothing, 21 percent on fabricated metal products, and 44 percent on motor vehicles.[19] From the perspective of overall US industry exports, none of the changes are large enough at the bilateral level to have a significant impact on total exports.

For Pakistan, the bilateral export gains are smaller and concentrated in textiles and clothing. Reflecting the comparatively large role that the

---

19. While Pakistan's applied tariffs have generally declined since 2001, tariffs in these sectors remain high. Earlier chapters in this report discuss recent changes in Pakistan's tariff schedule.

United States plays in Pakistan's bilateral trade profile, these translate into significant overall trade expansion in clothing. Pakistani exports of vegetables and fruits are also expected to grow but from a low base. Other sectors decline, indicating that the reform leads to significant reallocation of production resources, and not merely changes in the regional composition of trade.

The predicted changes in bilateral trade in services are positive but relatively small: export gains of 15 percent for the United States and 7 percent for Pakistan. Moreover, total US exports of services are predicted to decline, indicating that the increase in US service exports to Pakistan represents trade diversion. The model suggests two possibilities for the small changes. The first is that the trade flow barriers estimated by Dee, Hanslow, and Phamduc (2003) are relatively small (about 5 percent). The second is that other types of barriers (capital taxes and output taxes) are not region specific in GTAP, so it is possible that data and conceptual limits lead to an understatement of the potential for expansion of bilateral services trade.

The estimated changes in output volume by sector are presented in table 8A.7. These figures are useful for understanding the possible extent of structural adjustment that might be required under the agreement. In the United States, all sectors are only marginally affected by the proposed FTA. This suggests that US adjustment issues in response to the US-Pakistan FTA would be quite modest. In Pakistan the adjustments are likely to be more substantial, with significant output declines predicted in coal, oil, and gas, leather products, chemicals, and other manufactures. However, output gains are estimated in clothing, motor vehicles, and services. Overall, the FTA output adjustments seem manageable, especially when compared with the unilateral benchmark calculations, which suggest some very large adjustments.

A final issue of concern is how the benefits of the proposed FTA are likely to be spread across society. The GTAP framework deals with this issue in the Ricardian tradition, by estimating changes in the rewards to the primary factors (capital, labor, land) used in the production process. The estimated percentage changes in real factor rewards are presented in table 8A.8. In the United States, all effects are relatively minor. In Pakistan, however, important income changes are predicted. In particular, the model predicts a decrease in the returns to natural resources, suggesting that Pakistani farming households are likely to come under pressure from increased US agricultural exports. The returns to labor, both skilled and unskilled, also appear to fall. However, the returns to capital rise by a larger magnitude than the estimated fall in returns to labor.

Because the United States has recently signed several new FTAs, and is considering others, it is important to consider how those FTAs would affect our simulation outcomes. We consider a scenario in which the proposed US-Pakistan agreement is implemented simultaneously with other current and prospective FTAs that might enter into force by 2007, with the United States as the FTA hub. As mentioned above, the current US FTAs are with Australia, CAFTA-DR, Chile, Morocco, and Singapore; prospective partners for a US FTA are Korea, Malaysia, SACU, Switzerland, and Thailand.[20] The results are presented in tables 8A.9 through 8A.13.

The main result from table 8A.9 is that the presence of the other FTA partners slightly restrains expansion but otherwise does not substantially alter the predicted changes in bilateral trade between the United States and Pakistan. However, there are substantial increases in total US trade, reflecting the broader array of trading opportunities that arise under the hub formation. Similarly, while the overall welfare effect is only slightly reduced for Pakistan, the benefits are much greater for the United States from multiple FTAs owing to terms-of-trade improvement. Even so, the gains remain a very small fraction of US GDP, reflecting both low initial US barriers to trade and the relatively small economic size of its current and prospective FTA partners.

Table 8A.10 shows the estimated regional welfare effects. Under the multiple FTA scenario, the effects on certain countries are magnified, especially for the NAFTA partners, Western Europe, Japan, and China. The negative effects on nonmembers remain small in proportion to their GDP levels.

The regional trading pattern estimates in table 8A.11 indicate that, when the US-Pakistan FTA is considered in conjunction with other FTAs, several countries experience a loss of exports to the United States. This is particularly true for countries that are not US FTA partners. Moreover, CAFTA-DR and Morocco lose exports to Pakistan, because the hub-spoke structure does not eliminate barriers between Pakistan and other US partners, such as CAFTA-DR and Morocco. In our earlier discussion of the effects of a US-Pakistan FTA on third countries that do not have preferential access to the US market, we identified Bangladesh, India, and Sri Lanka as countries that might be adversely affected by a US-Pakistan bilateral FTA. It is worth highlighting that, when all US bilateral FTAs are considered, the impact on these countries is significantly larger than when a US-Pakistan FTA is considered in isolation.

While estimated changes in the sectoral patterns of trade and production (tables 8A.12 and 8A.13) are not significantly different from those already discussed (tables 8A.6 and 8A.7), there are some differences in the volume of total US trade, especially in processed rice, textiles and clothing, and other manufactures. However, tables 8A.12 and 8A.13 indicate that a large fraction of the projected trade changes are redirection, and that production changes remain relatively small, with the exception of grains and processed rice.

---

20. Egypt is also a prospective FTA partner but is not currently available in the GTAP database.

Summing Up

The quantitative results from the gravity and CGE models presented in this chapter offer two useful views of the economic prospects of a US-Pakistan FTA. The views concur in some respects that deserve emphasis. Importantly, the estimates from the two models concur in suggesting that an FTA between Pakistan and United States would significantly expand trade between the two countries. The overall gain in mutual trade is conservatively estimated at about 43 percent by the gravity model and at between 89 percent (US exports to Pakistan) and 36 percent (Pakistan exports to the United States) by the CGE model (averaging an increase of about 60 percent in bilateral two-way trade). In addition, both models agree that the expansion in bilateral trade would be focused in agriculture and manufactures. Improved business practices in Pakistan, in concert with the proposed US-Pakistan FTA, might further expand Pakistan's overall trade by as much as 35 percent, not only with the United States but also with other major trading partners.

The general equilibrium estimates of the GTAP model provide additional insights. The CGE model finds no improvement in overall economic welfare for the large US economy, but an appreciable improvement for Pakistan, estimated at 1.5 percent of GDP per annum. It also points to particular sectors in both countries that would benefit from the expansion of bilateral exports. These include grains, processed foods, chemicals, machinery and equipment (including electronic equipment), and other transport equipment in the United States, and textiles and clothing in Pakistan.

Adverse spillover effects arising from trade diversion under the hypothesized US-Pakistan FTA are small. Effects of appreciable magnitude are confined mainly to the Central American economies, Korea, the Philippines, and certain economies in South Asia (principally Bangladesh, India, and Sri Lanka). In all cases, however, the adverse impacts are minor (less than 0.1 percent of GDP).

Finally, the results of the GTAP model suggest that liberalization of services trade between Pakistan and the United States would not lead to substantial economic gains for either country. This result seems at odds with the thrust of "deeper integration" under other US FTAs and, more generally, the wave of RTAs worldwide. An explanation for this result may lie in the still elementary and underdeveloped framework of the domestic and international services economy in the GTAP model. It may also lie in the model's absence of more sophisticated dynamic linkages between foreign direct investment and international trade in both goods and services.

Appendix 8A

Table 8A.1 Gravity model estimates for total trade without and with US-Pakistan trade integration and openness, 1962–99

Variable	1962–99		1990–99		1995–99	
	Without	With	Without	With	Without	With
Constant	−18.89***	−18.03***	−7.18***	−6.15***	−11.53***	−10.12***
Distance	−0.79***	−0.81***	−0.77***	−0.80***	−0.77***	−0.79***
Joint GDP	0.73***	0.73***	0.54***	0.53***	0.64***	0.63***
Joint GDP per capita	−0.07***	−0.08***	−0.26***	−0.27***	−0.41***	−0.41***
Common language	0.17***	0.12***	0.21***	0.14***	0.22***	0.15***
Common border	0.50***	0.49***	1.04***	1.01***	1.11***	1.09***
Landlocked	−0.18***	−0.19***	−0.51***	−0.52***	−0.40***	−0.42***
Island	0.10***	0.08***	0.34***	0.34***	0.40***	0.43***
Land area	−0.12***	−0.13***	−0.07***	−0.08***	−0.05***	−0.07***
Common colonizer	−0.07**	−0.01	−0.12***	−0.03	0.00	0.09
Colony	0.73***	0.73***	0.30*	0.30*	0.18	0.18
Ever a colony	1.71***	1.77***	0.98***	1.06***	0.76***	0.85***
Common country	0.24	0.21	−0.65	−0.75	(dropped)	(dropped)
Currency union	0.81***	0.79***	1.54***	0.66***	(dropped)	(dropped)

GSP	−0.10***	−0.10***	0.30***	0.27***	0.05	0.06**
EU and US RTAs (11)	0.12***	0.12***	0.20***	0.20***	0.65***	0.67***
Other HIC RTAs (10)	0.24***	0.24***	0.33***	0.34***	0.35***	0.37***
MIC and LIC RTAs (39)	0.54***	0.55***	−0.20***	−0.12***	−0.28***	−0.18***
Joint TI index					0.45***	0.41***
US-Pakistan trade		1.23**		0.55		−0.27
US openness	1.48***	1.48***		1.47***		1.42***
Pakistan openness	−0.93***	−0.93***		−0.92***		−1.00***
R-squared	0.40	0.41	0.34	0.35	0.40	0.41
Observations (thousands)	940	940	263	263	64	64
Groups (thousands)	61	61	44	44	22	22

***, **, * indicate that the coefficients are statistically significant at the 99, 95, and 90 percent levels, respectively.

GSP = generalized system of preferences
HIC, MIC, LIC = high-, middle-, low-income countries, respectively
RTA = regional trade agreement
TI index = Transparency International's corruption index

Notes: Table shows estimates for total trade in all commodities and manufactures (Standard International Trade Classification, SITC 0 through 9). Regressand is log real trade. Distance, joint GDP, joint GDP per capita, land area, and joint TI index are measured in log terms. Estimated year effects are not reported. Numbers in parentheses indicate how many RTAs are covered by the separate RTA variables. Groups are numbers of country pair–commodity combinations for which trade exists in the data sample.

Source: Authors' calculations based on generalized least squares estimation of the Rose (2004) gravity model with random effects, using a combined version of the Rose (2004) and Feenstra et al. (2005) datasets.

Table 8A.2   Gravity model estimates by major commodity categories without and with US-Pakistan trade integration and openness, 1962–99

Variable	Food, beverages, and tobacco (SITC 0 and 1)					
	1962–99		1990–99		1995–99	
	Without	With	Without	With	Without	With
Constant	–13.62***	–12.61***	–3.75***	–2.69***	–7.09***	–5.66***
Distance	–0.66***	–0.68***	–0.62***	–0.65***	–0.61***	–0.63***
Joint GDP	0.59***	0.58***	0.41***	0.41***	0.46***	0.45***
Joint GDP per capita	–0.11***	–0.12***	–0.23***	–0.24***	–0.30***	–0.30***
Common language	0.22***	0.16***	0.22***	0.15***	0.27***	0.21**
Common border	0.58***	0.57***	1.07***	1.05***	1.14***	1.11***
Landlocked	–0.23***	–0.25***	–0.48***	–0.50***	–0.44***	–0.47***
Island	0.08**	0.06	0.31***	0.30***	0.32***	0.36***
Land area	–0.06***	–0.08***	–0.03***	–0.05***	0.01	–0.01
Common colonizer	–0.15**	–0.08	–0.18*	–0.10	0.04	0.15
Colony	0.49***	0.50***	0.55	0.54	0.44	0.44
Ever a colony	2.08***	2.15***	1.28***	1.36***	1.02***	1.11***
Common country	0.98	0.95	–0.70	–0.80	(dropped)	(dropped)
Currency union	0.82***	0.80***	1.92***	1.03*	(dropped)	(dropped)
GSP	–0.03***	–0.03***	0.39***	0.36***	0.21***	0.22***
EU and US RTAs (11)	0.15***	0.16***	0.11***	0.12***	0.59***	0.61***
Other HIC RTAs (10)	0.32***	0.32***	0.36***	0.37***	0.41**	0.42**
MIC and LIC RTAs (39)	0.31***	0.32***	–0.27***	–0.20***	–0.35***	–0.26***
Joint TI index					0.41***	0.38***
US-Pakistan trade		0.64		–0.52		–1.40
US openness		1.76***		1.51***		1.48***
Pakistan openness		–1.06***		–0.94***		–1.12***
R-squared	0.32	0.33	0.28	0.29	0.36	0.37
Observations (thousands)	194	194	53	53	13	13
Groups (thousands)	12	12	9	9	4	4

Raw materials (SITC 2 and 4)					
1962–99		**1990–99**		**1995–99**	
Without	**With**	**Without**	**With**	**Without**	**With**
−16.62***	−16.04***	−6.19***	−5.53***	−9.46***	−8.70***
−0.58***	−0.59***	−0.48***	−0.50***	−0.54***	−0.55***
0.67***	0.67***	0.41***	0.40***	0.48***	0.47***
−0.22***	−0.23***	−0.21***	−0.22***	−0.31***	−0.32***
−0.04	−0.08	0.03	−0.01	−0.01	−0.04
0.32***	0.31***	1.01***	0.99***	1.08***	1.06***
−0.18***	−0.19***	−0.43***	−0.44***	−0.44***	−0.45***
0.08**	0.07*	0.21***	0.21***	0.29***	0.31***
−0.07***	−0.08***	0.01	0.00	0.05***	0.03**
−0.15**	−0.09	0.16*	0.22**	0.33*	0.37**
0.42***	0.42***	0.09	0.08	0.16	0.16
1.19***	1.23***	0.50***	0.55***	0.57***	0.61***
−0.19	−0.21	−1.61	−1.68	(dropped)	(dropped)
0.76***	0.75***	0.59	0.03	(dropped)	(dropped)
−0.18***	−0.18***	0.05	0.04	−0.02	−0.01
0.05	0.06*	0.21***	0.21***	0.46***	0.47***
0.21***	0.21***	0.20*	0.21**	0.18	0.19
0.52***	0.53***	−0.04	0.01	−0.03	0.02
				0.39***	0.37***
	2.34**		1.04		0.16
	0.93***		0.85***		0.71***
	−0.96***		−0.70***		−0.67***
0.31	0.31	0.27	0.27	0.32	0.33
162	162	43	43	11	11
11	11	7	7	4	4

(table continues next page)

Table 8A.2 Gravity model estimates by major commodity categories without and with US-Pakistan trade integration and openness, 1962–99 *(continued)*

	Mineral fuels and lubricants (SITC 3)					
	1962–99		1990–99		1995–99	
Variable	Without	With	Without	With	Without	With
Constant	−11.13***	−10.40***	−3.26***	−2.36***	−6.56***	−5.13***
Distance	−1.02***	−1.04***	−0.85***	−0.87***	−1.07***	−1.09***
Joint GDP	0.29***	0.29***	0.27***	0.26***	0.44***	0.44***
Joint GDP per capita	0.44***	0.43***	0.04	0.03	−0.21***	−0.23***
Common language	−0.29***	−0.33***	−0.01	−0.08	0.30**	0.25*
Common border	0.51***	0.50***	1.10***	1.09***	1.42***	1.41***
Landlocked	−1.33***	−1.35***	−1.29***	−1.31***	−1.11***	−1.14***
Island	0.47***	0.46***	0.58***	0.57***	0.87***	0.90***
Land area	0.19***	0.18***	0.16***	0.15***	0.16***	0.13***
Common colonizer	0.74***	0.79***	0.76***	0.85***	0.69**	0.76**
Colony	0.73***	0.73***	−0.07	−0.08	0.27	0.26
Ever a colony	1.00***	1.05***	0.22	0.30	0.37	0.47
Common country	−0.79	−0.81	−1.13	−1.21	(dropped)	(dropped)
Currency union	0.71***	0.70***	0.66	0.02	(dropped)	(dropped)
GSP	−0.36***	−0.35***	−0.27***	−0.29***	−0.39***	−0.35***
EU and US RTAs (11)	−0.39***	−0.39***	−0.14*	−0.14*	0.12	0.16
Other HIC RTAs (10)	0.30**	0.30**	−0.13	−0.11	0.50	0.56
MIC and LIC RTAs (39)	0.35***	0.36***	0.17	0.23**	0.07	0.19
Joint TI index					0.13**	0.07
US-Pakistan trade		0.73		−0.75		−1.72
US openness		0.95***		1.10***		1.40***
Pakistan openness		−0.69***		−0.87***		−1.86***
R-squared	0.33	0.34	0.26	0.27	0.37	0.40
Observations (thousands)	61	61	17	17	5	5
Groups (thousands)	5	5	3	3	2	2

***, **, * indicate that the coefficients are statistically significant at the 99, 95, and 90 percent levels, respectively.

Notes: Regressand is log real trade. Distance, joint GDP, joint GDP per capita, land area, and joint TI index are measured in log terms. Estimated year effects are not reported. Numbers in parentheses indicate how many RTAs are covered by the separate RTA variables. Groups are numbers of country-pair-commodity combinations for which trade exists in the data sample.

Source: Author's calculations based on generalized least squares estimation of the Rose (2004) gravity model with random effects, using a combined version of the Rose (2004) and the Feenstra et al. (2005) datasets.

Manufactures (SITC 5 through 8)					
1962–99		**1990–99**		**1995–99**	
Without	**With**	**Without**	**With**	**Without**	**With**
–24.61***	–23.78***	–11.37***	–10.35***	–17.42***	–16.14***
–0.98***	–1.00***	–1.01***	–1.04***	–1.03***	–1.05***
0.95***	0.95***	0.74***	0.73***	0.89***	0.88***
0.09***	–0.10***	–0.34***	–0.35***	–0.56***	–0.56***
0.32***	0.27***	0.27***	0.21***	0.24***	0.18***
0.59***	0.58***	1.19***	1.16***	1.13***	1.11***
–0.06***	–0.07***	–0.52***	–0.53***	–0.36***	–0.38***
0.01	–0.01	0.36***	0.36***	0.41***	0.44***
–0.23***	–0.24***	–0.15***	–0.16***	–0.14***	–0.15***
–0.14***	–0.08**	–0.28***	–0.18***	–0.15*	–0.06
0.79***	0.80***	0.38	0.38	0.18	0.17
2.11***	2.16***	1.44***	1.52***	1.02***	1.10***
0.49	0.47	–0.80	–0.89	(dropped)	(dropped)
0.67***	0.65***	1.70***	0.76**	(dropped)	(dropped)
–0.07***	–0.07***	0.49***	0.47***	0.15***	0.17***
0.22***	0.23***	0.33***	0.34***	0.92***	0.94***
0.35***	0.35***	0.46***	0.47***	0.40***	0.42
0.71***	0.71***	–0.31***	–0.23***	–0.36***	–0.26***
				0.65***	0.61***
	1.31*		1.49**		0.90
	1.53***		1.59***		1.42***
	–0.84***		–1.00***		–1.03***
0.57	0.57	0.51	0.51	0.66	0.66
461	461	133	133	31	31
28	28	21	21	11	11

Table 8A.3 Estimated changes in key economywide variables for the United States and Pakistan: CGE model

Variable	United States			Pakistan		
	Initial value (millions of dollars)	Bilateral FTA (percent change or millions of dollars)	Unilateral benchmark	Initial value (millions of dollars)	Bilateral FTA (percent change or millions of dollars)	Unilateral benchmark
Total import value	1,288,130	-0.1	2.8	14,993	16.1	32.7
From partner	3,748	36.3	16.3	1,272	90.8	9.0
From rest of world	1,284,382	-1.1	1.5	13,722	9.1	34.9
Total export value	880,543	0.5	6.7	14,179	-6.3	13.1
To partner	1,242	89.3	11.5	3,595	36.3	11.7
To rest of world	879,301	0.4	6.6	10,584	-20.7	13.6
Tariff revenue	19,919	392	-19,919	2,159	-152	-2,159
From partner	282	-282	-282	84	-84	-84
From rest of world	19,636	674	-19,636	2,075	-68	-2,075
Welfare as percent of GDP	9,983.5	0	-0.1	81.6	1.5	0.7
Total equivalent variation		-1,003	-11,243		1,237	602
Allocative efficiency		-371	1,639		627	895
Terms of trade		-632	-12,882		610	-294

Source: Initial data from the GTAP6 database (Dimaranan and McDougall 2005). Authors' estimates from simulation results.

Table 8A.4 Estimated changes in net welfare by country or region: CGE model (millions of dollars)

Country/region	Initial GDP (billions of dollars)	Bilateral FTA			Unilateral benchmark					
					United States			Pakistan		
		Total	Allocative efficiency	Terms of trade	Total	Allocative efficiency	Terms of trade	Total	Allocative efficiency	Terms of trade
Australia	350.3	22	2	20	196	7	190	4	0	4
New Zealand	49.8	2	1	1	73	0	73	3	0	3
China	1,060.2	−9	13	−22	2,307	314	1,993	43	10	33
Hong Kong	165.2	8	4	4	55	−71	125	−15	0	−15
Japan	4,017.9	9	35	−26	1,855	294	1,561	−34	17	−51
South Korea	408.5	−11	6	−17	898	93	805	39	9	30
Bangladesh	45.5	−12	−6	−6	202	97	104	0	0	−1
India	458.6	−18	−10	−8	233	83	150	35	8	27
Sri Lanka	15.6	−7	0	−7	158	20	138	12	1	11
Pakistan	81.6	1,237	627	610	184	30	154	602	895	−294
Chile	65.0	2	1	1	52	0	52	3	0	2
Rest of South America	1,176.4	50	12	38	877	198	679	2	−7	9
CAFTA-DR	102.2	−14	−11	−3	858	356	502	−6	−4	−2
Western Europe	8,228.2	41	144	−102	5,340	408	4,932	−51	−33	−18
Eastern Europe	817.9	18	12	6	465	9	455	7	−4	11
Morocco	32.9	3	2	2	22	7	15	−4	−1	−3
SACU	10.0	−1	0	−1	32	3	29	−1	0	−1
Rest of world	1,624.4	56	19	36	1,729	56	1,673	205	18	187

(table continues next page)

217

Table 8A.4 Estimated changes in net welfare by country or region: CGE model (millions of dollars) (continued)

Country/region	Initial GDP (billions of dollars)	Bilateral FTA			Unilateral benchmark					
					United States			Pakistan		
		Total	Allocative efficiency	Terms of trade	Total	Allocative efficiency	Terms of trade	Total	Allocative efficiency	Terms of trade
Indonesia	140.6	1	3	−1	293	−67	360	32	−5	37
Malaysia	86.9	5	15	−10	165	−46	212	117	−4	121
Philippines	67.3	−9	−4	−5	224	46	178	−2	0	−2
Singapore	84.8	21	2	19	16	−23	40	7	−2	8
Thailand	111.6	1	1	1	280	−42	323	16	1	15
Vietnam	31.1	2	1	1	152	72	80	1	0	1
ASEAN	522.5	22		1,130	171					
Canada	703.7	80	13	67	−869	43	−912	9	3	6
United States	9,983.5	−1,003	−371	−632	−11,243	1,639	−12,882	−156	−36	−120
Mexico	599.0	−5	−25	20	−1,199	−124	−1,075	2	2	0
NAFTA	11,286.2	−927			−13,311			−145		
World total	30,518.9	471			3,355			869		

ASEAN = Association of Southeast Asian Nations
CAFTA-DR = Central American Free Trade Agreement–Dominican Republic
NAFTA = North American Free Trade Agreement
SACU = Southern African Customs Union

Source: Initial data from the GTAP6 database (Dimaranan and McDougall 2005). Estimates from simulation results.

Table 8A.5 Estimated changes in the regional pattern of exports: CGE model (percent change)

Country/region	Initial value (billions of dollars)			Bilateral FTA			Unilateral benchmark			
							United States		Pakistan	
	Total	To United States	To Pakistan	Total	To United States	To Pakistan	Total	To United States	Total	To Pakistan
Australia	72.3	8.6	0.3	0	-0.1	6.8	0.3	3.8	0	-11.8
New Zealand	18.1	2.8	0	0	-0.1	7.8	0.4	5.9	0	12.0
China	379.4	108.3	0.9	0	-0.3	12.8	1.0	8.2	0	45.4
Hong Kong	98.0	20.4	0.1	0	-0.2	3.4	0.6	8.2	0	6.4
Japan	448.0	123.7	0.8	0	-0.3	12.7	0.4	4.0	0.1	64.8
South Korea	175.4	37.2	0.5	0	-0.3	11.9	0.6	6.4	0.1	57.4
Bangladesh	7.8	2.9	0	-0.1	-1.0	5.3	2.8	19.3	0.1	18.6
India	60.3	12.2	0.6	0	-0.5	9.9	0.4	2.3	0.1	35.7
Sri Lanka	6.4	2.4	0.1	0	-0.9	10.8	1.9	20.2	0.1	53.7
Pakistan	14.2	3.6		-6.3	36.3		1.5	16.1	7.5	
Chile	21.7	4.0	0	0	-0.1	3.5	0.2	1.6	0	-0.7
Rest of South America	187.6	49.4	0.2	0	-0.1	7.7	0.4	3.2	0.1	20.2
CAFTA-DR	34.1	13.4	0	0	-0.4	5.2	2.0	13.7	0	0.2
Western Europe	2,655.5	309.1	3.2	0	-0.2	9.9	0.3	3.1	0	24.3
Eastern Europe	341.3	24.2	0.3	0	-0.1	7.9	0.2	0.8	0	14.1
Morocco	11.2	1.1	0	0.1	-0.1	5.8	0.3	1.9	0	-29.7
SACU	6.2	0.5	0	0	-0.6	5.9	1.0	28.9	0	5.7
Rest of world	555.4	114.7	4.0	0	-0.2	7.5	0.5	2.8	0.1	24.7

(table continues next page)

Table 8A.5 Estimated changes in the regional pattern of exports: CGE model (percent change)*(continued)*

Country/region	Initial value (billions of dollars)			Bilateral FTA			Unilateral benchmark			
							United States		Pakistan	
	Total	To United States	To Pakistan	Total	To United States	To Pakistan	Total	To United States	Total	To Pakistan
Indonesia	68.0	11.4	0.2	0	-0.4	8.9	0.7	10.4	0.1	75.8
Malaysia	124.4	24.0	0.5	0	-0.2	9.7	0.3	3.0	0.1	146.8
Philippines	37.8	11.5	0	0	-0.3	9.6	0.1	5.5	0	30.3
Singapore	110.3	17.8	0.6	0	-0.2	11.8	0.2	1.1	0	26.0
Thailand	79.4	17.2	0.2	0	-0.3	10.6	0.3	5.9	0.1	53.2
Vietnam	15.3	1.4	0	0	-0.1	4.7	0.2	5.1	0	33.9
ASEAN	435.1	83.3	1.6	0	-0.2	10.5	0.3	4.6	0	74.8
Canada	265.1	198.0	0.1	0	-0.1	7.2	-1.0	-2.2	0	11.3
United States	880.5		1.2	0.5		89.3	4.3		0.1	8.8
Mexico	164.2	129.4	0	0	0	5.0	-0.5	-1.8	0	13.2
NAFTA	1,309.8	327.3	1.4	0.3	-0.1	78.5	2.6	-2.1	0	9.2
World total	6,838.0	1,249.1	14.3	0.1	-0.1	16.1	0.8	2.7	0.1	32.2

Source: Initial data from the GTAP6 database (Dimaranan and McDougall 2005). Estimates from simulation results.

Table 8A.6 Estimated changes in the sectoral pattern of exports: CGE model (percent change)

Country/region	United States Initial value (millions of dollars) Total	To Pakistan	United States Bilateral FTA Total	To Pakistan	Unilateral benchmark	Pakistan Initial value (millions of dollars) Total	To United States	Pakistan Bilateral FTA Total	To United States	Unilateral benchmark
Grains	9,633	31	0.6	159.8	1.5	180	7	−15.6	−0.8	6.3
Vegetables and fruits	5,017	2	0.2	30.0	1.0	190	5	−6.9	29.0	8.8
Other agriculture	14,703	97	0.6	54.3	2.7	274	22	−14.6	−12.2	11.2
Forestry and fisheries	1,497	0	0.1	104.3	0.9	34	4	−8.0	−10.9	9.3
Coal, oil, and gas	4,251	1	0.2	243.1	2.7	203	16	−36.5	−38.6	42.1
Processed rice	463	0	1.0	107.5	2.5	464	5	−12.5	−7.3	−0.4
Other food products	28,204	38	0.8	336.2	1.5	467	23	−20.6	−16.3	−5.8
Textiles	12,449	9	1.1	227.7	5.4	5,440	1,555	−3.9	43.8	6.4
Wearing apparel	4,995	2	1.1	471.5	9.4	2,122	1,007	15.7	65.2	2.5
Leather products	1,893	0	1.1	306.9	18.8	358	15	−38.0	−5.1	−11.8
Wood products	8,206	2	0.6	250.3	1.5	74	32	−24.1	−23.9	−2.5
Paper products	20,026	17	0.5	103.0	0.7	22	3	−23.8	−24.6	0.4
Chemicals	104,314	129	0.5	97.4	1.3	434	13	−21.3	−18.4	12.0
Minerals and metals	32,032	17	0.6	282.2	1.6	130	10	−29.1	−27.5	−1.7
Fabricated metal products	14,848	3	0.6	427.2	1.2	90	29	−33.2	−30.5	−3.2
Motor vehicles	56,726	6	0.3	824.9	−0.1	7	1	−22.2	−23.1	7.4
Other transportation equipment	51,796	69	0.9	115.0	2.5	115	1	−31.8	−32.4	1.1
Electronic equipment	110,411	37	0.7	244.7	2.6	18	1	−32.0	−32.8	12.4
Machinery and equipment	164,865	130	0.9	226.9	2.3	191	37	−36.1	−36.6	−0.2
Other manufactures	14,446	13	0.9	167.0	3.5	403	102	−31.7	−28.9	−4.4
Nontraded services	4,082	8	0.7	34.7	1.6	112	12	−27.0	−27.4	−11.8
Traded services	215,685	630	−0.1	15.1	11.1	2,850	695	−3.7	7.1	20.0

Source: Initial data from the GTAP6 database (Dimaranan and McDougall 2005). Estimates from simulation results.

Table 8A.7 Estimated changes in the sectoral pattern of production: CGE model (percent change in volume)

Sector	United States			Pakistan		
	Initial value (millions of US dollars)	Bilateral FTA	Unilateral benchmark	Initial value (millions of US dollars)	Bilateral FTA	Unilateral benchmark
Grains	27,782	0.3	0.4	5,634	−1.5	−0.7
Vegetables and fruits	25,749	0.1	0.1	6,314	−0.3	−0.9
Other agriculture	144,090	0.1	−0.2	13,671	−1.1	−2.6
Forestry and fisheries	21,513	0.1	−0.1	2,701	1.3	0.2
Coal, oil, and gas	112,595	0.1	0.1	2,258	−10.5	−13.6
Processed rice	2,138	0.3	−0.6	4,189	−1.5	−0.4
Other food products	734,887	0.1	−0.3	6,010	−4.7	−16.3
Textiles	143,198	0.1	−6.9	10,929	−4.4	0.2
Wearing apparel	108,886	0.2	−8.2	2,306	9.5	0.8
Leather products	15,715	0.5	−14.7	678	−27.5	−15.8
Wood products	224,967	0.1	0.0	614	−0.9	0.9
Paper products	388,245	0.1	0.0	1,366	−4.0	−8.2
Chemicals	854,532	0.2	−0.6	7,826	−7.4	−10.6
Minerals and metals	376,428	0.3	−0.7	4,030	−4.5	−12.1
Fabricated metal products	286,697	0.2	−0.5	2,008	1.1	−2.3
Motor vehicles	462,140	0	−0.7	1,070	5.7	−33.5
Other transportation equipment	191,991	0.4	0.9	1,187	−4.3	−7.2
Electronic equipment	347,350	0.4	1.2	648	−3.6	−8.0
Machinery and equipment	778,853	0.3	0	2,835	−4.0	−7.1
Other manufactures	63,713	0.4	0.1	1,444	−10.4	−6.1
Nontraded services	2,475,607	0	−0.1	16,819	9.0	11.4
Traded services	9,978,422	−0.1	0.2	44,039	0.9	2.3

Source: Initial data from the GTAP6 database (Dimaranan and McDougall 2005). Estimates from simulation results.

Table 8A.8 Estimated changes in real returns to factors of production: CGE model (percent change at constant prices)

Factor	United States		Pakistan	
	Bilateral FTA	**Unilateral benchmark**	**Bilateral FTA**	**Unilateral benchmark**
Land	0.6	0.2	–4.0	–6.9
Unskilled labor	–0.3	–0.1	–2.7	0.1
Skilled labor	–0.3	0	–6.0	–2.7
Capital	–0.3	–0.1	15.8	18.6
Natural resources	0.6	0.6	–22.9	–31.7

Table 8A.9 Estimated changes in key economywide variables under current and proposed US FTAs: CGE model

Variable	United States	Pakistan	Chile	Australia	Singapore	Morocco	CAFTA-DR	SACU	Korea	Malaysia	Switzerland	Thailand
Total import value (percent change)	1.5	14.0	2.5	0.9	1.4	8.5	9.9	6.8	6.5	4.0	0.9	3.0
From partner(s)	16.7	72.2	32.2	12.7	-2.0	132.3	46.3	37.0	42.7	28.4	17.7	52.0
From rest of world	-0.5	8.6	-4.0	-1.9	2.0	-0.1	-1.5	4.2	-1.8	0.5	-1.2	-2.7
Total export value (percent change)	2.3	-7.6	1.1	0.2	2.2	-4.4	6.6	-2.2	10.5	2.5	0.5	1.0
To partner(s)	27.7	22.9	7.5	7.2	5.4	-3.7	35.9	51.3	25.2	9.2	3.5	19.6
To rest of world	-1.2	-18.0	-0.3	-0.7	1.6	-4.5	-12.3	-7.3	6.6	0.9	0	-4.2
Tariff revenue (millions of US dollars)	-4,283.4	135.9	-239.7	-438.4	-0.6	-161.5	-910.5	-18.1	-7,996.5	-684.0	-565.8	-724.2
From partner(s)	-3,402.2	-83.6	-188.6	-331.6	-0.4	-85.0	-839.2	-25.2	-3,803.9	-378.5	-323.5	-443.2
From rest of world	-881.2	219.5	-51.0	-106.8	-0.2	-76.5	-71.3	7.1	-4,192.6	-305.5	-242.3	-281.0
Welfare as a percent of GDP	0	1.4	0.2	0	-0.2	0.8	1.6	1.4	0.2	0.8	0	0.5
Total equivalent variation (millions of US dollars)	3,204.1	1,115.8	116.4	-31.1	-171.8	258.2	1,629.9	142.4	793.2	709.3	-26.6	553.7
Allocative efficiency	-223.3	608.8	55.9	-2.3	-128.8	138.3	773.3	67.9	2,162.8	491.5	-32.5	-33.1
Terms of trade	3,427.4	507.1	60.5	-28.8	-43.0	120.0	856.6	74.5	-1,369.5	217.8	5.8	586.8

CAFTA-DR = Central American Free Trade Agreement–Dominican Republic
SACU = Southern African Customs Union

Table 8A.10 Estimated changes in net welfare by region, multiple US FTAs: CGE model

Country	Initial GDP (billions of dollars)	Multiple US FTAs[a] (millions of dollars)		
		Total	Allocative efficiency	Terms of trade
Australia	348.7	−31.1	−2.3	−28.8
New Zealand	49.5	−58.5	3.1	−61.5
China	1,054.2	−1,063.0	−426.0	−637.0
Hong Kong	158.3	207.6	−89.7	297.3
Japan	4,006.1	−1,039.9	−498.1	−541.8
South Korea	406.5	793.2	2,162.8	−1,369.5
Bangladesh	45.3	−70.3	−33.8	−36.5
India	456.2	−247.1	−79.2	−167.8
Sri Lanka	15.5	−52.0	−9.5	−42.6
Pakistan	81.1	1,115.8	608.8	507.1
Chile	64.7	116.4	55.9	60.5
Rest of South America	1,172.1	−524.0	−204.7	−319.3
CAFTA-DR	101.4	1,629.9	773.3	856.6
Western Europe	7,941.2	−2,114.4	−661.8	−1,452.6
Switzerland	238.0	−26.6	−32.5	5.8
Eastern Europe	812.8	−257.9	−74.4	−183.5
Morocco	32.6	258.2	138.3	120.0
SACU	9.9	142.4	67.9	74.5
Rest of world	1,615.9	−319.9	−105.2	−214.8
Indonesia	140.1	−93.9	24.7	−118.6
Malaysia	86.1	709.3	491.5	217.8
Philippines	66.9	−123.3	−42.9	−80.4
Singapore	83.4	−171.8	−128.8	−43.0
Thailand	111.1	553.7	−33.1	586.8
Vietnam	30.8	11.6	5.2	6.4
ASEAN	518.3	885.6		
Canada	702.0	−434.4	−94.6	−339.8
United States	9,965.5	3,204.1	−223.3	3,427.4
Mexico	597.8	−622.5	−80.2	−542.3
NAFTA	11,265.3	2,147.3		
World total	30,393.6	1,492.0		

a. The FTA scenario for the United States assumes implementation of the FTAs identified in table 8A.9.

Note: Bold type designates current or prospective US FTA partners.

Source: Initial data from GTAP6 database (Dimaranan and McDougall 2005). Estimates from simulation results.

Table 8A.11 Estimated changes in the regional pattern of exports, multiple US FTAs: CGE model

Country/region	Initial value (billions of US dollars)			Multiple US FTAs[a] (percent change in value)		
	Total	To United States	To Pakistan	Total	To United States	To Pakistan
Australia	72.1	8.6	0.3	0.2	7.2	6.0
New Zealand	18.1	2.8	0	-0.4	1.1	7.9
China	377.7	108.1	0.9	-0.3	-1.1	11.3
Hong Kong	98.0	20.4	0.1	-0.2	-2.1	5.8
Japan	446.8	123.6	0.8	-0.2	0.1	12.3
South Korea	174.9	37.1	0.5	10.5	25.2	21.8
Bangladesh	7.8	2.9	0	1.1	-8.3	6.0
India	60.1	12.1	0.6	-0.4	-2.8	7.8
Sri Lanka	6.4	2.4	0.1	-0.7	-7.4	8.8
Pakistan	14.1	3.6		-7.6	22.9	
Chile	21.6	4.0	0	1.1	7.5	1.2
Rest of South America	187.2	49.4	0.2	-0.2	-0.7	6.9
CAFTA-DR	34.1	13.3	0	6.6	35.9	-6.3
Western Europe	2,540.4	294.1	2.9	-0.2	-0.1	9.0
Switzerland	106.8	14.6	0.3	0.5	3.5	10.4
Eastern Europe	340.3	24.2	0.3	-0.1	-0.2	6.8

Morocco	11.2	1.1	0	-4.4	-3.7	-3.7
SACU	6.2	0.5	0	-2.2	51.3	1.9
Rest of world	554.0	114.5	4.0	-0.2	-1.0	6.2
Indonesia	67.8	11.3	0.2	-0.3	-2.7	6.5
Malaysia	124.1	24.0	0.5	2.5	9.2	12.4
Philippines	37.7	11.5	0.0	-0.2	-2.0	10.1
Singapore	110.1	17.8	0.6	2.2	5.4	13.1
Thailand	79.1	17.1	0.2	1.0	19.6	5.1
Vietnam	15.2	1.4	0	-0.1	0.2	6.3
ASEAN	434.0	83.1	1.6	1.4	7.2	10.5
Canada	264.7	197.7	0.1	-0.2	-0.3	7.5
United States	879.7		1.2	2.3		70.6
Mexico	163.9	129.2	0.0	-0.2	-0.4	7.2
NAFTA	1,308.3	326.9	1.4	1.5	-0.4	62.4
World total	6,820.0	1,247.6	14.3	0.5	1.4	14.0

a. The FTA scenario for the United States assumes implementation of the FTAs identified in table 8A.9.

Note: Bold designates current or prospective US FTA partners.

Source: Initial data from GTAP6 database (Dimaranan and McDougall 2005). Estimates from simulation results.

Table 8A.12 Estimated changes in the sectoral pattern of exports, multiple US FTAs: CGE model (percent change in value)

Sector	United States					Pakistan				
	Initial value (millions of dollars)		Multiple US FTAs[a]		Unilateral benchmark	Initial value (millions of dollars)		Multiple US FTAs[a]		Unilateral benchmark
	Total	To Pakistan	Total	To Pakistan		Total	To United States	Total	To United States	
Grains	9,633	31	26.9	125.8	1.5	180	7	−9.5	20.1	6.3
Vegetables and fruits	5,017	2	0.7	21.0	1.0	190	5	−5.7	36.6	8.8
Other agriculture	14,703	97	20.3	35.3	2.7	274	22	−15.3	−4.5	11.2
Forestry and fisheries	1,497	0	0.6	98.5	0.9	34	4	−7.6	−9.3	9.3
Coal, oil, and gas	4,251	1	1.7	237.0	2.7	203	16	−33.3	−34.9	42.1
Processed rice	463	0	41.4	92.8	2.5	464	5	−11.9	−14.9	−0.4
Other food products	28,204	38	8.9	296.0	1.5	467	23	−20.8	−14.2	−5.8
Textiles	12,449	9	17.4	196.0	5.4	5,440	1,555	−5.5	31.8	6.4
Wearing apparel	4,995	2	26.9	453.3	9.4	2,122	1,007	10.3	49.8	2.5
Leather products	1,893	0	7.2	288.4	18.8	358	15	−35.6	−6.3	−11.8
Wood products	8,206	2	2.1	238.4	1.5	74	32	−20.1	−19.6	−2.5
Paper products	20,026	17	1.5	96.5	0.7	22	3	−21.1	−21.0	0.4
Chemicals	104,314	129	2.4	92.6	1.3	434	13	−19.6	−16.2	12.0
Minerals and metals	32,032	17	3.6	268.9	1.6	130	10	−26.4	−24.4	−1.7
Fabricated metal products	14,848	3	2.3	401.3	1.2	90	29	−30.0	−26.9	−3.2
Motor vehicles	56,726	6	2.4	793.9	−0.1	7	1	−19.5	−20.1	7.4
Other transport equipment	51,796	69	−0.7	104.8	2.5	115	1	−26.7	−26.6	1.1
Electronic equipment	110,411	37	−0.5	230.0	2.6	18	1	−28.5	−29.6	12.4
Machinery and equipment	164,865	130	2.2	214.0	2.3	191	37	−32.6	−32.9	−0.2
Other manufactures	14,446	13	13.5	152.7	3.5	403	102	−28.7	−25.5	−4.4
Nontraded services	4,082	8	−0.3	30.1	1.6	112	12	−24.0	−24.0	−11.8
Traded services	215,685	630	−1.0	−6.9	11.1	2,850	695	−6.1	−14.6	20.0

a. The FTA scenario for the United States assumes implementation of the FTAs identified in table 8A.9.

Source: Initial data from GTAP6 database (Dimaranan and McDougall 2005). Estimates from simulation results.

Table 8A.13 Estimated changes in the sectoral pattern of production, multiple US FTAs: CGE model[a]
(percent change in volume)

Sector	United States	Pakistan	Chile	Australia	Singapore	Morocco	CAFTA-DR	SACU	Korea	Malaysia	Switzerland	Thailand
Grains	7.5	-1.1	1.7	-0.6	1.5	-3.1	-5.4	-7.8	-26.7	6.5	-0.3	0.2
Vegetables and fruits	-1.1	-0.3	1.6	0.3	1.3	-0.5	-1.8	-5.8	5.9	3.8	0	-0.2
Other agriculture	1.5	-1.1	0.7	-1.1	-0.2	0	-1.7	-3.5	-0.8	-3.5	-0.2	-0.4
Forestry and fisheries	0	1.1	0.3	0.1	-0.7	6.6	-0.8	-2.3	4.7	3.8	0.1	-1.1
Coal, oil, and gas	0.1	-9.1	0.8	0.1	7.3	-13.8	-8.0	-6.8	1.2	-0.6	0.5	-0.3
Processed rice	7.2	-1.4	0.1	0.3	0.6	-0.8	-5.3	-5.5	2.0	16.4	-3.9	0.8
Other food products	0.2	-5.0	0.4	0.5	0.9	-1.0	-2.9	-5.0	19.5	8.5	-0.5	-1.8
Textiles	-1.2	-5.1	1.2	0.9	22.5	-3.4	41.3	33.7	36.2	41.5	0.9	14.0
Wearing apparel	-1.2	5.6	1.4	1.0	44.7	0.4	37.9	53.1	41.2	81.2	6.3	21.7
Leather products	-1.1	-25.7	1.4	0.6	9.1	1.4	-9.8	-7.9	47.7	9.7	3.2	26.3
Wood products	0	-0.2	1.4	-0.2	4.9	-0.7	-11.2	-4.3	1.6	4.9	0.2	-6.5
Paper products	0.1	-3.5	-0.5	-0.2	3.3	-4.4	-6.5	-6.2	2.2	-0.1	0	-2.3
Chemicals	0.3	-6.6	1.0	-0.2	4.6	-3.7	-5.7	-4.6	5.2	2.8	0.6	-1.9
Minerals and metals	0.3	-3.5	1.8	-0.2	3.7	0.1	-11.8	-0.1	4.8	3.6	0.7	-3.1

(table continues next page)

Table 8A.13 Estimated changes in the sectoral pattern of production, multiple US FTAs: CGE model[a]

(percent change in volume) (continued)

Sector	United States	Pakistan	Chile	Australia	Singapore	Morocco	CAFTA-DR	SACU	Korea	Malaysia	Switzerland	Thailand
Fabricated metal products	0	1.4	0.9	-0.1	3.2	0.1	-10.1	1.1	6.3	3.7	1.7	-4.2
Motor vehicles	0.1	6.2	0.5	-0.3	2.7	2.9	-3.2	-1.7	5.1	2.9	0.6	-0.4
Other transportation equipment	-0.3	-2.9	2.0	0.6	6.5	-3.4	-10.1	-1.9	9.1	7.3	0.5	2.5
Electronic equipment	-0.7	-2.4	-4.5	0.3	2.4	-4.7	-20.9	1.7	3.2	3.5	-0.1	-4.2
Machinery and equipment	0.2	-2.8	0.7	0	5.5	-0.3	-18.5	3.0	4.7	6.0	1.0	-2.3
Other manufactures	2.8	-9.2	0.9	0.1	3.3	-2.8	-11.1	-9.9	10.8	4.3	-1.3	-3.3
Nontraded services	0.1	8.8	1.5	0.3	-0.6	10.6	4.0	13.1	-1.2	-0.3	0.3	2.3
Traded services	-0.1	0.9	-1.2	-0.1	-1.8	-0.9	-1.5	1.2	-3.5	-7.3	-0.3	-1.7

CAFTA-DR = Central American Free Trade Agreement–Dominican Republic
SACU = Southern African Customs Union

a. The FTA scenario for the United States assumes implementation of the FTAs identified in table 8A.9.

Source: Initial data from GTAP6 database (Dimaranan and McDougall 2005). Estimates from simulation results.

9

Conclusion

Several recent events have tested relations between the United States and Pakistan. The discovery in 2004 of a nuclear proliferation network that supplied technology and materials to Iran, Libya, and North Korea, headed by renowned Pakistani scientist A. Q. Khan, and the mild response of Pakistan's government increased tensions. The killing of Pakistani civilians by US forces in January 2006 during an antiterrorist strike on the northwest frontier spurred a massive outburst of anti-American feeling. Anti-American sentiments were also displayed in February 2006, in the wake of the Danish cartoon incident, and again in March 2006 during President George W. Bush's visit to Islamabad. Other events continue to cast a shadow. Drug-related insurgents in Baluchistan and al Qaeda forces on the Afghan-Pakistan border are extremely troublesome. Iran's drive for nuclear weapons adds another concern, since geography and history contribute to close relations between Pakistan and Iran.[1]

These "negatives" are offset, however, by Pakistan's critical role as a Muslim ally in the US war against terrorism. Because of this important role, geopolitical considerations will take precedence over others—

---

1. In March 2006 President Bush clarified the US position on cooperation between South Asia and Iran. For the moment, the United States objects only to the prospect of nuclear cooperation with Iran, particularly in areas that could have a military application. The president's statement implied that the United States would not object to cooperation in other critical areas, and specifically mentioned fossil energy. "Our beef with Iran is not the pipeline, our beef with Iran is . . . they want to develop a nuclear weapon and I believe a nuclear weapon in the hands of the Iranians will be very dangerous for all of us" (BBC News, March 4, 2006).

including the economic issues examined in this book. In other words, geopolitics will largely determine the course of US-Pakistan relations—and the fate of any US-Pakistan FTA proposal. But a US-Pakistan FTA offers a vehicle for extending the bilateral relationship beyond mutual security concerns to the economic arena.

The case for increased trade and investment cooperation between the United States and Pakistan fundamentally rests on the proposition that closer ties could anchor the reform process in Pakistan. Economic reform, based on market principles, can create new and better jobs, and can, over time, serve as a bulwark against Islamic radicalism.

As we outlined in chapter 1, relations between Pakistan and the United States have alternated during the past 50 years between episodes of close partnership and sharp friction, reflecting the ups and downs of global and regional geopolitics. Since September 11, 2001, Pakistan's evolution has become a top US foreign policy priority, and the administration has repeatedly expressed a keen interest in Pakistan's *own* path toward political and economic reform. Both countries believe that democracy and freedom will play a decisive role in the struggle against radical Islam, a shared commitment cited by President Bush in a speech at the Asia Society, when he called on President Pervez Musharraf to deliver on his commitment to open, free, and fair elections in 2007.[2] The close relationship between the two countries has not been derailed despite instances of episodic violence such as those cited above.

The geopolitical considerations, together with Pakistan's evolution toward democracy, will decisively shape the prospects for an FTA. Beyond those preconditions, chapter 1 briefly addressed possible economic concerns. We argued that the new global wave of FTAs is less about forming tightly knit geographic units around a major power and more about criss-cross commercial networks spanning the globe. In this setting, a US-Pakistan FTA would complement the US strategy of competitive liberalization that in time could reshape commercial relations across South Asia. We observed that, because Pakistan is the second largest Muslim country in the world after Indonesia and an essential bridge between the Middle East and South Asia, a US-Pakistan FTA would reflect America's post–September 11 foreign policy priorities. We explained that an FTA can deliver real economic benefits to both Pakistan and the United States, as high barriers that limit trade in both directions are scaled back and eventually eliminated. We dispelled doubts concerning the issue of timing: A US-Pakistan FTA should not disrupt the last lap of the WTO Doha Round,

---

2. See White House press release, "President Addresses Asia Society, Discusses India and Pakistan," February 22, 2006, available at www.whitehouse.gov. However, in contrast to the high expectations encouraged by that speech, democracy featured less prominently during President Bush's subsequent visit to Pakistan in early March 2006.

since FTA negotiations and ratification would likely follow comparable milestones in the Doha process.

Many US critics of the endeavor will point to Pakistan's weak performance on corruption, as well as its labor and environment practices, as reasons for backing away from an FTA. Pakistani critics will dismiss an agreement that cements economic ties with the United States. But the proposed FTA provides a platform for building on the reform process in Pakistan, a process that encompasses social as well as economic issues.

Indicators of the current low intensity of bilateral trade and investment relations could be construed as a reason not to enter into an FTA. But this is a circular argument, as trade barriers share part of the blame for the low level of commercial interchange. In 2004, for example, US exporters faced high duties to enter Pakistan's market, and Pakistani firms were the fifth largest contributor of US custom duties relative to imports.[3]

Agriculture will challenge negotiators, as discussed in chapter 2. US producers will want maximum access to a market with high growth potential, whereas Pakistan will not want to disrupt activities that provide employment and sustenance for the majority of its population. The United States will therefore focus on lowering and eventually eliminating tariffs, while Pakistan will also seek assistance to improve its capacity to ensure clean and safe agricultural shipments.

Lower barriers will adversely affect some producers that are accustomed to high protection, but long phaseout periods should be designed to allow adequate time for adjustment. In Pakistan, the sensitive products are likely to be wheat, corn, poultry, and vegetable oils. Sugar and tobacco will be sensitive import products for the United States. The sensitive list will also include dairy items in both countries. However, Pakistan and the United States share a mutual interest in liberalizing cotton and rice. The computable general equilibrium (CGE) model predicts significant gains for the United States in processed foods, and an increase in Pakistan's exports of fruits and vegetables. While negotiations are under way, sanitary and phytosanitary (SPS) and other regulatory measures that limit US imports of fruits and vegetables should be examined, and steps taken both to improve Pakistan's compliance and to remove unnecessary barriers.

Trade in textiles and clothing, examined in chapter 3, holds the key to a successful agreement. Market access for textiles and clothing will be Pakistan's foremost commercial interest. Without substantial US concessions, a US-Pakistan FTA would be a lopsided bargain and not politically acceptable to Pakistan. Leaders in Pakistan will need to advertise convincing market access benefits to enlist support from domestic stakeholders, and the prospects of increased textile and clothing exports will be essential to that effort.

---

3. In 2004 Pakistan ranked 51st as a source of US imports and 17th as a source of US customs duties.

Liberalization is not a one-way street, however. Textile and clothing barriers are high in both countries. A US-Pakistan FTA will result in new market opportunities for US as well as Pakistani producers. The agreement should therefore be crafted to promote vertical integration between US and Pakistani firms, and to make Pakistan an attractive sourcing option for the US retail market—goals that will entail comprehensive reciprocal liberalization. Short phaseout periods of up to six years should be available for sensitive items. "Yarn-forward" rules of origin should be applied, to ensure market opportunities for US textile producers, with a high de minimis margin for nonconforming yarns and fabrics. The agreement should also contain strong language on customs cooperation and illegal transshipment.

In addition to textiles and clothing, significant trade opportunities exist in "other manufactures," discussed in chapter 4. US barriers are not overly burdensome to the vast majority of Pakistan's manufactured exports (apart from textiles and clothing), but Pakistan applies some very high tariffs to a few items. Empirical simulations indicate that liberalization in this area will generate large export gains for US firms (particularly in chemicals and in machinery and mechanical equipment) as Pakistan lowers its barriers. Some Pakistani firms will need to adjust by finding new markets and adopting new production methods. In other FTAs, the United States has accepted long phaseouts for a few truly sensitive manufactured products.

The parties should agree to an ambitious target of immediate liberalization of 95 percent of existing two-way trade in other manufactures.[4] While this will entail a greater effort in Pakistan than in the United States, it will balance US concessions on textiles and clothing. Pakistan should eliminate nontariff barriers, including local content requirements, on other manufactures. With very limited exceptions, the United States should grant immediate duty-free access to all imports of other manufactures from Pakistan, particularly leather goods. Long phaseout periods (up to 10 years) should be reserved for truly sensitive items.

Efforts to include environmental and labor standards in trade agreements have proven quite controversial, as discussed in chapter 5. The harmonization of environmental standards to the highest level (often the US level) can unfairly penalize countries with limited means, such as Pakistan. Most labor standards, particularly those directed at workers engaged in making nontraded goods and services, are best determined at

---

4. Pakistan could go a long way toward fulfilling the liberalization target by granting immediate duty-free access on other manufactures that are not produced domestically or on items that currently enjoy duty-free treatment not reflected on the tariff schedule (e.g., aircraft and parts thereof). In fact, current US exports to Pakistan are not substantial for sensitive items such as construction materials, plastics and rubbers, articles and tools of base metals, and motor vehicles.

the national level. At the international level, fundamental labor and environmental standards should be agreed in international organizations or multilateral pacts, exemplified by the International Labor Organization (ILO) or the Montreal Protocol. Yet, since the 1990s, the US Congress has linked labor and environmental provisions with trade pacts, and a US-Pakistan FTA will follow this recent tradition.

With these practical realities in mind, we propose that a US-Pakistan FTA adopt the basic labor and environment standards and dispute settlement framework of the Central American Free Trade Agreement–Dominican Republic (CAFTA-DR), as discussed in chapter 5. Pakistan's federal and provincial governments should amend their statutes as necessary[5] and undertake more vigorous enforcement of labor legislation. Pakistani firms that export to the United States should adopt—and self-certify compliance with—codes of conduct for labor matters that reflect the ILO Declaration on Fundamental Principles and Rights at Work. Mechanisms for monitoring compliance with environmental regulations should be established and strengthened. This will require American support as well as the involvement of the Asian Development Bank.

Buy-national procurement rules and other restrictions exist at the federal and subfederal levels in both Pakistan and the United States, as summarized in chapter 6. The United States should grant unconditional most favored nation (MFN) rights for government procurement, at both the federal and state levels, to Pakistani firms, and Pakistan should reciprocate.[6] The United States should work toward extending its procurement coverage for products exported by Pakistan, such as textiles and clothing and medical instruments, with appropriate (but limited) waivers in the Buy American Act and the Berry amendment. Pakistan should become a signatory to the plurilateral WTO Government Procurement Agreement (GPA), with a schedule of commitments that mirrors those stipulated by the GPA for developing countries and those of CAFTA-DR for US partners.

Investment and services sector exchanges between Pakistan and the United States hold much potential, as discussed in chapter 7. While barriers and frictions in investment are relatively low, improving the confidence of foreign investors in Pakistan remains a paramount objective. The conclusion of a bilateral investment treaty (BIT) will be an important

---

5. For example, the Industrial Relations Ordinance (IRO) should conform with the ILO conventions ratified by Pakistan.

6. The US-Peru FTA contains an alternative approach for state procurement rules: Firms based in a given US state can access government procurement in Peru only if that state grants equivalent rights to Peruvian firms. In our view, this is a second-best approach to unconditional MFN status.

step in this direction—and possibly a prerequisite to FTA discussions.[7] However, investment promotion will also require strong provisions addressing corruption. In fact, as part of the BIT text or as a separate codicil, we recommend that treaty benefits be denied to investors that engage in significant corrupt practices.

In the context of the proposed FTA, Pakistan and the United States should renegotiate the existing bilateral income tax treaty to reduce sharply the withholding rates on dividends, interest, and royalties. The government of Pakistan should encourage foreign direct investment in a more varied spectrum of sectors, by extending its privatization plans to encompass state-owned firms that are currently exempt from the Monopolies and Restrictive Trade Practices Ordinance. Pakistan should also commit to nondiscriminatory tax collection methods.

In the services sectors, the US-Chile FTA serves as a model for what could eventually be accomplished between the United States and Pakistan. A good start for Pakistan would be to reduce barriers that restrict foreign insurance and reinsurance firms, and then to consider privatizing the state life insurance company. As in the US-Singapore FTA, a US-Pakistan FTA could phase out local presence requirements, limits on the number of services providers and on the value of services transactions, and restrictions on the number of persons that may be employed by a foreign services provider.

Our econometric analysis, reported in chapter 8, gives results from two models: a gravity model and a CGE model. The overall gain in two-way trade that would result from a US-Pakistan FTA is estimated at about 40 percent by the gravity model. The CGE model calculates a possible expansion of 50 percent in two-way trade, but the increase is more moderate when other US FTAs are considered (35 percent). Both models agree that the bilateral trade expansion would be focused in agriculture and manufactures. The CGE model further calculates that an FTA could deliver an appreciable rise in Pakistan's income, estimated at 1.5 percent of GDP per annum.

Particular sectors that would benefit from the expansion of bilateral exports include for the United States, grains, processed foods, chemicals, and machinery and equipment (including electronic equipment) and for Pakistan, textiles and clothing. Trade diversion under the hypothesized US-Pakistan FTA will be small.

Pakistan and India are the bedrock members of the South Asian Free Trade Area (SAFTA), discussed in appendix A. South Asia is a region with some of the world's lowest intensity of trade flows, both within the re-

---

7. Unfortunately the US-Pakistan BIT was not concluded during President Bush's visit to Islamabad in March 2006. Negotiations will continue, as both presidents considered the agreement a "key step" to the expansion of US-Pakistan economic ties.

gion and with other regions. Low intraregional trade reflects the difficult relationship between India and Pakistan as well as the import substitution strategies pursued by all South Asian countries until the 1980s. In the happiest of outcomes, a US-Pakistan FTA would inspire all SAFTA members to liberalize at a faster pace, both to avoid undesirable diversion of trade and investment and to emulate the best commercial practices adopted by Pakistan. Accelerated liberalization among SAFTA members would in turn complement a US-Pakistan FTA. If trade relations are normalized within South Asia, and barriers are slashed, then the region will become that much more attractive for foreign investment not only by American but also by European and Japanese corporations.

If SAFTA becomes the driving force of Pakistan's liberalization, a US-Pakistan FTA could complement regional reform. The bilateral FTA would ensure increased competition in the Pakistani market for a range of manufactured goods, and probably go beyond SAFTA in liberalizing services and curbing nontariff barriers. Both SAFTA and the US-Pakistan FTA can make Pakistan more attractive to foreign corporations, and generate new opportunities for the country's firms at home and abroad.

APPENDICES

Appendix A
Pakistan and South Asia

SHAHID JAVED BURKI

South Asia is a large region in terms of population but is relatively poor compared with other parts of Asia.[1] In 2003 the region's estimated population was 1.4 billion, and its combined GDP was $728 billion, measured at market exchange rates, or $3.7 trillion in terms of purchasing power parity (PPP). Average per capita income was only $530 in conventional terms and $2,493 in PPP terms, whereas the averages for the Association of Southeast Asian Nations (ASEAN) countries, for example, are $4,998 and $8,228 in conventional and PPP terms, respectively.

India is the region's predominant country and its largest economy. Since the 1990s, it has also experienced the region's fastest growth—with 1.2 billion people, the country had 77.5 percent of the region's population. In purchasing power terms, India accounted for 82 percent of the region's total income (table A.1) but only 68 percent of total regional trade.

As shown in tables A.2 and A.3, while trade-to-GDP ratios are relatively low in South Asia, the rate of trade growth in all countries except Pakistan was much higher than the rate of increase in domestic output. This means that the trade-to-GDP ratios were even lower in 1990 than

Shahid Javed Burki is the former minister of finance, government of Pakistan.

1. For this discussion, the South Asian region is defined to include all countries represented in the South Asian Association for Regional Cooperation (SAARC): Bangladesh, Bhutan, India, the Maldives, Nepal, Pakistan, and Sri Lanka. Although Afghanistan was invited (at the conclusion of the organization's summit in November 2005) to join the regional group, the country is not traditionally considered part of South Asia and is not included in this discussion.

Table A.1 Macroeconomic data for SAFTA countries, 2003

Country	Population (millions)	GDP (billions of dollars)		Per capita GDP (US dollars)		Trade	
		PPP[a]	Market exchange rate	PPP[a]	Market exchange rate	Total (billions of dollars)	Ratio to GDP[b] (percent)
Bangladesh	138.0	258	55.0	1,870	351	16.4	30
Bhutan	0.9	n.a.	0.6	n.a.	695	0.5	85
India	1064.0	3,062	571.0	2,877	542	127.0	22
Maldives	0.3	n.a.	0.6	n.a.	2,232	1.0	156
Nepal	25.0	35	6.0	1,420	240	2.5	42
Pakistan	148.0	303	78.0	2,040	520	25.0	32
Sri Lanka	19.0	72	18.0	3,740	930	12.8	99
South Asia total	1373.0	3,730	728.0	2,493	530	190.2	26

n.a. = not available

SAFTA = South Asian Free Trade Area

a. PPP refers to purchasing power parity (either GDP or GDP per capita), in which all goods and services are assigned US prices.
b. The ratio is calculated on the basis of GDP at market exchange rates.

Source: World Bank, *World Development Indicators 2005.*

Table A.2 Growth of trade, by value, in major South Asian economies, 1981–2004 (average annual percent growth rate)

Country	Exports	Imports
Bangladesh[a]	9.5	7.6
India	10.8	9.7
Nepal[b]	12.7	8.2
Pakistan[c]	8.8	6.3
Sri Lanka[d]	8.2	7.2

a. Data for 1999 not available.
b. Data for 2001 and 2002 not available.
c. Data for 1994 not available.
d. Data for 1994–98 not available.

Source: UN Statistics Division (2005).

today. Pakistan began to play catch-up beginning in the 2003–04 fiscal year, and in 2004–05 both exports and imports increased at double-digit rates.

By way of comparison, China in 2003 had a population of 1.288 billion, while its GDP in both conventional and PPP terms was considerably higher than India's—$1.23 trillion and $5.79 trillion, respectively.[2] Its GDP per capita, estimated at $1,100 at market exchange rates, was more than twice as high as that of South Asia. In PPP terms, China's income per head ($6,410) was three times greater than South Asia's ($2,493).

China scholars increasingly believe that the open trading system adopted by the country, since it began to reform its economy in the late 1970s, have helped it achieve and maintain high rates of economic growth. As discussed below, China has become a pivotal player in the redefined global industrial production system, a position made possible by the emphasis placed on trade. In contrast, the South Asian countries are considerably less open and less well integrated into the global system. In 2003 China had a trade-to-GDP ratio of 75 percent; South Asia's was only 26 percent, one-third that of China's.

---

2. In late 2005 the Chinese revised their GDP estimates, increasing GDP by more than 16 percent. China also increased its estimates for recent economic growth. Output is thus bigger and growing faster than previously thought. Estimates for 2006 suggest that China will overtake the United Kingdom to become the fourth largest economy in the world at market prices. In purchasing power terms it is already the second largest, with output about half that of the United States.

Table A.3 Trade of major South Asian economies, 2003
(billions of US dollars)

Country	Exports	Imports	Total trade	GDP	Trade-to-GDP ratio
Bangladesh	6.9	9.5	16.4	55.0	29.8
India	56.0	70.7	126.7	570.8	22.2
Nepal	0.7	1.8	2.5	5.9	41.7
Pakistan	11.9	13.0	24.9	77.6	32.1
Sri Lanka	5.1	6.7	11.8	17.8	66.3
South Asia total	80.6	101.7	182.3	727.1	25.3

Source: World Bank, *World Development Indicators 2005.*

There are several reasons why South Asia has lagged behind China and the other countries of East Asia. Among them is the region's troubled history, which is by far the most important reason. History weighs heavily on South Asia in the poor relations between India and Pakistan, the area's two largest and most developed economies. Also hampering the region's progress are its development strategies, pursued by all countries in the region from the late 1940s, when much of the area emerged from colonial rule, to the early 1990s. In the next section we discuss the historical impacts of the structure of the South Asian economies and of the composition and pattern of their trade in slowing regional integration.

In the late 1940s, when the mainland of South Asia was one country under colonial management, there was considerable trade among the areas that later became independent states—about half of the region's total trade was among these colonial parts. However, the growing difficulties between India and Pakistan reduced intraregional trade to the point that currently only one-twentieth of the area's total trade takes place among the countries in the region. This change had a profound impact on the structures of the South Asian economies. Will greater integration in South Asia reverse the region's pattern of concentrating on the export of goods and services to Europe and North America? This is clearly a fundamental development challenge for South Asian countries. The third section in this appendix addresses how a US-Pakistan free trade agreement (FTA) could help shape trade policy in South Asia, focusing on its implications for the reemerging South Asian Free Trade Area (SAFTA).

South Asia has also done poorly in accessing international markets and benefiting from the rapid expansion of global trade. In the fourth section, which assesses the pros and cons of regional trade arrangements, we briefly describe the evolving system of international production that has contributed to the greater integration of other developing regions—in particular East Asia and Eastern Europe—into the global economy. By contrast, in South Asia, India is the only economy that has carved out a niche for itself in the new global economic system. However, even after becoming an important player in outsourcing, Indian trade as a proportion of GDP remains small compared with China's. Would regional economic integration make South Asia a more attractive area for investment by multinational corporations and lead to greater integration in the global economy? What lessons can be drawn not only from South Asia's history but also from Europe's experience with regional integration? How might a South Asian trade agreement complement a US-Pakistan FTA? These are some of the questions discussed in this section.

The Weight of History

Politics of Trade

The most important reason for poor regional integration in South Asia has been intense hostility between India and Pakistan, dating from the time the two countries gained independence from colonial rule in 1947. Relations began to thaw only recently, following the 2004 summit of the South Asian Association for Regional Cooperation (SAARC) and a meeting between Pakistan's President Pervez Musharraf and India's then Prime Minister Atal Bihari Vajpayee on the summit's sidelines.

But much must still occur before the legacy of history can be overcome. Even two years after Prime Minister Vajpayee extended the hand of friendship to Pakistan at a public meeting in Srinagar (the capital of the disputed state of Kashmir), Delhi and Islamabad have made little progress in resolving their differences. Nonetheless leaders of the two countries continue to meet. President Musharraf met with Prime Minister Manmohan Singh, India's current leader, in New York in September 2004 and pledged to work toward creating a peaceful South Asian region. In November 2004 Prime Minister Singh traveled to Srinagar and reiterated his wish to work with Pakistan to improve the economic well-being of the more than 1 billion people in South Asia. Later in the same month, Prime Minister Singh and Pakistan's new prime minister, Shaukat Aziz, held discussions in New Delhi.

In 2005 President Musharraf took advantage of the Pakistani cricket team's visit to India to get himself invited to Delhi where he met with the Indian prime minister. In this meeting, the two leaders gave special attention to trade and pledged to remove barriers that had been created since 1949. The Singh-Musharraf statement issued after the meeting promised that the leaders would work toward peace and use dialogue to resolve their many outstanding issues. However, when President Musharraf and Prime Minister Singh met again in September 2005, in

New York, they found little common ground on which to resolve the various disputes that continue to sour relations.

On October 8, 2005, a significant portion of Azad Kashmir (the part of Kashmir under Pakistan's control) was devastated by an earthquake that took more than 80,000 lives, injured another 350,000 people, and displaced three-fourths of the area's population. But even this tragedy did not result in any major shifts in the troop positions of the two countries. Although five additional points were opened between the two parts of Kashmir, nothing much flowed through them—not people, nor trade, only a few relief goods.

In November 2005 the SAARC nations met for their 13th summit. The meeting was postponed twice—once because of the tsunami that caused havoc in Southeast and South Asia in December 2004, and again because of Indian unhappiness with political developments in Nepal. The communiqué issued after the meeting was silent on the subject of SAFTA; the omission was an indication that the free trade area would miss its promised launch on January 1, 2006.

It is not clear that there is yet a political environment in which the two sides can begin to concentrate their energies on promoting inter-country trade. On the other hand, some tangible progress in trade could create an environment in which the two rivals might work together.

Successful implementation of the proposed SAFTA might improve relations between the long-time antagonists and would also help restore health to the South Asian economy by removing distortions that resulted from both the 1947 partition of British India and the 1971 emergence of Bangladesh.

Under colonial rule most of South Asia was one country, with much of the physical infrastructure built to allow easy flow of goods and commodities among the provinces of British India. The British administration in India invested heavily in developing the irrigation systems in the provinces of Punjab and Sindh to feed the food-deficient parts of the empire. Between the latter part of the 18th century and the early 20th century, India was repeatedly ravaged by famines that took a heavy toll on the British domain. According to historian Niall Ferguson, "Another famine [after the one in 1780] in 1783 killed more than a fifth of the population of the Indian plains; this was followed by severe scarcities in 1791, 1801, and 1805" (Ferguson 2003, 53). The enormous loss of life caused by the famines created great anxiety in the India Office in London. Blue-ribbon Royal Famine Commissions were established after each major famine to devise a long-term solution to persistent food scarcities. Eventually, a strategy was adopted to increase India's domestic supply of food grain.

British planners saw that the vast tracts of virgin land in Punjab and Sindh could be cultivated by irrigating them with water from the well-endowed Indus river system. The strategy worked, and within a few decades the two regions were able to produce vast quantities of food grains surplus to their needs. But this surplus had to be transported to the northeast, especially the heavily populated provinces of Bengal and Bihar. To do this, the British invested in transport infrastructure—in particular farm-to-market roads, a system of roads connected to the fabled Grand Trunk Road that linked Kabul with Calcutta, railways, and the port of Karachi. These investments formed the basis for close economic integration of the various parts of what was then the British Indian Empire and what are now parts of the independent states of Bangladesh, India, and Pakistan. If regional economic integration ever succeeds, it should quickly restore the economic and trading system that existed before British India was divided into separate countries. It was politics that severed these links; it will take politics to restore them.

A further challenge arose in the way the waters of the Indus River system were divided between the successor states of India and Pakistan. A water dispute surfaced between the two newly independent countries in the early 1950s and almost brought them to war. Intense international diplomacy and the involvement of a consortium led by the World Bank salvaged the situation. The Indus Water Treaty of 1960 led to the assignment of three western rivers to Pakistan and three eastern rivers to India.[3]

The water issue was not the only dispute between India and Pakistan that had profound economic consequences for the region and inhibited trade between the two countries. In 1949, Pakistan refused to follow other countries of the "sterling area"[4] in devaluing its currency with respect to the US dollar; India, in return, refused to recognize the new exchange rate of 144 of its rupees to 100 Pakistani rupees and halted all trade with its neighbor. As a result, Pakistan was starved of most manufactured goods for daily consumption and launched a program of industrialization to achieve a measure of self-sufficiency. Had this trade war not occurred, Pakistan would not have industrialized as rapidly as it did—but it also would not have forsaken its comparative advantage in agriculture.[5] As suggested below, elimination of trade barriers among the countries of South Asia could rectify some of these developments and create an environment for the redevelopment of agriculture in Pakistan.

Import Substitution and Bureaucratic Controls

The growing political problems between India and Pakistan were not the only reason for meager intraregional trade in South Asia. All countries in

---

3. For a detailed account of the development of the dispute and its resolution, see Michel (1969).

4. The sterling area comprised the British colonies that had linked their currencies to the British pound. The sterling area comprised most of today's Commonwealth member countries.

5. For an elaboration of this view, see Burki (1980).

the region pursued import substitution approaches to economic development for nearly 40 years, from their independence in the late 1940s to the
adoption of greater openness in trade beginning in the mid-1980s. Consequently, following independence from British rule, trade among the countries fell from about 19 percent of the total in 1948, to about 4 percent by
the end of the 1950s, and to 2 percent by 1967 (World Bank 2004a, 20).

The share of intraregional trade in total trade began to increase only
after the countries abandoned import substitution in favor of general
trade liberalization. In recent years, the share of intraregional trade in total trade has increased to 4 percent (table A.4). Still, this increase is insignificant compared with trade among countries in other regions:
Intraregional trade accounted for 67 percent of the total for the European
Union; 62 percent for Canada, Mexico, and the United States (members of
the North American Free Trade Agreement); and 26 percent for ASEAN
members. South Asia's small degree of intraregional trade is even more
arresting when we consider that, at 25.3 percent for all of the countries in
the South Asia region, trade-to-GDP ratios are below world norms.

The dirigistic economic policies adopted by all countries in the region
have left another pertinent legacy. Jawaharlal Nehru, India's first prime
minister, following the advice of senior Indian economists as well as his
own instincts, brought socialist economic management to his country. As
a result of the support it had provided to Britain in the Second World
War, India had a highly developed bureaucratic system that could quickly
exercise control over the economy. During the war, India's bureaucrats
established public-sector enterprises for the war effort, producing goods
that could not be obtained readily from the market. The bureaucracy was
also responsible for procuring supplies for the soldiers while ensuring
that domestic shortages did not occur. To prevent price gouging, the bureaucracy ran an elaborate system of rationing and price controls. All this
machinery was at hand when Nehru launched the license raj. Developed
over three decades, the tentacles of this system left no corner of the Indian economy—old and established, or new and modern—untouched.[6]

For a decade and a half, Pakistan followed a different route, encouraging the private sector to help meet the acute shortages of consumer
goods created by the 1949 trade war with India. While encouraging private entrepreneurship, the state was generous in building a high wall of
trade protection. The state also established public financial institutions to
provide the private sector with cheap long-term capital. For a time, Pakistan operated a dual exchange rate system that gave rich incentives to
firms that set up import-substituting industries, while punishing firms
that sold their products in the international market.

---

6. An excellent description of the license raj and the damage it did to the Indian economy
appears in Das (2003).

Table A.4 South Asian intraregional trade as a share of total imports, total exports, and total trade, selected years (percent)

Country	Intraregional imports to total imports				Intraregional exports to total exports				Intraregional trade to total trade[a]			
	1990	1995	2000	2004	1990	1995	2000	2004	1990	1995	2000	2004
Bangladesh	9	16	8	20	2	2	1	2	7	10	5	13
Bhutan[b]	11	58	60	n.a.	10	88	82	n.a.	10	74	72	n.a.
India	0	1	1	1	3	5	4	5	2	3	3	3
Maldives	n.a.	18	23	21	n.a.	23	18	10	n.a.	18	22	19
Nepal[c]	30	34	38	54	14	19	45	54	26	31	40	54
Pakistan	2	1	2	3	4	3	3	4	3	2	3	3
Sri Lanka[d]	7	11	12	19	4	3	3	9	6	7	8	15
South Asia total[e]	2	4	3	4	3	5	4	5	3	4	4	4

n.a. = not available

a. To facilitate the reading of the table, the ratio of intraregional trade to total trade was measured equally at the country level and at the regional level (intraregional imports plus intraregional exports divided by total imports plus total exports). While this technique is accurate at the country level, at the regional level it overestimates the participation of regional trade as it leads to double counting of intraregional trade flows. Utilizing a formula that corrects for double counting in the numerator and the denominator, ntraregional trade would be estimated at less than 2.5 percent of total trade for any of the years displayed in the table.

b. Data for Bhutan were obtained from World Bank (2004a). Figures for 2000 correspond to 1998.

c. Due to lack of available data, 2004 figures for Nepal correspond to 2003. The low figure for Nepal's regional trade in the early 1990s reflects the "trade and transit" crisis with India, an economic sanctions episode in which India closed a number of key trade and transit points with Nepal.

d. Due to lack of available data, 1995 and 2000 figures reported for Sri Lanka correspond to 1994 and 1999, respectively.

e. Excludes Bhutan. 1990 intraregional figures for Maldives were obtained as "mirror data" (i.e., exports of partners to Maldives), while figures for total exports were obtained from the WTO statistics database. Figures for Nepal and Sri Lanka correspond to the nearest available year as indicated in previous notes.

Source: UN Statistics Division (2005).

Then in 1972–74 Zulfikar Ali Bhutto, an avowed socialist, took Pakistan in a sharply different direction with the extensive nationalization of private assets. His administration took control of 31 large-scale industries, virtually all financial institutions, all large-scale trading companies, and eventually even small agroproduction enterprises. By the middle of the 1970s, the grip of the Pakistani state on the economy was as tight as the hold in India. Sheikh Mujibur Rahman, the first president of Bangladesh, finding no reason to experiment with a system of economic governance different from those of his neighbors, also brought bureaucratic socialism to his country. Thus, by about the mid-1970s, South Asia had closed itself off to the world economy.

At this point, several small countries in East Asia began to open their economies to foreign trade and to external capital flows. These two entirely different approaches to economic management profoundly influenced the economic fortunes of East and South Asia. First the East Asian miracle economies beginning in the early 1970s, and later China starting in the mid-1980s, enjoyed rapid increases in their GDPs, sharp growth in per capita income, and significant declines in the incidence of poverty. The South Asian economies, on the other hand, experienced growth rates not much higher than the rate of population increase. There was, consequently, only modest growth in per capita income and a steady increase in the rate of poverty.

Fortunately, as a result of recent changes in policy, the larger countries in the region are now more open to international trade. In 2003 Sri Lanka was the most open, with a trade-to-GDP ratio of 66 percent. The corresponding ratio for Nepal was 42 percent; for Pakistan, 32 percent; for Bangladesh, 30 percent; and for India, 22 percent.[7] But despite these improved ratios, there is relatively little trade among the countries of the region (as indicated in tables A.4 and A.5).

Will the reforms undertaken in the mid-1980s, but not always consistently pursued, enable South Asians to close the yawning gap between their economic situation and that of East Asia? This will depend on continued policy initiatives that lead to greater openness, better integration into the global economic system, and improved regional integration.

From Autarky to Relative Openness

First Sri Lanka in the 1970s and then India, Bangladesh, and Pakistan in the early 1990s abandoned trade protectionism in favor of openness as the strategy for development and poverty alleviation. India's shift was prompted by the foreign exchange crisis in 1991 and prodding by the In-

---

7. The lower figure for India is actually typical for most of the large Asian countries with the exception of China.

Table A.5 South Asian intraregional trade, 2004 (millions of US dollars)

Importer/exporter	Bangladesh	Bhutan[a]	India	Maldives	Nepal[b]	Pakistan	Sri Lanka
Bangladesh	—	3	1,594	0	6	198	13
Bhutan	3	—	84	nr	1	0	nr
India	54	70	—	0	342	158	386
Maldives	0	nr	42	—	nr	2	60
Nepal	3	1	737	nr	—	3	0
Pakistan	43	0	505	0	1	—	39
Sri Lanka	9	nr	1,344	17	1	135	—
South Asia total	112	74	4,306	18	351	496	499

nr = neither country reports

a. Exports for Bhutan are based on partner data (mirror statistics). There are discrepancies between free on board (f.o.b) and cost, freight, insurance (c.i.f) values in mirror statistics.

b. Due to lack of available data 2004 figures for Nepal actually correspond to 2003.

Source: UN Statistics Division (2005).

ternational Monetary Fund (IMF), which had developed a new approach under the label of Washington Consensus.[8] The Washington Consensus called for a program of fiscal austerity, privatization, and market liberalization. While the countries of Latin America plunged into these reforms, South Asians adopted a measured—perhaps too measured—approach. According to Joseph Stiglitz, "the Washington Consensus policies were designed to respond to the very real problems in Latin America, and made considerable sense. . . . When trade liberalization—the lowering of tariffs and elimination of other protectionist measures—is done the right way and at the right pace, so that new jobs are created as inefficient jobs are destroyed, there can be significant efficiency gains" (Stiglitz 2002).

South Asian governments also responded to the way development institutions such as the World Bank interpreted the remarkable performance of the "miracle economies" of East Asia (World Bank 1993). In 1970 Korea's trade-to-GDP ratio was 32 percent; it increased to 66 percent in 1988. For Malaysia, another miracle economy, the ratio in the same period increased from 89 percent to 109 percent (World Bank 1993, 39).

There was now a model available next door that held promise for South Asia. The export-oriented growth policies adopted by the East Asians were widely credited for their phenomenal economic growth in the quarter century before the Asian financial crisis of 1997:

> Some analysts have, with hindsight, attributed these achievements to unique cultural and geographical circumstances. But there was little evidence at the outset that East Asian economies would achieve spectacular results. In the 1950s even trade optimists were export pessimists and did not anticipate that Korea's exports would grow four times as fast as world trade during the next thirty years. (World Bank 1993)[9]

The East Asian economic miracle had a profound impact on the thinking of policymakers in South Asia. They were now prepared to accept openness in place of discredited import-substitution policies. For a decade—from the mid-1980s to about the mid-1990s—most of the major economies in the South Asia region undertook reforms to achieve greater openness.

But the effort stalled, particularly in India, after 2000. Old habits die hard, and strong vested interests that had survived the demise of the license raj applied political pressure to slow the reform process. Reformists, however, persisted. Momentum resumed with large cuts in industrial tariffs by India between 2002 and February 2004.

According to a recent World Bank study, "other developments—Pakistan's comprehensive liberalization of its trade policies since 1996–97 (in-

---

8. For a recent discussion of the Washington Consensus, see Williamson (2004).

9. Among this group of analysts was the Oxford economist Ian Little (1982).

cluding its agricultural trade policies), and Sri Lanka's potential to resume long-deferred reforms as prospects improve of ending its civil war—contribute to a regional picture of very mixed achievement but widely shared responsibility" (World Bank 2004a, 1). As a result of these measures, Pakistan and Sri Lanka are now the least protected markets in the region, with a top customs duty rate of 25 percent and an average customs duty, including other protective rates, of 18.8 percent for Pakistan. India, the region's largest economy, also has relatively high rates of protection (see table A.6), and despite low average tariffs, the Bangladeshi economy is also highly protected through other duties and other protective rates.

South Asia: A Poorly Integrated Area

Since the 1960s, developing countries have carved out a prominent place in the evolving global system of both production and trade. The two developments are closely linked. The global production system, based on the activities of some 60,000 multinational corporations (MNCs), now encompasses a number of East Asian countries other than those in the developed world, but does not yet include South Asia to any significant extent.[10] This is doubtless because multinationals choose to locate on the basis of various "environmental" features, prominently including economic policies and labor force characteristics.

Even the simplest operations, such as the production of garments, are now broken into several steps, frequently in different countries.[11] By splitting the final product into several intermediate products and components, MNCs are able to lower costs and maximize returns. They play on various kinds of arbitrages—wages, skills, knowledge, and fiscal incentives being the most important—and locate the manufacture of parts and components in countries that have a comparative advantage in each segment of production.

10. The term "global production system" is used by the United Nations Conference on Trade and Development (UNCTAD) in its annual World Investment Report to describe the way a large number of US, Western European, and Japanese firms have evolved into MNCs.

11. According to a story in The Economist, published on the eve of the lapse of the Multi-Fiber Arrangement (MFA) that governed trade in textiles and clothing for several decades, "The shirt on your back probably had an exotic life before it reached you. Say you bought it in the United States and the label said it was 'Made in Sri Lanka.'" However, before leaving Sri Lanka for the United States, it may already have traveled to many places across the developing world. It may well been made from Chinese fabric, woven in China from fiber imported from Pakistan, cut in China, and sewn in Sri Lanka with buttons imported from China. The final packing may have been done in Hong Kong." See "The Looming Revolution," The Economist, November 13, 2004, 91.

Table A.6 Tariff structures in South Asia (percent)

Item	India, 2004	Pakistan, 2002–03	Bangladesh, 2004–05[a]	Sri Lanka 2004	Nepal, 2003
Average MFN customs duty rate[b]	22.2	17.3	16.3	11.3	13.7
General top customs duty rate[c]	30.0	25.0	25.0	27.5	29.5
Tariff lines with specific duties	5.3	0.9	0	1.2	0.6

MFN = most favored nation

a. Tariff data as of June 2004. These figures reflect tariff changes announced in the country's fiscal 2005 budget on June 10, 2004, which indicated a significant move toward the reduction of protection via the reduction of the top rate to 24, a move to three nonzero tariff bands, and the rationalization of supplementary duties.
b. Other protective taxes are applied to some imports. Their incidence is considerable in the case of Bangladesh and Nepal.
c. The schedules of South Asian countries include higher rates than those listed under the "general top duty rate." For example, imports of vehicles and certain parts thereof to Pakistan face duties ranging from 35 to 90 percent.

Source: World Bank (2004a).

East Asian countries have become major suppliers of parts and components in this dispersed system. This is one reason why China now runs a sizable trade deficit with the countries of East Asia and has a large trade surplus with the United States. In 2005, while China ran a trade surplus of $104 billion with the United States, the most important destination of its final products, it had significant deficits with suppliers of intermediate products. China had a combined deficit of $106 billion with four East Asian countries—$52 billion with Taiwan, $38 billion with South Korea, $8 billion with Malaysia, and $6 billion with Thailand.

The scale and direction of trade is also profoundly influenced by the trade system—which partly explains how developing nations increased their share of world trade from about one-fifth in 1960 to about one-third in 2004. During this time, international trade as a whole was expanding at unprecedented rates. Growth in exports outpaced growth in output in every region. Among developing countries, the East Asian region outperformed the rest. South Asia, on the other hand, did relatively less well. Although the share of exports in output increased over the period 1980–2000, South Asia has the lowest share of trade in GDP of any region except the Middle East and North Africa. Nonoil export shares of the East Asian and Pacific region increased from 18 percent in 1980, to 25 percent in 1990, and to 34 percent in 2000. The corresponding shares for South Asia were 8, 9, and 14 percent, respectively.

India is the only South Asian country that has effectively made a place for itself in the rapidly changing global economy. However, even India has succeeded in only one sector of global commerce—information technology, for which it is a major locus of outsourcing for large corporations based in America and Europe. In the space of a few days in December 2005, three of the biggest companies in the United States—JPMorgan Chase, Intel, and Microsoft—announced plans to create a total of more than 7,500 jobs in India in high-value areas such as research and development and processing of complex derivative trades. This move signaled that outsourcing to India had moved beyond simple and relatively low-skilled projects such as call centers and medical and legal administrative transactions. For some big US companies, what began as an interesting experiment has become a core strategy. For example, under JPMorgan's plans, 20 percent of the global workforce of its investment bank will be in India by the end of 2007.

Why were American and European corporations, in particular those operating in the fast developing and changing service sector, attracted to India? For JPMorgan, the attractions of India are not just costs—which industry analysts estimate at about 40 percent below US levels[12]—but also the caliber of staff. According to the head of operations at JPMorgan's investment bank, "The quality of people we hire is extraordinary and their level of loyalty to the company unbeatable."[13]

Hesitant Steps Toward Regional Integration

Exports of the major South Asian economies have historically been directed at countries far removed from the area. The United States was the major destination of South Asian exports of goods and commodities, accounting for 36 percent of Bangladesh's total exports, 29 percent of Pakistan's, and 21 percent of India's. There was a different pattern for the area's imports. For both Bangladesh and Pakistan, China became the primary source of imports; for India, the United States was the largest single supplier. Tables A.7a and A.7b provide a detailed breakdown of the destination and origin of South Asian exports and imports.

Then in 1985, largely at the urging of President Zia ur Rahman of Bangladesh, the South Asian countries decided to establish a regional arrangement intended to produce greater economic cooperation among them. SAARC extended membership to seven countries—Bangladesh,

---

12. See David Weighton, "Movement of Tasks Overseas Jump Up Skill Claim," *Financial Times Survey: The World 2006*, January 25, 2006, 4.

13. Veronique Weil, as quoted in Weighton, "Movement of Tasks," 4.

Table A.7 Exports and imports of SAFTA countries, 2004

Destination of exports (percent of total exports)

Destination	Bangladesh	India	Maldives	Nepal[a]	Pakistan	Sri Lanka
China and Hong Kong	2	11	0	4	7	2
European Union	59	22	14	9	30	32
Japan	1	3	8	1	1	3
United States	26	17	20	29	23	34
Other destinations	13	48	57	58	39	30
All destinations (millions of dollars)	5,797	79,846	170	653	13,379	5,485

Source: UN Statistics Division (2005).

Source of imports (percent of total imports)

Source	Bangladesh	India	Maldives	Nepal[a]	Pakistan	Sri Lanka
China and Hong Kong	18	8	3	10	17	14
European Union	10	17	10	6	14	16
Japan	5	3	2	2	6	5
United States	3	6	1	1	10	3
Other sources	64	66	84	80	53	62
All sources (millions of dollars)	8,537	108,264	642	1,802	17,949	7,880

SAFTA = South Asian Free Trade Area

a. Bhutan was excluded due to lack of recent data.
b. Figures for Nepal correspond to 2003.

Source: UN Comtrade, 2004.

Bhutan, India, Maldives, Nepal, Pakistan, and Sri Lanka. These members agreed to a charter with the following objectives:

(a) to promote the welfare of the peoples of South Asia and to improve their quality of life; (b) to accelerate economic growth, social progress and cultural development in the region and to provide all individuals the opportunity to live in dignity and to realize their full potentials; (c) to promote and strengthen collective self reliance among the countries of South Asia; (d) to contribute to mutual trust, understanding and appreciation of one another's problems; (e) to promote active and mutual assistance in the economic, social, cultural, technical and scientific fields; (f) to strengthen cooperation with other developing countries; (g) to strengthen cooperation among themselves in international forums on matters of common interests; and (h) to cooperate with international and regional organizations with similar aims and purposes.[14]

A secretariat was set up in 1986 in Katmandu, the capital of Nepal, headed by a secretary general and one director from each member country to facilitate the work of the organization. The secretariat was not at first asked to work on issues related to economic cooperation and integration. But in April 1993 the council of ministers signed an agreement to form the SAARC Preferential Trading Arrangement (SAPTA), which went into effect in December 1995—and was followed by three rounds of preferential tariff reductions.

Concluded in 1995, SAPTA-1 covered only 6 percent of traded goods (about 226 products at the 6-digit level of the Harmonized Schedule of Tariffs, or HS). The important issue of nontariff barriers was left for a later date. SAPTA-2, concluded in 1997, was slightly more ambitious, covering 1,800 HS 6-digit items and incorporating provisions to ease some nontariff barriers. SAPTA-3, signed in 1998, was the most ambitious of the three agreements, covering 2,700 items. Work on SAPTA-4 was initiated in 1999 but was put on hold after the change of regime in Pakistan on October 12, 1999. Politics had once again interrupted the advance of regional integration in South Asia.

However, after the SAARC itself was stalled in 2001–02 because of continuing hostility between India and Pakistan, India concluded bilateral agreements with its smaller neighbors to increase trade. As a consequence, the total value of regional trade increased rapidly during the late 1980s and most of the 1990s, but not the share of regional trade in total trade. This was principally because of unilateral trade liberalization by countries on India's borders and large appreciations of the exchange rates of the peripheral countries relative to the Indian rupee. Most of the increased trade was one way, with large increases in exports from India, especially to Bangladesh and Sri Lanka. This growth in regional trade had little to do with the granting of regional trade preferences under SAPTA.

The South Asian Free Trade Area

At SAARC's 12th summit, held in Islamabad, Pakistan, in January 2004, the seven heads of state of the member nations took a major step toward regional economic integration: They agreed to launch SAFTA by January 1, 2006. This step was meant to have been taken earlier: At their summit in 1997, SAARC leaders had agreed to launch SAFTA by 2001. The five-year delay was caused by a series of developments: the rapid deteriora-

---

14. See www.saarc-sec.org (accessed February 8, 2006).

tion of relations between India and Pakistan following nuclear tests by the two countries in May 1998, the military takeover in Pakistan in October 1999, and the near war between the two nations in 2001–02, when more than a million soldiers were massed along the Indo-Pakistan border. Tensions eased starting in April 2003, when Atal Bihari Vajpayee, then prime minister of India, pledged to work toward creating a peaceful South Asian region.

SAFTA is a traditional trade agreement in that it does not include some of the nontrade issues incorporated in other regional trade agreements (RTAs) (and in that sense, South Asia lags behind its peers). SAFTA covers tariff reductions, rules of origin, safeguards, institutional structures, and dispute settlement. It also calls for the adoption of trade facilitation measures such as harmonization of standards and mutual recognition of test results, harmonization of customs procedures, and cooperation in improving transport infrastructure. These measures can help significantly reduce the transaction costs of regional trade.

As shown in table A.8, the SAFTA tariff reduction program stipulates average weighted tariffs of no more than 20 percent by the region's more developed economies—India, Pakistan, and Sri Lanka—within two years of the implementation of the agreement. Within five years after the completion of the first phase, India and Pakistan will adjust their tariffs to between 0 and 5 percent. The region's least developed countries—Bangladesh, Bhutan, Maldives, and Nepal—are required to have average weighted tariffs of no more than 30 percent within two years, but may be allowed eight years for the second downward adjustment. Sri Lanka will be allowed six years for the second phase. India, Pakistan, and Sri Lanka will thus reduce their tariffs on imports from regional partners to the agreed low levels no later than January 1, 2009. The agreement also calls for the elimination of all quantitative restrictions for products on the tariff liberalization list. While member states have been allowed to develop lists of sensitive items that would not be subjected fully to the stipulated tariff cuts, the number of products to be included in the country lists would be subject to review every four years.

The Islamabad Declaration established institutional mechanisms to oversee the implementation of SAFTA. A ministerial council will be the highest decision-making authority while a committee of experts (CoE) will closely monitor the implementation of the agreement and resolve disputes. The CoE will report to the ministers every six months on the progress of the agreement, which is to be fully implemented by 2015 (SAARC 2004).

After the Islamabad summit, member countries made significant progress toward concordance on rules of origin and "sensitive" lists, but not on compensation for members that fear the loss of revenue once SAFTA is in place, or that request technical assistance for dealing with transition issues. The CoE met several times following the 2004 summit

Table A.8 Planned phased tariff cuts on intra-SAFTA trade

SAARC country	First phase[a] January 2006– January 2008	Second phase[a]	
		January 2008– January 2013 for non-LDCs	January 2016 for LDCs
LDCs: Bangladesh, Bhutan, Maldives, and Nepal	Reduce maximum tariff to 30 percent		Reduce tariffs to the 0 to 5 percent range in eight years (equal annual reductions recommended, but not less than 10 percent).
Non-LDCs: India, Pakistan, and Sri Lanka[c]	Reduce maximum tariff rate to 20 percent	Reduce tariffs to the 0 to 5 percent range in five years.[b] Reduce tariffs to 0 to 5 percent for products of the LDCs within three years.	

LDC = least developed country
SAARC = South Asian Association for Regional Cooperation
SAFTA = South Asian Free Trade Area

a. These phased tariff cuts for intra-SAFTA trade may not apply to items on each country's "sensitive list."
b. It is recommended that reductions be done in equal installments, with at least a 15 percent reduction of the base tariff per year.
c. Sri Lanka is allowed six years to reduce its tariffs to the 0 to 5 percent range.

Source: World Bank (2004a).

and was expected to hold its concluding session in July 2005. Indeed, there were high expectations that the heads of government would make sufficient progress during SAARC's 13th summit (scheduled for January 2005) to ready the region for the launch of SAFTA on January 1, 2006. Unfortunately, both nature and politics intervened. The summit was postponed to early February 2006 to allow the governments of the affected countries to deal with the tsunami tragedy of December 26, 2004. Then, in February 2005, the king of Nepal removed his country's prime minister and assumed the role of chief executive. This elicited a very negative response from Indian Prime Minister Manmohan Singh, who announced that he would not attend a summit at which the Nepalese king would be present as the head of government. India also pointed to a series of skirmishes between the government and opposition parties in Bangladesh as a security problem, and demanded that the meeting at Dhaka be rescheduled.

Scheduling the summit, therefore, became a political issue. In early February 2005, Chandrika Kumaratunga, the Sri Lankan president, visited Islamabad to sign agreements and protocols with Pakistan, including an FTA. At the banquet for the visiting head of state, President Musharraf declared that "Pakistan believes that we need to inject more seriousness into SAARC, which is for the benefit of all South Asian countries and postponement of the summit does not augur well for the effectiveness of this organization."[15]

The 13th SAARC summit meeting was finally held in November 2005 at Dhaka, Bangladesh. The governments did not take up the issue of the timely launch of SAFTA, instead leaving the CoE to finalize recommendations on the various issues that had to be resolved before the agreement could be implemented. No new date was set for the inauguration of SAFTA. Although the agreement had been ratified by five SAARC countries in order for it to become effective in January 2006, Pakistan and Sri Lanka delayed ratification until early 2006. Pakistan was the last country to ratify SAFTA in February 2006.

Pros and Cons of Regional Trade Arrangements

Among the three approaches to increasing trade among countries, purists prefer unilateral action not contingent on the granting of reciprocity by trading partners.[16] The second-best approach is to conduct negotiations on the removal of barriers to cross-border trade in the context of multilateral rounds, such as the Tokyo and Uruguay Rounds under GATT auspices, and the ongoing WTO Doha Development Round. According to the purists' line of thinking, the least satisfactory approach is to start with bilateral or regional integration as a first step in easing constraints on global trade.

Notwithstanding the skepticism of purists, regional agreements have proliferated. The number of bilateral FTAs and regional trade agreements (RTAs) has more than quadrupled since 1990, rising to about 230 in 2004 (World Bank 2004b). Trade between FTA and RTA partners now constitutes nearly 40 percent of the world total.

As countries reduce tariffs across the board, however, the value of preferences decline and trade facilitation acquires more importance. As a recent World Bank study emphasizes, "trade policies are one element—and often a relatively minor one—of the overall costs of trade" (World Bank 2004c, 21). Three key components of trade facilitation are worthy of

---

15. "Pakistan, Sri Lanka See Boost in Trade," *Dawn*, February 9, 2005.

16. The Indian economist Jagdish Bhagwati is one of the most articulate exponents of this point of view. For his approach to international trade see Bhagwati (2002).

attention: customs clearance, transport, and standards. Costs of trade, which include custom procedures, port bottlenecks, and conformity to standards, can amount to 30 to 105 percent of the tariff on trade. Lowering these costs can have beneficial impacts as important as those accruing from eliminating tariffs.

Unlike several factors that increase the transaction costs of international trade, there is general agreement about good customs procedures. The World Customs Organization has developed a list of best practices, which the Kyoto Convention commits its signatories to implement. A review of initiatives to modernize customs in the South Asian region suggests a number of areas where change and modernization would be productive. These include (a) aligning customs codes and international standards, (b) simplifying and harmonizing procedures, (c) bringing all tariff structures in line with the international harmonized tariff classification, (d) striving for transparency, (e) adopting and effectively implementing the WTO customs valuation agreement, and (f) establishing joint border posts.

The second broad area of facilitation concerns improvements in transport, where inefficiencies can be costly. In the Andean Community, for instance, trucks spend more than half of their journey time at border crossings (Prado 2001). It is estimated that each day lost to transport delays is equivalent to a tax of about 0.5 percent on the value of trade worldwide. The situation in the developing world is much worse (Hummels 2000). In recent years a number of transport and trade facilitation agreements have been negotiated—as part of, or in conjunction with, an FTA or RTA—to ease the movement of goods and services across borders.

One way to introduce efficiency in the transport sector is to encourage compensation among the partners in a regional arrangement. But this requires legal frameworks and effective enforcement mechanisms, both of which take time and resources to achieve. For instance, the European Union fully implemented such agreements only in 1985, 28 years after the signing of the Treaty of Rome. Yet many would agree that the time and resources required are worth it, as the option of legal action under regional treaties can help in the effective implementation of transport agreements. In the European Union, for example, the European Court of Justice has played an important role.

The third important series of trade facilitation measures includes the formulation and implementation of systems of standards, quality assurance, accreditation, and metrology. To reduce the negative consequences of divergent standards, WTO members have agreed to discipline the use of mandatory standards by governments. The scope of this discipline is relatively modest: The governments have committed themselves to transparency of their standards regimes and equal treatment of all trading partners. Until now, according to a recent World Bank study, "RTAs in the developing world have not realized their full potential for overcoming standards-related obstacles to regional or global trade, although some slow progress is evident, such as in Mercado Común del Sur (Mercosur). That is likely to change as the WTO Agreements on Technical Barriers to Trade and Sanitary and Phytosanitary Measures come into full practical application, and as the importance of reforming standards systems in developing countries gains prominence. In the meantime, several principles can contribute to successful cooperation in standards and conformity assessment procedures" (World Bank 2004b, 89).

New FTAs and RTAs, including those between developed and developing countries (also called North-South agreements), are addressing issues that go beyond trade—investment rights, labor and environmental laws, and, in some cases, political openness.[17] Most South-South agreements, however, focus on merchandise trade, and tend to treat services, investment, and intellectual property rights unevenly or ignore them altogether. Agreements such as those of ASEAN and Mercosur have not provided specifically for liberalization of services beyond the arrangements that have resulted from unilateral actions by the member states or that are included in multilateral accords such as the WTO General Agreement on Trade in Services (GATS).

Services should be included in RTAs because they play a large role in the economies of developing countries and attract foreign investment. According to a recent study on economic integration in Latin America, controlling for other factors, countries with fully liberalized financial and telecommunications sectors grew annually on average about 1.5 percentage points faster than other countries (Mattoo and Sauvé 2004). Liberalizing services allows more suppliers to compete in the regional market, lowering prices and increasing efficiency. And including services in trading agreements does not erode government revenues because, in contrast to goods, the movement of services across international borders is normally not taxed.

Do RTAs attract more investment? The World Bank recently investigated the effects of 238 FTAs and RTAs (along with other variables) on foreign direct investment (FDI) inflows for 152 countries over a period of 22 years, from 1980 to 2002. In general the Bank found that the countries that were open (measured as the ratio of trade to GDP) grew more rapidly, were more stable (measured by rates of inflation), and attracted greater amounts of FDI. On average, a 10 percent increase in market size associated with an RTA produces a 5 percent increase in FDI. However,

---

17. Although some North-North agreements, such as the recent expansion of the European Union, have incorporated labor standards, most North-South and South-South agreements are confined to intrafirm movements of professionals. They do not substantially increase access for temporary workers, skilled or unskilled.

the study underscored that an RTA cannot substitute for an adequate investment climate (World Bank 2004b).

Analysts who support RTAs as stepping-stones toward free international trade maintain that geographic proximity is a good reason to encourage them. In supporting the "natural bloc" concept, some trade experts have used gravity models[18] to argue that proximity and combined market size are good determinants of the quantum of trade.[19] It is natural for neighboring countries to have intense trade relations.

But proximity has not worked in South Asia, where intraregional trade remains an insignificant component of total trade and, it has been argued, is not a good enough reason to expend a great deal of political and bureaucratic energy in moving toward regional integration in South Asia (Lahiri 1998). This discussion therefore comes to a different conclusion: Given the long history of intraregional trade when the now independent states were part of the British Indian Empire, some of the old trade patterns could be reestablished once the right environment for them is created.

This conclusion is also supported by the results from Dean DeRosa's gravity model estimation for the post–Uruguay Round period 1995–99, presented in table A.9. The explanatory variables in the gravity model remain much the same as before (see chapter 8), including the three RTA variables (see table B.1 for descriptions of the variables).[20]

The overall explanatory power of the present gravity model results (R-squared = 0.54) is somewhat higher than found previously (R-squared = 0.40) (see table 8A.1), but the profile of individual coefficient estimates, and their significance, remains much the same, with the possible exception of the coefficient estimates for the RTA variables. Although the coefficient estimate for the middle- and low-income country RTA variable (–0.27) is nearly identical to the previous estimate (–0.28) and remains significant, the coefficients for the other two RTA variables (both positive and significant) are about 50 percent higher than found previously.

Using the coefficients obtained in the new gravity model estimation, DeRosa has calculated predicted-to-actual intra-SAPTA trade ratios (table A.10) and predicted-to-actual global trade ratios of SAPTA members (table A.11). One consistent finding in the intra-SAPTA calculations is that actual

---

18. These models draw their name from Newtonian physics in that trade flows between two countries increase in proportion to their economic mass (as measured by their respective GDPs) and are constrained by the friction between them (proxied by the distance between them) due to transaction and other costs.

19. See, for instance, Frankel, Stein, and Wei (1997) and chapter 8 of this report.

20. The joint Transparency International variable, which is designed to measure the extent of corruption in the two partner countries, was dropped in the calculations presented in tables A.10 through A.12 because data were available only for India and Pakistan in South Asia.

Table A.9 Gravity model estimates for aggregate trade in South Asia, 1995–99

Variable	Estimate
Constant	−10.40***
Distance	−0.96***
Joint GDP	0.73***
Joint GDP per capita	−0.39***
Common language	0.31***
Common border	1.32***
Landlocked	−0.77***
Island	0.40***
Land area	−0.11***
Common colonizer	−0.04
Colony	0.26
Ever a colony	1.37***
Common country	−1.11
Currency union	1.39***
GSP	0.58***
EU and US RTAs (11)	1.04***
Other HIC RTAs (10)	0.59***
MIC and LIC RTAs (39)	−0.27***
R-squared	0.54
Observations (thousands)	43
Groups (thousands)	10

***, **, * indicate that the coefficients are statistically significant at the 99, 95, and 90 percent levels, respectively.

GSP = generalized system of preferences

HIC, MIC, LIC = high-, middle-, low-income country

RTA = regional trade agreement

Notes: Regressand is log real trade. Distance, joint GDP, joint GDP per capita, and land area are measured in log terms. Estimated year and country effects are not reported. Numbers in parentheses indicate how many RTAs are covered by the separate RTA variables. Groups are numbers of country pair–commodity combinations for which trade exists in the data sample.

To investigate intra-SAPTA trade using the Rose (2004) gravity model, it was necessary to refine the trade data compiled from the Feenstra et al. (2005) dataset. Most important, the trade data were recompiled to individually identify exporting countries and importing countries (in table 8.1, bilateral trade flows between specific country pairs were simply combined). Additionally, the trade data were recompiled on a total basis—that is, aggregating trade flows over all categories of commodities, manufactures, and other traded goods (SITC 0 through 9). Finally, it should be noted that the bilateral and world trade of both Bhutan and the Maldives is not reported in the Feenstra et al. dataset. Moreover, close inspection of the trade data reveals little or no reported trade between some SAPTA partners (for example, Bangladesh and Nepal).

Source: Dean DeRosa's calculations based on generalized least squares estimation of the Rose (2004) gravity model with random effects, using a combined version of the Rose (2004) and the Feenstra et al. (2005) datasets.

Table A.10 Predicted versus actual SAPTA intraregional trade, 1999
(millions of US dollars, based on 1995–99 estimates)

	Importer				
Exporter	Bangladesh	India	Nepal	Pakistan	Sri Lanka
Predicted trade					
Bangladesh	n.a.	2,316	n.a.	469	n.a.
India	2,316	n.a.	322	3,141	296
Nepal	n.a.	322	n.a.	20	n.a.
Pakistan	469	3,141	20	n.a.	46
Sri Lanka	n.a.	296	n.a.	46	n.a.
Actual trade					
Bangladesh	n.a.	78	0[a]	27	0[a]
India	628	n.a.	143	128	490
Nepal	0[a]	189	n.a.	0.6	0[a]
Pakistan	118	68	1.0	n.a.	101
Sri Lanka	0[a]	44	0[a]	35	n.a.
Predicted-to-actual trade					
Bangladesh	n.a.	29.6	n.c.	17.3	n.c.
India	3.7	n.a.	2.3	24.6	0.6
Nepal	n.c.	1.71	n.a.	31.5	n.c.
Pakistan	4.0	46.1	14.1	n.a.	0.5
Sri Lanka	n.c.	6.7	n.c.	1.3	n.a.

n.a. = not applicable. Trade predictions are not made when no trade is recorded between two countries. When the exporter and importer are the same country, there is no international trade.

n.c. = not calculated. Observations that are recorded as "0" are dropped from the calculation of ratios.

SAPTA = SAARC Preferential Trading Arrangement

SAARC = South Asian Association for Regional Cooperation.

a. Trade values that are not reported are often recorded as "0" although a small amount of trade may take place.

Note: See table 8A.1 for coefficients of independent variables used in the gravity model estimations.

Source: Dean DeRosa's calculations based on generalized least squares estimation of the Rose (2004) gravity model with random effects, using a combined version of the Rose (2004) and Feenstra et al. (2005) datasets.

trade between members falls far below predicted values. For example, Pakistan's exports to India are 46 times less than the gravity model would predict, and its imports from India, Nepal, and Bangladesh are also much lower than predicted. Turning to global trade, while both India and Sri Lanka appear to enjoy better trade performance than generally predicted by the gravity model, Pakistan, Bangladesh, and Nepal do not.[21]

---

21. Of course, Sri Lanka and India do not compare favorably to China on this metric, but China is an outlier in gravity model equations.

Table A.11 Predicted versus actual global trade of SAPTA members, 1999
(millions of US dollars, based on 1995–99 estimates)

| Country | GDP | Predicted | | | Actual | | Predicted/actual |
		(X+M)	(X+M)/GDP	(X+M)	(X+M)/GDP	(X+M)/GDP
Bangladesh	48,301	14,445	0.30	10,106	0.21	1.43
India	449,846	58,810	0.13	81,467	0.18	0.72
Nepal	5,012	2034	0.41	1,177	0.23	1.73
Pakistan	70,598	22,703	0.32	15,324	0.22	1.48
Sri Lanka	15,698	4,972	0.32	8,512	0.54	0.58

M = imports
X = exports

Note: See table 8A.1 for coefficients of independent variables used in the gravity model estimations.

Source: Dean DeRosa's calculations based on generalized least squares estimation of the Rose (2004) gravity model with random effects, using a combined version of the Rose (2004) and Feenstra et al. (2005) datasets.

As shown in table A.11, Pakistan's predicted trade-to-GDP ratio is 32 percent, while the actual ratio is 22 percent, and Bangladesh's ratio is almost identical to that of Pakistan. Of the five regional members included in the estimate, only Nepal falls shorter of its predicted trade ratio than Pakistan. These results underscore the great potential for Pakistan to increase both its intraregional and global trade.

Even at this early stage of analysis of the possible economic outcome of SAFTA, it is important to underscore that the success of the contemplated regional arrangement will also depend on noneconomic outcomes. As the late Robin Cook, former foreign minister of Britain, said of the signing of the European Constitution, "Pause for a while to contemplate the remarkable transformation of European politics which made this event possible. Most of the countries sitting together in the same council chamber have been at war with each other in living memory, and repeatedly in the century that preceded it." At the same time he noted that progress toward increasing economic and political associations among the countries of Europe was not always easy: "[The] appeal [of opponents] to past millennium betrays what drives their resistance to European integration—a misplaced nostalgia for the outdated world of freestanding nations. It is an era that has vanished. We are all interdependent now."[22]

---

22. Robin Cook, "A Strong Europe—or Bush's Feral US Capitalism," *The Guardian*, October 29, 2004, 26.

Could a regional trading arrangement in South Asia, such as the one envisaged under SAFTA, set in motion the same kind of dynamism that has brought the countries of Europe together in the European Union? The answer will have to await the passage of time. But the brief overview above of economic development in the South Asian region underscores the point made by Robin Cook: The weight of much historical baggage has to be cast off before countries in a region that has suffered a great deal of conflict can begin to work together. Thus our focus has been on relations between India and Pakistan—how they have improved recently after deteriorating for so long, and how SAFTA might help to bring about greater economic cooperation between them and among all the countries in the region.

For Pakistan, an FTA with the United States could complement SAFTA by increasing its trade both within South Asia and with the rest of the world. A US-Pakistan FTA could also push the reform process among SAFTA member countries as they see the benefits that Pakistan gains by opening up. A US-Pakistan FTA would be one of several US FTAs with a single regional partner, such as the US agreements with Singapore, Australia, Colombia, and Peru. A US-Pakistan FTA and the successful launch of SAFTA will ensure increased competition between US and Indian suppliers in the Pakistani market for a range of manufactured goods. Ultimately, the desired outcome is progress toward better economic policies, and both agreements can make positive contributions toward that goal.

Conclusion

There is no doubt that the successful launch of SAFTA—the delayed inauguration occurred in July 2006—will bring about profound changes in the economies of South Asia. Some of these changes were investigated by a team of economists that worked on a US Agency for International Development (USAID)–sponsored project that resulted in a report on the *South Asian Free Trade Area: Opportunities and Challenges* (USAID 2005). According to the report's chapter on Pakistan, the most significant impact of SAFTA will be a sharp increase in Pakistan's international trade as a proportion of GDP. Including trade with Afghanistan (which would be conducted mostly through formal channels), total international trade for Pakistan could increase at a rate of 10 to 12 percent per year in the next 10 years; in real terms this would mean an increase from the present $34 billion to $90 billion. Trade with India is likely to increase tenfold from the current $2 billion (including informal trade) to $20 billion. In other words, of the $58 billion increase in total trade projected for this period, some $18 billion—or almost 31 percent of the increase—could come from Pakistan's new trade with India.

Table A.12 Current and projected value of Pakistan's trade, 2004 versus 2014 (billions of US dollars)

Type of trade	2004			2014		
	Exports	Imports	Total	Exports	Imports	Total
Formal	14.0	18.0	32.0	43.0	47.0	90.0
Informal	0.5	1.0	1.5	n.a.	n.a.	n.a.
Total	14.5	19.0	33.5	43.0	47.0	90.0
Trade-to-GDP ratio (percent)			30.0			42.0

n.a. = not available

Source: Burki and Akbar (2005).

Agriculture and light engineering products will become important export items, while industrial raw material and capital equipment will become important import items. Agriculture should regain some of the importance it had 50 years ago, at the time of Pakistan's independence from Britain. With transit trade earning more foreign exchange , the transport sector should benefit through the modernization of the trucking, processing, warehousing, and packaging industries. Pakistan could also see a major increase in tourism as Indians begin to visit holy sites.

Some of the changes in the projected value of Pakistan's bilateral trade are presented in table A.12, and changes in the destinations of Pakistan's trade are shown in table A.13. In this scenario, the share of the United States declines from one-fifth of Pakistan's total trade to about one-eighth, while the share of India increases more than fourfold. However, if Pakistan simultaneously opens its economy through a bilateral FTA with the United States, there could be a large absolute expansion in bilateral US-Pakistan trade, even as Pakistan's commerce with the SAFTA countries grows at a faster pace.

The USAID project also discussed the impact of SAFTA on India and other countries of South Asia. India's trade expansion is likely to take the form of gains in intraindustry movement of goods, possible vertical integration, and industrial restructuring. Gains from SAFTA can be augmented for India and the other member countries if its scope is broadened to include infrastructure development and liberalization of investment and services.

Table A.13 Projected destinations of Pakistan's trade, 2004 versus 2014

(percent share of total trade)

Country	2004	2014
Afghanistan	5	9
Dubai	6	n.a.
India	5	22
Saudi Arabia	10	12
United Kingdom	4	3
United States	19	12
Subtotal	49	58

n.a. = not available

Source: Burki and Akbar (2005).

Appendix B
Technical Aspects of the Gravity and Computable General Equilibrium Models

DEAN DeROSA and JOHN P. GILBERT

Gravity Model

As mentioned in chapter 8, the gravity model analysis underlying this study is based on a dataset specially constructed by joining the elements of two large datasets developed by other researchers. The first of these is an extensive gravity model dataset developed by Andrew Rose (2004) that covers aggregate bilateral merchandise trade between 178 countries from 1948 to 1999 (with gaps and excluding Taiwan and some centrally planned economies), compiled from the International Monetary Fund's (IMF) *Directions of Trade Statistics*. The bilateral trade figures in the Rose dataset are averages of free on board (f.o.b) export and cost, insurance, freight (c.i.f) import data in US dollars, deflated by the US consumer price index.

The Rose dataset also includes the "core" and regional trade agreement (RTA) explanatory variables discussed in chapter 8 and identified in tables 8A.1 and 8A.2.[1] The core explanatory variables are drawn from several standard sources, including the CIA's *World Factbook*, the IMF's *International Financial Statistics*, Penn World Table, and World Bank's *World Development Indicators*.[2]

Dean DeRosa is a visiting fellow at the Institute for International Economics. John P. Gilbert is associate professor of economics in the Department of Economics, Utah State University, Logan, Utah.

1. The US-Pakistan trade integration and openness dummy variables were compiled for the present study and added to the dataset by the authors.

2. See CIA's *World Factbook*, www.cia.gov; IMF's *International Financial Statistics*, http://ifs.apdi.net/imf; Penn World Table, http://pwt.econ.upenn.edu; and World Bank's *World Development Indicators*, www.worldbank.org.

To provide the Rose gravity model and dataset with somewhat greater analytical depth, the Rose dataset was concorded with bilateral merchandise trade data at the 1-digit Standard International Trade Classification (SITC) level, taken from the highly disaggregated bilateral trade dataset compiled by Feenstra et al. (2005). The Feenstra et al. dataset covers bilateral trade data for 1962–2000, organized by 4-digit SITC (Revision 2) categories. In contrast to the Rose trade data, world trade flows in the Feenstra et al. dataset are drawn from United Nations data sources and are based primarily on reporter-country import data (supplemented as possible where import data gaps occur by reporter country export data). The Feenstra et al. (2005) dataset covers a somewhat smaller number of trading countries than does the Rose dataset, especially during the period 1984–2000, when the bilateral trade of only 72 countries is represented in the dataset (but still accounts for 98 percent of world exports during 1996–2000).

For the present study, the Feenstra et al. (2005) world trade data were aggregated to the 1-digit SITC level by country pairs and deflated by the US consumer price index (1983 = 100). After transforming these real trade flows to natural logarithmic terms, they were finally integrated with the Rose data using a concordance between the UN (Feenstra et al.) country codes and IMF (Rose) country codes. In the process, we took account of all adjustments to the UN trade data reported by Feenstra et al. (2005), except the estimated redistribution of value added in trade between China and Hong Kong, separately reported in Feenstra et al. (2005). Lost in the process, however, were disaggregated trade flows for the former Soviet bloc countries, some less developed countries, and Taiwan, for which no UN (Feenstra et al.) or IMF (Rose) country codes were available. The separate UN country codes for former West Germany and present-day Germany were merged in the Feenstra et al. (2005) dataset before integrating the two datasets, thus preserving pre-1991 observations on the bilateral disaggregated trade of West Germany (including with Pakistan).

Finally, as also discussed in chapter 8, the explanatory variables in the Rose dataset are augmented by more up-to-date and comprehensive information about 60 bilateral and regional trade agreements involving the European Union and the United States, other high-income countries, and middle- and low-income countries worldwide, based on the official notifications to the World Trade Organization of the membership and start date of the agreements reported in Crawford and Fiorentino (2005). The explanatory variables in the Rose dataset are also augmented by the inclusion of a variable for the integrity of business practices by pairs of trading countries. This last explanatory variable is constructed from the ranking of countries by the extent of their corrupt business practices, as based on the perceptions of international businessmen and financial journalists compiled and reported annually since 1995 by Transparency International (www.transparency.org).

Table B.1 Gravity model regression variables, 1962–99

Regression variable	Description
Dependent variable	Log value of bilateral trade by 1-digit SITC, real US dollars
Distance	Log of distance
Joint GDP	Log of product of real GDPs
Joint GDP per capita	Log of product of real GDPs per capita
Common language	Common language dummy
Common border	Land border dummy
Landlocked	Number of countries landlocked (0/1/2)
Island	Number of island countries (0/1/2)
Land area	Log of product of land areas
Common colonizer	Dummy for common colonizer post-1945
Colony	Dummy for country pairs currently in colonial relationship
Ever a colony	Dummy for country pairs ever in colonial relationship
Common country	Dummy for same nation/perennial colonies
Currency union	Strict currency union dummy
GSP	GSP dummy
EU and US RTAs	Dummy for European Union and 10 RTAs with EU or US hubs
Other HIC RTAs	Dummy for 10 other high-income country RTAs
MIC and LIC RTAs	Dummy for 39 middle- and low-income country RTAs
Joint TI index	Log of product of Transparency International corruption index
US-Pakistan trade	Dummy for US-Pakistan trade
US openness	Dummy for US trade with all partners
Pakistan openness	Dummy for Pakistan trade with all partners

GSP = generalized system of preferences
RTA = regional trade agreement

Notes: Dependent variable based on bilateral trade flows drawn from the Feenstra et al. (2005) dataset. RTAs and US-Pakistan trade and openness variables constructed by the authors.

Sources: Rose (2004); Feenstra et al. (2005); Crawford and Fiorentino (2005); Transparency International (2005).

Table B.1 describes the regression variables included in the combined Feenstra et al. and Rose datasets, and table B.2 identifies the bilateral and regional trade agreements (RTAs) covered by the three combined RTA variables constructed for the gravity model analysis in chapter 8.

Table B.2 Regional trade agreements, 1962–99

Agreement	Date of entry into force	Type of agreement	Combined RTA regression variable
EU (Treaty of Rome)	January 1, 1958	Customs union	EU and US RTAs
EFTA (Stockholm Convention)	May 3, 1960	Free trade agreement	Other HIC RTA
Central American Common Market	October 12, 1961	Customs union	MIC and LIC RTAs
Tripartite Agreement	April 1, 1968	Preferential arrangement	MIC and LIC RTAs
EU–Switzerland and Liechtenstein	January 1, 1973	Free trade agreement	EU and US RTAs
PTN	February 11, 1973	Preferential arrangement	MIC and LIC RTAs
EU-Iceland	April 1, 1973	Free trade agreement	EU and US RTAs
EU-Norway	July 1, 1973	Free trade agreement	EU and US RTAs
Caricom	August 1, 1973	Customs union	MIC and LIC RTAs
Bangkok Agreement	June 17, 1976	Preferential arrangement	MIC and LIC RTAs
EU-Algeria	July 1, 1976	Free trade agreement	EU and US RTAs
Patcra	February 1, 1977	Free trade agreement	Other HIC RTAs
Sparteca	January 1, 1981	Preferential arrangement	Other HIC RTAs
LAIA	March 18, 1981	Preferential arrangement	MIC and LIC RTAs
Anzcerta	January 1, 1983	Free trade agreement	Other HIC RTAs
Gulf Cooperation Council	July 1, 1983	Preferential arrangement	MIC and LIC RTAs
US-Israel	August 19, 1985	Free trade agreement	EU and US RTAs
Andean Community	May 25, 1988	Preferential arrangement	MIC and LIC RTAs
GSTP	April 19, 1989	Preferential arrangement	MIC and LIC RTAs
Laos-Thailand	June 20, 1991	Preferential arrangement	MIC and LIC RTAs
Mercosur	November 29, 1991	Customs union	MIC and LIC RTAs
AFTA	January 28, 1992	Preferential arrangement	MIC and LIC RTAs
EFTA-Turkey	April 1, 1992	Free trade agreement	Other HIC RTAs
EFTA-Israel	January 1, 1993	Free trade agreement	Other HIC RTAs
Central European FTA	March 1, 1993	Free trade agreement	MIC and LIC RTAs
Armenia–Russian Federation	March 25, 1993	Free trade agreement	MIC and LIC RTAs
Kyrgyz Republic–Russian Federation	April 24, 1993	Free trade agreement	MIC and LIC RTAs
EU-Romania	May 1, 1993	Free trade agreement	EU and US RTAs
EFTA-Romania	May 1, 1993	Free trade agreement	Other HIC RTAs
EFTA-Bulgaria	July 1, 1993	Free trade agreement	Other HIC RTAs
Melanesian Spearhead Group	July 22, 1993	Preferential arrangement	MIC and LIC RTAs
EU-Bulgaria	December 31, 1993	Free trade agreement	EU and US RTAs
NAFTA	January 1, 1994	Free trade agreement	EU and US RTAs
Georgia–Russian Federation	May 10, 1994	Free trade agreement	MIC and LIC RTAs
Comesa	December 8, 1994	Preferential arrangement	MIC and LIC RTAs
Commonwealth of Independent States	December 30, 1994	Free trade agreement	MIC and LIC RTAs
Romania-Moldova	January 1, 1995	Free trade agreement	MIC and LIC RTAs

(table continues next page)

Table B.2 *(continued)*

Agreement	Date of entry into force	Type of agreement	Combined RTA regression variable
Kyrgyz Republic–Armenia	October 27, 1995	Free trade agreement	MIC and LIC RTAs
Kyrgyz Republic–Kazakhstan	November 11, 1995	Free trade agreement	MIC and LIC RTAs
SAPTA	December 7, 1995	Preferential arrangement	MIC and LIC RTAs
Armenia-Moldova	December 21, 1995	Free trade agreement	MIC and LIC RTAs
EU-Turkey	January 1, 1996	Customs union	EU and US RTAs
Georgia-Ukraine	June 4, 1996	Free trade agreement	MIC and LIC RTAs
Armenia-Turkmenistan	July 7, 1996	Free trade agreement	MIC and LIC RTAs
Georgia-Azerbaijan	July 10, 1996	Free trade agreement	MIC and LIC RTAs
Kyrgyz Republic–Moldova	November 21, 1996	Free trade agreement	MIC and LIC RTAs
Armenia-Ukraine	December 18, 1996	Free trade agreement	MIC and LIC RTAs
Canada-Israel	January 1, 1997	Free trade agreement	Other HIC RTAs
Israel-Turkey	May 1, 1997	Free trade agreement	MIC and LIC RTAs
Canada-Chile	July 5, 1997	Free trade agreement	Other HIC RTAs
Eurasian Economic Community	October 8, 1997	Customs union	MIC and LIC RTAs
Kyrgyz Republic–Ukraine	January 19, 1998	Free trade agreement	MIC and LIC RTAs
Romania-Turkey	February 1, 1998	Free trade agreement	MIC and LIC RTAs
EU-Tunisia	March 1, 1998	Free trade agreement	EU and US RTAs
Kyrgyz Republic–Uzbekistan	March 20, 1998	Free trade agreement	MIC and LIC RTAs
Georgia-Armenia	November 11, 1998	Free trade agreement	MIC and LIC RTAs
Bulgaria-Turkey	January 1, 1999	Free trade agreement	MIC and LIC RTAs
CEMAC	June 24, 1999	Preferential arrangement	MIC and LIC RTAs
Georgia-Kazakhstan	July 16, 1999	Free trade agreement	MIC and LIC RTAs
Chile-Mexico	August 1, 1999	Free trade agreement	MIC and LIC RTAs

AFTA = ASEAN Free Trade Area
Anzcerta = Australia–New Zealand Closer Economic Relations Trade Agreement
ASEAN = Association of Southeast Asian Nations
Caricom = Caribbean Community
CEMAC = Economic and Monetary Community of Central Africa
Comesa = Common Market for Eastern and Southern Africa
EFTA = European Free Trade Association
GSTP = General System of Trade Preferences among Developing Countries
HIC, MIC, LIC = high-, middle-, low-income country
LAIA = Latin American Integration Association
Mercosur = Southern Cone Common Market
NAFTA = North American Free Trade Agreement
Patcra = Agreement on Trade and Commercial Relations between Australia and Papua New Guinea
PTN = Protocol Relating to Trade Negotiations among Developing Countries
SAPTA = SAARC Preferential Trade Arrangement
Sparteca = South Pacific Regional Trade and Economic Cooperation
SAARC = South Asian Association for Regional Cooperation

Sources: Crawford and Fiorentino (2005); table B.1.

Estimating Techniques

As might be expected, the estimation of gravity models using cross-sectional time-series data presents some complex and difficult problems in econometric methodology (Egger 2002, Hsiao 2003). Essentially, ordinary least squares regression is unsatisfactory because it does not admit possible unobserved effects related to the combinations of commodities and pairs of trading countries in the dataset. As a consequence, the analysis reported in chapter 8 utilizes a random-effects variant of the gravity model, using generalized least squares (GLS) as the estimating technique. For a discussion of the application of the GLS technique to a random-effects regression model, see Hsiao (2003). An important assumption of the random-effects approach, embodied in the estimation results reported in chapter 8, is that the unobservable random-effects variable is uncorrelated with the observed explanatory variables included in the regression equation.

CGE Model

As mentioned in chapter 8, our computable general equilibrium (CGE) model is based on the Global Trade Analysis Project (GTAP) framework, a publicly available model that is widely adopted. The GTAP model is a multiregion, multisector model that assumes perfect competition and constant returns to scale. Bilateral trade is handled via the Armington assumption, which treats goods from alternative sources as imperfect substitutes. Import demand functions are separated by agent (sometimes called the Salter specification).[3] Production conditions are modeled using "nested" constant elasticity of substitution (CES) functions,[4] and intermediate goods are used in fixed proportions.[5] Representative household demand takes into account changes in demand structures as incomes rise.[6] These and other aspects of the GTAP model are fully documented in Hertel (1997) and on the GTAP Web site at www.gtap.org. Recent surveys of the application of CGE mod-

---

3. In other words, the aggregate household, government, investor, and each firm all make their own individual choices about how much of each intermediate input to source domestically and how much to import.

4. The CES function treats primary factors of production (capital, skilled and unskilled labor, natural resources, and land) as imperfect substitutes in the production process, with a single elasticity describing substitutability between all factor pairs. Intermediate inputs are used in fixed proportion to output.

5. For any given proportional change in output, intermediate input will grow by the same proportion. The input-output coefficients are obtained from the input-output tables routinely produced by statistical agencies in most economies, and constructed for the few regions where the data are unavailable.

6. Changes in demand structure are modeled by so-called nonhomothetic demand functions.

els to regional trade negotiations include Scollay and Gilbert (2000, 2001), Gilbert and Wahl (2002), Robinson and Thierfelder (2002), and Lloyd and MacLaren (2004).

Base Data

The base data for the simulations are drawn from the GTAP6 database (final release), which represents the world economy as of 2001 and is the most complete dataset available. The database contains input-output representations of individual economies, obtained from national statistical agencies, and international trade and income data from the UN Comtrade database and the World Bank, respectively. The GTAP6 database improves significantly on GTAP5 by incorporating new protection data from the AMAD and MacMaps databases. The latter feature bilateral tariffs, so regional trading agreements in place at 2001 are fully integrated. Full database documentation can be found in Dimaranan and McDougall (2005).

Aggregation Strategy

While the GTAP6 database features 87 regions and 57 sectors, it must be aggregated for reasons of computational efficiency. The aggregations we have chosen are shown in table B.3.

The GTAP6 database does not contain Pakistan as an individual economy. Instead Pakistan is grouped in the "rest of South Asia" category, which comprises Pakistan, Maldives, and Bhutan. The input-output data for this region are constructed from that of similar neighboring economies. Protection and macroeconomic data represent the members of the group directly. Because Pakistan is by far the dominant member of the "Rest of South Asia" category (roughly 85 percent of the region's GDP), we have treated the results for this region as approximating the effects for Pakistan. This should be kept in mind for all references to Pakistan throughout this section.

The approach taken in constructing the aggregation was to rank the total exports of the United States and Pakistan as well as the bilateral exports of the two countries, and then use this ranking, along with "natural" sectoral groupings, to aggregate the data. A similar approach was followed for regional aggregation, where care was also taken to include current US partners in the North American Free Trade Agreement as well as new and prospective US FTA partners, in addition to regional trading partners of Pakistan.[7]

---

7. New US partners are Australia, Chile, Morocco, Singapore, partners in the Central American Free Trade Agreement–Dominican Republic, Bahrain, and Oman; prospective US partners are Korea, Malaysia, Southern African Customs Union partners, Switzerland, and Thailand. (Egypt is also a prospective US FTA partner, but is not covered in the GTAP6 database and therefore was not considered in our calculations.)

Table B.3 Aggregation scheme for GTAP6 database

Sectoral aggregation	Regional aggregation
Grains	Australia
Vegetables and fruits	New Zealand
Other agriculture	China
Forestry and fisheries	Hong Kong
Coal, oil, and gas	Japan
Processed rice	South Korea
Other food products	Bangladesh
Textiles	India
Wearing apparel	Sri Lanka
Leather products	Pakistan
Wood products	Chile
Paper products	Rest of South America
Chemicals	CAFTA-DR
Minerals and metals	Western Europe
Fabricated metal products	Eastern Europe
Motor vehicles	Morocco
Other transportation equipment	SACU
Electronic equipment	Indonesia
Machinery and equipment	Malaysia
Other manufactures	Philippines
Nontraded services	Singapore
Traded services	Thailand
	Vietnam
	Canada
	United States
	Mexico
	Rest of world

GTAP = Global Trade Analysis Project
CAFTA-DR = Central American Free Trade Agreement–Dominican Republic
SACU = Southern African Customs Union

Data Adjustments

While agricultural protection data in GTAP6 are excellent, services protection data are limited. Philippa Dee, Kevin Hanslow, and Tien Phamduc (2003) have published their estimates of barriers to services trade at the aggregate level. In this study, we split services into traded and nontraded categories, following the classification adopted by Dee et al. (2003), and use the estimates of services barriers from that study. These barriers are implemented using several trade policy instruments (import tax equivalents, export tax equivalents, taxes on output, and taxes on domestic capital). The various tax rates were imposed on the GTAP6 dataset prior to the major simulation using the Altertax procedure. This procedure fixes the current account balance and uses parameters such that all key shares in the model remain constant when the new taxes are imposed while ensuring that the database remains consistent.

References

Akhtar, Mahboob. 2005. Cotton Production in Pakistan and Role of Trading Corporation of Pakistan in Price Stabilization. Lecture Delivered at the International Cotton Advisory Committee on 10–19 May, 2005. www.icac.org.

Aksoy, M. A., and J. C. Beghin, eds. 2006. *Global Agricultural Trade and Developing Countries*. Washington: The World Bank.

Allgeier, Peter. 2004. Written Statement of Ambassador Peter F. Allgeier, Deputy US Trade Representative, before the Committee on Finance, June 15, 2004, Washington.

Anderson, Kym, and Valenzuela, Ernesto. 2006 (forthcoming). Do Global Trade Distortions Still Harm Developing Country Farmers?" *Review of World Economics* 143, no. 1.

ADB (Asian Development Bank). 2002. *Pakistan: Country Strategy and Program 2002–2006*. Manila. www.adb.org (accessed December 23, 2005).

ADB (Asian Development Bank)/OECD (Organization for Economic Cooperation and Development) Anti-Corruption Initiative for Asia and the Pacific. 2004. Thematic Review on Provisions and Practices to Curb Corruption in Public Procurement: Self-Assessment Report Pakistan. www.oecd.org (accessed September 6, 2005).

BEA (US Bureau of Economic Analysis). 2005. *Survey of Current Business* (September). Washington.

Bhagwati, Jagdish, ed. 2002. *Going Alone: The Case for Relaxed Reciprocity in Freeing Trade*. Cambridge: MIT Press.

Burki, Shahid Javed. 1980. *Pakistan: A Nation in the Making*. Boulder: Westview Press.

Burki, Shahid, and Mohammed Akbar. 2005. Pakistan. In *South Asian Free Trade Area: Opportunities and Challenges*. Washington: US Agency for International Development.

Choi, Inbom, and Jeffrey Schott. 2001. *Free Trade between Korea and the United States*. Washington: Institute for International Economics.

CIA (US Central Intelligence Agency). 2006. *The World Factbook: Pakistan*. www.cia.gov (accessed December 1, 2005).

Commerce Division of the Embassy of Pakistan. 2005. First Round of Negotiations between the Islamic Republic of Pakistan and the People's Republic of China: Agreed Minutes. August 15–16, 2005.

Council of Economic Advisers. 2004. *Economic Report of the President*. Washington: US Government Printing Office.

Crawford, Jo-Ann, and Roberto V. Fiorentino. 2005. *The Changing Landscape of Regional Trade Agreements.* WTO Discussion Paper 8. Geneva: World Trade Organization.

CRS (Congressional Research Service). 2001. *NAFTA Labor Side Agreement: Lessons for the Worker Rights and Fast-Track Debate.* Washington. http://ncseonline.org (accessed December 23, 2005).

CRS (Congressional Research Service). 2005. *Pakistan-U.S. Relations.* CRS Issue Brief for Congress. Washington.

Das, Gurucharan. 2003. *India Unbound.* New Delhi: Penguin.

Dee, Philippa, Kevin Hanslow, and Tien Phamduc. 2003. Measuring the Cost of Barriers to Trade in Services. In *Trade in Services in the Asia-Pacific Region*, ed. Takatoshi Ito and Anne O. Krueger. Chicago: University of Chicago Press.

Dimaranan, Betina, and Robert A. McDougall, eds. 2005. *Global Trade, Assistance, and Protection: The GTAP6 Database.* Center for Global Trade Analysis. West Lafayette, IN: Purdue University.

EIU (Economist Intelligence Unit). 2004. *Country Profile: Pakistan.* London.

Egger, Peter. 2002. An Econometric View on the Estimation of Gravity Models and the Calculation of Trade Potentials. *World Economy* 25, no. 2 (February): 297–312.

Elliott, Kimberly Ann. 2004. *Labor Standards, Development, and CAFTA.* Washington: Institute for International Economics.

Elliott, Kimberly Ann, and Richard B. Freeman. 2003. *Can Labor Standards Improve under Globalization?* Washington: Institute for International Economics.

Esty, Daniel C., Marc Levy, Tanja Srebotnjak, and Alexander de Sherbinin. 2005. *2005 Environmental Sustainability Index (ESI): Benchmarking National Environmental Stewardship.* New Haven: Yale Center for Environmental Law and Policy. http://sedac.ciesin. columbia.edu (accessed December 23, 2005).

European Commission. 2004. *Report on US Barriers to Trade and Investment* (December). Brussels.

Export Promotion Bureau of Pakistan. 2005a. Assistance for Relocation of Industries. Public Notice no. 4(4)/2004/PPI. www.epb.gov.pk (accessed November 2005).

Export Promotion Bureau of Pakistan. 2005b. *Pakistan's Export Strategy.* www.epb.gov.pk.

FAO (UN Food and Agriculture Organization). 20035. *Livestock Sector Brief: Pakistan* (June). www.fao.org (accessed July, 2006).

Feenstra, Robert C., Robert E. Lipsey, Haiyan Deng, Alyson C. Ma, and Hengyong Mo. 2005. *World Trade Flows: 1962–2000.* NBER Working Paper 11040. Cambridge, MA: National Bureau of Economic Research.

Ferguson, Niall. 2003. *Empire: How Britain Made the Modern World.* London: Allen Lane.

Ferrantino, Michael J. 2006. *Policy Anchors: Do Free Trade Agreements Serve as Vehicles for Developing-Country Policy Reform?* Washington: US International Trade Commission.

Frankel, J. A, E. Stein, and S. J. Wei. 1997. *Regional Trading Blocs in the World Economic System.* Washington: Institute for International Economics.

Galal, Ahmed, and Robert Z. Lawrence. 2005. *Anchoring Reform with a US-Egypt Free Trade Agreement.* Washington: Institute for International Economics.

Gereffi, Gary. 2001. Global Sourcing in the U.S. Apparel Industry. *Journal of Textiles and Apparel, Technology and Management* 2, no. 1 (Fall).

Gereffi, Gary, and Olga Memedovic. 2003. *The Global Apparel Value Chain: What Prospects for Upgrading by Developing Countries.* Vienna: United Nations Industrial Development Organization.

Gilbert, J., and T. Wahl. 2002. Applied General Equilibrium Assessments of Trade Liberalization in China. *World Economy* 25, no. 5: 697–731.

Gillson, Ian, Colin Poulton, Kelvin Balcombe, and Sheila Page. 2006. *Understanding the Impact of Cotton Subsidies on Developing Countries.* Overseas Development Institute Working Paper. www.odi.org (accessed July 2006).

Government of Pakistan. 2000. *Pakistan 2000 Agricultural Census.* Islamabad: Statistics Division, Ministry of Economic Affairs and Statistics.

Government of Pakistan. 2002. Custom General Order no. 12 of 2002. Islamabad: Central Board of Revenue.

Government of Pakistan. 2003. *Poverty Reduction Strategy Paper*. Islamabad.

Government of Pakistan. 2005a. *Pakistan Economic Survey 2004–2005*. Islamabad.

Government of Pakistan. 2005b. *Trade Policy 2005–06: Import Policy Order*. Islamabad: Ministry of Commerce.

Government of Pakistan. 2005c. *Textile Vision 2005*. Islamabad.

Greenaway, David, and Scott Milner. 2002. Regionalism and Gravity. *Scottish Journal of Political Economy* 49: 574–85.

Heritage Foundation. 2005. Index for Economic Freedom. www.heritage.org (accessed November 30, 2005).

Hertel, Thomas, ed. 1997. *Global Trade Analysis: Modeling and Applications*. New York: Cambridge University Press.

Hoekman, Bernard, and Michel Kostecki. 1995. *The Political Economy of the World Trading System: From GATT to WTO*. Oxford: Oxford University Press.

HRCP (Human Rights Commission of Pakistan). 2004. *State of Human Rights in 2003*. www.hrcp-web.org (accessed January 23, 2006).

HRCP (Human Rights Commission of Pakistan). 2005a. *State of Human Rights in 2004*. www.hrcp-web.org (accessed January 23, 2006).

HRCP (Human Rights Commission of Pakistan). 2005b. Bonded Labor Database. www.hrcp-web.org (accessed December 23, 2005).

Hsiao, Cheng. 2003. *Analysis of Panel Data*. Cambridge, UK: Cambridge University Press.

Hufbauer, Gary C., and Kimberly Ann Elliott. 1994. *Measuring the Costs of Protection in the United States*. Washington: Institute for International Economics.

Hufbauer, Gary C., and Jeffrey J. Schott. 2005. *NAFTA Revisited: Achievements and Challenges*. Washington: Institute for International Economics.

Hufbauer, Gary C., and Yee Wong. 2005. *China Bashing 2004*. International Economics Policy Brief PB04-5. Washington: Institute for International Economics.

Hummels, D. L. 2000. *Time as a Trade Barrier*. GTAP Working Paper 18. Purdue University: Center for Global Trade Analysis.

Huntington, Samuel P. 1993. The Clash of Civilizations? *Foreign Affairs* 72, no. 3: 22–28.

Huntington, Samuel P. 1996. *The Clash of Civilizations and the Remaking of World Order*. New York: Touchstone.

ICFTU (International Confederation of Free Trade Unions). 2002. *Report for the WTO General Council Review of Trade Policies of Pakistan*. Brussels. www.icftu.org (accessed December 21, 2005).

ICFTU (International Confederation of Free Trade Unions). 2004. *Pakistan: Annual Survey of Violations of Trade Union Rights*. Brussels. www.icftu.org (accessed December 21, 2005).

ICFTU (International Confederation of Free Trade Unions). 2005. *Pakistan Trade Union Centres Unite in New Organisation*. July 9, 2005. Brussels. www.icftu.org (accessed December 21, 2005).

ILO (International Labor Organization). 2002. *A Future Without Child Labour*. Geneva. www.ilo.org (accessed December 18, 2005).

ILO (International Labor Organization). 2005a. *Review of Annual Reports Under the Follow-up to the ILO Declaration on Fundamental Principles and Rights at Work*. Geneva. www.ilo.org (accessed December 18, 2005).

ILO (International Labor Organization). 2005b. *A Global Alliance Against Forced Labour*. Geneva. www.ilo.org (accessed December 23, 2005).

IMF (International Monetary Fund). 2003. *Government Finance Statistics Yearbook*. Washington.

IMF (International Monetary Fund). 2005. *Asia and Pacific Regional Outlook: September 2005*. Washington.

James, Clive. 2005. *Global Status of Commercialized Biotech/GM Crops: 2005*. ISAAA Briefs 34-2005. Ithaca, NY: International Service for the Acquisition of Agri-Biotech Applications.

Kux, Dennis. 2001. *The United States and Pakistan 1947–2000: Disenchanted Allies.* Washington: Woodrow Wilson Center.

Lahiri, S. 1998. Controversy: Regionalism versus Multilateralism. *Economic Journal* 108: 1126–27.

Lall, Sanjaya. 2004. *Benchmarking Pakistan's Competitive Performance.* Manila: Asian Development Bank.

Library of Congress. 1994. *Country Study: Pakistan.* Washington. http://lcweb2.loc.gov.

Little, Ian M. D. 1982. *Economic Development.* New York: Basic Books.

Lloyd, P. J., and D. MacLaren. 2004. Gains and Losses from Regional Trading Agreements: A Survey. *Economic Record* 80, no. 251: 445–97.

Mattoo, Aaditya, and Pierre Sauvé. 2004. Regionalism and Trade in Services in the Western Hemisphere: A Policy Agenda. In *Integrating the Americas,* eds. Antoni Estevadeordal, Dani Rodrik, Alan Taylor, and Andrés Velasco. Cambridge, MA: Harvard University Press.

Michel, Aloys. 1969. *The Indus River.* New Haven: Yale University Press.

MTI (Singapore Ministry of Trade and Industry). 2003. Information Paper on the US-Singapore Free Trade Agreement, May 16, 2003. www.mti.gov.sg.

National Association of Manufacturers. 2005. *U.S. Companies Invest in High-Wage Overseas Markets.* Washington. www.nam.org.

National Tariff Commission of Pakistan. 2005. Preliminary Determination and Levy of Provisional Antidumping Duty on Import of Polyester Filament Yarn Originating in and/or Exported from the Republic of Indonesia, the Republic of Korea, Malaysia and the Kingdom of Thailand. A.D.C. no. 07/2005/NTC/PFY. www.ntc.gov.pk (accessed July 2006).

Nordas, Hildegunn K. 2004. *The Global Textile and Clothing Industry Post the Agreement on Textiles and Clothing.* Discussion Paper 5. Geneva: World Trade Organization.

OECD (Organization for Economic Cooperation and Development). 2003. *Agricultural Policies in OECD Countries: Monitoring and Evaluation.* Paris.

OECD (Organization for Economic Cooperation and Development). 2004a. PSE/CSE database 2004. Paris. www.oecd.org (accessed July 2006).

OECD (Organization for Economic Cooperation and Development). 2006. *United States: Report on Competition Law and Institutions.* Paris.

Orden, David, Abdul Salam, Reno Dewina, Hina Nazli, and Nicholas Minot. 2006. *The Impact of Global Cotton Markets on Rural Poverty in Pakistan.* Background Paper Series 8. Islamabad: Asian Development Bank, Pakistan Resident Mission.

Pakistan Central Board of Revenue. 2005a. Pakistan Customs Tariff 2005–06. www.cbr.gov.pk (accessed July 2006).

Pakistan Central Board of Revenue. 2005b. Exemption from Customs Duty on Import of Specified Goods (Non-Survey Based). SRO 567. Customs Active/Operative Notifications/SROs: Import. www.cbr.gov.pk.

Pakistan Central Board of Revenue. 2005c. Exemption from Customs Duty and Sales Tax on Import of Specified Machinery, Equipment, Apparatus and Items. SRO 575. Customs Active/Operative Notifications/SROs: Import. www.cbr.gov.pk.

Pakistan Central Board of Revenue. 2005d. Exemption from Customs Duty on Import of Raw Materials, Sub-components, Components, Sub-assemblies and Assemblies, for Manufacture of Specified Goods (Survey based). SRO 565. Customs Active/Operative Notifications/SROs: Import. www.cbr.gov.pk.

Pakistan Federal Bureau of Statistics. 2005. *Census of Manufacturing Industries 2000–01.* www.statpak.gov.pk.

Pakistan Finance Division. 2005. *Pakistan Economic Survey 2004–05.* Islamabad: Government of Pakistan.

Pakistan Ministry of Foreign Affairs. 2004. *Year Book 2003–2004.* Islamabad.

Panagariya, Arvind. 2000. Preferential Trade Liberalization: The Traditional Theory and New Developments. *Journal of Economic Literature* 38, no. 2: 287–331.

Parliament of Australia Senate. 2004. *Final Report of Select Committee on the Free Trade Agreement Between Australia and the United States of America.* www.aph.gov.au (accessed November 5, 2005).

People's Republic of China, Ministry of Commerce. 2005. Agreement on the Early Harvest Program for the Free Trade Agreement between the Government of the People's Republic of China and the Government of the Islamic Republic of Pakistan. http://english. mofcom.gov.cn (accessed September 2005).

Prado, M. 2001. *Pasos Fronterizos en la Comunidad Andina.* Washington: Inter-American Development Bank.

Promopak. 2001. *Supply and Demand Survey Report on Agro Products and Processed Foods.* Geneva: International Trade Center.

PPRA (Public Procurement Regulatory Authority). 2004. Public Procurement Rules 2004. www.ppra.org.pk (accessed September 6, 2005).

Regmi, A., M. Gehlhar, J. Wainio, T. Vollrath, P. Johnston, N. Kathuria. 2005. *Market Access for High Value Foods.* Agricultural Economic Report 840. Washington: US Department of Agriculture.

Robinson, S., and K. Thierfelder. 2002. Trade Liberalization and Regional Integration: The Search for Large Numbers. *Australian Journal of Agricultural and Resource Economics* 46, no. 4: 585–604.

Rose, Andrew K. 2004. Do We Really Know that the WTO Increases Trade? *American Economic Review* 94, no. 1: 98–114.

SAARC (South Asian Association for Regional Cooperation). 2004. Islamabad Declaration. Islamabad.

Salazar-Xirinachs, Jose M., and Jaime Granados. 2004. The US–Central America Free Trade Agreement: Opportunities and Challenges. In *Free Trade Agreements: US Strategies and Priorities,* ed. Jeffrey J. Schott. Washington: Institute for International Economics.

Schnepf, Randy. 2005. *Background on the U.S.-Brazil WTO Cotton Subsidy Dispute.* CRS Report for Congress RL32571. http://fpc.state.gov (last accessed July 2006).

Schott, Jeffrey J. 2004a. Free Trade Agreements: Boon or Bane of the World Trading System? In *Free Trade Agreements: US Strategies and Priorities,* ed. Jeffrey J. Schott. Washington: Institute for International Economics.

Schott, Jeffrey J. 2004b. Reviving the Doha Round. Paper for the Institute for International Economics. Washington: Institute for International Economics. www.iie.com.

Scollay, Robert, and John Gilbert. 2000. Measuring the Gains from APEC Trade Liberalization: An Overview of CGE Assessments. *World Economy* 23, no. 2: 175–93.

Scollay, Robert, and John Gilbert. 2001. *New Regional Trading Arrangements in the Asia Pacific?* Washington: Institute for International Economics.

Stiglitz, Joseph. 2002. *Globalization and Its Discontents.* New York: W. W. Norton & Company.

Sutherland, Peter, Jagdish Bhagwati, Kwesi Botchwey, Niall FitzGerald, Koichi Hamada, John H. Jackson, Celso Lafer, and Thierry de Montbrial. 2004. *The Future of the WTO: Addressing Institutional Challenges in the New Millennium.* Geneva: World Trade Organization.

Transparency International. 2005. *Pakistan: Progress Report Ending July 31, 2005.* Karachi.

UNCTAD (United Nations Conference on Trade and Development). 2004a. *The Generalized System of Preferences.* New York: United Nations.

UNCTAD (United Nations Conference on Trade and Development). 2004b. *World Investment Report 2004: The Shift Toward Services.* Geneva.

UNCTAD (United Nations Conference on Trade and Development). 2005. *World Investment Report 2005: Transnational Corporations and the Internationalization of R&D.* Geneva.

UNIDO (United Nations Industrial Development Organization). 2005. Online Data Access: Pakistan. www.unido.org (accessed November 6, 2005).

UN Statistics Division. 2005. UN Commodity Trade Statistics Database (UN Comtrade). http://unstats.un.org (accessed November 2005).

USAID (US Agency for International Development). 2005. *South Asian Free Trade Area: Opportunities and Challenges.* Washington.

US CBP (US Customs and Border Protection). 2003. Top IPR Seizures by Top Trading Partner and Commodity. www.cbp.gov (accessed November 2005).

US CBP (US Customs and Border Protection). 2004. *2004 Year-End Textile Status Report for Absolute Quotas: Pakistan.* www.cbp.gov (accessed December 2005).

US CBP (US Customs and Border Protection). 2005a. *What Every Member of the Trade Community Should Know About: NAFTA for Textiles and Textile Articles.* www.cbp.gov (accessed November 2005).

US CBP (US Customs and Border Protection). 2005b. *Daily Textile Status Report for Absolute Quotas: China (Mainland).* www.cbp.gov (accessed December 2005).

US Census Bureau. 1990. *Statistical Abstract of the United States: 1990* (110th Edition).Washington: US Government Printing Office.

US Census Bureau. 1993. *Statistical Abstract of the United States: 1993* (113th Edition).Washington: US Government Printing Office.

US Census Bureau. 2001. *Statistical Abstract of the United States: 2001* (121st Edition).Washington: US Government Printing Office.

US Census Bureau. 2004. *Statistical Abstract of the United States: 2004-2005* (124th Edition). Washington: US Government Printing Office.

US Census Bureau. 2005. *Geographic Area Statistics: 2003, Annual Survey of Manufactures.* Washington: US Government Printing Office.

US Commercial Service. 2001. *Pakistan Country Commercial Guide, Fiscal 2002.* Washington: Department of Commerce.

USDA (US Department of Agriculture). 2002a. *SPS Accomplishments Report, Fiscal 2002.* Washington. www.aphis.usda.gov (accessed July 2006).

USDA (US Department of Agriculture). 2002b. *2002 Census of Agriculture.* Washington. www.nass.usda.gov (accessed July 2006).

USDA (US Department of Agriculture). 2005a. *Pakistan Grain and Feed: Wheat and Rice Update.* Quarterly Report 2005. Washington.

USDA (US Department of Agriculture). 2005b. *Food Aid Reports.* www.fas.usda.gov (accessed July 2006).

US Department of Commerce. 2003. *The U.S. Textile and Apparel Industries: An Industrial Base Assessment.* Report to Congress (October). www.bis.doc.gov. (accessed July 2006).

US Department of Commerce. 2005a. Final Results of Sunset Reviews and Revocation of Antidumping Duty Orders and Countervailing Duty Orders on Cotton Shop Towels from Bangladesh, the People's Republic of China, and Pakistan. 70 FR 18362. http://ia.ita.doc.gov (accessed July 2006).

US Department of Commerce. 2005b. Statement on CITA Decision Regarding Requests for Safeguard Action on Imports of Textiles and Apparel from China. *Commerce News* 23, November 2005.

US Department of Commerce. 2005c. *Pakistan: Import Tariffs and Taxes.* OTEXA Foreign Market Information. http://web.ita.doc.gov (accessed January 2006).

US Department of Commerce. 2005d. *Sector Summary for Textiles and Apparel in the North American Free Trade Agreement (NAFTA).* http://otexa.ita.doc.gov.

US Department of State, Bureau of Democracy, Human Rights and Labor. 2002. *Country Reports on Human Rights Practices: Pakistan 2001.* Released March 4, 2002. www.state.gov (accessed December 18, 2005).

US Department of State, Bureau of Democracy, Human Rights and Labor. 2004. *Country Reports on Human Rights Practices: Pakistan 2003.* Released February 25, 2004. www.state.gov (accessed December 18, 2005).

US Department of State, Bureau of Democracy, Human Rights and Labor. 2005. *Country Reports on Human Rights Practices: Pakistan 2004.* Released February 28, 2005. www.state.gov (accessed December 18, 2005).

USITC (US International Trade Commission). 1998. *Production Sharing: Use of U.S. Components and Materials in Foreign Assembly Operations, 1994–1997.* Publication no. 3146. Washington.

USITC (US International Trade Commission). 2000. *Cotton Shop Towels from Bangladesh, China, and Pakistan*. Publication no. 3267. Washington.

USITC (US International Trade Commission). 2004a. Textiles and Apparel: Assessment of the Competitiveness of Certain Foreign Suppliers to the U.S. Market. Investigation no. 332-448. Washington.

USITC (US International Trade Commission). 2004b. The Economic Effects of Significant U.S. Import Restraints. Fourth Update 2004. Investigation no. 332-325, Publication 3701. Washington.

USITC (US International Trade Commission). 2005a. Interactive Tariff and Trade Dataweb. Washington. http://dataweb.usitc.gov (accessed November 2005).

USITC (US International Trade Commission). 2005b. Official Harmonized Tariff Schedule of the United States 2005. Washington. www.usitc.gov.

USTR (US Trade Representative). 2000. Jordan Free Trade Agreement. Washington. www.ustr.gov.

USTR (US Trade Representative). 2003a. Special 301 Watch List. Washington. www.ustr.gov (accessed November 2005).

USTR (US Trade Representative). 2003b. Singapore Free Trade Agreement: Text of the Agreement. Washington. www.ustr.gov (accessed November 6, 2005).

USTR (US Trade Representative). 2003c. Chile Free Trade Agreement: Final Text. Washington. www.ustr.gov (accessed July 15, 2005).

USTR (US Trade Representative). 2004a. Advisory Committee Report to the President, the Congress and the United States Trade Representative on the U.S.-Australia Free Trade Agreement (FTA). Washington. www.ustr.gov (accessed November 2005).

USTR (US Trade Representative). 2004b. *National Trade Estimate of Foreign Trade Barriers: Pakistan*. Washington. www.ustr.gov (accessed November 2005).

USTR (US Trade Representative). 2004c. CAFTA-DR Final Text. Washington. www.ustr.gov (accessed November 2005).

USTR (US Trade Representative). 2004d. Final Text of the Morocco Free Trade Agreement. Washington. www.ustr.gov (accessed November 6, 2005).

USTR (US Trade Representative). 2004e. Final Text of the U.S.-Australia Free Trade Agreement. Washington. www.ustr.gov (accessed November 6, 2005).

USTR (US Trade Representative). 2004f. Bahrain FTA Final Text. Washington. www.ustr.gov (accessed November 2005).

USTR (US Trade Representative). 2004g. U.S.-Morocco Free Trade Agreement: Textile and Apparel Provisions. Washington. www.ustr.gov (accessed November 6, 2005).

USTR (US Trade Representative). 2005a. *National Trade Estimate of Foreign Trade Barriers: Pakistan*. Washington. www.ustr.gov (accessed November 2005).

USTR (US Trade Representative). 2005b. Memorandum of Understanding between the Governments of the United States and the People's Republic of China Concerning Trade in Textile and Apparel Products. Washington. www.ustr.gov (accessed November 2005).

USTR (US Trade Representative). 2005c. Benefits from Establishing Quotas on Certain Chinese Apparel Exports to the United States. Washington. www.ustr.gov (accessed November 2005).

USTR (US Trade Representative). 2005d. *Textiles: United States to Compete with Asia*. Washington. www.ustr.gov (accessed November 6, 2005).

USTR (US Trade Representative). 2005e. CAFTA Facts: Comparison of the Labor Provisions in the US-Jordan, CAFTA-DR, and Morocco FTAs. Washington. www.ustr.gov (accessed December 18, 2005).

USTR (US Trade Representative). 2005f. The Facts on CAFTA and Government Procurement. Washington. www.ustr.gov (accessed December 18, 2005).

Vargo, Regina. 2003. Prepared Witness Testimony: Ms. Regina K. Vargo. The House Committee on Energy and Commerce. http://energycommerce.house.gov.

Williamson, John. 2004. A Short History of the Washington Consensus. Paper commissioned by Fundación CIDOB for a conference titled From the Washington Consensus Toward a New Global Governance, Barcelona, September 24–25. www.iie.com.

Woolgar, Tony. 2004. Submission from the Textile, Clothing and Footwear Union of Australia (TCFUA) to the Senate Select Committee on the Free Trade Agreement between Australia and the United States of America. www.aph.gov.au (accessed November 6, 2005).

World Bank. 1993. *The East Asian Miracle: Economic Growth and Public Policy*. Washington.

World Bank. 2004a. *Trade Policy in South Asia: An Overview*. Report No. 29949. Washington.

World Bank. 2004b. *World Development Indicators 2004*. Washington.

World Bank. 2004c. *Global Economic Prospects: Trade, Regionalism and Development*. Washington.

World Bank. 2005. *Remittances: Development Impact and Future Prospects*. Washington. http://publications.worldbank.org.

WEF (World Economic Forum). 2005. Global Competitiveness Report: Growth Competitiveness Index (GCI) 2005. Geneva. www.weforum.org (accessed November 30, 2005).

World Organization for Animal Health (OIE). 2005. Geographical Distribution of List A Diseases. Paris. www.oie.int. (accessed December 12, 2005).

World Organization for Animal Health (OIE). 2005. Animal Health Status Worldwide in 2004. Paris.

WTO (World Trade Organization). 1996. United States—Measures Affecting Imports of Women's and Girls' Wool Coats. DS 32. www.wto.org (accessed November 28, 2005).

WTO (World Trade Organization). 2001a. United States—Transitional Safeguard Measure on Combed Cotton Yarn from Pakistan. DS 192. www.wto.org (accessed October, 2005).

WTO (World Trade Organization). 2001b. *Report of the Working Party on the Accession of China*. WT/MIN(01)/3. Geneva.

WTO (World Trade Organization). 2002a. *Trade Policy Review: Pakistan* (January). Geneva.

WTO (World Trade Organization). 2002b. United States—Sub-Central Government Entities which Procure in Accordance with the Provisions of this Agreement. October 16, 2002. WT/Let/431. Geneva. www.wto.org (accessed November 30, 2005).

WTO (World Trade Organization). 2004a. *Trade Policy Review: United States* (January). Geneva: World Trade Organization.

WTO (World Trade Organization). 2004b. *Trade Policy Review: Sri Lanka* (March). Geneva.

WTO (World Trade Organization). 2005a. Regional Trade Agreements. www.wto.org (accessed November 7, 2005).

WTO (World Trade Organization). 2005b. Statistics Database. www.wto.org (accessed November 21, 2005).

WTO (World Trade Organization). 2005c. Statistics on Antidumping. www.wto.org (accessed November 6, 2005).

WTO (World Trade Organization). 2005d. United States Notification to WTO Committee on Anti-Dumping Practices. Report number G/ADP/N/126/USA (March). Geneva.

WTO (World Trade Organization). 2005e. *Country Profiles: Pakistan*. Geneva.

WTO (World Trade Organization). 2005f. Information to be Notified to the Committee Where a Safeguard Investigation Is Terminated with No Safeguard Measure Imposed. Report no. G/SG/N/9/PAK/1 (October). Geneva.

World Trade Review. 2005. Antidumping/Safeguards: CBR Move to Stop Furniture Dumping, December 1–15, 2005. www.worldtradereview.com.

Index

Other Publications from the **Peterson Institute**

79 Trade Relations Between Colombia
and the United States
Jeffrey J. Schott, editor
August 2006   ISBN 978-0-88132-389-4
80 Sustaining Reform with a US-Pakistan
Free Trade Agreement
Gary C. Hufbauer and Shahid Javed Burki
November 2006   ISBN 978-0-88132-395-5

BOOKS

IMF Conditionality* John Williamson, editor
1983   ISBN 0-88132-006-4
Trade Policy in the 1980s* William R. Cline, ed.
1983   ISBN 0-88132-031-5
Subsidies in International Trade*
Gary Clyde Hufbauer and Joanna Shelton Erb
1984   ISBN 0-88132-004-8
International Debt: Systemic Risk and Policy
Response*   William R. Cline
1984   ISBN 0-88132-015-3
Trade Protection in the United States: 31 Case
Studies* Gary Clyde Hufbauer, Diane E. Berliner,
and Kimberly Ann Elliott
1986   ISBN 0-88132-040-4
Toward Renewed Economic Growth in Latin
America* Bela Balassa, Gerardo M. Bueno, Pedro-
Pablo Kuczynski, and Mario Henrique Simonsen
1986   ISBN 0-88132-045-5
Capital Flight and Third World Debt*
Donald R. Lessard and John Williamson, editors
1987   ISBN 0-88132-053-6
The Canada-United States Free Trade Agreement:
The Global Impact*
Jeffrey J. Schott and Murray G. Smith, editors
1988   ISBN 0-88132-073-0
World Agricultural Trade: Building a Consensus*
William M. Miner and Dale E. Hathaway, editors
1988   ISBN 0-88132-071-3
Japan in the World Economy*
Bela Balassa and Marcus Noland
1988   ISBN 0-88132-041-2
America in the World Economy: A Strategy for
the 1990s*   C. Fred Bergsten
1988   ISBN 0-88132-089-7
Managing the Dollar: From the Plaza to the
Louvre*   Yoichi Funabashi
1988, 2d. ed. 1989   ISBN 0-88132-097-8
United States External Adjustment
and the World Economy*
William R. Cline
May 1989   ISBN 0-88132-048-X
Free Trade Areas and U.S. Trade Policy*
Jeffrey J. Schott, editor
May 1989   ISBN 0-88132-094-3

Dollar Politics: Exchange Rate Policymaking
in the United States*
I. M. Destler and C. Randall Henning
September 1989   ISBN 0-88132-079-X
Latin American Adjustment: How Much Has
Happened?*   John Williamson, editor
April 1990   ISBN 0-88132-125-7
The Future of World Trade in Textiles and
Apparel*   William R. Cline
1987, 2d ed. June *1999*   ISBN 0-88132-110-9
Completing the Uruguay Round: A Results-
Oriented Approach to the GATT Trade
Negotiations*   Jeffrey J. Schott, editor
September 1990   ISBN 0-88132-130-3
Economic Sanctions Reconsidered (2 volumes)
Economic Sanctions Reconsidered:
Supplemental Case Histories
Gary Clyde Hufbauer, Jeffrey J. Schott, and
Kimberly Ann Elliott
1985, 2d ed. Dec. 1990   ISBN cloth 0-88132-115-X
                              ISBN paper 0-88132-105-2
Economic Sanctions Reconsidered: History and
Current Policy   Gary Clyde Hufbauer,
Jeffrey J. Schott, and Kimberly Ann Elliott
December 1990   ISBN cloth 0-88132-140-0
                              ISBN paper 0-88132-136-2
Pacific Basin Developing Countries: Prospects for
Economic Sanctions Reconsidered: History
and Current Policy   Gary Clyde Hufbauer,
Jeffrey J. Schott, and Kimberly Ann Elliott
December 1990   ISBN cloth 0-88132-140-0
                              ISBN paper 0-88132-136-2
Pacific Basin Developing Countries: Prospects
for the Future*   Marcus Noland
January 1991   ISBN cloth 0-88132-141-9
                              ISBN paper 0-88132-081-1
Currency Convertibility in Eastern Europe*
John Williamson, editor
October 1991   ISBN 0-88132-128-1
International Adjustment and Financing: The
Lessons of 1985-1991* C. Fred Bergsten, editor
January 1992   ISBN 0-88132-112-5
North American Free Trade: Issues and
Recommendations*
Gary Clyde Hufbauer and Jeffrey J. Schott
April 1992   ISBN 0-88132-120-6
Narrowing the U.S. Current Account Deficit*
Alan J. Lenz/*June 1992*   ISBN 0-88132-103-6
The Economics of Global Warming
William R. Cline/*June 1992*   ISBN 0-88132-132-X
US Taxation of International Income: Blueprint
for Reform*   Gary Clyde Hufbauer,
assisted by Joanna M. van Rooij
October 1992   ISBN 0-88132-134-6
Who's Bashing Whom? Trade Conflict
in High-Technology Industries
Laura D'Andrea Tyson
November 1992   ISBN 0-88132-106-0

Measuring the Costs of Visible Protection
in Korea* Namdoo Kim
November 1996 ISBN 0-88132-236-9
The World Trading System: Challenges Ahead
Jeffrey J. Schott
December 1996 ISBN 0-88132-235-0
Has Globalization Gone Too Far?
Dani Rodrik
March 1997 ISBN paper 0-88132-241-5
Korea-United States Economic Relationship*
C. Fred Bergsten and Il SaKong, editors
March 1997 ISBN 0-88132-240-7
Summitry in the Americas: A Progress Report
Richard E. Feinberg
April 1997 ISBN 0-88132-242-3
Corruption and the Global Economy
Kimberly Ann Elliott
June 1997 ISBN 0-88132-233-4
Regional Trading Blocs in the World Economic
System Jeffrey A. Frankel
October 1997 ISBN 0-88132-202-4
Sustaining the Asia Pacific Miracle:
Environmental Protection and Economic
Integration Andre Dua and Daniel C. Esty
October 1997 ISBN 0-88132-250-4
Trade and Income Distribution
William R. Cline
November 1997 ISBN 0-88132-216-4
Global Competition Policy
Edward M. Graham and J. David Richardson
December 1997 ISBN 0-88132-166-4
Unfinished Business: Telecommunications
after the Uruguay Round
Gary Clyde Hufbauer and Erika Wada
December 1997 ISBN 0-88132-257-1
Financial Services Liberalization in the WTO
Wendy Dobson and Pierre Jacquet
June 1998 ISBN 0-88132-254-7
Restoring Japan's Economic Growth
Adam S. Posen
September 1998 ISBN 0-88132-262-8
Measuring the Costs of Protection in China
Zhang Shuguang, Zhang Yansheng,
and Wan Zhongxin
November 1998 ISBN 0-88132-247-4
Foreign Direct Investment and Development:
The New Policy Agenda for Developing
Countries and Economies in Transition
Theodore H. Moran
December 1998 ISBN 0-88132-258-X
Behind the Open Door: Foreign Enterprises
in the Chinese Marketplace
Daniel H. Rosen
January 1999 ISBN 0-88132-263-6

Toward A New International Financial
Architecture: A Practical Post-Asia Agenda
Barry Eichengreen
February 1999 ISBN 0-88132-270-9
Is the U.S. Trade Deficit Sustainable?
Catherine L. Mann
September 1999 ISBN 0-88132-265-2
Safeguarding Prosperity in a Global Financial
System: The Future International Financial
Architecture, Independent Task Force Report
Sponsored by the Council on Foreign Relations
Morris Goldstein, Project Director
October 1999 ISBN 0-88132-287-3
Avoiding the Apocalypse: The Future
of the Two Koreas
Marcus Noland
June 2000 ISBN 0-88132-278-4
Assessing Financial Vulnerability: An Early
Warning System for Emerging Markets
Morris Goldstein, Graciela Kaminsky,
and Carmen Reinhart
June 2000 ISBN 0-88132-237-7
Global Electronic Commerce: A Policy Primer
Catherine L. Mann, Sue E. Eckert, and Sarah
Cleeland Knight
July 2000 ISBN 0-88132-274-1
The WTO after Seattle
Jeffrey J. Schott, editor
July 2000 ISBN 0-88132-290-3
Intellectual Property Rights in the Global
Economy Keith E. Maskus
August 2000 ISBN 0-88132-282-2
The Political Economy of the Asian Financial
Crisis Stephan Haggard
August 2000 ISBN 0-88132-283-0
Transforming Foreign Aid: United States
Assistance in the 21st Century
Carol Lancaster
August 2000 ISBN 0-88132-291-1
Fighting the Wrong Enemy: Antiglobal Activists
and Multinational Enterprises
Edward M. Graham
September 2000 ISBN 0-88132-272-5
Globalization and the Perceptions of American
Workers
Kenneth F. Scheve and Matthew J. Slaughter
March 2001 ISBN 0-88132-295-4
World Capital Markets: Challenge to the G-10
Wendy Dobson and Gary Clyde Hufbauer,
assisted by Hyun Koo Cho
May 2001 ISBN 0-88132-301-2
Prospects for Free Trade in the Americas
Jeffrey J. Schott
August 2001 ISBN 0-88132-275-X

19 Reforming the IMF for the 21st Century
    Edwin M. Truman, editor
    April 2006   ISBN 0-88132-387-X
                          ISBN 978-0-88132-387-0

WORKS IN PROGRESS

A US–Middle East Trade Agreement:
A Circle of Opporunity?
Robert Z. Lawrence
Reference Rates and the International
Monetary System
John Williamson
Reform in a Rich Country: Germany
Adam S. Posen
Second among Equals: The Middle-Class
Kingdoms of India and China
Surjit Bhalla
Global Forces, American Faces:
US Economic Globalization at the Grass
Roots   J. David Richardson
The Future of Chinese Exchange Rates
Morris Goldstein and Nicholas R. Lardy
The Arab Economies in a Changing World
Howard Pack and Marcus Noland
Economic Regionalism in East Asia
C. Fred Bergsten
The Strategic Implications of China-Taiwan
Economic Relations
Nicholas R. Lardy
Financial Crises and the Future
of Emerging Markets
William R. Cline

US Taxation of International Income, 2d ed.
Gary Clyde Hufbauer and Ariel Assa
Prospects for a Sri Lanka Free Trade
Agreement
Dean DeRosa
Prospects for a US-Indonesia Free Trade
Agreement   Gary Clyde Hufbauer
and Sjamsu Rahardja
Workers at Risk: Job Loss from Apparel,
Textiles, Footwear, and Furniture
Lori G. Kletzer
Economic Sanctions Reconsidered, 3d. ed.
Kimberly Ann Elliott, Gary C. Hufbauer,
and Jeffrey J. Schott
The Impact of Global Services Outsourcing
on American Firms and Workers
J. Bradford Jensen, Lori G. Kletzer,
and Catherine L. Mann
Rethinking US Social Security:
Drawing on World Best Practices
Martin N. Baily and Jacob Kirkegaard
Policy Reform in Mature Industrial
Economies
John Williamson, ed.
The Impact of Financial Globalization
William R. Cline
Banking System Fragility
in Emerging Economies
Morris Goldstein and Philip Turner
Competitiveness of the United States
and Other Industrial Countries
Martin N. Baily, Robert Z. Lawrence,
and Gary C. Hufbauer

**Australia, New Zealand,
and Papua New Guinea**
D. A. Information Services
648 Whitehorse Road
Mitcham, Victoria 3132, Australia
Tel: 61-3-9210-7777
Fax: 61-3-9210-7788
Email: service@dadirect.com.au
www.dadirect.com.au

India, Bangladesh, Nepal, and Sri Lanka
Viva Books Private Limited
Mr. Vinod Vasishtha
4737/23 Ansari Road
Daryaganj, New Delhi 110002
India
Tel: 91-11-4224-2200
Fax: 91-11-4224-2240
Email: viva@vivagroupindia.net
www.vivagroupindia.com

**Mexico, Central America, South America,
and Puerto Rico**
US PubRep, Inc.
311 Dean Drive
Rockville, MD 20851
Tel: 301-838-9276
Fax: 301-838-9278
Email: c.falk@ieee.org

Southeast Asia *(Brunei, Burma, Cambodia,
Indonesia, Malaysia, the Philippines,
Singapore, Taiwan, Thailand, and Vietnam)*
APAC Publishers Services PTE Ltd.
70 Bendemeer Road #05-03
Hiap Huat House
Singapore 333940
Tel: 65-6844-7333
Fax: 65-6747-8916
Email: service@apacmedia.com.sg

Canada
Renouf Bookstore
5369 Canotek Road, Unit 1
Ottawa, Ontario KIJ 9J3, Canada
Tel: 613-745-2665
Fax: 613-745-7660
www.renoufbooks.com

Japan
United Publishers Services Ltd.
1-32-5, Higashi-shinagawa
Shinagawa-ku, Tokyo 140-0002
Japan
Tel: 81-3-5479-7251
Fax: 81-3-5479-7307
Email: purchasing@ups.co.jp
*For trade accounts only. Individuals will find
Institute books in leading Tokyo bookstores.*

Middle East
MERIC
2 Bahgat Ali Street, El Masry Towers
Tower D, Apt. 24
Zamalek, Cairo
Egypt
Tel. 20-2-7633824
Fax: 20-2-7369355
Email: mahmoud_fouda@mericonline.com
www.mericonline.com

**United Kingdom, Europe
(including Russia and Turkey), Africa,
and Israel**
The Eurospan Group
c/o Turpin Distribution
Pegasus Drive
Stratton Business Park
Biggleswade, Bedfordshire
SG18 8TQ
United Kingdom
Tel: 44 (0) 1767-604972
Fax: 44 (0) 1767-601640
Email: eurospan@turpin-distribution.com
www.eurospangroup.com/bookstore

**Visit our Web site at:
www.petersoninstitute.org
E-mail orders to:
IIE mail@PressWarehouse.com**